Corporate Social Responsibility and the Paradoxes of State Capitalism

DISLOCATIONS

General Editors: August Carbonella, *Memorial University of Newfoundland*; Don Kalb, *University of Bergen & University of Utrecht*; Linda Green, *University of Arizona*

The immense dislocations and suffering caused by neoliberal globalization, the retreat of the welfare state in the last decades of the twentieth century, and the heightened military imperialism at the turn of the twenty-first century have raised urgent questions about the temporal and spatial dimensions of power. Through stimulating critical perspectives and new and cross-disciplinary frameworks that reflect recent innovations in the social and human sciences, this series provides a forum for politically engaged and theoretically imaginative responses to these important issues of late modernity.

Recent volumes:

Volume 33
Corporate Social Responsibility and the Paradoxes of State Capitalism: Ethnographies of Norwegian Energy and Extraction Businesses Abroad
Edited by Ståle Knudsen

Volume 32
Glimpses of Hope: The Rise of Industrial Labor at the Urban Margins of Nepal
Michael Hoffmann

Volume 31
Bulldozer Capitalism: Accumulation, Ruination, and Dispossession in Northeastern Turkey
Erdem Evren

Volume 30
Facing the Crisis: Ethnographies of Work in Italian Industrial Capitalism
Edited by Fulvia D'Aloisio and Simone Ghezzi

Volume 29
Big Capital in an Unequal World: The Micropolitics of Wealth in Pakistan
Rosita Armytage

Volume 28
Fifty Years of Peasant Wars in Latin America
Edited by Leigh Binford, Lesley Gill, and Steve Striffler

Volume 27
Brazilian Steel Town: Machines, Land, Money and Commoning in the Making of the Working Class
Massimiliano Mollona

Volume 26
Claiming Homes: Confronting Domicide in Rural China
Charlotte Bruckermann

Volume 25
Democracy Struggles: NGOs and the Politics of Aid in Serbia
Theodora Vetta

Volume 24
Worldwide Mobilizations: Class Struggles and Urban Commoning
Edited by Don Kalb and Massimiliano Mollona

For a full volume listing, please see the series page on our website:
https://www.berghahnbooks.com/series/dislocations

Corporate Social Responsibility and the Paradoxes of State Capitalism

Ethnographies of Norwegian Energy
and Extraction Businesses Abroad

Edited by Ståle Knudsen

Published in 2023 by
Berghahn Books
www.berghahnbooks.com

© 2023, 2026 Ståle Knudsen
First paperback edition published in 2026

All rights reserved. Except for the quotation of short passages
for the purposes of criticism and review, no part of this book
may be reproduced in any form or by any means, electronic or
mechanical, including photocopying, recording, or any information
storage and retrieval system now known or to be invented,
without written permission of the publisher.

Library of Congress Cataloging-in-Publication Data
Names: Knudsen, Ståle, 1963- editor.
Title: Corporate social responsibility and the paradoxes of state capitalism : ethnographies of Norwegian energy and extraction businesses abroad / edited by Ståle Knudsen.
Description: New York : Berghahn Books, 2023. | Series: Dislocations ; Volume 33 | Includes bibliographical references and index.
Identifiers: LCCN 2022059186 (print) | LCCN 2022059187 (ebook) | ISBN 9781800738737 (hardback) | ISBN 9781800738744 (ebook)
Subjects: LCSH: Petroleum industry and trade—Government policy—Norway. | Gas industry—Government policy—Norway. | Petroleum industry and trade—Foreign ownership—Government policy—Norway | Social responsibility of business—Norway. | Energy industries—Norway—History.
Classification: LCC HD9575.N62 C67 2023 (print) | LCC HD9575.N62 (ebook) | DDC 338.2/728/09481—dc203/eng/20230203
LC record available at https://lccn.loc.gov/2022059186
LC ebook record available at https://lccn.loc.gov/2022059187

British Library Cataloguing in Publication Data
A catalogue record for this book is available from the British Library

EU GPSR Authorized Representative
LOGOS EUROPE, 9 rue Nicolas Poussin, 17000, LA ROCHELLE, France
Email: Contact@logoseurope.eu

ISBN 978-1-80073-873-7 hardback
ISBN 978-1-83695-121-6 paperback
ISBN 978-1-80073-874-4 epub
ISBN 978-1-80073-987-1 web pdf

https://doi.org/10.3167/9781800738737

This work is published subject to a Creative Commons Attribution Noncommercial No Derivatives 4.0 License. The terms of the license can be found at http://creativecommons.org/licenses/by/4.0/. For uses beyond those covered in the license contact Berghahn Books.

Contents

List of Illustrations — vii

Preface

Introduction   Bringing the State Back In: Corporate Social Responsibility and the Paradoxes of Norwegian State Capitalism in the International Energy and Extraction Industries   1
Ståle Knudsen, Dinah Rajak, Siri Lange, and Isabelle Hugøy

Part I. Setting the Scene: Introduction and Framing of CSR in the Norwegian Context

Chapter 1   Rethinking Access: Key Methodological Challenges in Studying Energy Companies   39
Ingrid Birce Müftüoğlu, Ståle Knudsen, Ragnhild Freng Dale, Oda Eiken Maraire, Dinah Rajak, and Siri Lange

Chapter 2   *Samfunnsansvar* Is Not CSR: Mapping Expectations and Practices of (Corporate) Social Responsibility in Norway   63
Oda Eiken Maraire and Isabelle Hugøy

Chapter 3   Dynamics of Localized Social Responsibility: A Case from Agder, Norway   92
Eldar Bråten

Chapter 4   Model of a Model: Norsk Hydro at Home and Abroad   115
Ståle Knudsen

Part II. Ethnographies of Norwegian Corporations' Engagement with CSR

Chapter 5 Traveling, Translation, Transformation: On Social Responsibility and the Nordic Model in China 137
Emil A. Røyrvik

Chapter 6 Between Social Footprint and Compliance, or "What IBAMA Wants": Equinor Brazil's Social Sustainability Policy 163
Iselin Åsedotter Strønen

Chapter 7 Gender, Regulation, and Corporate Social Responsibility: The Case of Equinor's Social Investments in Tanzania 193
Siri Lange and Victoria Wyndham

Chapter 8 Exporting the Norwegian Model through the "Capacity Building" of a Local Union Branch: The Case of Equinor in Tanzania 219
Siri Lange

Chapter 9 Staging Mutual Dependencies: Energy Infrastructure and CSR in a Norwegian Petroleum Town 244
Ragnhild Freng Dale

Chapter 10 Standardizing Responsibility through the Stakeholder Figure: Norwegian Hydropower in Turkey 268
Ståle Knudsen, Ingrid Birce Müftüoğlu, and Isabelle Hugøy

Chapter 11 The "Nordic Model" in the Middle East Oil Fields: How Shareholder Value Eclipses Corporate Responsibility 295
Synnøve Bendixsen

Conclusion Inactive State Ownership and the Nordic Model Recast as "Values" 322
Ståle Knudsen

Index 335

Illustrations

Figures

2.1.	Enacting *samfunnsansvar* during a pandemic. © Isabelle Hugøy	71
2.2.	Trends in media use of the concepts CSR and *samfunnsansvar*. © Oda Eiken Maraire and Nina Bergheim Dahl	78
8.1.	Equinor's office building outside Oslo. © Siri Lange	229
8.2.	The office of the National Union of Mine and Energy Workers in Tanzania (NUMET). © Siri Lange	231
9.1.	Audience members gathered for Equinor's Snøhvit anniversary in Hammerfest, August 2017. © Ragnhild Freng Dale	246
10.1.	Localizing IFC standards in Turkey. © Statkraft	275
10.2.	"Good Neighbors." © Bahadir Sezegen	280
11.1.	View from a village close to the Tawke field. © Synnøve Bendixsen	307

Tables

0.1.	Overview of corporations discussed in the case studies. © Ståle Knudsen	5
7.1.	Overview of stakeholders and relevant policy documents. © Siri Lange	203
7.2.	Overview of Equinor's social investments in Tanzania 2014–18. © Siri Lange	209

Map

9.1.	Map showing the location of the two currently producing fields operated from Hammerfest. © Tom Chudley	249

PREFACE

Ståle Knudsen

This is a book about the possibilities and limitations of corporate responsibility in the context of the neoliberal global economy.[1] We focus on how transnational Norwegian energy and extractive industries handle corporate social responsibility (CSR) when they operate abroad. With significant state ownership and embeddedness in the Nordic societal model, Norwegian capitalism is sometimes considered particularly benign. Is this reflected in the way Norwegian corporations handle operations abroad? Our search for an answer has resulted in a series of ethnographic case studies of major Norwegian corporations' activities around the world (part II). As a backdrop for the case studies, we review important dimensions of the historical and Norwegian context for the way in which corporations maneuver, such as the notion of *samfunnsansvar* (societal responsibility), the political economy of industrial development in Norway, state ownership, and the Nordic model (part I).

Most books are long in the making: this one is no exception. The idea for the project from which this book has emerged was sparked during a lunch conversation between Siri Lange and me, ten years ago. We secured funding first for a pre-study (from the University of Bergen and the Chr. Michelsen Institute) and subsequently for a full-scale research project. The project, Energethics—Norwegian Energy Companies Abroad: Expanding the Anthropological Understanding of Corporate Social Responsibility, ran from 2015 to 2019 and was funded by a FRIPRO grant from the Research Council of Norway (grant no. 240617). A set of articles from this project was published in *Focaal* in 2020, corresponding to the introduction and chapters 6, 8, and 10 in this volume. In addition to these chapters, the Energethics team has crafted several new chapters (chapters 1, 2, 4, 7, 9, and 11) for this book, and we have elicited two chapters from other scholars working on related issues (chapters 3 and 5). Of the articles published in *Focaal*, chapters 6 and 10 have by and large only seen minor changes when carried over to this book, while the introduction has been thoroughly overhauled and updated and chapter 8 considerably restructured.

The Energethics case studies originally addressed Norwegian energy corporations' work on CSR abroad (and in the periphery of Norway; see chapter 9). With the realization that Norsk Hydro, a major Norwegian extractive industries corporation, has played a crucial role as a model in the Norwegian context, we have added two chapters focusing on this corporation, thus expanding the scope beyond energy. This is, however, not reflected in all chapters, such as in chapter 1, which addresses methods and has previously been published. In our estimation, though, the considerations we make in the methods chapter would hold for studies of Norsk Hydro as well.

In addition to the funding from the Research Council of Norway, I also want to acknowledge here support from the University of Bergen, especially for funding the costs of language editing and for making the book open access (additional funding for open access was granted by the Western Norway Research Institute and the Norwegian University of Science and Technology). Two reviewers read the whole manuscript thoroughly and provided many helpful suggestions, for which we are very grateful. I also want to express my gratitude to our always reliable language editor, Katharine Wheeler, who has been through most chapters at least once.

The majority of the case studies in the book concern the oil and gas corporation, Equinor. From its formation as a state corporation in the early 1970s and until 2018, when it changed its name, it was known as Statoil. In order not to confuse the reader, we have chosen to refer to the corporation as Equinor throughout, even when we consider its activities before 2018.

Notes

1. Earlier versions of six of the chapters have previously been published as articles:

    Introduction: Knudsen, Ståle, Dinah Rajak, Siri Lange, and Isabelle Hugøy. 2020. "Bringing the State Back In: Corporate Social Responsibility and the Paradoxes of Norwegian State Capitalism in the International Energy Sector." In Theme Section, "Corporate Social Responsibility and the Paradoxes of State Capitalism," edited by Ståle Knudsen and Dinah Rajak. *Focaal—Journal of Global and Historical Anthropology* 88: 1–21.

    Chapter 1: Müftüoğlu, Ingrid B., Ståle Knudsen, Ragnhild F. Dale, Oda Eiken, Dinah Rajak, and Siri Lange. 2018. "Rethinking Access: Key Methodological Challenges in Studying Energy Companies." *Energy Research & Social Science* 45 (November): 250–57.

    Chapter 6: Strønen, Iselin. 2020. "Between Social Footprint and Compliance, or 'What IBAMA Wants': Equinor Brazil's Social Sustainability policy." In Theme

Section, "Corporate Social Responsibility and the Paradoxes of State Capitalism," ed. Ståle Knudsen and Dinah Rajak. *Focaal—Journal of Global and Historical Anthropology* 88: 40–57.

Chapter 7: Lange, Siri, and Victoria Wyndham. 2021. "Gender, Regulation, and Corporate Social Responsibility in the Extractive Sector: The Case of Equinor's Social Investments in Tanzania." *Women's Studies International Forum* (84): 102434.

Chapter 8: Lange, Siri. 2020. "Doing Global Investments the Nordic Way: the 'Business Case' for Equinor's Support to Union Work among Its Employees in Tanzania." In Theme Section, "Corporate Social Responsibility and the Paradoxes of State Capitalism," ed. Ståle Knudsen and Dinah Rajak. *Focaal: Journal of Global and Historical Anthropology* 88: 22–39.

Chapter 10: Knudsen, Ståle, Ingrid B. Müftüoğlu, Isabelle Hugøy. 2020. "Standardizing Responsibility through the Stakeholder Figure: Norwegian Hydropower in Turkey." In Theme Section, "Corporate Social Responsibility and the Paradoxes of State Capitalism," ed. Ståle Knudsen and Dinah Rajak. *Focaal—Journal of Global and Historical Anthropology* 88: 58–75.

— Introduction —

BRINGING THE STATE BACK IN: CORPORATE SOCIAL RESPONSIBILITY AND THE PARADOXES OF NORWEGIAN STATE CAPITALISM IN THE INTERNATIONAL ENERGY AND EXTRACTION INDUSTRIES

Ståle Knudsen, Dinah Rajak, Siri Lange, and Isabelle Hugøy

Through a focus on the practices and politics of corporate social responsibility (CSR), this book examines comparatively how transnational companies (TNCs), the state, and the world economic order are linked in complex ways in energy industries. Our focus on energy and extraction corporate operations arises from their considerable environmental, social, and economic footprints (which CSR policies attempt to mitigate); further, states take a particular interest in energy due to its crucial role in society. While both proponents and critics of CSR have focused on the "business case" for CSR, anthropological debates have stressed how private corporations mobilize the language and practice of CSR and sustainability as (neoliberal) techniques to bypass the state, depoliticize conflicts, and take on the role of moral guardians. In the Nordic countries, however, the states have taken the lead role in promoting CSR and sustainability and expect Norwegian-based TNCs to act responsibly when "going global." The Nordic context—through which large energy corporations have been closely associated with the national project, the welfare state, and have significant state ownership—challenges conventional thinking about public versus private sector agendas and disrupts assumptions about how state politics and corporate interests interact in the exercise of social responsibility.

At the same time, Norwegian energy and extraction TNCs are intrinsically incorporated into the logics and workings of global capitalism along with the modes/norms of transnational corporate culture it generates. Norwegian energy corporations, which to a large extent are state owned, started operating abroad around 1990. This was a consequence of the opening up of international markets as well as deregulation at home and a perceived need to internationalize Norwegian state capital. While working far from home, these energy corporations relate and adapt to local and national particularities in their places of operation. At the same time, the standards and procedures for CSR or sustainability (as it is now more commonly cast within the extractive and energy sectors) to which they relate are set and managed by international institutions.

Most of the contributions in this book explore ethnographically the performance of corporate responsibility by Norwegian energy and extraction companies. They reveal how the relationship between transnationalism, state power, and local politics plays out in different ways in diverse contexts. In this introduction, we contextualize these cases in a broader theoretical and historical discussion of the ways in which debates about social responsibility are shaped by the competing forces of global political economy, state ownership, and national interest. We explore the relationship between transnational corporate capitalism and the Nordic model of welfare capitalism and state ownership, between global diversification and notions about Norway as the "humanitarian superpower." The ethnographic chapters follow a collection of chapters that set the scene, providing background on the Norwegian context. The relation between the concept, CSR, and its common Norwegian translation, *samfunnsansvar* (societal responsibility), is discussed in chapter 2. Chapter 3 provides a historical ethnography of a Norwegian company town where the state plays only a minor role, probing the analytical challenges of discussing CSR in the Norwegian context—a thread followed in later chapters of the book. This historical backdrop is enriched in chapter 4 through a review of how the Norwegian corporation Norsk Hydro has been a model for state ownership and CSR.

It is conventional wisdom and theoretical assumption that the Nordic model informs a better kind of global capitalism. Bringing ethnographic insights from a range of geographic contexts, this collection questions to what extent the Nordic model actually travels with the corporations when they operate abroad, even when the corporations are wholly or partly state owned. There are good reasons to question this, particularly when we consider what it takes for a corporation to succeed internationally.

In the theoretical discussion that follows, we outline two significant moves beyond the current state of anthropological studies of CSR. First, we resituate the state (which has remained a missing piece of the puzzle when it comes to critical analyses of CSR) as central to our understanding of what CSR *does* both for companies themselves and its target publics (whether local communities, employees, "host" or "home" governments). We argue that positioning the politics of the state as key to the unfolding policy landscape of CSR results in richer and more accurate analysis of both the intended and unintended outcomes of CSR practice. Second, we do not assume that the variegated practices of CSR can be fully understood as (purely) neoliberal governance techniques. This becomes evident when we account for how CSR is performed in the Nordic context. Our approach considers global political economy and historicizes the relationship between state, capital, and CSR. This expanded, and admittedly ambitious, framing enables us to ask: what can we learn about the relationship between state, capital, and corporate responsibility by studying state-owned Norwegian energy corporations operating abroad?

CSR and the State

The concept of CSR and the practices that come with it have distinctive roots in the business environment of the United States. CSR gained international popularity during the 1980s and 1990s, but, like other traveling models, it adapted to local circumstances. Both proponents and critics of CSR have primarily considered CSR a business strategy. While proponents have focused on "proving" the business case for CSR, critical studies view CSR as part and parcel of the global neoliberal shift in policies. The putative association of CSR with neoliberalism is one of the key reasons why the role of the state in relation to CSR has largely remained unseen. The result has been an oversimplified story about CSR as a technique of neoliberal governance for bypassing or usurping the role of the state. Drawing largely on work produced by the Energethics project, this collection sets out to problematize this stock story and interrogate more closely the intersection of CSR, state politics, and global capitalism.

There is not scope in this introduction for a comprehensive review of the anthropology of CSR (see Dolan and Rajak 2016), but it is important to note that anthropological studies of CSR have argued that CSR should be seen as a broad, evolving, and flexible set of practices and languages through which businesses variously attempt to position themselves as ethical actors. Thus, depending on context, sector, time, and local particularities, CSR may mean different things and can be "best understood as a boundary object" (Smith 2021: 5; see also chapter 2). Ethnographic work in this field has shown the diverse ways that corporations use the language and practice of ethics to contain and respond to the various challenges and conflicts generated by their activities. This literature has explored how CSR policies emerged out of corporate accommodation to critiques of their environmental and social impacts (and of the neoliberal economic reforms of the 1980s more generally) and evolved into a set of techniques through which companies claim to foster local sustainable development in direct interaction with relevant local communities (Kirsch and Benson 2010; Welker 2009).

The discourse of CSR has been dynamic and adaptive. In recent years, in response to converging crises of the commodity downturn, climate change action, and depleting reserves, there has been a shift within the broader energy and extraction sectors from the register of responsibility to an emphasis on sustainability and risk management in articulating a CSR agenda. At the same time this shift has arguably been in response to growing critique of corporate colonial paternalism enacted through CSR (see, e.g., Chong 2018; Rajak 2011; Welker 2014). To many critics and practitioners alike, CSR retained too much of the philanthropic tradition it was meant to replace, prompting the language to shift toward "sustainability" and "environmental, social, and governance" (ESG) risks. A major claim by business and in management theory is that the handling of corporate responsibility should be embedded or mainstreamed within corporate management processes—within the very DNA of the company—from geological prospecting to risk assessment to financial forecasting.

The latest shift in the language of business responsibility from CSR to ESG has coevolved with the emergence of an expanding field for business ethics constituted by international codes, conventions, and consultancy; this new institutional landscape has generated extensive machinery for reporting and auditing, as detailed in chapter 10. While CSR primarily developed within a neoliberal (Anglo-American) context, these new international frameworks are more influenced by other states and actors. Since these international institutions generally have no power over the corporations other than affecting their reputation, state law and regulations remain the primary mechanisms for sanctioning the work of TNCs.

However, a key insight from ethnographies of corporate ethics is that TNCs increasingly bypass the state—both at home and in their countries of operation—through local enclaving (Ferguson 2005) or

Table 0.1. Overview of corporations discussed in the case studies.

Corporation	Main activity	Ownership	Size (market capitalization range 2010–2022) billion USD	Global presence	Employees	Chapter(s) addressed
Equinor (until 2018 Statoil)	Oil and gas extraction	Listed, 67% state	40–120	30 countries	21 000	1, 6, 7, 8, 9
Statkraft	Hydro-power, wind, solar, electricity trade	100% state owned, corporatized	Total assets 1.5–3.5*	20 countries, mainly Europe, Brazil	4 800	10
Norsk Hydro	Aluminum, energy	34% State, 7% Government Pension Fund Norway, no other large shareholders	4–20	40 countries, main countries Norway and Brazil	31 000	4, 5
DNO ASA	Oil and gas extraction	No state ownership, RAK Petroleum 45%, of which DNO executive chairman Bijan Mossavar-Rahman controls around 40%. Overall little Norwegian ownership, but leadership and board to a large extent Norwegian.	0.25–2.5	Middle East (mainly Iraq), Norway, UK	1 000	11

Sources: https://companiesmarketcap.com/, https://ycharts.com/companies/DTNOF/market_cap, company websites. * Since the shares of Statkraft are not publicly traded, it is not possible to calculate market capitalization. These numbers represent total assets 2017–21, https://www.tradingview.com/symbols/BMFBOVESPA-STKF3/financials-balance-sheet/total-assets/. © Ståle Knudsen partnership with nonstate actors (Gardner 2012), thereby claiming "a kind of collective moral guardianship over people," especially where states are incapable of furthering the ideals of development, freedom, democracy, and the like (Rajak 2011: 55). Often, corporations have been seen to "take on the role of states" by funding and operating basic services, such as schools, health facilities, and transport infrastructure, through CSR programs. Accordingly, studies of CSR tend to be characterized by the absence, rather than the presence, of the state.

We reexamine this position, asking whether state entities can take an active role in shaping the CSR of TNCs, be it in their country of origin or of operation. In the actualized practice of CSR, the boundary between the corporation and state may be difficult to pinpoint, and CSR may be interwoven with other interactions between the corporation, public authorities, and locals (see, e.g., Welker 2014; Rogers 2015). By offering comparative cases across fully state-owned companies (Statkraft), publicly listed companies with significant state shareholding (Equinor and Norsk Hydro), as well as corporations without state ownership (chapters 3 and 11), we raise a set of key questions: Can, in fact, both state-owned and partially state-owned energy and extraction companies pursue and implement corporate ethics by governance techniques that do not rely on and promote market rule, commodification, and privatization as regulatory frameworks evolve from the focus on CSR to ESG? Do corporations without state ownership, but which are based in the corporate culture of Norway, practice CSR differently? Finally, the chapters in this book look beyond the actors and institutions producing CSR from above (both private and governmental), to examine how CSR can be claimed "from below" or become domesticated (Knudsen 2015).

Neoliberal Globalization and the State

In recent anthropological scholarship, there has been much focus on neoliberalism as a traveling and hegemonic model. The idea of neoliberalism and how it can be studied has of course been highly contested,[1] but it still underpins the way in which we think about and study state, capital, corporations, and a whole range of other issues under the current global situation. At a policy level and in public debate, the notion of the free market as being at odds with the state has been hegemonic. Even analysts have tended to give normative privilege to one or the other side in the dichotomy. "Neoliberal" is freely and flexibly used in a normative way by those skeptical of any kind of "marketization" or capitalism (Flew 2012).

A typical contemporary example of state versus market thinking is Mariana Mazzucato's influential book, *The Entrepreneurial State: Debunking Public vs. Private Sector Myths* (2018). She presents her work as a challenge to "conventional wisdom" concerning the role of government in the economy and as an attempt to reestablish confidence in the public sector (2018: xxiii). Referring especially to Polanyi (2001 [1944]), she acknowledges the critical role of "states in *shaping* and *creating* markets" (Mazzucato 2018: 15), thus seemingly going beyond the public-private distinction. Yet, the "conventional wisdom" she refers to is clearly an Anglo-American neoliberal-inspired view on the limited role the public (or the state) should have in the economy, and her strategy for attacking that convention is to give more weight to the state side of the dichotomy. Although she contends that her "book is an open call to change the way we talk about the State" (2018: 213), state and business remain two very distinct spheres, and there is nothing between or beyond.

Even though the *Varieties of Capitalism* approach (Ingham 2011: 215; Hall and Soskice 2001) differentiates between the ideal types of liberal market economies (LME) and coordinated market economies (CME), not all possible capitalisms can be situated on a straight axis between these two poles. Systems that are not LME are not simply characterized by a strong state; a variety of other actors may take important roles—be they trust/banks, labor unions, guilds—and the level of state involvement may be of very different kinds. Norway, France, Russia, and China all have strong state involvement in the economy, but the organization of their societies and economies are certainly very different.

Thus, within this dichotomous framework it is difficult to engage in nuanced thinking about the Nordic model. There are several good reasons for questioning the narrative about the free market as being at odds with the state. First, readings of foundational texts on neoliberalism tend to be simplistic, reproducing assumptions about the logic of neoliberal capital and governance in ways that overlook the nuances and countervailing trajectories of specific context. Second, work on the history of managerialism as well as comparative studies of governance techniques challenge such conventional readings of neoliberalism by exposing alternative trajectories in governance that do not "fit" the "off-the-shelf" neoliberal model. And, finally, contemporary shifts in the global political economy destabilize the stock story of state versus market. Below we discuss these three issues in more detail.

A variety of approaches to neoliberalism inform ethnographic work on contemporary economy and society. While the foundational (though very different) texts of Harvey and Foucault continue to dominate the scene,[2] readings of both approaches tend to assume the existence of a global program of neoliberalism that overdetermines all social processes, so that, for example, every instance of CSR will solely be seen as a tool of capital. A closer reading of both Harvey and Foucault supports a more nuanced rendering of neoliberalism.

Although he claims that "the continuous circulation of capital … functions … as the engine of the totality" (Harvey 2017: 113), Harvey holds that different "moments" (of which he identifies seven, including "institutional frameworks") are autonomous and independent and argues that in Marx's work there is "no prime mover, but a mess of often contradictory movements across and between the different moments that have to be uncovered and worked out" (Harvey 2017: 114). This is certainly more dynamic and less deterministic and reductionist than structural-deterministic Marxist approaches that see neoliberalism as a global process steered by the interest of capital. While we acknowledge the crucial power of capitalist and class dynamics, we stress that, here as with all societies, the development of contemporary capitalist societies involves other forces and dynamics often overlooked as a result of the preoccupation with the workings of capital. Crucially, these multifaceted dynamics of governance (and the social struggles that determine them) are not reducible to the pursuit of profit and of the so-called logic of capital.

Yet despite Harvey's concession that "a dialectical relation between territorial [i.e., state] and capitalistic logics of power" (Harvey 2003: 183) exists, he does not really explore the logic and agency of government. Harvey and other Marxist-inspired approaches to neoliberalism tend to restrict the working of the state and governance to a function of "the dynamics of capital accumulation and the networks of class power" (Harvey 2005: 76; see also Ingham 2011).

When thinking about governance under neoliberal conditions, Foucauldian theories of governance have been particularly influential. While Foucault was interested in "the art of government" in his exploration of neoliberalism (Foucault 2008), studies inspired by his approach typically stress how the reflexive practice of governance increasingly enacts "competitiveness, commercial rationale and risk calculation" (Hilgers 2011: 358) as the main logics in the art of government. "Neoliberal governance" is set to work in a grand narrative about a global program for the "marketization of everything" and inculcation of "neoliberal subjectivities."

This is a simplified articulation of Foucault's nuanced and historically situated understanding of neoliberalism. A closer reading of his lectures reveals that he did not think that there was only one way that "enterprise society" could be organized. Foucault outlined how North American and German neoliberalisms could be seen as two different, contextually dependent answers to the questions of how to "not govern too much" while balancing freedom and security. While arguing for "making the market, competition, and so the enterprise, into what could be called the formative power of society" (Foucault 2008: 148), the ordoliberals considered that competition "is not a principle on which it would be possible to erect the whole of society" (Foucault 2008: 243). They also wanted an active social policy and "a *Vitalpolitik*, a politics of life" (Foucault 2008: 148), through which was organized a "political and moral framework" distinct from the rules of competition (Foucault 2008: 243).

Thus, both Harvey and Foucault, in different and distinct ways, envision how capital, markets, states, and other social actors are configured relative to each other, resulting in distinctive socio-economic-political formations. Such "economic-institutional ensembles" can take many forms, even when organized for markets and fostering *homo* æconomicus (Foucault 2008: 147); the Nordic model may be considered one such "ensemble." Still, we consider that Harvey's approach tends toward assuming "global" dynamics ("capital ... functions ... as the engine of the totality"), whereas Foucault's approach gravitates toward totalities ("ensembles"). Both may give credence to simplistic analyses where CSR is seen to be derived directly from neoliberal capitalist and/or governance logics.

Drawing on Reidar Grønhaug's theory of social fields, Bråten elaborates in chapter 3 an approach that to lesser extent assumes particular global dynamics or social totalities. Identifying "social fields" (resembling "moments" in Harvey's approach) with different "scales" and characterized by certain logics or dynamics—"proper dynamics" in Grønhaug's terminology—he endeavors a historical-ethnographic analysis of the way social responsibility is configured and how it changes over time in a Norwegian community dominated by a privately owned shareholding company. This approach, which is implicitly adopted by most chapters in this collection, is more sensitive to empirical variation yet can support analytical rigor and comparison. Indeed, Bråten concludes that "CSR [is] inextricably [tied] to the proper dynamics of corporations. Despite its variegated surface forms, I take CSR to be ontologically rooted in (thus logically secondary to) the proper dynamic of capitalist production" (Bråten: 110). Taking this approach also keeps us from reifying, for example, the Nordic model and the Nordic context that affords one particular polity that has fostered corporations with special characteristics. Corporations have different trajectories in different polities, and neither state, corporations, nor capitalism can be taken for granted.

Diversifying Theories of Governance

The second reason for questioning the narrative about a global hegemonic neoliberalism relates to a tendency to read all contemporary governance as neoliberal. Although we have argued above that Foucault's analysis of neoliberalism usefully enables approaches that do not assume an overarching global and hegemonic neoliberalism, we also acknowledge a significant limitation of Foucault's work on neoliberalism in that he was primarily interested in the emergence of certain *ideas* about governance. He did not pursue in any detail how and to what extent the neoliberal rationalities were implemented; in an aside, Foucault (2008: 144) simply states that the ordoliberals' preferred policy "could not be strictly applied in Germany" due to the ballast of earlier economic policies. Perhaps it is this character of his work that has made it so easy to read a global program of neoliberal governance into it. Detailed historical and ethnographic studies have, however, demonstrated that governance techniques that we tend to consider neoliberal often have other origins and are designed for other purposes.

Just as new public management, audits, cost-benefit calculations, and the like are generally considered neoliberal governance techniques (Knafo et al. 2019), so we suggest that CSR as operationalized by Norwegian state energy corporations shows a similar genealogy to particularly Nordic styles of governance and managerialism. "Rather than enforce market-like mechanisms," the ambition of professional management was to empower policy makers and top managers in large organizations through the "use [of] optimization as a tool for governance" (Knafo et al. 2019: 246, 247). The complex management models that emerged out of this, especially "stage gate process" (Lenfle and Loch 2009: 12), are today central to the work of public authorities and large corporations alike—including Equinor, Norsk Hydro, and Statkraft—and are mirrored in the processes of standardization and ethical performance management and reporting that are the bedrock of CSR. The authors explain why this managerial tradition later has come to be seen as neoliberal by the fact that "the rhetoric of neoliberal theory was later re-appropriated by those promoting managerial practices of governance and who presented their framework as a means to produce 'market-like logics'" (Knafo et al. 2019: 247–48).

Equally, we draw on insights from comparative ethnography on China (Nonini 2008; Kipnis 2008) and post-Soviet studies (Collier 2011; Lampland 1995, Rogers 2015), which have also made crucial strides in disrupting the grand narrative of neoliberalism. Donald Nonini criticizes anthropological assertions that China is becoming neoliberal, challenges claims that universalize neoliberalization, and "argues for a different and more complex anthropological understanding of how state formation, politics, cultural practices, and economic transformations are related to one another" (Nonini 2008: 147). Kipnis, taking issue especially with Rose's approach (e.g., 1999), convincingly conveys how the comprehensive audits system in Chinese schools has its own unique trajectory and (nonmarket) rationale and is not a result of diffusion of neoliberal rationality. Kipnis holds that in place of pursuing the alleged diffusion of a "regime of truth," we should, rather, explore the scientism that informs and legitimizes many different audit systems, the performance of which should be seen as "techniques for manipulating local social relations" (Kipnis 2008: 282). Thus, in place of explaining all new forms of governance that involve auditing, statistics, metrics, competition, and the like as neoliberal, we may be well advised to focus rather on management, bureaucratization, governance, standardization, rationalization, and scientism—that is, ways of "seeing like a governing agent" (Kipnis 2008: 282), to paraphrase Scott (1998). What are considered neoliberal governance techniques are often complex mergers of models with separate trajectories and purposes.

Shifts in Global Political Economy

The final reason for questioning the neoliberal account is the current shift in the global economic system. With the rise of China, new protectionist policies in the United States, and a turn to more authoritative governments, there emerges a realization that there must be other ways of configuring capital, markets, and the state than those that are articulated in the standard narrative about neoliberalization modeled on pervasive Anglo-American ideas about the state and (private) capital. Keith Hart has suggested that the "neoliberal hegemony may be cracking." He argues that "a swing back to state intervention is now more likely than any time in the last four decades" but also asks, "What is the state now and where can it be found?" (Hart 2018: 546).

That question is perhaps best answered by problematizing the classic state-society duality and "[treating] state and non-state governmentality within a common frame" (Ferguson and Gupta 2002: 994). Indeed, James Ferguson and Akhil Gupta argue that it is precisely through nonstate actors (including both local NGOs and international organizations) that state power is reconfigured, as states attempt to extend their authority across new scales, creating networks of transnational governance, and "stake their claim to superior generality and universality" (2002: 996). Rather, the questions must be: Where can governance be found? How do these models of governance travel? While Ferguson and Gupta do not consider TNCs at all in their exploration of transnational governance, we argue that TNCs are key sites (and purveyors) of governance on a national and global scale, a role authorized and validated by the discourse of CSR/corporate citizenship, and are thus key to understanding the relation between capital and governance. The case study on Statkraft in this collection, for instance, explores governance as it is enacted in the complex interface between the Norwegian state, the corporation, international institutions and standards, and the Turkish state.

Most studies of contemporary governance start from the premise that neoliberal models travel from Global North to South (or global economic center to periphery), establishing themselves in new places in a form of (neoliberal) bureaucratic imperialism. Jamie Peck and Nik Theodore (2015) challenge this assumption, arguing that progressive governance policies, now often developed in the Global South, may become traveling models and spread rapidly to other jurisdictions. Sometimes these compete, sometimes they merge with policies that will usually be considered neoliberal.

Following their lead, we hope in this collection to provide a counterbalance to the preoccupation with the workings of governance and capital in so called archetypal neoliberal states or in the ways in which weak states are captured/sidelined by TNCs. Rather, we focus on corporations working out of Norway, a developed economy with a strong state ostensibly less impacted by neoliberal logic than most other Western states. Below we discuss the "actually existing" Nordic model as an assemblage of different governance techniques and actors, admittedly increasingly informed by neoliberal doctrines but with its own unique histories and characters. We make the claim that it makes sense to think about the Nordic societies as unique and not representing only versions of the neoliberal model. The Nordic model, while adopting models from the outside, may also harbor governance techniques that can more (chapter 5) or less (chapter 11) successfully travel elsewhere. Thus, we ask, do the Norwegian energy corporations we have studied take with them techniques of governance that can be identified as particular to the Norwegian context (such as strong union representation, the consensus model, or egalitarian ethos) when working abroad? For example, a key question that motivates Lange's study of the Norwegian oil giant, Equinor, in this collection, is how (and to what extent) the company attempts to introduce the Nordic "consensus model" of union representation and employment relations in their greenfield operations in Tanzania.

The Nordic Model

We have argued the importance of problematizing the public-private distinction and historicizing the relationship between state, capital, and CSR. Accordingly, in the following sections, we first make the argument that it makes sense to talk about a Nordic model and explain why by outlining the emergence and characteristics of the model. Subsequent sections review reforms of the Norwegian state since the 1980s and the evolving policy for state-owned corporations, which we show to be driven by accelerating internationalization of Norwegian capital and interests. Chapter 4 further explores the Nordic model through the lens of Norsk Hydro, which in many respects has been a model for the Nordic model in Norway.

The Nordic model is a result of the particular trajectories of political and economic developments in the Nordic countries during the last one to two hundred years. We focus here on Norway, where a progressive constitution from 1814, the relative lack of both nobility and powerful bourgeoisie, a decentralized petty bourgeoisie, and independent municipalities and co-ops have facilitated the emergence of a relatively egalitarian society. Yet, industrialization from the 1880s onward resulted in the same kinds of tensions and unrest as in other European countries between emerging capitalists and laborers. Many years of strife ended when the major labor union and the employers' organization agreed to the "Major Agreement" (*Hovedavtalen*) in 1935, which set the rules for how to manage relations between parties. With the state also involved, the basis was set for a tripartite cooperation that would be deepened after the war and find its most comprehensive solutions in the "income-political settlements" (*inntektspolitiske oppgjør*) during the 1970s when the deals included not only salaries but also comprehensive adjustments of the welfare system, pensions, employee representation on company boards, and so forth. This basic structure of the tripartite cooperation remains in place.

Similar developments took place in the other Nordic countries, which can be said to share the following characteristics: "(1) exceptionally egalitarian and democratic political traditions, (2) the welfare state and (3) labor market politics and regulations" (Ervasti et al. 2008: 3). Although the kind of state involved in the tripartite cooperation has sometimes been characterized as the "corporatist state," the Nordic corporatist state does not substitute for but adds to democratic mechanisms. The "state" is not a strong central state (e.g., the French state) but rather is "remarkably decentralized, and the commitments of the welfare state seem to be exceptionally well embedded in institutions under local, popular control" (Vike 2012: 128).

The political left in Norway has increasingly appropriated the model—now referring to the "Norwegian societal model"—and, in addition to the structural and economic variables mentioned above, considers core values such as trust, cooperation, consensus, openness, community (*fellesskap*), gender equality, and egalitarianism to be constitutive and to guarantee the success of the model. There is widely shared trust in the state; the leading labor union, LO, emphasizes the value of the "communal state" (*fellesskapsstaten*). While the Nordic/Norwegian model is thus associated with certain values and norms—a certain "culture"—we think it unwise to try to discern whether these values and norms are a result or cause of the social-regulatory dimensions of the model. It makes no sense to try to identify "essential" Nordic values, but if there is a single element that, were it removed from the model, would render it "non-Nordic," we would say it is the influence that the labor movement has on capital and the state. Beyond that, the Nordic model is contested and unstable and has had uneven penetration even within Norway, as demonstrated in Bråten's chapter. It is a moving target, but, also, potentially transferable. *The Economist*[3] suggests that other countries may learn from the "new Nordic model," which "begins with the individual rather than the state," with openness and a willingness to reform.

"Toward a Better Organized State"

Since the 1980s and at times in the vanguard, the Nordic countries have enacted significant reforms—experimenting with and developing new ways of creating and governing markets[4]—that are often considered of a neoliberal character (for Sweden, see Harvey 2005 and Fulcher 2015). In Norway, reforms of the state were discussed and implemented to some extent before neoliberal ideas about the role of the state started to circulate and then accelerated after internationalization gained momentum. The initial driver was not related to capitalist dynamics but rather was found in dynamics largely internal to the Norwegian state, with concerns surfacing already in the 1960s related to "modernization" and "efficiency" in the state and to the mixing of different roles within the same agencies (Herning 2009: 68). Policies such as internal independence/devolution (*fristilling*) within state governance, management by objectives (*målstyring*), and corporatization (see Herning 2009: 11–12) were seen as natural and realistic tools to modernize the state.

Beyond the internal dynamics, the seemingly ubiquitous presence of the state across all dimensions of life resulted in the growth of a popular countermovement, which brought the Conservative Party to power in the early 1980s, ousting the Labor Party, which had dominated politics since World War II. Significant reforms were implemented and were not overturned when the Labor Party came back into power.

The momentum for reform was channeled into the green paper "A Better Organized State" (Prop. 5 1989), arguably the single most important green paper ever in Norway. It contended that societal, demographic, and technological changes in Norway necessitated considerable reforms of the state in order to maintain its efficiency and legitimacy. Overall, the report emphasizes the importance and implications of internationalization (see, e.g., 40–41, 42), for example, arguing for the organization of state-owned corporations as stock-based firms since that is a form that is "well known and acknowledged nationally as well as internationally" (Prop. 5 1989: 155).

The combined impact of pressure from within the state as well as a political and ideological shift toward policies reminiscent of the "Third Way" eventually resulted in significant corporatization and privatization of state agencies and assets. This also implied huge shifts in the relation between the state and major national entities involved in energy production and resource extraction.

Globally, the oil and gas sector is not capitalist—or at least not owned by private capital. While the "seven sisters" once controlled most of the sector, the tide turned in the 1960s and 1970s so that, now, "the role of state enterprises is stronger than ever" (Victor, Hults, and Thurber 2012: 3). Although "state control over oil waned" during the 1990s (Victor, Hults, and Thurber 2012: 7), national oil companies (NOC) control roughly two-thirds of global oil and gas reserves and production. Most of these are inextricably enmeshed with the state apparatus, largely operate within their home countries, and are not listed companies with tradable shares. Until the 1980s, such was the case for Equinor, which is considered one of the more successful among the national oil corporations, as well as for the state and municipal agencies responsible for hydropower production in Norway. Internationally Statkraft is, however, more of an anomaly, since it remains completely state owned in a sector—electricity production and distribution—that to a much larger extent has been privatized.

Although strong ties to the Norwegian state and society remain, Equinor and Statkraft became more independent as they started operating abroad, corporatized, and (partly) privatized. Equinor is therefore among the few NOCs that "are commercially minded entities little different from their private sector international oil company ... counterparts" (Victor et al. 2012: 3). Thus, Equinor represents a kind of hybrid between an NOC and the Anglo-American oil companies.

Although internationalization spurred liberalization in the organization of the economy, the total thrust of the reforms never was as dramatic and deep as in the "iconic" neoliberal experiments. The actors who initiated and fought for reform and restructuration of stage agencies were not necessarily ideologically motivated by a neoliberal program, and "agencification and corporatization have a much longer history [in Norway] than the NPM reform movement" (Lægreid, Roness, and Rolland 2013: 670). Managers of state agencies and state enterprises also lobbied actively for corporatization (e.g., Statkraft, see Nilsen and Thue 2006) and privatization (e.g., Equinor, see Sæhter 2017), first to facilitate a management less restrained by state bureaucratic structures, then to be able to internationalize. Norsk Hydro, over which the state had (by choice) less influence, could more easily internationalize by adapting to an international business environment, thereby emerging as a model for other Norwegian corporations venturing abroad (see chapter 4).

Thus, the corporatization of Statkraft (1992) and partial privatization of Equinor (2001) were not results of a neoliberal policy for "marketization" but, rather, answers to historically specific challenges. "Internationalization" was one such particular historic challenge experienced by the management in these corporations from the late 1980s onward. And, despite these reforms, it still makes sense to talk about a particular Nordic/Norwegian "economic-institutional ensemble," where the basic architectures of the tripartite model and of the welfare state are in place, to the extent that in the North Sea oil economies "Norwegian trade unions remain important actors (beyond the wildest dreams of their UK counterparts)" (Cumbers 2012: 238).

State Ownership: Professional and (In)active

Although state ownership of oil and gas corporations is now more the rule than the exception globally, the anthropological literature has not explored the way in which states manage their ownership or identified what consequences that may have for corporate responsibility. Before we do so, this section provides a brief outline of the nuts and bolts of state ownership and the Norwegian government's claim that they pursue a transparent, pragmatic, "professional," and "active" ownership policy in the context of internationalization.

First, it is important to note that, even compared with the other Nordic countries,[5] state capitalism has been particularly important in Norway. The Norwegian state and municipalities have been heavily involved in transport, postal services, energy and telecommunications, and industry, especially after World War I (Lie 2016). When oil extraction started during the early 1970s, the state controlled most dimensions of the sector. The successful incorporation of the oil industry into the Nordic model probably contributed to the relative success of the oil economy, avoiding Dutch disease and the resource curse. State ownership—or, more precisely, public ownership—is now much higher in Norway than in any other Western European and OECD country. Public institutions in Norway own approximately one-third of all equity in Norway,[6] and the Norwegian state owns 35 percent of the shares on the Oslo Stock Exchange. Five out of the six most valuable corporations on the Oslo Stock Exchange are controlled by the Norwegian state (Lie, Mykelbust, and Norvik 2014: 86).

State ownership in Norway has largely developed pragmatically during the last few decades (Lie et al. 2014; Lie 2016). The current state ownership policy is a political compromise: large and relatively "active" state ownership (favored by the left) versus state ownership managed with discipline, commercial "professionalism," and little involvement from the state (favored by the right) (Lie 2016: 924). "Professionalism" denotes "businesslike management" as well as noninvolvement by the state. This is partly related to the legacy of the so-called Kings Bay case,[7] which toppled the government in 1963 (Lie et al. 2014) and instituted an unwritten rule in Norwegian state governance that representatives from the government (politicians as well as civil servants) must not have central roles in state-owned businesses. Thus, *that* state ownership is significant is widely accepted, while *how* the state exerts its ownership has been a bone of contention. There has been disagreement particularly over how much the state should interfere (be "active") in the operation of its corporations (see chapter 4, this volume).

Since the early 2000s, the state's ownership of corporations has become "objectified," with a consolidated focus and apparatus for making ownership visible and governable through a suite of instruments and rules: a Department of Ownership was established within the Ministry of Trade and Industry; guidelines for the overall ownership policy have been outlined in dedicated white papers; occasional reports set out governmental "ownership policies"; an annual ownership report summarizes results for all companies (seventy-five in 2017) in which the state has full or partial ownership.[8]

For the largest "commercial" state-owned corporations, adhering to the state's ownership policy has primarily meant producing revenue for the shareholder-state. Yet, from the first white paper addressing state ownership, there has been a consistent focus on the importance of globalization and internationalization, actualizing debate about ethics in new ways (Meld. St. 61 [1996–97]). Experience has shown that active ownership quickly comes up against a perceived need to abide by the rules of international capitalism. Some of the international activities of Equinor, such as tar sands extraction in Canada, have been controversial abroad and at home. Equinor again became the focus of intense media and public attention when it was revealed that it had an accumulated loss amounting to 20 billion euros from their investments in the United States.[9] Another example is the scandal that erupted in 2018 relating to Hydro's handling of a toxic water spill from their facilities in Brazil. While the case has been brought to the Norwegian parliament, Stortinget, the government has declined to instruct or in any other way put pressure on Equinor (Sæther 2017: 304; Lie et al. 2014: 87) or Hydro (chapter 4). Demonstrating to the world (aka the global finance markets) that the Norwegian state pursued "professional" noninterfering ownership was considered crucial. Thus, the new, consolidated, and professional way to govern ethics of the state-owned corporations is for the state to articulate through white papers and ownership reports clear "expectations" or rules for responsible corporate conduct.

CSR as State Matter for Global Engagement

"Corrupt countries line up for Statoil" claimed an article in the major Norwegian daily *Aftenposten* in 2006.[10] Equinor (previously Statoil), Telenor, Statkraft, Norsk Hydro—all among the largest Norwegian corporations and all with state ownership—have each been involved in scandals in their overseas operations. This has been a serious issue for the reputation of the corporations and of the Norwegian state, and members of parliament have been concerned that Norway's reputation abroad may be harmed (Ihlen 2011: 14–16). The scandals have been addressed in several white papers on state ownership. Norsk Hydro's failed attempt to establish a bauxite-producing facility in Orissa, India, during the 1990s due to local resistance and global media exposure was discussed in the governmental white paper on CSR (Meld. St. 10 [2008–9]: 43) as an example of why Norwegian corporations need more comprehensive CSR strategies to address "complex challenges" and higher expectations in the "international civil society community." A 2004 green paper considers that "the state's legitimacy may be reduced, for example as lawmaker or in cases that relate to foreign policy, if the state through its role as owner does not pursue high standards in this field" (Prop. 53 2003–4: 16). As the Norwegian state increasingly operates as an international capitalist, can it maintain the high ethical standards embedded in the Nordic model while aligning that with the international image of Norway as a humanitarian superpower?

Maraire and Hugøy, reviewing in chapter 2 the development of the language of CSR in policy papers, argue that it is this context—the problems that Norwegian, often state-owned, corporations have faced in acting responsibly abroad—that has molded thinking about CSR in Norway. The formalization of CSR was a government initiative with the establishment of KOMPAKT in 1998, which was "a consultative body consisting of the traditional corporatist partners as well as NGOs and academia, with the explicit goal of providing a forum for discussion" (Gjølberg 2010: 212). Importantly, this consultative body has from the start been embedded within the Ministry of Foreign Affairs and is tasked "to strengthen the Government's basis for developing policy and for decision-making in the area of CSR, with particular emphasis on international issues."[11]

Globalization and internationalization induced both Norwegian and Russian energy and extraction businesses to engage with CSR, but in very different ways and with dissimilar results. Whereas CSR became a tool for managing messy realities for Norwegian corporations when operating abroad (but not at home) and at an increasing remove from the Norwegian state, CSR was mobilized in the Perm region of Russia during the 2000s in efforts to coordinate state-corporation relations, resulting in "an interpenetration of corporation and state that was far more thorough and extensive than we find elsewhere" (Rogers 2015: 176). Thus, "in the Volga federal district ... this was the primary way in which 'the state' reemerged [sic] in the 2000s" (2015: 158). This illustrates the point that CSR is a highly flexible governance technique that can be mobilized in a wide range of different political economies, or economic-institutional ensembles, based on different motivations, and having divergent results even though internationalization is the primary driver.

Two interrelated claims have been made about CSR in the Nordic countries, the first represented by the idea, expressed by, for example, managers at Statkraft, that "we are CSR, we do not need CSR in Norway" since much of what CSR policies try to achieve is "already in place" in the Nordic countries (see chapter 2). The second claim is that the Nordic model makes Norwegian corporations well prepared for competition in an international arena (Ihlen 2011: 48). This seems to be confirmed by the high score and many prizes Nordic corporations receive for their CSR work (Strand, Freeman, and Hockerts 2015).

However, it has also been argued that the "Nordic state-market-society model" is at odds with the American "business case" model of CSR, which implicitly grants discretionary powers to businesses, acknowledges unions only as "stakeholders," and "can appear illegitimate in the context of the 'Nordic normative legacy'" (Gjølberg 2010: 210). Unions in Norway—as in the rest of the Nordic countries and in much of Europe—tend to take a critical stance toward CSR. They are particularly concerned about the way in which CSR sidesteps or ignores the institutionalization of workers' rights in laws and regulations, making voluntary important societal concerns that should be required and regulated (Trygstad and Lismoen 2008). So, was the Nordic model the foundation when the government came to develop CSR policies for state-owned corporations?

Successive governments since 2001 have expected corporations with state ownership to take a leading role in work on CSR (Meld.

St. 132 [2006–7]: 64). The white paper on "CSR in a Global Economy" elaborated some of the rationale: "To an increasing extent, Norwegian companies are engaging in commercial activities in, and trade with, countries that are affected by political instability, widespread poverty or corruption" (Meld. St. 10 [2008–9]: 7). For the last ten years, there has been increased focus on CSR in the dialogue between the state and its companies and in ownership reports. The move toward the business case for CSR is well illustrated by a statement by Monica Mæland, Conservative minister for trade and industry, who stated that "to be good corporations and give high returns in the long run, they need to handle their social responsibility (*samfunnsansvar*) in a good way" (*Aftenposten*, 16 April 2016).

Thus, the Norwegian state does not expect corporations to adhere to some specific Nordic or Norwegian model for CSR but, rather, requires corporations in which the state has significant ownership and that have overseas operations to be serious about CSR by signing on to the Global Compact, following the OECD responsible business conduct recommendations for multinational corporations, taking up ILO's core conventions, and applying Global Reporting Initiative (GRI) reporting standards (Meld. St. 27 [2013–14]: 81). A "Nordic concern" about CSR is, perhaps paradoxically, addressed by expecting corporations to adhere to "universal" standards and mechanisms.

A number of various international conventions and institutions are in place to guide businesses and other organizations to behave as responsibly as possible. While chapter 10 discusses in some detail how Statkraft relates to international standards, it is outside the scope of this introduction to review these frameworks, except for mention of a few general characteristics and trends. First, adherence to most of the standards and principles is voluntary. Even though sustainability reporting is increasingly becoming compulsory, it is not supported by any sanctions other than "naming and blaming." Second, there is a distinction between standards that one may sign on to and submit annual CSR reports to, such as UN Global Compact and the reporting framework GRI, and standards that provide tools for actual guidance in the field—the most widely used being the WB International Financial Corporation's Performance Standards. Third, a new industry has burgeoned to serve and feed the appetite for "sustainability reporting" over the last five to ten years, leading to proficiency in sustainability reporting as a particular skill and making for a larger role for audit firms in consulting and advising on sustainability issues.

At the same time, international standards clearly play different roles in different industries and different contexts. While oil (and gas) extraction has been an international business for 150 years, with both the resource, capital, and know-how being highly mobile, oil TNCs seem paradoxically to be less restricted by international standards and frameworks than hydropower corporations that, until a few decades ago, were primarily confined to national markets. Hydropower, oil, and gas provide different material-technical properties, with dissimilar scaling potentials, resulting in divergent energy-producing activities that involve a variety of constellations of capital-state-international relations.

Oil and gas, together with other extractive industries, have typically been controlled by shareholder and state funding, and the primary response to local resistance and environmental activism and the like has typically unfolded as classical CSR and a concern with local content. Hydropower, on the other hand, grew from local disconnected projects, gradually becoming networked into national electricity systems often controlled by the state. Development of hydropower was embedded within national developmental policies. With electrification considered crucial for development, large dam projects came to be iconic elements in the development drive of emerging economies from the 1960s onward. Since such development initiatives were often supported by the World Bank or regional development banks (such as the Asian Development Bank) rather than private capital, resistance and controversies more readily became internationalized. This in turn stimulated the evolution and use of international standards, such as the International Finance Corporation's (IFC) Performance Standards in the hydropower sector, as discussed in chapter 10.

With intensifying global concern for climate change, the reputational challenge has shifted significantly in favor of hydropower and its important role in the green transition. When Norwegian hydropower engaged in its first projects beyond Europe in the 1990s, they were typically "large dam" projects that came with challenges such as large-scale human resettlement. These projects also typically took place within a developmental aid framework, stimulated partly by Norway's drive to become a humanitarian superpower.

A Humanitarian Superpower Pursuing Global Business

When large Norwegian corporations operate abroad, they do so in a context in which Norway plays an important role in the domains of peace, aid, humanitarian efforts, and climate change diplomacy.

Do Norwegian business and Norwegian humanitarian diplomacy impact each other? Is the way in which Norwegian corporations handle CSR in their operations abroad influenced by Norway's other engagements globally? With Norwegian business expanding abroad during the last couple of decades, potential for convergence, cooperation, or tension has increased.

Norwegian foreign direct investment had a slow start in the 1960s and did not become significant until 1985 (Hveem 2009: 384).[12] During the 1990s the total accumulated Norwegian direct investment abroad increased by 500 percent (Stråtveit 2015: 24), with Norway becoming a net exporter of capital investments in 1995 (Hveem 2009: 384). From 2000 to 2012, Norwegian foreign direct investment tripled, to reach 135 billion euros in 2012 (Stråtveit 2015: 26) and 186 billion euros in 2019.[13] These numbers exclude the so-called "Oil Fund" (Government Pension Fund Global), which is a pure investment fund of now (November 2022) around 1.25 trillion euros. The larger share of Norwegian direct investments abroad is undertaken by corporations that have significant state ownership, such as Statoil, Statkraft, Norsk Hydro, Telenor, and Yara (Lie et al. 2014: 111).

Norway may be unique in Europe when it comes to the role of state capital in foreign investments. If we turn to Asia, however, we find some interesting similarities between the ways in which Norwegian and Chinese state capital is set to work abroad. Both took off during the 1990s, both seek profit, and both Norwegian (as shown by our research) and Chinese (Lee 2017) state-owned corporations are sensitive to local circumstances. However, given the very different positions in the global economy as well as diverging state trajectories and geopolitical alignments, dissimilarities surpass similarities. (Surplus) Chinese state capital is generally set to work as state loans, which come with the condition that Chinese entrepreneurs are contracted for the project that the loan funds. (Surplus) Norwegian state capital, on the other hand, is first and foremost set to work in the "Oil Fund," which is not used strategically for political gains and, secondly, through state ownership in corporations active abroad. While Norwegian state capital primarily seeks revenues and is sometimes conjoined with the Norwegian state's humanitarian ambitions, Chinese state capital is deployed to pursue political interests and access to resources (e.g., minerals). Thus, Norwegian state-owned TNCs are in many respects more similar to privately owned (shareholding) TNCs than to Chinese state-owned TNCs. As Lee cogently notes, "ownership categories … are poor guides to corporate objectives" (Lee 2017: 4).

Corporate management within state agencies was the main driver for the internationalization of Norwegian state capital (Sæther 2017; Nilsen and Thue 2006). Limited investment opportunities in Norway prompted the corporations to look abroad. The authorities did not look unfavorably on this development (Lie et al. 2014: 111). Since 1990, state capital surplus was primarily invested abroad (to prevent "Dutch disease") through the "Oil Fund." In 1996, Labor prime minister Thorbjørn Jagland determined that internationalization would also make it more difficult for the state to secure tax income. He considered that this could be offset by securing the state—as shareholder—income through investment in Norwegian corporate investments abroad (Sejersted 1999: 98n179). This was reiterated in the 2000/2001 New Year speech of Labor premier Stoltenberg implicitly urging Statkraft to explore projects abroad: "The time for construction of new large hydropower plants in Norway is over."[14]

While Hydro was fully corporatized when it started operating abroad in the 1970s, for both Statkraft and Statoil the perceived need to move abroad was a decisive factor in stimulating corporatization (or "corporate normalization"). This started in Statoil in 1988 (Thurber and Istad 2012), which, under a Labor government, became a partly privatized and listed company in 2001. Statoil first learned international operations by partnering closely with BP during the 1990s and merged with the oil and gas section of Norsk Hydro in 2008 to better compete internationally. The most recent shift in corporate identity came in May 2018 when Statoil took its new name, Equinor. The name change also makes state ownership less obvious. In the case of Statkraft, international expansion was motivated not only by limitations on further investments in Norway but also by structural changes in the European power supply system.

How is Norwegian (state) capitalism abroad related to Norway's other international engagements? In 2020, the volume of Norwegian aid was 39.5 billion NOK (NORAD[15]), only 2 percent of (accumulated) Norwegian direct investment abroad. Still, Norway donated 1.11 percent of its Gross National Income (GNI) to Official Development Assistance[16]—a higher percentage of GNI than any other country. Norway has played a central role in a number of peace negotiations (see, e.g., Stokke 2012), and its charge of the Nobel Peace Prize no doubt contributes to Norway's association with peace internationally and locally. Overall, by "doing good," the "humanitarian superpower" Norway is trying to take an international role that far exceeds the relative size of its population, particularly now that it has a seat on the UN Security Council. Norwegian governments have consistently supported global governance, especially through the UN. In its efforts for aid, peace, and humanitarian assistance, the state has often been involved with Norwegian NGOs and academicians.

While these efforts may seem altruistic, some of Norway's donation to the international community can be seen as an instrument for legitimizing continued oil production in Norway. Government policy has, for instance, sought to fulfil climate policy obligations by supporting initiatives to make reductions in CO_2 emissions abroad. Thus, Norway is the world's biggest supporter of REDD+ (Reducing Emissions from Deforestation and Degradation).[17] Sometimes, when the stakes are high, economic interests are clearly prioritized over the image of a peace-loving nation that cares about the world. After the Nobel Prize Committee in 2010 awarded the Peace Prize to the Chinese dissident Liu Xiaobo, China's sanctions so drastically reduced exports from Norway to China (Kolstad 2019) that the Norwegian government refused to meet with the Dalai Lama when he visited Norway in 2014.

In the first phase of Norwegian development cooperation, Norway's aid policies were not much intertwined with the interests that Norway's foreign policy pursued and were based on long-term bilateral commitments to a few selected countries. From the early 1990s this began to change. Norwegian aid gradually became a central part of Norwegian foreign policy, and funds were increasingly directed toward countries in conflict and to global funds (Sørbø 2020). The Norwegian vision of "development" has been inspired by Amartya Sen and the idea that individual economic and political freedom, along with respect for human rights, is the "core criteria" for development (Dale 2018). "This vision of development, which Norway has subscribed to for a long time, has in common with the 'Nordic model' that cooperation will result in a better society. [But, t]he kind of conflicts of interests that were part of Norway's path to a welfare society are not part of this model" (Dale 2018: 5). The violence and scale of strikes as well as the government's willingness to deploy police and military force to repress them in the early 1930s (Bals 2021) is underplayed. Furthermore, it has recently come to light that, in 1919, all political parties in Stortinget and the employers' confederation supported extensive concessions to the labor unions—such as the eight-hour workday—since they feared an imminent communist revolution (Rasmussen and Knutsen 2021).

Thus, the Nordic model emerged through conflict and contestation between labor and capital. While capital was forced to be "responsible," high moral standards and mutual responsibility between employers and employees have come to be considered key characteristics of the Nordic model. While CSR marks our starting point for a discussion about state, capital, and responsibility, we consider it fruitful to cast a wider net because the corporations themselves increasingly shy away from the concept and because Norwegian corporate responsibilities are often considered to be profoundly embedded in the Nordic model as well as in notions of *samfunnsansvar* (chapter 2). A narrow focus on CSR limits our ability to explore how corporations manage the dilemma between profits and ethics. Therefore, some case studies do not so much discuss examples of CSR as focus on "thick" relations of responsibility (chapter 9) or on ways in which corporations seek to make the Nordic model travel (chapters 5 and 8).

Accordingly, the ethnographic chapters in part II start with cases that demonstrate relatively successful CSR activities or transfer of the Nordic model. Subsequent case studies range from corporations that operate more or less as any other large transnational business to an example of a particularly cynical company. Along this trajectory, corporations are discussed in sequence: Norsk Hydro (chapters 4 and 5), Equinor (chapters 6–9), Statkraft (chapter 10), and DNO (chapter 11). Although it contains some ethnographic and other material, part I should not be considered as containing case studies from Norway. Its role is to prepare the reader for the case studies of part II by providing relevant analytical, historical, and Norwegian context.

Overview of the Chapters

Chapter 1, on methods, argues that a multimethod and reflexive approach can help social scientists reflect on frictions in corporate encounters, and more importantly, that attention to these frictions is in fact a gateway to new insights about the field. The chapter thus questions dominant assumptions within anthropology of what constitutes "access" and discusses how multiple approaches to "access," which consider the positionality of the researcher and fluidity of research fields along with attention to power dynamics, can shape the sort of knowledge that is produced when studying transnational energy companies.

In chapter 2, Oda Eiken Maraire and Isabelle Hugøy explore expectations and conceptualizations of the originally Anglo-American concept "corporate social responsibility" in Norway through an analysis of newspaper articles and state documents. By outlining how CSR and its common Norwegian translation, *samfunnsansvar* (societal responsibility), travel, translate and develop differently in policy and public discourse, they argue that, in policy discourse, *samfunnsansvar* has moved away from its cultural resonance and increasingly adapted to an international discourse of CSR. Considering that the cultural resonance inherent in *samfunnsansvar* persists in public discourse, this creates a dynamic space between *samfunnsansvar* and CSR that gives corporations and state institutions in Norway the opportunity for strategic and rhetorical maneuvering.

The Norwegian context and the analytical challenges of studying CSR in a Nordic context is further explored in chapter 3, in which Eldar Bråten discusses community-oriented social responsibility as it was practiced by one publicly listed, nonstate hydroelectric power company in Norway until the 1970s. The case demonstrates that private capital may forge "responsible" social contracts, even in the context of a deep welfare state, and that it did so prior to the "branding" of responsibility as CSR. Adopting a morphogenetic approach, Bråten traces the dynamics through which local forms of CSR emerged while also addressing the analytical entailments of viewing CSR practices and discourses as emergent forms rather than coherent entities. Analyzing the complexities and contingencies of the company's local involvements, Bråten concludes that CSR should be understood as a derivative phenomenon—logically, temporally, and in terms of social constitution.

The importance of the example set by or granted to the Norwegian corporation, Norsk Hydro, for the development of state policies and corporate strategies related to responsibilities of Norwegian capital abroad is explained by Ståle Knudsen in chapter 4. The story of Norsk Hydro, here elaborated particularly around the handling of its involvement in a recent scandal in Brazil, is indicative of general developments in the relation between corporations, industrial capital, the state, and the Nordic model in Norway. Zooming in on Norsk Hydro will thus guide the reader toward an understanding of many of the main dynamics, dilemmas, challenges, and tensions involved when taking Norwegian (state) capital and/or the Nordic model abroad.

The first of the ethnographic case studies tells the story of a particularly strong and explicit mobilization of the Nordic model in globalized corporate practice. In chapter 5, Emil Røyrvik investigates how Norsk Hydro's core ideas and practices associated with the Nordic model play out in their operations in the authoritarian state of China, focusing on issues related to democratic ideals and socially responsible operations in the workplace. He goes on to argue that the extant literature on the international "export" of the Nordic model fails to sufficiently consider the social practices of travel and translations on the ground that is documented in the chapter. The study finds core ideas and elements of the Norwegian model—in particular, the Nordic tradition of implicit CSR—to be functioning dynamically as a living reality Hydro's China venture and beyond.

In the first of four chapters on Equinor, Iselin Strønen shows in chapter 6 how, in order to get their license to operate very profitable offshore operations in Brazil, Equinor has had to comply with Brazilian state requirements to fund and operate CSR projects. This case study explores in detail one such project, in which poor fisherwomen are being trained and empowered to pursue alternative livelihoods and interact with political and public institutions, and traces the involvement of Brazilian state institutions and consultancy-NGOs and their ideologies. Paradoxically, this project received the internal reward for the best CSR project in Equinor in 2016 despite being one of very few Equinor CSR projects that was not voluntary and that they did not design themselves.

Moving to another of Equinor's major foreign operations, the case from Tanzania tells a very different story than that from Brazil. In Tanzania, Equinor has for several years been on the brink of making its largest overseas investment ever. While the final investment decision is expected but not yet realized, the corporation has maneuvered itself as well as possible relative to authorities, local communities, and workers in a context of Tanzania as one of the most important recipients of Norwegian aid throughout many decades. Siri Lange and Victoria Wyndham show in chapter 7 that company ownership by a state that profiles itself as a champion in gender equality does not in itself lead to gender-sensitive social investments. The main "beneficiaries" of Equinor's social investments in Tanzania are men, but this fact is disguised by using gender-neutral language in CSR reporting. They argue that the national regulations of host countries and perceptions of risk as well as the need to gain "a social license to operate" from host communities mean that the gendered dimensions of CSR in the petroleum sector differ in important ways from other sectors. In the chapter that follows, Siri Lange tells the unique story of Equinor's decision to actively encourage and support the formation of a local union branch among its Tanzanian employees. With support from of the Norwegian union, Equinor has involved the Tanzanian union branch in a logic of training and encouragement reminiscent of the social interaction structured by the political economy of aid and "capacity building."

Turning the gaze back toward Norway and Equinor's operations in the Norwegian Arctic, Ragnhild Freng Dale in chapter 9 examines how the content and performance of CSR takes a different form in the company's home region than in its operations abroad. Through the event of a ten-year anniversary of the Snøhvit project, she draws out the mutual dependency between the company and the host community of Hammerfest. Less exposed but critical to this relationship is the role of the state and industry regulations, which became visible in the tensions between Equinor's strategic plans for a new Barents Sea oil field and the Finnmark region's expectations of local content.

In the case study of Statkraft in Turkey, in chapter 10, Ståle Knudsen and his coauthors consider, through a multisited approach, how the corporation manages one of its hydropower projects in Turkey by employing various standards. Tasked by its owner—the Norwegian state—to primarily pursue profit and guided only by very general expectations concerning CSR, Statkraft has selected to apply the performance standards of IFC, while they report (as required by the state) according to GRI standards. However, use of these standards is flexible and pragmatic, and in the process, "stories" become as important for reporting as standards, while the heterogeneous and disjointed CSR field in Statkraft is tenuously held together by the enigmatic figure of the stakeholder.

Among the case studies, chapter 11 stands out in its description of a Norwegian transnational oil company that shows particular disregard for the Norwegian state's "expectations." Synnøve Bendixsen discusses the operations of the privately held company, DNO (Det Norske Oljeselskap, the Norwegian Oil Company), in the Kurdistan Region of Iraq and in Yemen. These two cases, as in other areas where DNO operates outside of Norway, are characterized by weak states, high degrees of conflict, nonfunctioning democratic institutions, and high levels of inequality. Bendixsen argues that, in focusing on shareholder value, DNO takes an instrumental approach to CSR. Yet, the lack of adherence to Norwegian authorities' expectations—including not complying with the recommendations of the Norwegian OECD contact point for responsible business concerning a case where DNO was criticized for its treatment of employees in Yemen—has brought few penalties and sanctions, for example in terms of access to new licenses on the Norwegian shelf.

Despite the critiques raised against DNO by various institutions, news coverage of the cases from Iraq and Yemen reported in chapter

11 has been very patchy and of low impact. This illustrates a larger point, namely that the internationalization of Norwegian business, in particular the petroleum sector, has made reporting more challenging for news media that lack the resources and knowledge that corporations can muster (Baumberger and Slaatta 2011; Sæther 2017: 238–82). News media tend to use one source to report the activities of Equinor and other corporations abroad: the corporations themselves. As anthropologists, we have resources that journalists usually do not possess: relevant foreign language skills (such as Turkish, Swahili, Portuguese), country knowledge, networks, and time. Thus, we should be better placed to ply deeper into the intricate relations between corporations, states, and communities. On the other hand, anthropologists are not at liberty to use all the methods of journalism. Studying energy and extraction corporations operating abroad anthropologically comes with particular challenges. That is the topic of the next chapter.

Acknowledgments

Research on which this chapter rests has been conducted within the frames of the project Energethics (2015–19), funded by a FRIPRO grant from the Research Council of Norway (grant no. 240617).

Ståle Knudsen is professor in the Department of Social Anthropology, University of Bergen, Norway. He was leader of the project Energethics (2015–19), from which this book emerges. Knudsen has, since the early 1990s, done ethnographic fieldwork in Turkey, and his publications include the monograph *Fisheries in Modernizing Turkey* (Berghahn, 2009).

Dinah Rajak is reader in anthropology and international development at the University of Sussex. She is the author of *In Good Company: An Anatomy of Corporate Social Responsibility* (Stanford University Press, 2011) and coeditor of *The Anthropology of Corporate Social Responsibility* (Berghahn, 2016).

Siri Lange holds a PhD in social anthropology and is a professor in the Department of Health Promotion and Development (HEMIL) at the University of Bergen, Norway. Prior to joining HEMIL, Lange was a senior researcher at the Chr. Michelsen Institute (CMI) in Bergen (2002–17). Lange has published extensively on social, economic, and political issues in Tanzania.

Isabelle Hugøy was a research assistant for the Energethics project, and since 2020 she has been a doctoral fellow in the Department of Social Anthropology, University of Bergen, Norway. Her doctoral project deals with human-soil relations and explores how soil is actualized across different knowledge registers in the context of efforts to decarbonize agricultural sectors in Norway and Costa Rica.

Notes

An earlier version of this chapter was published as: Knudsen, Ståle, Dinah Rajak, Siri Lange, and Isabelle Hugøy. 2020. "Bringing the State Back In: Corporate Social Responsibility and the Paradoxes of Norwegian State Capitalism in the International Energy Sector." In Theme Section, "Corporate Social Responsibility and the Paradoxes of State Capitalism," edited by Ståle Knudsen and Dinah Rajak. *Focaal—Journal of Global and Historical Anthropology* 88: 1–21.

1. See, e.g., debate in *Social Anthropology* 20(1)–21(1).
2. There are also other approaches: see Hilgers 2011 for an overview; see Waquant 2012 for an approach informed by Bourdieu.
3. "Northern Lights," *The Economist*, 2 February 2013.
4. One important example: with a new energy legislation in 1991, the electricity sector in Norway was the first to deregulate in Europe (Nilsen and Thue 2006; Herning 2009; Angell and Brekke 2011).
5. Sweden had from an early date much more private capital and "remained thoroughly capitalist, exhibiting one of the highest levels of concentrated and family capital ownership in the world" (Ingham 2011: 188), with around fifteen families controlling 70 percent of the Stockholm Stock Exchange (Lie 2016: 924).
6. Same level as in Russia and China. France and Italy 10 percent, Germany 2 percent, UK insignificant (Meld. St. 27 [2013–14]: 31, 36, 37). These numbers exclude the so-called Oil Funds: Government Pension Fund Norway and Government Pension Fund Global (the last valuing 1.25 trillion euro in November 2022).
7. For the Kings Bay affair, see: https://en.wikipedia.org/wiki/Kings_Bay_Affair.
8. For an overview (in Norwegian) of these documents, see: https://www.regjeringen.no/no/tema/naringsliv/statlig-eierskap/andre-relevante-dokumenter/id737457/?expand=factbox2602523.
9. "De hemmelige Equinor-rapportene," *DN Magasinet*, 6 May 2020.
10. "Korrupte land i kø for Statoil," *Aftenposten*, 21 December 2006, accessed 25 November 2015.
11. https://www.regjeringen.no/en/topics/foreign-affairs/business-cooperation-abroad/innsikt/kompakt_en/id633619/, accessed 9 April 2019.
12. This depiction ignores the Norwegian shipping sector, which has long been internationally active but has not made significant investments abroad.
13. https://www.ssb.no/en/utenriksokonomi/fordringer-og-gjeld-overfor-utlandet/statistikk/direkteinvesteringer, accessed 15 October 2021.
14. https://www.regjeringen.no/no/dokumentarkiv/Regjeringen-Stoltenberg-I/smk/Taler-og-artikler-arkivert-individuelt/2001/statsministerens_nyttarstale_2001/id264461/, accessed 8 April 2020.
15. https://www.norad.no/aktuelt/nyheter/2021/slik-var-norsk-bistand-i-2020/, accessed 15 October 2021.

16. https://www.regjeringen.no/en/historical-archive/solbergs-government/Ministries/ud/news1/2021/recordhigh_assistance/id2844317/, accessed 15 October 2021.
17. Svarstad and Benjaminsen, 30 December 2018, https://www.dagsavisen.no/nye meninger/equinors-klimamaskerade-1.1254458.

References

Agnell, Svein I., and Ole A. Brekke. 2011. *Frå kraft versus natur til miljøvenleg energi? Norsk vasskraftpolitikk i eit hundreårsperspektiv* [From power versus nature to environmentally friendly energy? Norwegian hydropower politics in a hundred-year perspective]. Report 3/2011, Uni-Rokkansenteret, Bergen.

Bals, Jonas. 2021. *Streik! – En historie om strid, samhold og solidaritet* [Strike! – A history about strife, unity and solidarity]. Oslo: Res Publica.

Baumberger, Berit E., and Tore Slaatta, 2011. "Norsk oljejournalistikk—Statoils utenlandsvirksomhet som transnasjonalt nyhetsbeite" [Norwegian oil journalism—Statoil's foreign activities as a transnational news field]. *Norsk Medietidsskrift* 18(1): 41–60.

Benson, Peter, and Stuart Kirsch, 2010. "Capitalism and the Politics of Resignation." *Current Anthropology* 51(4): 459–86.

Chong, Kimberly. 2018. *Best Practice: Management Consulting and the Ethics of Financialization in China*. Durham, NC: Duke University Press.

Collier, Stephen J. 2011. *Post-Soviet Social: Biopolitics, Neoliberalism, Social Modernity*. Princeton, NJ: Princeton University Press.

Cumbers, Andrew. 2012. "North Sea Oil, the State and Divergent Development in the UK and Norway." In *Flammable Societies: Studies on the Socio-economics of Oil and Gas*, edited by John-Andrew McNeish and Owen Logan, 221–42. London: Pluto.

Dale, Svein. 2018. *Myter om Bistand*. [Myths about aid]. Civita-notat: Civita.

Dolan, Catherine, and Dinah Rajak, eds. 2016. *The Anthropology of Corporate Social Responsibility*. New York: Berghahn Books.

Edgecliffe-Johnson, Andrew. 2019. "Beyond the Bottom Line." *Financial Times*, 4 January 2019.

Ervasti, Heikki, Torben Fridberg, Mikael Hjerm, Olli Kangas, and Kristen Ringdal. 2008. "The Nordic Model." In *Nordic Social Attitudes in a European Perspective*, edited by Heikki Ervasti, Torben Fridberg, Mikael Hjerm, and Kristen Ringdal, 1–20. Cheltenham: Edward Elgar.

Ferguson, James. 2005. "Anthropology and its Evil Twin: 'Development' in the Constitution of a Discipline." In *The Anthropology of Development and Globalization: From Classical Political Economy to Contemporary Neoliberalism*, edited by Marc Edelman and Angelique Haugerud, 140–54. Oxford: Blackwell.

Ferguson, James, and Akhil Gupta. 2002. "Spatializing States: Toward an Ethnography of Neoliberal Governmentality." *American Ethnologist* 29(4): 981–1002.

Flew, Terry. 2012. "Michael Foucault's *The Birth of Biopolitics* and the Contemporary Neoliberalism Debates." *Thesis Eleven* 108(1): 44–65.

Foucault, Michel. 2008. *The Birth of Biopolitics: Lectures at the Collège de France 1978–1979*. Translated by Graham Burchell. Basingstoke: Palgrave.

Fulcher, James. 2015. *Capitalism. A Very Short Introduction. Second Edition*. Oxford: Oxford University Press.

Gardner, Katy. 2012. *Discordant Development: Global Capitalism and the Struggle for Connection in Bangladesh*. London: Pluto Press.

Garsten, Christina, and Kerstin Jacobsson. 2011. "Post-political Regulation: Soft Power and Post-political Visions in Global Governance." *Critical Sociology* 39(3): 421–37. https://doi.org/10.1177/0896920511413942

Gjølberg, Maria. 2010. "Varieties of Corporate Social Responsibility (CSR): CSR Meets the 'Nordic Model.'" *Regulation and Governance* (3): 203–29. https://doi.org/10.1111/j.1748-5991.2010.01080.x

Hall, Peter, and David Soskice, eds. 2001. *Varieties of Capitalism*. Oxford: Oxford University Press.

Hart, Keith. 2018. "AFTER 2008: Market Fundamentalism at the Crossroad." *Cultural Anthropology* 33(4): 536–46. https://doi.org/10.14506/ca33.4.03

Harvey, David. 2005. *A Brief History of Neoliberalism*. Oxford: Oxford University Press.

———. 2017. *Marx, Capital and the Madness of Economic Reason*. London: Profile Books.

Herning, Linn Kira Kolsrud. 2009. "'Fra etat til konsern': En historisk-komparativ studie av den norske stats engasjement i norsk nettbasert infrastruktur fra 1970 til 2006" ["From agency to enterprise": A historical-comparative study of the Norwegian state's involvement in Norwegian network-based infrastructure from 1970 to 2006]. MA thesis, Department of Archeology, Conservation, and History, University of Oslo.

Hilgers, Mathieu. 2011. "The Three Anthropological Approaches to Neoliberalism." *International Social Science Journal* 202: 351–63. https://doi.org/10.1111/j.1468-2451.2011.01776.x

Hveem, Helge. 2009. "Norske utenlandsinvesteringer og norsk (utenriks)politikk: Dårlig forbindelse?" [Norwegian foreign direct investments and Norwegian (foreign) policy: Poor connection?]. *Internasjonal Politikk* 67(3): 381–412. https://www.idunn.no/ip/2009/03/art01

Ingham, Geoffrey. 2011. *Capitalism, Key Concepts*. Cambridge: Polity Press.

Ihlen, Øyvind. 2011. *Samfunnsansvar på Norsk: Tradisjon og kommunikasjon* [CSR in Norwegian. Tradition and communication]. Bergen: Fagbokforlaget.

Kipnis, Andrew. 2008. "Audit Cultures: Neoliberal Governability, Socialist Legacy, or Technologies of Governing." *American Ethnologist* 35(2): 275–89. https://doi.org/10.1111/j.1548-1425.2008.00034.x

Knafo, Samuel, Sahil Jai Dutta, Richard Lane, and Steffen Wyn-Jones. 2019. "The Managerial Lineages of Neoliberalism." *New Political Economy* 24(2): 235–51. https://doi.org/10.1080/13563467.2018.1431621

Knudsen, Ståle. 2015. "Corporate Social Responsibility in Local Context: International Capital, Charitable Giving and the Politics of Education in Turkey." *Southeast European and Black Sea Studies* 15(3): 369–390.

Kolstad, Ivar. 2019. "Too Big to Fault? Effects of the 2010 Nobel Peace Prize on Norwegian Exports to China and Foreign Policy." *International Political Science Review* 41(2): 207–23.

Lampland, Martha. 1995. *The Object of Labor: Commodification in Socialist Hungary*. Chicago: Chicago University Press.

Lee, Ching Kwan. 2017. *The Specter of Global China: Politics, Labor, and Foreign Investment in Africa*. Chicago: University of Chicago Press.

Lenfle, Sylvain, and Cristoph Loch. 2009. "Lost Roots: How Project Management Settled on the Phased Approach (and Compromised Its Ability to Lead Change in Modern Enterprises)." In INSEAD Working Paper Series. Fontainbleau, France: INSEAD—the business school of the world. http://dx.doi.org/10.2139/ssrn.1501176

Lie, Einar. 2016. "Context and Contingency: Explaining State Ownership in Norway." *Enterprise and Society* 17(4): 904–30. https://doi.org/10.1017/eso.2016.18

Lie, Einar, Egil Myklebust, and Harald Norvik. 2014. *Staten som kapitalist: Rikdom og eierskap for det 21. århundre* [The state as a capitalist. Wealth and ownership in the 21st century]. Oslo: Pax forlag A/S.

Lægreid, Per, Paul G. Roness, and Vidar Rolland. 2013. "Agencification and Corporatization in Norway 1947–2011." *International Journal of Public Administration* 36(9): 659–72.

Mazzucato, Mariana. 2018. *The Entrepreneurial State: Debunking Public vs. Private Sector Myths*. Penguin Books.

Meld. St. 61. 1996–97. *Om eierskap i næringslivet* [About ownership in the business world]. White Paper from Ministry of Trade and Industry, Government of Norway.

Meld. St. 22. 2001–2. *Et mindre og bedre statlig eierskap* [A smaller and improved state ownership]. White Paper from Ministry of Trade and Industry, Government of Norway.
Meld. St. 13. 2006–7. *An Active and Long-Term State Ownership.* White Paper from Ministry of Trade and Industry, Government of Norway.
Meld. St. 10. 2008–9. *Corporate Social Responsibility in a Global Economy.* White Paper from Ministry of Foreign Affairs, Government of Norway.
Meld. St. 27. 2013–14. *Diverse and Value-Creating Ownership.* White Paper from Ministry of Trade, Industry and Fisheries, Government of Norway.
Nilsen, Yngve, and Lars Thue. 2006. *Statens Kraft 1965–2006* [The state's power 1965–2006]. Oslo: Universitetsforlaget.
Nonini, Donald M. 2008. "Is China Becoming Neoliberal?" *Critique of Anthropology* 28(2): 145–76. https://doi.org/10.1177/0308275X08091364
OAGN. 2016–17. *Riksrevisjonens kontroll med forvaltningen av statlige selskaper for 2015* [The Office of the Auditor General's control of the management of state-owned companies for 2015]. Oslo: Office of the Auditor General of Norway.
OECD. 2017. "Development Co-operation Report 2017." Data for development Paris: OECD.
Peck, Jamie, and Nik Theodore. 2015. *Fast Policy: Experimental Statecraft at the Thresholds of Neoliberalism.* Minneapolis: University of Minnesota Press.
Polanyi, Karl. 2001 [1944]. *The Great Transformation: The Political and Economic Origins of Our Time.* Boston: Beacon Press.
Prop. 5. 1989. *En bedre organisert stat* [A better organized state]. Green Paper from the Ministry of Administration, Government of Norway.
Prop. 53. 2003–4. *Statens eierskap i Statkraft SF* [State ownership in Statkraft SF]. Green Paper from Ministry of Trade and Industry, Government of Norway.
Rajak, Dinah. 2011. *In Good Company: An Anatomy of Corporate Social Responsibility.* Stanford, CA: Stanford University Press.
Rasmussen, Magus B., and Carl H. Knutsen. 2021. *Reforming to Survive: The Bolshevik Origins of Social Policies.* Cambridge: Cambridge University Press.
Rogers, Douglas. 2015. *The Depths of Russia: Oil, Power, and Culture after Socialism.* Ithaca, NY: Cornell University Press.
Rose, Nikolas. 1999. *Powers of Freedom: Reframing Political Thought.* New York: Cambridge University Press.
Scott, James C. 1998. *Seeing like a State: How Certain Schemes to Improve the Human Condition Have Failed.* In Yale Agrarian Studies Series, edited by James C. Scott. New Haven, CT: Yale University Press.
Sejersted, Francis. 1999. *Systemtvang eller politikk: Om utviklingen av det oljeindustrielle kompleks i Norge* [Systems forcing or politics. About the development of the oil-industrial complex in Norway]. Oslo: Universitetsforlaget.
Smith, Jessica M. 2021. *Extracting Accountability: Engineers and Corporate Social Responsibility.* Cambridge, MA: The MIT Press.
Stokke, Kristian. 2012. "Peace-Building as Small State Foreign Policy: Norway's Peace Engagement in a Changing International Context." *International Studies* 49(3&4): 207–31. https://doi.org/10.1177/0020881714532334
Strand, Robert, R. Edward Freeman, and Kai Hockerts. 2015. "Corporate Social Responsibility and Sustainability in Scandinavia: An Overview." *Journal of Business Ethics* 127:115. https://doi.org/10.1007/s10551-014-2224-6
Stråtveit, Torstein. 2015. "'Norge ut i verden': En kartlegging av norsk utgående direkteinvestert kapital 1990–2012" ["Norway abroad": A survey of Norwegian foreign direct invested capital 1990–2012]. MA thesis. Bergen: University of Bergen.
Sæther, Anne Karin. 2017. *De beste intensjoner: Oljelandet i klimakampen* [The best of intentions: The oil country in the climate struggle]. Oslo: Cappelen Damm AS.

Sørbø, Gunnar. 2020. *Norsk bistand er i en spagat mellom retorikk og virkelighet: Bistandsaktuelt*. https://bistandsaktuelt.no/arkiv-kommentarer/2020/eks-cmi-direktor-gunnar-sorbo-om-problemer-og-utviklingstrekk-i-norsk-bistand/

Thurber, Mark C., and Benedicte T. Istad. 2012. "Norway's Evolving Champion: Statoil and the Politics of State Enterprise." In *Oil and Governance: State-Owned Enterprises and the World Energy Supply*, edited by David G. Victor, David R. Hults, and Mark C. Thurber, 599–654. Cambridge: Cambridge University Press.

Trygstad, Sissel, and Håvard Lismoen. 2008. *Fagbevegelsen og CSR* [The labor movement and CSR]. Fafo-notat. Oslo: Fafo.

Victor, David G., David R. Hults, and Mark C. Thurber. 2012. "Introduction and Overview." In *Oil and Governance: State-Owned Enterprises and the World Energy Supply*, edited by David G. Victor, David R. Hults, and Mark C. Thurber, 3–31. Cambridge: Cambridge University Press.

Vike, Halvar. 2012. "Varianter av vest-europeiske statsformasjoner" [Variants of Western European state formations]. *Norsk antropologisk tidsskrift* 23(2): 126–42.

Wacquant, Loic. 2012. "Three Steps to a Historical Anthropology of Actually Existing Neoliberalism." *Social Anthropology* 20(1): 66–79.

Welker, Marina. 2009. "'Corporate Security Begins in the Community': Mining, the Corporate Responsibility Industry and Environmental Advocacy in Indonesia." *Cultural Anthropology* 24(1): 142–79.

———. 2014. *Enacting the Corporation: An American Mining Firm in Post-authoritarian Indonesia*. Berkeley: University of California Press.

— Part I —

SETTING THE SCENE

Introduction and Framing of CSR
in the Norwegian Context

— Chapter 1 —

RETHINKING ACCESS
Key Methodological Challenges in Studying Energy Companies

Ingrid Birce Müftüoğlu, Ståle Knudsen, Ragnhild Freng Dale, Oda Eiken Maraire, Dinah Rajak, and Siri Lange

Introduction

Energy is deeply embedded in society, and the way it is produced, distributed, and consumed has consequences for the way we live our lives. Yet, the multifaceted social and material relations that this involves tend to elude scientific description and analysis. Among the primary reasons for this elusiveness are the barriers we encounter when studying energy companies. Firstly, energy companies are considered close to the cogwheels and power of society, and more so than corporations in other fields they confront demands from both political spheres and civil society to attain sustainability and to take responsibility for bringing society through the "green transition." Debates regarding the need for more energy, financial profit, and increasing rates of unemployment add to the complexity of these goals. Another important factor that might entrench corporate barriers is the constant development of energy technology, which can change the operations and structure of the energy industry within a short timeframe. Lastly, national and international policies, agreements, and guidelines are under constant negotiation. Increasing visibility has pushed energy companies to develop sophisticated communication strategies, which enable flexible positioning in the face of criticism. These are among the dimensions that must be accounted for when researching energy companies today. The sum of these societal and environmental dimensions can indeed create challenges for social scientists who choose to study energy companies.

So, which methodological measures can make us better equipped to understand the role of energy companies? Participant observation and ethnographic methods hold potential for prying open corporate self-representation in an exploration of the relations of power and politics that determine flows of energy and extractive capital at the global and local levels. Ethnographic methods help us move past structural analyses to locate the agents and processes at work within economies of energy production and to identify tensions and dynamics both within the corporation and at the interface with society. Enabling us to look beyond the virtual, and actual, walls of energy companies, such methods help us understand how energy corporations work and how decisions are made and justified. Further, these methods illuminate the interaction of personal values and institutional norms, individual agency, and structural constraints that shape the development and management of energy supply chains.

Ethnographic methods require reflexivity, pushing the researcher to question methodological prerequisites, which, in the case of ethnography on energy companies, may be to ask what it *means* to look beyond the walls of energy companies, and how social scientists should study cultural, structural, ethical, and social aspects of energy when the corporate walls are high and usually well guarded. When we enter the field of energy companies, the researchers' initial expectations to access, reflections on positionality, and power relations between academia and business are challenged, thus arguably necessitating a reconsideration of key anthropological methodological insights for further exploration: What can be considered "good" access for a social scientist in this research field? What are the power relations between academia and business at present? Is reflexivity an essential tool in studying a field that, to a large extent, exercises power and affects all aspects of society and people's lives?

We will reflect on these enquiries by demonstrating how we came to question dominant assumptions within anthropology of what constitutes "access" in ethnographic work that focuses on energy companies. To do so, we will first present the research project Energethics, on which our methodological reflections are built and our take on multisited ethnography is based. Then we will critically discuss how to understand "access" when studying energy companies. We suggest that the term should be de-anchored from conventional understandings of access to allow us as researchers to reflect and adapt to the flux we must negotiate in the field. We show how multiple approaches to "access"—which takes into account the positionality of the researcher, fluidity of research fields along with attention to power dynamics, and "strategic intimacy" with energy company employees—can shape the sort of knowledge that is produced when studying energy companies. The overall objective of the article is to show how a creative and active ethnographic approach produces new knowledge about energy corporations while simultaneously creating new challenges in relation to how to approach this particular field of study. In doing so, we also argue that anthropological ethnographic research, in its particularity and attention to the complexity of contexts, has the potential to strengthen the literature on energy companies and extractive industries.

Energy Companies and the "Social Life" of Corporate Social Responsibility (CSR)

The methodological discussions in this chapter draw on the anthropological project Energethics,[1] which ran from 2015 to 2019, and the experiences from the fieldwork of research team members with reference to Norwegian energy industry presence in Turkey, London, Oslo, Tanzania, and Northern Norway. In Energethics, we studied energy companies by investigating corporate social responsibility (CSR) strategies and practices of energy companies based in Norway, representing varying degrees of state ownership: Statkraft (100 percent state owned, hydropower), Statoil, now Equinor (67 percent state owned, hydrocarbons), and DNO ("The Norwegian Oil Company," 100 percent private, hydrocarbons). An important aspect of Energethics was that it sought to explore the field where the companies operate and not just the companies in and of themselves. Multisited ethnography enabled us to empirically track the production, circulation, reformulation, and outcomes of CSR policy and practice in Norwegian energy companies abroad, from boardrooms to operations, from the sites of formal policymaking to the sites of implementation in different locations around the world. This multisited approach to the "flow," negotiation, and localization of CSR can arguably provide insight into how energy corporations work, and the CSR "take" on studying energy companies is certainly not unusual among social anthropologists (Barry 2013; Benson and Kirsch 2010; Cross 2011; Frynas 2009; Rajak 2011a; Welker 2009; Welker 2014).

During the last twenty-five to thirty-five years, Norwegian energy companies have increasingly "gone global," and many of the projects in which these companies invest have involved significant, and sometimes contested, environmental and social issues in energy frontiers. Investment strategies have raised a number of ethical, social, environmental, and political concerns that have been high on the public and political agenda. Energy transnational corporations (TNCs) as well as Norwegian firms relate to these societal, cultural, political, and economic challenges of energy investments, productions, and infrastructures by developing policies for corporate ethics, often conceptualized as CSR. In Norway, the energy sector, in cooperation with the state, has been at the forefront in adapting to global standards for CSR. Anthropological studies have argued that CSR should be seen as a broad, evolving, and flexible set of practices and languages through which businesses variously attempt to position themselves as ethical actors. As such, we may consider CSR as a particularly adaptable discourse, which, over the past two decades, has evolved to respond to and incorporate new ideas and challenges, encompassing movements that often start out as alternative or even oppositional to the corporate world. The language and practice of CSR has thus increasingly become embedded in international conventions and institutions, such as the UN Global Compact, OECD Corporate Responsibility Guidelines, and the Global Reporting Initiative (GRI).

What we see from emergent ethnographic work in this field are the various ways in which corporations use the language and practice of ethics to contain and respond to the different kinds of challenges generated by their activities. Examples include the ecological crisis, conflicts concerning labor rights and local expectations of jobs, the problem of dependency and Dutch disease, and increasing corruption and conflict over resources. CSR policies largely evolved out of corporate accommodation to critiques of the environmental and social impacts of neoliberal economic reforms of the 1980s (Rajak 2011a). In the later years, CSR strategies have increasingly involved governance techniques whereby the companies claim to foster local sustainable development in direct interaction with relevant local communities. Thus, claims Noel Castree (2008: 147), CSR is often "actualized in tandem with" free market environmentalism. CSR, as practiced by most TNCs, may therefore be considered neoliberal governmentality.

In the Energethics project, we critically explored this position, asking whether and to what extent CSR can be claimed "from below" or by governmental entities, and whether state-owned energy companies can pursue and implement corporate ethics by governance techniques that do not rely on market rule and privatization (see the introduction for a more elaborate discussion). Thus, our starting point has been that the role of the state is central to understanding CSR dynamics, whether defined by its presence or, at times, its absence from the debate. As we elaborated in the introduction, national oil companies control roughly two-thirds of global oil and gas, and Equinor is considered one of the more successful among these national oil corporations. Statkraft, however, is more of an anomaly since it remains 100 percent state owned in a sector—electricity production and distribution—that has to a much larger extent been privatized. Both Equinor and Statkraft argue that working with and supporting the state in Norway is in their very DNA and that, therefore, they find it natural to pursue the same strategy abroad. Fieldwork on these companies was thus conducted not only on the impact of the corporations' projects in Turkey, Tanzania, and Northern Norway but also on the way in which CSR was handled at various levels of the corporations and in the relevant contexts in which they operate. The project took us to places such as Oslo, Bergen, Stavanger, Ankara, and London and methodologically involved a variety of approaches, including analyzing reports, white papers, and guidelines and tracking the performance of CSR through the circuit of conventions, policy forums, and award ceremonies, which constitute the elite "global" arena of corporate citizenship.

This flexible approach strays from central aspects in conventional anthropological ethnography where thorough and long-term participant observation is the preferable method. The discipline's historical intensity of "studying down" has shaped the methodological framework, while studying corporations demands a reinventing of anthropology, something Laura Nader anticipated decades ago. In "Up the Anthropologist" she writes: "What if, in reinventing anthropology, anthropologists were to study the colonizers, rather than the colonized, the culture of power rather than the culture of the powerless, the culture of affluence rather than the culture of poverty?" (Nader 1972 [1969]: 289). Also in later years, anthropologists have experienced how the solid tradition on "studying down" has set its marks on the ethnographic know-how. Karen Ho (2016: 29) considers that "studying up fostered for me a critical re-framing of anthropology's fundamental assumptions, challenges, and possibilities because it necessitated pulling apart methodological and theoretical tools that were forged through the process and contexts of studying the marginalized, and recalibrating their directionality and use."

Compared to traditional anthropological ethnography, multisited ethnography might come through as an opportunistic approach to the field where energy companies operate, but at the same time it is necessary to grasp the "social life" of CSR. There are, interestingly, parallels between the anthropological multisited way of approaching the field and the way in which multinational energy companies themselves operate in a field that encompasses national laws/policies and international nonjuridical guidelines on "soft" risk assessment and performance. Both Equinor and Statkraft perform and report CSR across sites bound together by new energy investments and infrastructures. Energy projects are dependent on a "smooth" flow across sites and beyond borders, especially because legitimation of projects depends so much on stakeholder involvement, meaning that the CSR department's key activity is to create and implement strategies for ethical business conduct across different sites, including main offices, country offices, and local communities, in relation to governments, NGOs, and civil society (for an elaboration of this, see especially chapter 10). The fields across which corporations must produce smoothness are nearly always uneven, and ethnographic methods are, we argue, especially suited to explore how they perform this work.

Using multisitedness to approach energy companies' multinational operations initially opens up for a common understanding between researchers and corporations, creating meeting points where ethnography can be conducted. As such, similarities in approaches gives access to arenas for communication, cooperation, and even knowledge production between academia and energy corporations regarding international energy development, responsibility, and ethics. Still, at a certain point during fieldwork, after the initial conversations and meetings, both the researcher and the representative for the corporation somehow realize that the meaning of "site" is fundamentally different for each. While corporations treat multiple sites in their production chain according to a strict hierarchical structure with headquarters at the top, researchers treat all sites as equal. Talking insightfully about "sites" and "globalization" with corporate representatives might initially be interpreted by the researcher as an opening to a corporation's inner life, only to realize that common language opens nothing beyond an instrumental entry to the field of study, pushing the ethnographic scope to the periphery of the corporate practice. Research language that initially speaks to and then gradually adapts to the corporation may contribute toward legitimatizing the corporations' position and reputation in society while having a negative effect on the need to develop a relevant critical language, which could facilitate an evidence-based dialogue about and with energy companies. To maintain a reflexive position toward the similarities between this project's multisited academic approach and the corporate approach to the multinational energy field has been a central methodological challenge, especially because the unpredictable movement between getting close to and feeling distanced from the corporate body made us question the meaning of "access" in this particular field of study.

Access and Flexibility

Trying to gain access to the energy companies, the Energethics research team found that our expectations of what "access" meant and required in return was a methodological challenge in itself. After establishing communication with the Norwegian energy companies, our main contact persons in Equinor and Statkraft made it clear that cooperation would have to be reciprocal and that the company would need to benefit in some way. Often, leveraging or demonstrating our knowledge or previous experience was needed to secure access. Samuel Coleman (1996) addresses "why they let me in," suggesting that if a corporation sees the ethnographer as a possible asset to the business, they will be more likely to grant access. Without explicitly framing it as a methodological challenge, Greg Urban and Kyung-Nan Koh (2013: 140) emphasize that "contemporary anthropological research necessitates 'giving back' [to the corporation, because] few corporations are eager to allow access to those whose research does not contribute to the corporation's goals." The importance of giving the corporations an opportunity to "check facts" before we published articles was often brought up in conversation with both Equinor and Statkraft employees. During interviews, the interviewer sometimes experienced being tested by corporate interviewees, who made statements concerning certain pivotal events in ways that demanded that the anthropologist choose a side in their response (Choy 2011: 1–4). For example, we were expected to say what *we* think of a specific initiative to ensure local content in a project—such as a sponsored event or the number of locally employed youth—or give our opinion of the new roads or buildings that were built in conjunction with the company's regional activity. In such situations, where our informants clearly expect us to agree with certain points of view, our responses shape their perceptions of our motives, and with that determine how and what information is shared.

After several experiences similar to those described above, we soon realized that our main contacts in Equinor and Statkraft, who were very professional, friendly, and helpful, were not so much at our disposal to help us gain access to relevant processes and arenas in the corporation; rather, they kindly guided us toward what they considered to be "CSR in a nutshell" in the company. They directed us toward "key informants" who were managers in the CSR departments or key CSR employees in the field. From their perspective, all relevant information about CSR could be untangled by interviewing a few employees. If we talked to employees without approval from our appointed contact person, we received mostly gentle but sometimes stern reminders to limit our conversations to the approved contacts. Our main contacts were gatekeepers as well as our closest dialogue partners in the company.

When we had an impression that we had gained "good access," being let into a project and able to observe CSR in practice in the local communities where the companies had invested, it was orchestrated by the gatekeepers with a rationale that "this particular project" gave an impression of how CSR was "done" at its best within the company. In a certain sense, they treated us as a combination of consultants and auditors. After this discovery—that good access mostly meant access carefully orchestrated by the companies—we had to reconsider the meaning of access. It became clear to us that our expectations of "good access" as opposed to "poor access" were affected by a notion of peeking behind the curtains, gaining close insights into the everyday work life of employees through participant observation in meetings, lunches, and seminars and by "hanging out" during or after work appointments.

When we first started the project, "access" was one of the main themes discussed within the research team, and we may have had a rather superficial understanding of what access implied. It is fair to say that we evaded an explicit move toward conducting the necessary concept clarifications; rather, we spoke of access as if we all had the same expectations of eventually cracking the business code, of being "let in." Although we did not envision total immersion in the daily activities of the corporations, we did imagine that the development of the project depended on "gaining access," and we emphasized the practical problems concerning gaining access rather than asking the obvious: "What does access mean?" Although it now seems naïve, we did—to varying degrees—aim for and hope to somehow gather crucial, behind-the-scenes information revealing new knowledge about business and CSR. Our ideas about access were obviously informed by classical anthropological ideals about "becoming one of them," "hanging out with the informants," and the like. At one of the first meetings with our contact person in Statkraft, for instance, we asked him how we could go about being among the office staff at the headquarters in Oslo and at the country office in Istanbul. We also asked him if we could join some of the CSR staff on their journeys to Turkey and other relevant places. We tried to convey our flexibility. He did not quite turn us down but postponed answering, and after a year of maneuvering our inquiries in other directions, the dialogue about "insider" access gradually ceased.

So, when access to corporate offices is at best precarious, expanding ethnographic research to the wider field to which corporate employees relate has proven to open new vistas. Arenas, such as conventions, policy forums, and award ceremonies, offer a critical sphere where energy executives reach out beyond the walls of the company, albeit in ways that are often highly ritualized and orchestrated. Nevertheless, such sites have an important ethnographic value in their own right, giving us access to flows and negotiation of concepts, knowledge, and models, as well as articulation of power relations—broadening our understanding of who is relevant in the field. The venues at which we meet are important not only as places to observe others but also as places to be seen. Though these conference rituals are not equal to observing the inner workings of company dynamics, conference participation shapes our access to company employees and representatives as arenas that are also meeting places at the intersection of business, academia, and policy. By registering and paying the conference fee (often a barrier in itself, due to the high fees levied),[2] dressing and acting like the rest of the delegates, we gain access both to the "onstage" conference presentations and the "offstage" conversations and informal business encounters that take place around it. Naturally, these informal encounters are not offstage even if they give the appearance of being so but are arenas where the researcher can engage in networking and observations.

Further, fieldwork at such sites can reveal the ritualized and performative dynamics of CSR, which are, we suggest, crucial to establishing it as development orthodoxy.[3] It is here that we begin to disentangle the agency of various actors—from captains of industry to representatives of the "grassroots," from business schools to UN agencies—involved in the production of this powerful discourse; we begin to see how the shift from agonistic to collaborative, from conflictual to consensual, is achieved. Within these arenas, corporate executives come together with representatives of global NGOs, the growing army of CSR consultants, and dozens of small firms or nonprofits (the boundary between which is often blurred). Participants extol the virtues of bi-, tri-, or multisector partnerships, develop standards, and present case studies recounting their engagement with the local communities who represent the targets of their ethical behavior. Such gatherings unfold as highly ritualistic theaters of virtue (Rajak 2011b) in which awards for the best corporate citizen are presented and inspiring stories of social responsibility are told. These rituals are elements in the construction of narratives that structure the processes of the CSR world. As Maurice Bloch (1992) argues, ritual can serve to constrain contestation while inviting participants to share in and thus validate a particular worldview. Put another way, they compel consensus while mystifying the dynamics of power at work. Rituals of corporate morality thus play an important role in generating particular ways of seeing and understanding on the part of people involved in the CSR industry and should be seen as a new and significant dimension of corporate power.

Official conventions rarely pass under the radar of civil society, which sometimes engages in its own counterperformances. Participants at Ethical Corporation's 2016 convention in London were greeted with a banner, courtesy of the London Mining Network, that said "The Oxymoron Appreciation Society proudly presents 'The Responsible Extractives Summit 2016.'" Perhaps they had been reading Benson and Kirsch's article on "Corporate Oxymorons" (2009). It took some time for the hotel to borrow some ladders and construction workers from a building site opposite to take it down. During the panel on "Stranded Assets," questions flashed up on the big screen polling the audience with, "Is climate change good or bad for the extractive industries?" An awkward pause followed. After some time, the facilitator glanced over his shoulder and exclaimed: "Oh, sorry! That should have read 'Is the climate change convention good or bad for the extractive industries?'" "In our company, we have a very good story to tell" was a frequent refrain among oil executives at events, such as Responsible Extractives 2016, both in their public performance and in individual conversations over coffee or outside of the conference circuit. Of course, the line between public performance and individual narrative is in no way clear, and if "inside ethnography" relies on waiting for a key informant to "break ranks" from, for instance, the dominant discourse of sustainability in big oil, then we will certainly hit a wall. The smooth surface of energy companies belies these subsurface fissures but has proved far more impenetrable in recent years. For researchers trying to find a way to get beyond these surfaces, there is an implicit way of discussing access where the goal is to gain access.

It was the comparative dimension of the Energethics project that eventually made us realize that practical access to the field of study and access to relevant knowledge about energy companies were different things, which we had conflated. Discussing within the group variations in "degree of access" and strategies for addressing access challenges in case studies that were to some extent interlinked through our main contacts in the companies, we realized that the access issue actually taught us something about the way in which the companies work. Knowledge about business and CSR does not necessarily depend on practical access to the inner workings of the corporation, or what several scholars coin as methodological challenges: busy corporate work schedules, sensitivity to publicity, the distracting presence of an ethnographer, and restrictions to entry and on participant observation (Rohlen 1974; Nader 1972 [1969]; Gusterson 1995; Ho 2016). Rather than taking for granted that these are obstacles for the researcher to develop knowledge about energy companies, the methodological challenges experienced and discussed by anthropologists since the 1960s can be viewed as basic knowledge about the field that one tries to understand. The busy corporate work schedules, for instance, might tell us something important about how corporate time is organized compared to, for example, academic time, which can be regarded as access to interesting aspects of the field we study rather than a challenge to gain access. One of the most obvious examples of "failure to access" in the project was the impossibility for us to visit Statkraft's largest hydropower project outside of Norway, located in southeastern Turkey. While the reluctance to facilitate our visit to the project site may relate to concerns about reputation and perhaps mounting challenges for their CSR work, we came to realize that one of the major reasons was concern for (our) security. This, in turn, sensitized us to the importance of security and safety and, together with other observations, stimulated us to explore the companies' concerns and narratives about safety, ultimately leading us to analyze risk management—which has emerged as one of the major topics in the project and which we have explored further by other means in other contexts. Thus, what we initially thought of as lack of access actually provided us with basic information about the corporations' varied surfaces, flows, and concerns. We found that the key methodological challenge across all cases in the research project was that we had not fully reflected on the meaning of access in this particular field. The methodological challenge was in fact a theoretical one.

While Peter Benson and Stuart Kirsch (2010: 464) claim that ethnographers risk co-optation when doing fieldwork in corporate offices because they have a tendency "to emphasize and identify with their subjects," our exploration of alternative models and methodologies for studying the field in which these energy companies engage provides means to negotiate this risk. This includes bringing our critical sensibilities to the methodological tools anthropologists use, such as "gaining access" and "maintaining a reflexive stand." However, the meaning of "good access" obviously depends on one's research agenda and research questions. If the aim is to understand the motivations, experiences, and meaning of life within a corporation—including, for example, corporate employee perspective on energy and sustainability—then a "deeper" kind of access is required to gather relevant data. If instead the aim is to explore the way in which the corporation engages the wider fields of energy policy, CSR discourses, reporting regimes, and the like—in short, the role of corporations in society—other methods that come with other criteria for access are called for. In our experience, not gaining the expected access might instead be considered a door opener into important knowledge about what the companies did not want us to know. If we reconsider the meaning of "good access" and focus more on what the corporations endeavor to avoid telling and showing, we get insight into the implicit "flow" of CSR (Barry 2013). What is made visible and readable and how access is navigated both from our side and from a company's and its employees' side are relevant methodological considerations. "Access" can be given and withdrawn, therefore the company's ability to control the information and the different ways in which they make information accessible to us are observations that are appropriate to coin as "good access" in this particular field of study.

Control of information and the way in which access is navigated are not necessarily guided by purely instrumental considerations only. A thorough methodological reappraisal should critically assess our own positionality, including how we may be embedded in and—willingly or not—be "intimate with" representatives from the energy corporations. Below, we discuss this with reference to what it implies to be Norwegian researchers studying Norwegian energy.

Searching for Access through Multiple Positioning

When following energy companies' CSR work across sites, the researcher's search for relevant positions in order to gain access are ever changing. Sometimes seen as a potential asset or a stakeholder by the companies we study, the researcher's positioning is constantly negotiated and challenged. However, with anthropology's historical intensity of "studying down," for example looking into local communities and grassroots initiatives in the face of energy infrastructure and climate change (see, for example, Sawyer 2004; Gardner 2012; Kirsch 2014; De Neve 2009; Dolan and Scott 2009; Li 2010; Gilberthorpe 2013), the methodological framework has also been shaped by this particular focus (Ho 2016: 30). Hugh Gusterson argues that "participant observation is a research technique that does not travel well up the social structure" (1995: 115). While corporations shift between "reaching out" and raising their defenses, we are compelled to find new creative methodological strategies for research, sometimes mobilizing our identities as researchers creatively to establish alternative arenas for fieldwork. We arranged several dialogue workshops, to which we invited representatives of the companies as well as other relevant "stakeholders." These workshops—lasting a day or two—gave us the opportunity to interact on a different basis with representatives of energy companies and to observe interaction between them and other actors (state, NGOs, academia).

Thus, to understand how energy corporations work from the inside, we shifted our methods beyond conventional participant observation to constantly negotiate the barriers we encounter in the field. Doing fieldwork at Equinor's investment area in Tanzania, for instance, Norwegian researchers were initially considered "foreigners" by local employees (see chapters 7 and 8). Switching from Tanzania to Equinor sites in Norway put us in a completely different position, and our research might even be considered self-ethnography of sorts. Norwegians have grown up with the idea that the oil that this company extracts secures our economic future through the Government Pension Fund Global (the so-called "Oil Fund"). To demonstrate the enormous size of the fund, journalists at times spell out the fund's worth per capita, making us all petro-millionaires. For those of us living in western Norway, we encounter Equinor in our daily lives, where we have learned the offshore work schedules of the parents of our children's best friends. A man in his early sixties, a friend of a friend, has been offered a compensation package with a monthly salary higher than a full professor's wage for the rest of his life in addition to his state pension if he is willing to voluntarily quit his position. We learn such news with a mix of moral indignation and envy. Equinor and the rest of the industry has, particularly during boom times, operated outside of the economic realities that the rest of us relate to. The company sponsors cultural events, science competitions for children, and student festivals where we might get an

Equinor stamp on our wrist—a physical mark (albeit temporary) of this company's "omnipresence" in our country.

In Tanzania and Brazil, it is easier to create distance to everyday life under Equinor's influence. As anthropologists, we are in a position to gain access to lower-level employees—and to the Tanzanian and Brazilian national discourses in general—that many of the company's Norwegian staff and managers do not have. Although our ease of local access may in some cases seem threatening, it also makes us more attractive partners, since we may share information and an understanding of local perceptions that they would otherwise not have access to. This again requires a level of care with regards to the information we disclose to the higher-ranking employees. Equinor specifically stated that they were interested in learning more about the public's opinion of their company and that our research project could be helpful in this regard. Our dual capacity thus meant that our access to knowledge about local contexts put us in a position wherein access might be given to other parts of the company's workings.

Balancing multiple positions resulted in Equinor offering us access to their training sessions in Dar es Salaam, which gave us an opportunity to observe communication between company staff and Tanzanian civil servants, academics, and representatives for the corporation, as well as how the Tanzanian participants engaged in a counterhegemonic discourse during lunch breaks. The majority of the seminar participants were Tanzanian, and during the lunch breaks, the discussions quickly switched to Swahili. Being perceived as a Tanzanian and able to engage in the discussions in Swahili, the researcher quickly became part of the "us" in the "us" versus "them" discussions that dominated lunch conversations. There was a heated discussion of how the Equinor seminars were a calculated way for international oil companies to spread information about their agenda in the country. There was mistrust among participants of the company's intentions in the country, criticisms of their lack of skill transfer and poor CSR initiatives, and skepticism around the expenses they had incurred in the country so far.[4] This openness and discussion of the participants' blatant mistrust of Equinor depends on the researcher's flexible positionality, being able to blend in with both locals and corporate staff. However, applying multiple positions, changing direction whenever needed in search for access to a field difficult to grasp, makes the researcher accountable for how changing positionality affects access and, even more important, the knowledge that is produced when access is pursued through multiple positionalities.

As one of the researchers in the Energethics project has a background as a campaigner and frequently appears in public debates about the climate crisis, financial and environmental risks of new petroleum fields, and oil sponsorship in the arts and academia in Norway, the methodological positioning becomes even more ambivalent. The "researcher" position is mostly expected to be neutral in Norway, where embedded research on the energy sector from an "activist" position is not a well-known methodology. Though critical perspectives on the industry from the social sciences are not uncommon (see, for example, Dale and Andersen 2018; Ryggvik and Kristoffersen 2015), there is a tacit expectation of "role separation." Working in the north of Norway, where the environmental groups are smaller and less organized than in the south (Jentoft 2013: 440)—and where Oslo-based NGOs are viewed with a certain suspicion—our researcher did *not* solely align herself within the "environmental movement" but sought an equivocation where she engaged both with the industry and environmental groups. Still, the moniker "activist" is not always one you choose—it is also one that is ascribed based on associations with such groups and that might shut down discussion because you are assumed to be committed to a preconceived idea. This was particularly true for our researcher as texts with her signature are easily found by doing a Google search. While this "bias" might restrict access in some domains, association with activism and advocacy allows for a wider engagement with how company employees engage with our questions and respond to critical engagement within academic research.

Moving between different contexts and events makes it possible to trace how people in the industry and environmental groups relate to each other on as well as off the record. During the Barents Sea Conference of 2016, where there was no visible on-the-ground protest taking place, national NGOs kept an eye on what was going on from afar. When Equinor and other companies presented a new report on weather conditions in the Barents Sea, Greenpeace was quick to challenge them in the media, accusing them of undercommunicating the risks in the area. The disagreement turned into a radio debate on the state channel, NRK, where Equinor insisted it had a "responsible approach"—one of its core values—based on fifty years of experience as a company. At the conference, we discussed this with some employees. They were confident that they had "won" the radio debate and told us how Greenpeace had *not* presented well. The Twitter feeds of Greenpeace and other environmentalists told a different story: Equinor had made outrageous and irresponsible statements. They had each performed before and convinced different audiences—and now Equinor's representatives were working on convincing us. They kept referring to CEO Eldar Sætre by his first name, insisting that "Eldar is really concerned about the climate" and a very different leader from Helge Lund. Lund was Equinor's CEO from 2004 to 2014 and took the company into foreign investments that have proven both controversial and expensive, allegedly losing 20 billion USD in the United States before pulling out (see conclusion). "Eldar," from what they told us, was different, someone who was serious about Equinor being a sustainable company, with the offshore windmills in Scotland as a prime example.

As Kim Fortun (2001: 6) found in her work as ethnographer and advocate after the Bhopal disaster, a methodology of working within advocacy can trace transnational connections and how corporate events move across countries, where "oscillation between different sources of data became an important research strategy." Different materials become traces of longer-term engagements: public discussions, op-eds, interviews, conferences, demonstrations, actions, newspapers, and everyday lives in the proximity of the energy operations. The activist status also gives different entry to how the companies are seen by other groups concerned with energy projects (such as environmental NGOs), and people in the local contexts where they operate, who might seek to share their disagreements with someone they feel understands their conflicted relationship to the industry. Such encounters were frequent during our fieldwork, where different people would confide in us their frustration, skepticism, or outright rage toward the company, which they would not voice in town for fear of falling out with neighbors, while others would display an ambivalence and others again outright praise of company activities.

As a methodological tool, the activist-researcher position requires a constant negotiation. It is in no way an escape from the risk of co-optation (cf. Benson and Kirsch 2010) but rather highlights how we as researchers may find ourselves becoming part of the company's strategy or "risk management" whether or not we signal an explicit position of advocacy. Moving between spheres with a willingness to engage with agendas without necessarily signing on to them, *not* being "neutral," produces knowledge of how energy companies treat different stakeholders and how they engage in public debates in Norway as part of their operations.

Strategic Intimacy

Reflexivity concerning our own shifting position in the search for access gave us particular insight into how the corporate staff we encountered positioned themselves toward us. We were often met by employees who managed to balance a strategic and professional appearance with an intimate twist. This particular position blurred our view over the corporate landscape and made access a shifting asset rather than something we gained over time.

Opinions are divided about the internationalization of fully or partly state-owned companies in Norway. Equinor has been heavily criticized for their investments abroad, which have been controversial for a number of reasons in addition to contributing relatively little to the company's overall income. Statkraft has lost enormous sums on failed projects, a fact negatively commented upon in the media. Cost cutting and downsizing of the staff in Norway is sometimes held up against the "waste of money" that is taking place when these companies invest abroad. While both companies have internationalized in recent years, the great majority of company staff is still Norwegian. Norway is a society characterized by a high degree of interpersonal trust. Equinor employees who have been interviewed in Norwegian have to a very large degree come across as frank and open about various challenges, and they seem to take for granted that we as researchers know where to draw the line as to what can be publicized and what can't. This is in marked contrast to the international staff posted in Norway. Such staff have a more corporate air and prefer to refer to official documents and polices rather than to real life events. These observations highlight a methodological problem encountered when examining the elite agencies of actors within institutions that are enabled or constrained by managerial systems. While intimacy may be articulated also in internationalized "high-circle" corporate spheres, such as at international conferences and fairs, this intimacy should be interpreted in the context of how corporate representatives are situated in the field. Corporate representatives obviously must maneuver tensions or ambivalence between corporate and personal identity and agenda, but methodologically it is important not to disentangle the person from the corporation.

During the previous super-cycle when oil prices and earnings were high, we experienced how researchers benefit from the sense of corporate infallibility and complacency. It produced a strangely unguarded openness at a point when, as one of Equinor's media and

PR executives told us, "It was like selling water in the desert—you don't have to bother with the customer—the stuff just disappears and money appears in your bank account ... and so we let ourselves eat too many cakes when times were good."

Boom times yielded to downturn, with oil prices plummeting from 120 USD a barrel to below 30 USD at the lowest. According to insiders, corporate arrogance and profligacy gave way to corporate austerity and job losses, especially within the "expendable" functions such as sustainability, and a time of much greater circumspection. This is a sign of the times but also indicative of a new sophistication in the practice and discourse of CSR, now dubbed *sustainability*, in which engagement with researchers is welcomed yet tightly controlled, "dialogue" is open, yet company personnel are careful to stay on message. While the question of where the individual ends and the corporation begins, ethically, socially, and politically, is an interesting one, it can also be a diversion. Even those moments of apparent spontaneous confessional—the breaking of ranks from the corporate line to admit failures of responsibility, impotence, and frustration at the impending existential crisis of climate change, for example—have become part of the ritual of public performance on the CSR/sustainability circuit. "We really dropped the ball on that one, it wasn't good for us, but also on a personal level it felt immensely frustrating to have to let people down because the company had made a decision that was effectively beyond my control," an executive with one of the top ten global oil companies said in a moment of apparently painful candor. Catharsis comes quickly, however, through the quasi-public ritual of corporate confessional: "But it's at these times that I think we really learn from our mistakes, we paid the price heavily in reputational capital and, next time, those of us on the 'soft' (i.e., CSR, external relations) side will have a bit more influence with the 'hard side.'"

Thus, it may be difficult to trace the connection between individual agency and corporate agency and agendas. While the former might at times appear at odds with the latter, it can serve to sustain it in unexpected ways. Internal conflicts and differences can be productive rather than disruptive in the company's power to achieve its aims. Yet it relies, as Jessica Smith (2021) has elaborated in her study of engineers' CSR work, on the embodied work of individuals who play between the scales of the personal responsibility and institutional responsibility. Thus, they embody the ethical agency of the corporation as well as the supposed systemic limits or impediments to realizing its self-proclaimed vision of a sustainable future. Time and again we were told by executives, from sustainability managers to vice presidents: "We are all allies, we are on the same side of the table"; "We want a future for our grandchildren too"; "We're all members of WWF"; or, "Like our CEO always says, we have children too, I am worried too, I care about this too." The apparent intimacy of such statements belies their strategic value to the company. They seem to speak of internal tensions and ethical contestations rather than structural coordination. Yet, this seemingly casual intimacy is rehearsed and effective. It can be, we suggest, highly strategic, a reaffirmation of the political role of CSR work rather than evidence of the failure of the company to fully socialize managers of outlying units. As such, defenses rise, leaving the researcher skating (or sliding) over the top if relying only on corporate statements and reports. How companies relate to the world beyond their walls, be it the "impacted communities," national states, or civil society, and the techniques they deploy in handling critics differ from company to company. This has posed particular obstacles to analyzing responsibility as a terrain of agency in which we can locate nodes of power and decision-making and trace routes of causality.

Conclusion

Doing ethnographic research on energy corporations is not impossible, but it is challenging. Their role in society can be fruitfully explored ethnographically if certain methodological challenges are comprehensively and reflexively addressed. While we hold that a multisited approach is required to explore the way in which energy corporations interact with society, we have also come to realize that this comes with particular challenges and possibilities. The main methodological challenge we initially experienced was "gaining access." We have argued that the combination of a comparative method within the project and critical reflexivity about what access means stimulated us to rethink methodology and access and ultimately gave new directions to our analytic work. The heightened sensibility concerning methodology has implied scrutinizing our positionality as researchers; being flexible, sometimes taking the role of advocacy, and being drawn into strategic intimacy. Handling this obviously requires certain cultural and linguistic skills. For instance, the characters of most case studies require the researchers to handle three languages fluently. But this reflexive multisited approach also means working against strongly held ideas about ethnographic fieldwork, such as long time stays in one place, and "hanging out" with locals. Thus, our research has involved a high degree of personal flexibility, more semi-structured interviews than participation, noncontinuous involvement with our interlocutors, mapping infrastructures of extensive geographical extent or opaque character, being present at or attending activities that involve alternative forms of socialites (social media, websites, documents, video meetings, etc.), and even creatively designing situations where we can interact with and observe company representatives.

We have had to reconsider access to the field in the conventional anthropological meaning of "peeking behind the curtain," seeking different kinds of data collection: the reporting regime of corporations, the importance of creating evidence for CSR activities, and the importance of branding. However, the methodological challenge was not so much to break loose of our initial expectation to access but to realize that what we had taken for granted as methodological obstacles was, in fact, important knowledge about corporations, such as concerns about security and safety. Reflexivity was a key methodological tool throughout that allowed us to maintain awareness of our own expectations and implicit insights about energy companies and to apply these experiences to examine the boundaries between society and corporations. And if we don't reflect critically on the "sameness" when we argue that multisited methodology is a pre-requisite for access since corporate operations are multisited, we may be seduced into thinking that researchers and corporate representatives look similarly on the world, whereas the latter may tend to think within a more hierarchal or core/periphery framework.

Rather than the day-to-day workings in company offices, we explore the narratives they produce when facing external criticism and dialogue, striving to detail, unpack, and situate the patterns that emerge when tracing companies from corporate offices to local sites and back. As researchers in one way or the other are regarded as externals and sometimes as stakeholders, sometimes as risks, we are indeed embedded in the narratives produced and performed by energy companies. By giving "attention to complexity, contradiction and the contexts that enable and limit even the most powerful among us" (Ho 2016: 45), whether company employee or researcher, these interactions have become integral to our understandings of how CSR is handled by energy companies. While we consider that the approach we have sketched here should contribute toward improving our knowledge of the way in which energy corporations interact with society, we also realize that the ideal of gaining "full knowledge" of this interaction is as problematic as "good access." Nobody, not even those centrally positioned in the company, has "full knowledge" of the corporation and its immediate environment, and corporations are likely much more complex, chaotic, and unstable entities than their self-presentations often convey. Energy corporations interact in a society that rapidly changes policies, attitudes, and practices concerning energy, and we therefore suggest that further reflexive thinking about methodological challenges concerning the study of the interaction of energy corporations with society should focus more closely on how we can address the temporal dimension, keeping in mind that "corporate time" may be quite different from "academic time."

Acknowledgments

This chapter has previously been published with the same title and by the same authors in *Energy Research and Social Science* 45 (2018): 250–57. Only minor changes have been made to the text when adapting it for the book. We acknowledge the support of the Research Council of Norway, research grant number 240617.

Ingrid Birce Müftüoglu holds a PhD in ethnology and has done research within various fields, including the women's movement in Norway, nationalism in Turkey, and corporate social responsibility of Norwegian energy companies abroad. She is now working as a senior research and policy adviser.

Ståle Knudsen is professor in the Department of Social Anthropology, University of Bergen, Norway. He was leader of the project Energethics (2015–19), from which this book emerges. Knudsen has, since the early 1990s, done ethnographic fieldwork in Turkey, and his publications include the monograph *Fisheries in Modernizing Turkey* (Berghahn, 2009).

Ragnhild Freng Dale is a social anthropologist and senior researcher with the Western Norway Research Institute (Vestlandsforsking). Her research interests include energy infrastructure, petroleum, climate transitions, and community impacts, predominantly in Norway and Sápmi. She holds a PhD from the Scott Polar Research Institute at the

University of Cambridge and is a member of the Young Academy of Norway.

Oda Eiken Maraire was a research assistant for the Energethics project. She is currently a PhD candidate in the Department of Social Anthropology, University of Bergen, Norway, and part of the research project "Urban Enclaving Futures." With a focus on the real estate industry, her doctoral project explores imaginaries of future urban living and homemaking practices in affluent areas of Johannesburg, South Africa.

Dinah Rajak is reader in anthropology and international development at the University of Sussex. She is the author of *In Good Company: An Anatomy of Corporate Social Responsibility* (Stanford University Press, 2011) and coeditor of *The Anthropology of Corporate Social Responsibility* (Berghahn, 2016).

Siri Lange holds a PhD in social anthropology and is a professor in the Department of Health Promotion and Development (HEMIL) at the University of Bergen, Norway. Prior to joining HEMIL, Lange was a senior researcher at the Christian Michelsen Institute (CMI) in Bergen (2002–17). Lange has published extensively on social, economic, and political issues in Tanzania.

Notes

1. Full title: "Norwegian Energy Companies Abroad: Expanding the Anthropological Understanding of Corporate Social Anthropology." Energethics website: https://www.uib.no/en/project/energethics.
2. Costs for energy conferences may often be upward of eight hundred USD for a few days, including a conference dinner and other informal events. Researchers are sometimes able to negotiate or request a reduction in price, as the companies are aware that the income difference and spending allowance between academia and the corporate world is enormous, and they do want to include academicians in these events to preserve the democratic flow between different sectors in Norwegian society.
3. "Development orthodoxy" refers to the position of CSR now being firmly established as a central component of the development policy mainstream, which to a large extent goes unquestioned these days, when only a decade ago many development insiders were still rather ambivalent about such a key role for big business in development.
4. Data in this paragraph provided by research assistant Maria Njau.

References

Barry, Andrew. 2013. *Material Politics: Disputes along the Pipeline*. West Sussex: Wiley Blackwell.

Benson, Peter, and Stuart Kirsch. 2009. "Corporate Oxymorons." *Dialectical Anthropology* 34(1): 45–48.

———. 2010. "Capitalism and the Politics of Resignation." *Current Anthropology* 51(4): 459–86.

Bloch, Maurice. 1992. *Ritual, History and Power: Selected Papers in Social Anthropology*. London: Athlone Press.

Castree, Noel. 2008. "Neoliberalising Nature: The Logics of Deregulation and Reregulation." *Environment and Planning* 40: 131–52.

Choy, Timothy. 2011. *Ecologies of Comparison: An Ethnography of Endangerment in Hong Kong*. Durham, NC: Duke University Press.

Coleman, Samuel. 1996. "Obstacles and Opportunities in Access to Professional Work Organizations for Long-Term Fieldwork: The Case of Japanese Laboratories." *Human Organization* 55(3): 334–43.

Cross, Jamie. 2011. "Detachment as a Corporate Ethic: Materializing CSR in the Diamond Supply Chain." *Focaal: Journal of Global and Historical Anthropology* 60: 34–46.

Dale, Brigt, and Gisle Andersen. 2018. "Til Dovre faller? Norsk olje og grønn omstilling" [Until the mountains of Dovre crumble? Norwegian oil and the green transition]. In *Grønn omstilling: Norske veivalg* [Green transition: Norwegian crossroads], edited by Grete Rusten and Håvard Haarstad. Oslo: Universitetsforlaget.

De Neve, Geert. 2009. "Power, Inequality and Corporate Social Responsibility: The Politics of Ethical Compliance in the South Indian Garment Industry." *Economic and Political Weekly* 44(22): 63–72.

Dolan, Catherine, and Linda Scott. 2009. "Lipstick Evangelism: Avon Trading Circles and Gender Empowerment in South Africa." *Gender and Development* 17(2): 203–18.

Fortun, Kim. 2001. *Advocacy after Bhopal: Environmentalism, Disaster, New Global Orders*. Chicago: University of Chicago Press.

Frynas, Jedrzej G. 2009. *Beyond Corporate Social Responsibility: Oil Multinationals and Social Challenges*. Cambridge: Cambridge University Press.

Gardner, Katy. 2012. *Discordant Development: Global Capitalism and the Struggle for Connection in Bangladesh*. London: Pluto Press.

Gilberthorpe, Emma. 2013. "In the Shadow of Industry: A Study of Culturization in Papua New Guinea." *Journal of the Royal Anthropological Institute* 19(2): 261–78.

Gusterson, Hugh. 1995. "Exploding Anthropology's Canon in the World of the Bomb." In *Studying Elites Using Qualitative Methods*, edited by Rosanna Hertz and Jonathan B. Imber, 187–205. London: Sage.

Ho, Karen. 2016. "'Studying Up' Wall Street: Reflections on Theory and Methodology." In *Researching amongst Elites: Challenges and Opportunities in Studying Up*, edited by Luis L. M. Aguiar and Christopher J. Schneider, 29–48. Abingdon: Routledge.

Jentoft, Svein. 2013. "På sporet av Nord-Norge" [On the trail of Northern Norway]. In *Hvor går Nord-Norge? Politiske tidslinjer* [Where does Northern Norway go? Political timelines], edited by Svein Jentoft, J. I. Nergård, and K. A. Røvik, 3: 431–44. Stamsund: Orkana Forlag.

Kirsch, Stuart. 2014. *Mining Capitalism: The Relationship between Corporations and Their Critics*. Ewing: University of California Press.

Li, Fabiana. 2010. "From Corporate Accountability to Shared Responsibility: Dealing with Pollution in a Peruvian Smelter-Town." In *Corporate Social Responsibility: Discourses, Practices, Perspectives*, edited by Ravi Raman. London: Palgrave Macmillan.

Nader, Laura. 1972 [1969]. "Up the Anthropologist: Perspectives Gained from Studying Up." In *Reinventing Anthropology*, edited by D. Hymes, 285–311. New York: Pantheon.

Rajak, Dinah. 2011a. *In Good Company: An Anatomy of Corporate Social Responsibility.* Palo Alto, CA: Stanford University Press.

———. 2011b. "Theatres of Virtue: Collaboration, Consensus, and the Social Life of Corporate Social Responsibility." *Focaal—Journal of Global and Historical Anthropology* 60: 9–20.

Rohlen, Thomas. P. 1974. *For Harmony and Strength: Japanese White-Collar Organization in Anthropological Perspective.* Berkeley: University of California Press.

Ryggvik, Helge, and Berit Kristoffersen. 2015. "Heating Up and Cooling Down the Petrostate: The Norwegian Experience." In *Ending the Fossil Fuel Era*, edited by Thomas Princen, Jack P. Manno, and Pamela L. Martin, 249–76. Cambridge, MA: MIT press.

Sawyer, Suzana. 2004. *Crude Chronicles: Indigenous Politics, Multinational Oil and Neoliberalism in Ecuador.* Durham, NC: Duke University Press.

Smith, Jessica M. 2021. *Extracting Accountability. Engineers and Corporate Social Responsibility.* Cambridge MA: MIT Press.

Urban, Greg, and Kyung-Nan Koh. 2013. "Ethnographic Research on Modern Business Corporations." *Annual Review of Anthropology* 42: 139–58.

Welker, Marina. 2009. "Corporate Security Begins in the Community: Mining, the Corporate Responsibility Industry and Environmental Advocacy in Indonesia." *Cultural Anthropology* 24(1): 142–79.

———. 2014. *Enacting the Corporation: An American Mining Firm in Post-authoritarian Indonesia.* Berkeley: University of California Press.

— Chapter 2 —

SAMFUNNSANSVAR IS NOT CSR

Mapping Expectations and Practices of
(Corporate) Social Responsibility in Norway

Oda Eiken Maraire and Isabelle Hugøy

This chapter explores how the originally Anglo-American concept of corporate social responsibility (CSR) is perceived and practiced in Norwegian contexts. While CSR was developed in the American corporate world as a management concept with philanthropic ideals, it gained widespread legitimacy globally, and today organizations as well as governments engage with CSR (Gjølberg 2010: 204), including the Norwegian government. Yet, the common Norwegian translation of CSR, in public media, national policy documents, and existing literature (e.g., Gjølberg 2010; Morsing, Midttun, and Palmås 2007), is *samfunnsansvar*, which directly translates to "societal responsibility." This translation excludes the corporate aspect and replaces "social" with "societal," thus arguably alluding to a particular shared meaning and cultural resonance that is not congruent with that of CSR. *Samfunnsansvar* in Norway is part of a shared, imagined ideal of morally correct behavior, an ideal that promotes all actors in society, regardless of socioeconomic status, to act responsibly and ethically for the collective good of society. Consequently, however, because *samfunnsansvar* is *also* applied when CSR is translated to Norwegian, taken-for-granted ideas of *samfunnsansvar* may influence public perceptions and expectations toward Norwegian corporations' responsibility and CSR practices. In short, we argue that *samfunnsansvar* is not the same as corporate social responsibility. This difference is often muted but has significant consequences.

This chapter provides important context to the subsequent ethnographic contributions in this volume by mapping how various actors across sectors in Norwegian society over time relate to and navigate what can be considered as competing responsibilities (Trnka and Trundle 2017). Based on document analysis of Norwegian newspaper articles[1] and official Norwegian state documents,[2] we show how multiple claims about responsibility exist simultaneously, and we contend that because of the discrepancy between *samfunnsansvar* and corporate social responsibility, there exists a tacit tension between national and international approaches as to how CSR is conceptualized and practiced in Norwegian contexts. In unpacking this tension, we consider CSR as an idea that travels (Gjølberg 2010) and that local, national, and international contexts make CSR travel and eventually enable CSR to become localized (e.g., Welker 2014) or domesticated (e.g., Knudsen 2015) in particular ways. The vast literature on CSR globally (e.g., Dolan and Rajak 2016; Habisch et al. 2005; May, Cheney, and Roper 2007; Moura-Leite and Padgett 2011; Smith 2021) and on CSR and *samfunnsansvar* in Norway (e.g., Ditlev-Simonsen, Hoivik and Ihlen 2015; Gjølberg 2010; Ihlen 2011; Nordhaug and Olsen 2010) focuses mainly on corporations' responsibility. We add to this existing literature by mapping expectations, perceptions, and values associated with the term *samfunnsansvar* in Norway *beyond* corporations as well as state institutions. By doing so, we show that the dynamic space between *samfunnsansvar* and CSR gives corporations as well as government institutions in Norway the opportunity for strategic and rhetorical maneuvering. Thus, following Trnka and Trundle (2017: 22), we contribute to the call to critically analyze how neoliberal responsibilization importantly "exists within a matrix of dependencies, reciprocities, and obligations."

First, we will give a brief overview of the international discourse on CSR before contextualizing the Norwegian concept—*samfunnsansvar*. Then we map the development of *samfunnsansvar* over time in both public (newspaper articles) and policy (state documents) discourses. While we acknowledge that the Norwegian organizational landscape is overlapping, we will for analytical purposes separate between public and policy discourse. Furthermore, we recognize the limitations of the Atekst database,[3] and therefore emphasize that we use the material to indicate certain trends about how *samfunnsansvar* is conceptualized and practiced. In mapping the developments of *samfunnsansvar*, we reference newspaper articles as examples of how CSR is embedded in a broader application of *samfunnsansvar* in Norway on the one hand. On the other hand, our analysis of Norwegian policy documents suggests that expectations toward corporations' *samfunnsansvar* gradually adapts to an international discourse of CSR that dominates until *samfunnsansvar* as well as the English concept of CSR eventually disappear from policy papers and are, around 2020, replaced by "sustainability" and "sustainable value creation." In this process, we argue that the conceptualization of *samfunnsansvar* in Norwegian policy discourse gradually moved away from its cultural resonance toward adapting to an international discourse of CSR that is highly corporatized and business oriented. Nevertheless, the cultural resonance and shared meaning of *samfunnsansvar* persists in public discourse. By outlining how *samfunnsansvar* and CSR move in relation to each other, we examine how nuances of competing responsibilities play out within and across various Norwegian contexts. To better understand the tensions that emerge when different models of thought come together, we ask: how do ideas of *samfunnsansvar* affect the way Norwegian corporations practice CSR, and how does *samfunnsansvar* inform the perception that Norwegian corporations are particularly good at CSR abroad?

Beyond CSR as Polysemic

In 1953, the American economics professor Howard R. Bowen was one of the first to conceptualize CSR in *Social Responsibility of the Businessman* (Bowen and Johnson 2013). Bowen argued that businesses were expected to take responsibility for the social welfare of the nation by producing social goods (May, Cheney, and Roper 2007: 5). In the United States, corporate philanthropy has been widely accepted as a strategy to fulfill social responsibilities, which has also influenced the acceptance of CSR. In the 1970s, the idea was that businesses should do what makes the world better and not just what is good for the business. During this time, the concept of CSR became well-known and widely incorporated into business strategies. In the same time period, others, such as Milton Friedman, were skeptical of giving businesses too much political power to define the allocation of resources through CSR strategies and argued that the foremost duty of a business was to increase shareholder value (May, Cheney, and Roper 2007: 5–6). This criticism may point to what has been called a "transatlantic divide" between American and European societies' translations and enactments of the CSR concept (Gjølberg 2010: 204). The regulatory role of governments is stronger in Europe compared to the United States. May, Cheney, and Roper therefore argue that CSR "required a multi-stakeholder approach rather than a purely shareholder-oriented one" (2007: 6) when it was first introduced in Western European societies.

Companies increasingly incorporate CSR as a risk management activity (see Morsing, Midttun, and Palmås 2007) and as a strategic component for value creation (see Louche, Idowu, and Filho 2010), or they emphasize sustainability in articulating a CSR agenda (see introduction). While sustainability and sustainable development are most prevalent,[4] environmental, social, and governance (ESG) (see introduction) is gaining attention. The EU taxonomy for sustainable activities currently under development is one example of the move toward ESG (Financial Stability, Financial Services, and Capital Markets Union 2020). These strategies are in line with what Auld, Bernstein, and Cashore (2008) define as the new CSR; that a company's CSR agendas are in line with the firm's core activities, as opposed to the old CSR where philanthropic activities often had little to do with a firm's core practices.

Since its conception, CSR thus continues to be redefined, challenged, critiqued, and embraced. There exists no uniform definition of CSR, but the definitions that do exist are partly congruent—encompassing social, environmental, and economic impacts to various degrees (Auld, Bernstein, and Cashore 2008; Dahlsrud 2006; Moura-Leite and Padgett 2011). Jessica Smith (2021) argues that CSR is to be understood as a boundary object. A boundary object is mobile in its interpretive flexibility on individual and group levels, where intersecting social worlds can agree about what it means without setting a consensus (Star and Griesemer 1989: 393). Thus, we understand CSR not only as a polysemic concept that entails different meanings, we also approach it as a boundary object by analyzing CSR as an idea that travels. It travels across continents, from industries to governments (Gjølberg 2010: 205) in particular ways and takes on multiple and context-dependent meanings in the process. CSR can facilitate collaboration before reaching a consensus as the object moves unproblematically between both vague and more specific understandings (Star 2010: 604). With the inherent flexibility of CSR even within the English language, it is not surprising that an additional interpretational void emerges when the concept is translated into other languages, such as Norwegian.

Samfunnsansvar is not CSR

Samfunnsansvar in Norway

Our analysis indicates that *samfunnsansvar* in Norway is part of a shared imagined ideal of morally correct behavior. This ideal promotes all actors in society, regardless of socioeconomic status, to act responsibly and ethically for the collective good of society. It is a sense of responsibility that an individual, a company, or an institution is expected to be aware of and to have, take, and enact. Ideally, one does not take *samfunnsansvar* with intentions of economic gain. It is a duty (as opposed to a right), which can be related to social, cultural, financial, or environmental issues. We will show how this shared ideal also entails other values, such as egalitarianism, collaboration, and *dugnad* (voluntary work). To grasp how this locally specific term is perceived and practiced, we draw on Smith's approach (2021) and understand *samfunnsansvar* as a boundary object (Star and Griesemer 1989). With reference to the vague, yet vigorous, common understanding given above, we will in the following show how *samfunnsansvar* can be applied across different "frames" (Reese 2007) to promote different agendas precisely because of a shared cultural meaning that resonates across social worlds. Frames are not static but persist over time. Frames consist of socially shared organizing principles and concepts that work symbolically to create meaning (Reese 2007: 150). In this chapter, we do not analyze different frames; our intention is rather to show how *samfunnsansvar* is a central tool that is used, consciously or unconsciously, across various frames to exemplify how its meaning is never discussed or questioned—it is taken for granted.

Norwegian public and policy discourse tend to interchange the terms *næringslivets samfunnsansvar* (societal responsibility of the corporate sector), *bedriftenes samfunnsansvar* (societal responsibility of corporations), and *samfunnsansvar*, but the latter term is most frequently applied in debates about corporate responsibility among politicians, corporate representatives, and actors in civil society (see figure 2.2). While the first two terms may appear to reflect the connotations with the Anglo-American term, CSR, given their reference to the corporate sector, we contend that the related word *samfunnsansvar* points to an important difference between Norwegian and Anglo-American understandings of responsibility. The direct translation of *samfunnsansvar* is societal (*samfunns-*) responsibility (*ansvar*). Societal (*samfunns-*) refers to a society or a group. *Samfunnsansvar* is an altruistic responsibility that an individual or an institution has toward society in general. An individual's responsibility toward another individual would not be considered *samfunnsansvar* unless it is expected by the society at large (e.g., to help an elderly neighbor with various chores). Øyvind Ihlen and Heidi von Weltzien Hoivik (2015: 116) connect the aforementioned linguistic detail to the traditionally positive attitude and tripartite collaboration between the state, companies, and trade unions.

Ihlen and Hoivik (2015) delineate how historical factors, such as early paternalism, small-scale businesses, pious Christianity, and debates regarding welfare measures influenced what they call "the heritage of 'business responsibility' in Norway" (2015: 110). They argue that, historically, financial and social values or concerns were not considered detached from one another. Through multiple examples of strategies that Norwegian companies used to build a relationship with their workers—such as building infrastructure and homes (Norsk Hydro), supporting labor unions, and funding the building of a church (Dale AS)—they argue that these efforts point to "a climate of mutual recognition, cooperation, and compromise, [that] would later come to dominate Norwegian economic life" (2015: 112–13). They emphasize, however, that conflicts also occurred. They delineate how the Norwegian government during the 1870s set an agenda to bring market liberalism in line with ethics "more strongly centered on the broader needs of society" (2015: 111). In Norway, it was the government that pushed for such policies rather than the voluntary efforts of business leaders, as was the case in the United States. Ihlen and Hoivik call these measures "seeds of CSR" (2015: 111). We consider these measures as traces of *samfunnsansvar*. Ihlen also links the Norwegian approach to *samfunnsansvar* as different from other countries due to the historically strong state ownership of large companies (Ihlen 2007: 45). As Knudsen describes in chapter 4, state ownership is a central component in the Hydro Model, which has become a model to follow for other companies with state ownership, also in dealings with responsibility. As a contrast to strong state ownership, Eldar Bråten shows in chapter 3 how the development of a cooperative model in a small Norwegian town had little involvement from the state. While this literature is mainly concerned with company practices, our analysis of news articles indicates that perceptions and practices of *samfunnsansvar* not only concern corporations and the state but all actors in society, regardless of socioeconomic status. The following examples support our argument that *samfunnsansvar* is not CSR.

Samfunnsansvar *as Collective Effort*

An opinion piece published in the national newspaper *Verdens Gang* (*VG*) following World War II is the first available article in the database to mention *samfunnsansvar* in public discourse. Bjarne Rabben writes:

> These are new times. We shall adapt from war to peace. ... Is the youth mature enough to be able to carry the *samfunnsansvar* and point out the direction and goal for our society? The question is not dictated by a mistrust to the youth, but from the desire that society—the state—must make the youth better suited to take on *samfunnsansvar* and the societal tasks. (Rabben 1945, translated by authors)

This quote illustrates that Rabben expects that both the nation's youth and the state take *samfunnsansvar*. It indicates a collective effort where everyone contributes (i.e., indirectly collaborates) regardless of a person or group's socioeconomic status. This, too, becomes prevalent in his partial leveling and blurred boundaries between the state and society.

Ideas of collective effort are also connected to democracy and gender in a piece from 1948 when the chairwoman of Norway's Working Women's National Association, Bergliot Lie, is quoted as saying: "We want to shoulder the *samfunnsansvar* with men. A true democracy cannot be truly efficient if women do not get their place in management" (*VG* 1948, translated by authors). In 1955, a magazine for the union officials of the largest workers' union in Norway, Landsorganisasjonen i Norge (LO), argues that state banks should expand because the loan agreements of private banks were not in line with set financial guidelines, thus they did not show *samfunnsansvar* (*VG* 1955). This points to the expectation that the state should be a leading figure in enacting *samfunnsansvar*. In 1968, a car expert alludes to ideas of individual responsibility for the greater collective good when talking about the importance of good car maintenance by stating that car owners and users have a significant *samfunnsansvar* (*VG* 1968). According to a statement from the Conservative Party's Youth Party in 1969, it is *samfunnsansvar* to make sure that all districts in Norway have access to doctors and dentists (*VG* 1969). In the 1980s, *samfunnsansvar* is linked to women's rights and gender equality, such as access to political and financial power and participation (e.g., Haslund 1984; Raumnes 1983).

The term also appears in the context of income settlements in 1984, which sparked a debate about the form of settlement (*oppgjørsformen*):

> Should LO and other trade unions be able to play a sensible and meaningful role for their members, ... this presupposes that one increasingly assumes independent *samfunnsansvar*. ... The modern economy requires active participation by all of us, so that we can solve the tasks for the common good. Therefore, we will maintain that the way forward is through cooperation, not through conflicts and strikes. (Aftenposten 1984, translated by authors)

The quote illustrates the value of cooperation in tripartite negotiations that designates the Nordic model (see introduction). Collaboration is also one of the core ideas in understandings of *samfunnsansvar*. It points to the individual responsibility that every citizen has toward society. It also evokes ideas of egalitarianism in the sense that everyone who is part of the society should dutifully participate and collectively collaborate for the common good. Other news articles discuss how schools have an overarching *samfunnsansvar* (Andersen 1985) and that the pupils will learn and expand their *samfunnsansvar* at school (Holtet 1986), suggesting again that *samfunnsansvar* is considered a value that guides expectations of morally correct behavior through an ideal interdependence between state institutions and individual citizens.

A more recent example of expectations toward enactments of *samfunnsansvar* arises from March 2020 when the COVID-19 pandemic reached Norway. The term was mentioned twice as often in Norwegian media in March compared to any other month in 2020. Similarly, mentions of the term *dugnad* increased over 300 percent from February 2020 to March 2020. *Dugnad* originates from Norse *dugnaðr*, meaning "to help," particularly in terms of contributing with physical labor on farms without financial compensation (Østberg 1925). *Dugnad* continues to connote ideas of collective acts of equally distributed voluntary unpaid help and support, usually within communities such as neighborhoods and local sports clubs (e.g., Simon and Mobekk 2019). The concept overlaps ideas of *samfunnsansvar* in the sense that every member of society is expected to take responsibility without economic gain for the individual and without there being a law or regulation stipulating the appropriate behavior in the relevant context. In the context of the pandemic, individual and voluntary precautions and efforts are a means to collaboratively get the disease under control (e.g., see figure 2.1). And when actions breach the imagined ideal of *samfunnsansvar* or *dugnad*, the concepts are used as a guiding value to hold the accused accountable. For example, in May 2021, when politicians and members of parliament were offered the vaccine for COVID-19 outside of the ordinary vaccine program, doctors, among others, expressed that this prioritization of vaccines

Figure 2.1. Enacting *samfunnsansvar* during a pandemic. As a measure to prevent the spread of COVID-19, the poster—"Keep distance in the kiosk. Show *samfunnsansvar*! Maximum 15 persons"—encourages people on a ferry on the west coast of Norway to enact *samfunnsansvar* by keeping physical distance from others, 2020. © Isabelle Hugøy.

was not in keeping with the national *dugnad* promoted by the government as it breached the value of equality (e.g., Folkvord and Lægland 2021).

In sum, the abovementioned examples indicate that *samfunnsansvar* is an all-encompassing concept with shared cultural resonance that is unquestioned and yet actively applied across various social worlds or frames (Reese 2007) to promote different agendas. As a boundary object (Star and Griesemer 1989), the concept's interpretive flexibility becomes evident when *samfunnsansvar*, on the one hand, is expected to be enacted by state institutions—through demands for equal rights and for equal access to state-provided healthcare—and, on the other hand, by individuals—women wanting to take *samfunnsansvar* and the importance of pupils learning about and how to enact *samfunnsansvar*. The desire for equal collective effort, egalitarianism, and (individual) duty that is conveyed through the examples (be they of state or private actors) suggests that the concept should be considered in relation to and as embedded within an entangled organizational web that characterizes the Norwegian society.

The complex and overlapping organizational landscape, according to Halvard Vike (2018), is a result of individuals who partake in several associations. Based on his fieldwork on local politics and structures in Norway in the 1990s, Vike argues that there are tight integrations between the state and civil society because "the municipalities constitute highly complex bureaucratic structures in communities where networks of kin, neighborhood, friendship, and membership in voluntary organizations overlap each other and tend to be very dense" (2018: 124). Social control in the local community "also worked through a sense of equal membership that became strongly reinforced as voluntary organizations became politicized and in part co-opted by the state" (2018: 119). Roles and responsibilities overlap and blur boundaries and are perhaps part of the reason, as Vike argues, why nongovernmental movements and organizations did not see themselves as "outside the state" (2018: 119). This alludes to a sense of egalitarianism that is also applicable to business in Norway. According to Ihlen and Hoivik, "Norwegian business institutions are not considered to be hubs of society, as is often the case from an Anglo-American perspective. Business is instead considered to be one of many institutions functioning *in* society, and is not always seen as the most important" (2015: 117). This cultural and structural difference indicates perceptions of a more egalitarian societal ideal as opposed to the perceived strong hierarchical structures in the American business sector.

With the various sectors of the Norwegian society being closely interlinked—exemplified through the continuous strong tripartite collaboration between the state, companies, and trade unions—no actor sees themselves as outside the state, and thus everyone—individual citizen, state institution, corporation—is expected to enact *samfunnsansvar*. It is an altruistic responsibility for society that does not necessarily take businesses into consideration. *Samfunnsansvar* is a complex concept constituted of various subjective perceptions and practices with a shared meaning, a *taken-for-grantedness*. It is used as a flexible interpretative tool to promote or frame arguments, consciously or unconsciously, that cover broad or specific issues at the same time as it resonates across social worlds. Because CSR does not evoke the same imagery and cultural resonance as *samfunnsansvar*, we argue that, in Norway, the acceptance of CSR was strongly influenced by interpreting it in relation to the already existing and all-encompassing concept *samfunnsansvar*. To explore this point, we will outline developments of *samfunnsansvar* and CSR in public and policy discourse to further reveal that *samfunnsansvar* is not the same as CSR.

Samfunnsansvar and CSR in Public and Political Discourse

Domesticating CSR

Until 1984, *samfunnsansvar* is rarely mentioned in newspapers. In 1984, *samfunnsansvar* was mentioned seventeen times, and in 1985, twenty-five times. The number of mentions continued to increase, reaching its peak in 2020 (3,195 times, seemingly due to the COVID-19 pandemic). *Bedriftenes samfunnsansvar* is first mentioned in an article in 1989 that discusses how corporations not only have a responsibility for the physical environment but also the cultural environment within the corporation and society at large (Egeland 1989). *Næringslivets samfunnsansvar* was first mentioned the following year in an opinion piece that argues that the exclusive focus on financial profits by corporate leaders in the 1980s is insufficient to develop good corporate culture (Abel 1990). *Næringslivets samfunnsansvar* appears again three (Jaklin 1993) and seven years (Føllesdal 1997) later, and both *næringslivets samfunnsansvar* and *bedriftenes samfunnsansvar* appear again in 1998 (Hellebust 1998; Hålien 1998). The inclusion of *bedriftenes-* and *næringslivets samfunnsansvar* around 1990 and the increase in mentions of *samfunnsansvar* from the late 1990s onward must be understood in the context of globalization and international trends of deregulating markets, privatization, and companies going abroad, which in turn had consequences for the Norwegian state's governance. Among these were the ethical challenges facing companies as they internationalized and invested abroad at a faster rate from the 1990s and civil society's demand for insight into the investments (Hveem 2009: 384).

Nevertheless, *samfunnsansvar* is absent from policy papers during the 1990s. What appears, however, is a rather vague definition of what responsibility entails in a white paper on state ownership in the corporate sector: "The companies themselves have the primary responsibility for ethical standards and for acting, both nationally and internationally, according to the values and attitudes that we as a nation adhere" (Meld. St. 61 [1996 97], translation by authors). Neither of the concepts, *samfunnsansvar* nor CSR, are used in this context. We propose that the white paper alludes to a tacit cultural resonance of *samfunnsansvar* rather than CSR.

In newspapers, we find a similar tendency in that the first newspaper article to mention corporate social responsibility appeared in 1999 (Knutzen 1999), and the abbreviation CSR in 2001 (Olsen 2001). The following quote by Jørn Bue Olsen (2001, translation by authors) explains the CSR concept by applying the already established concept *samfunnsansvar*: "Another current trend that large responsible companies work on is the so-called CSR concept—Corporate Social Responsibility. Big companies acknowledge their *samfunnsansvar* and take an active shared responsibility [*sosialt medansvar*] in societal development." In this opinion piece, the English concept, its abbreviation, and the Norwegian translation are all mentioned and used somewhat interchangeably. Olsen's interchanging use of the different terms may point to the perception that CSR has different associated meanings that are narrower than the broader cultural and historical resonance that *samfunnsansvar* entails. The application of CSR in this quote may intend to specify responsibility in context of the corporate sector while acknowledging that other actors also have (equal) responsibility.

This taken-for-granted understanding of *samfunnsansvar* is also prevalent within the Norwegian business sector. Before the Anglo-American CSR concept was part of the formal agenda for Norwegian companies, there was, according to several companies, an established consensus that they already enact *samfunnsansvar* and CSR. Director of GC Rieber and previous president of the Confederation of Norwegian Enterprise (NHO) Paul-Christian Rieber has even argued that *samfunnsansvar* is in the genes of most of the Norwegian corporate sector (Ihlen 2011: 133). In an interview, a representative from Aker Solutions expressed that "*samfunnsansvar* has always been on our agenda, even though it might not have been defined as *samfunnsansvar* before" (Luthen 2009 in Ihlen 2011: 11, translated by authors). This resonates with what Knudsen describes in chapter 4; although Hydro did not explicitly frame their practices as CSR, actors working both in and with Norwegian corporations consider the so-called "Hydro model" to be a good model for implementing CSR. Ihlen's (2011) study of Norwegian companies further illustrates that their attitudes toward CSR meant that they had only to document their existing practices and attitudes. Attitudes toward implementing CSR reporting regimes connoted with *samfunnsansvar* as an ideal that already existed in the Norwegian context. Moreover, a study— conducted from 2005 to 2008 with interviewees from government, unions, and business confederations across the Nordic nations—

concluded that CSR was considered as "largely irrelevant and superfluous in a domestic context" (Gjølberg 2010: 221). Interviewees believed that implementation of CSR domestically was "a return to the old days of paternalism and charity" (2010: 221), thus implying that there exists a tension between the expectations of CSR and *samfunnsansvar*. This irrelevance must also be seen in relation to the Nordic welfare model, which has largely replaced paternalism and the perception that legal frameworks, regulations, democracy, and the like are lacking or unsatisfactory in countries of operation (Gjølberg 2010; Ihlen 2011). It should be noted that, even within this literature, it is unclear how interlocutors use the terms, as the authors often translate *samfunnsansvar* to include corporate responsibility.

Albeit with a somewhat different formulation, this taken-for-grantedness of what responsibility entails, as exemplified in white paper number 61 (Meld. St. 61. [1996–97]), continues to be present in later governance publications, that is, after the introduction of the CSR concept in newspapers. In 2002, the Bondevik II administration established ten principles of good corporate governance, with one specifying that "selskapet skal være bevisst sitt samfunnsansvar" (Meld. St. 22 [2001–2]: 8), which directly translates to "the company shall be aware of its societal responsibility." The launch of the principles must be seen in the context of the international debate on corporate governance, which accelerated after accounting scandals in several companies in the late 1990s and early 2000s (Meld. St. 13 [2010–11]a). This eventually led to the establishment of an extensive framework of legislation and nonbinding guidelines for responsible business conduct (Meld. St. 13 [2010–11]a; Eierberetning 2003).[5] The Norwegian version of the principle also bears associations with formulations regarding *samfunnsansvar* in newspapers, namely "to be aware of one's societal responsibility" (å være sitt samfunnsansvar bevisst). This "awareness" is applied across a broad variety of topics in public discourse, including concerns regarding alcohol consumption (Linden 2016) and how Norwegian media must prioritize developing good reviewers of art and culture (Engelstad et al. 2017) to the responsibilities of insurance companies (Ness, Johnsrud, and Lundin 2002).[6] This suggests that *samfunnsansvar* is used as a central tool, consciously or unconsciously, to convey arguments across a variety of frames because it resonates to a type of responsibility that is implicitly understandable and emotionally charged. While there exists no English version of white paper number 22 (2001–2), a translation is offered in the white paper on state ownership published five years later: "The company shall recognize its responsibility to all shareholders and stakeholders in the company" (Meld. St. 13 [2006–7]: 22). However, the translation does not reflect the connotations given in the Norwegian phrasing. The discrepancy between the policy documents in Norwegian and English then makes visible the tacit tension between established framings of *samfunnsansvar* — of which anyone, regardless of their socioeconomic position, should "be aware" — and a globalized discourse of CSR with its focus on shareholders and stakeholders. The principles remained unchanged for years.

The abovementioned examples suggest that the interpretation of CSR was strongly informed by established meaning(s) of *samfunnsansvar*, rather than the other way around, in both public and policy discourse, when translated into Norwegian. CSR can therefore be considered as domesticated into the existing understanding of *samfunnsansvar* in these earlier white papers on ownership. This shows how competing responsibilities in some respects align. However, in the following, we illustrate that the usages and understandings of responsibility have evolved differently in public and policy discourse. While *samfunnsansvar* maintains a sociocultural ideal across sectors in public discourse, *samfunnsansvar* gradually becomes corporatized in policy discourse. By mapping developments in policy documents, we continue to argue that *samfunnsansvar* is not the same as CSR.

Frictions: Domesticating CSR and Corporatizing Samfunnsansvar

In the annual reports on ownership (*eierberetninger*), from the first report in 2002 to 2020, we observe that the government, over time, increasingly adapts to an internationalized understanding of CSR. The reports from 2002 to 2006 mention that the state expects companies to take *samfunnsansvar*, claiming that CSR has gained increased attention both nationally and internationally, and that being listed in globally acknowledged ethical standards is a sign of quality, which can contribute to value creation. In fact, the reports encourage and sometimes explicitly expect state-owned companies to specifically follow international standards and guidelines as well as keep up with international trends in CSR practices. This suggests that companies are expected to relate to an international understanding of responsibility and document it.

We believe that the strengthened focus on and adaption to a globalized discourse on CSR is related to the internationalization of companies, both foreign companies' investments in Norway and to the country's increased foreign direct investments abroad, which in 2006 corresponded to almost half of Norway's gross national product

(Hveem 2009: 384), and finally to the state's goals with its ownership in commercialized companies, namely value creation (*verdiskaping*) in a financial sense. The participation in various working groups related to the development of both the Norwegian Corporate Governance Board and the revision of the OECD Principles of Corporate Governance in 2004 and finally the adoption of the latter in 2005 (Eierberetning 2004) also emphasize the shift toward a globalized discourse on CSR. Although the Norwegian versions of reports and white papers on ownership only mention corporate social responsibility a few times while frequently applying *samfunnsansvar*, it is evident that *samfunnsansvar* is used in a manner that becomes increasingly formalized. As we will illustrate in more detail later in this section, the policy documents make a rhetorical move toward a language and logic of business. This development suggests that *samfunnsansvar* travels into the financial sphere where it is corporatized and becomes a business opportunity. Promotion of financial value creation is a frame to which *samfunnsansvar* in public discourse does not pertain. The conceptualizations of *samfunnsansvar* in policy discourse have thus shifted away from a responsibility for the collective (without economic intentions or compensation) to responsibility to shareholders and (financial) value creation and profit. This conceptualization does not mean a direct responsibility toward the shareholders. It entails incorporating CSR as a mechanism that ensures acceptable conduct toward the environment and stakeholders (such as local population and employees) to avoid risk and ensure profit. Thus, the ideal of altruism inherent in perceptions of *samfunnsansvar* persists when *samfunnsansvar* becomes part of corporate technology and logic. Because *samfunnsansvar* now is considered to stimulate value creation in the same way as CSR, we propose that state expectations of companies' work with CSR and follow-ups have both become more extensive *and* specified.

From the mid-2000s, there is an exponential growth in mentions of *samfunnsansvar* compared to the steady but slow increase during the previous decades. Mentions of *bedriftenes-* and *næringslivets samfunnsansvar* and CSR increase only slightly from the mid 2000s. Figure 2.2 indicates the prevalence of the terms in newspaper articles from 2000 and shows how use of *samfunnsansvar* exceeds that of *bedriftenes-* and *næringslivets samfunnsansvar* as well as CSR. With this graph, we are interested in the prevalence of *samfunnsansvar* in relation to the other terms and not the number of articles per se.

Altogether, 663 articles mention *samfunnsansvar* in 2005, a number that increases by approximately 40 percent the following year. In

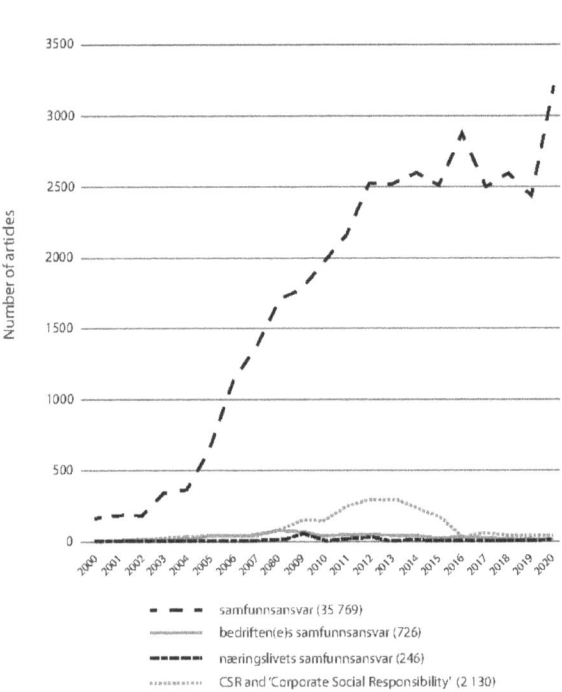

Figure 2.2. Trends in media use of the concepts CSR and *samfunnsansvar*. The graph shows how the terms move in relation to each other in the print editions of Norwegian newspapers from January 2000 to December 2020. Each graph shows all abbreviations of each term and total number of articles in this time period. The graph is constructed from data available in Atekst, 21 January 2021 © Oda Eiken Maraire and Nina Bergheim Dahl.

a random sample comparing the news articles from October 2005 and October 2006, most articles focused on companies' operations in Norway. A detailed review of these samples shows that roughly half of the mentions relate to corporations' *samfunnsansvar* (56.9 percent and 48.7 percent, respectively). In both time periods, only an approximate 12 percent of the articles speak of a collective societal or individual effort to enact *samfunnsansvar*. That *samfunnsansvar* is widely used as a shorthand for *næringslivets-* or *bedriftenes samfunnsansvar* and translation of CSR is further evidenced by the fact that about half of all mentions of *samfunnsansvar* in the Atekst database is categorized as relating to "economy and business" (other categories being politics, work life, etc.).[7]

Despite the ideal that all actors of society have an equal individual responsibility, the framing in newspaper articles indicates that to a large degree there is an expectation that the state should be a leading figure in practicing *samfunnsansvar*. As an example, in a piece responding to the publication of a document that expresses the government's politics on ownership issues ("*Regjeringens Eierpolitikk*"), journalist and political commentator Marie Simonsen stated that "one could assume that there would be an essential difference between a private and a state owner of a company, that the latter would take its *samfunnsanvar* more seriously and would be willing to pay the price" (Simonsen 2007, translated by authors). Simonsen criticized both the government and Minister of Trade and Industry Dag Terje Andersen for prioritizing financial revenues at the expense of other ambitions, such as the environment and research and development. She also claimed that the state seemed to be less concerned about environmental issues in companies operating abroad compared to domestic operations and, therefore, did not enact *samfunnsansvar* as expected. This expectation must be considered in relation to the government's explicit ambition that companies owned fully or partially by the Norwegian state should "be leading on work with ethics and *samfunnsansvar*" (Meld. St. 13 [2006–7]: 55, translated by authors). And further, that the state's legitimacy might be weakened in its other roles as a legislator or in foreign policy affairs if it does not, in its ownership role, meet high standards related to *samfunnsansvar* (Meld. St. 13 [2006–7]: 55). This supports Ihlen and Hoivik's (2015) argument that, in Norway, such policies were first impelled by the government and not the corporate sector. The aspirations toward high standards in acting responsibly is arguably also linked to the image of Norway as a humanitarian superpower (see introduction).

In the 2007 ownership report, Minister of Trade and Industry Dag Terje Andersen states that one of his main priorities is to "follow up the companies' efforts to assume their *samfunnsansvar*" (Eierberetning 2007: 5, translated by authors) and that companies must operate with high ethical standards. Andersen further contends that the ministry has met with most of its companies to talk about how they handle their responsibility. The report published in 2008 marks a significant increase, with mentions of *samfunnsansvar* being doubled from twenty-four in the 2007 report to forty-eight. The significant increase may be due to the global financial crisis, which enhanced attention to corporate governance (Meld. St. 13 [2010–11]a), thus also corporate responsibility, resulting in the publishing of the first white paper on *næringslivets samfunnsansvar* (Meld. St. 10

[2008–9]) by the Ministry of Foreign Affairs (thus indicating a focus on international operations).

In the first and, so far, only white paper on the theme, the government's understanding of *næringslivets samfunnsansvar*, which they translate into CSR in the English version, includes that companies integrate "*social and environmental concerns into their day-to-day operations, as well as in their dealings with stakeholders. CSR means what companies do on a voluntary basis beyond complying with existing legislation and rules in the country in which they are operating*" (Meld. St. 10 [2008–9]: 7, italics in original). However, in the Norwegian version of the white paper, *næringslivets samfunnsansvar*, *bedriftenes samfunnsansvar*, and *samfunnsansvar* are used interchangeably throughout. The interchangeable use of the terms is also apparent in newspapers. Furthermore, the frequency of use of the different terms also suggests that *samfunnsansvar* is the preferred term. Between 1945 and 2020,[8] *samfunnsansvar* is mentioned in 36,818 news articles compared to *bedriftenes samfunnsansvar* and *næringslivets samfunnsansvar*, which are referred to in 730 and 250 news articles respectively. In the same period, 927 articles mention corporate social responsibility, and 1,205 articles contain the abbreviation CSR starting in 2001.

We believe that the frequent use of *samfunnsansvar* and shifts in terms are due not only to the lack of abbreviations in Norwegian for *næringslivets-* or *bedriftenes samfunnsansvar* but also to the cultural resonance inherent in *samfunnsansvar*. This taken-for-grantedness of the concept is evident in the October samples from 2005 and 2006, where *samfunnsansvar* is described as something that corporations must simply "take," "show," or "enact" without explicitly defining what that responsibility entails. In existing literature, an inherent correlation between *samfunnsansvar* and business is often taken for granted (e.g., Gjølberg 2010; Nordhaug and Olsen 2010). In one instance, *samfunnsansvar* is translated to "*responsibility of business in/towards society*" (Ditlev-Simonsen, Hoivik, and Ihlen 2015: 181, italics in original), thus muting the difference between the concepts. Again, this suggests that the connotations engrained in *samfunnsansvar* make it effective, consciously or unconsciously, in conveying arguments across a variety of frames. We therefore contend that the numbers derived from the archive illustrate that CSR in Norwegian discourses is informed by established, yet vague, understandings of *samfunnsansvar* and is hence domesticated, as exemplified earlier.

The various terms associated with responsibility connote different meanings. This is also apparent in the English version of the same white paper, in which social responsibility and corporate social responsibility are used interchangeably. We suggest that this points to the inherent tension between *samfunnsansvar* and CSR in the Norwegian context. A tension in understandings and practices of companies' responsibilities also appears: "Although a number of companies and organizations have made considerable progress in integrating social responsibility into their business practice, there is still a need for increased awareness, greater knowledge and broader involvement" (Meld. St. 10 [2008–9]: 7). There is a prevailing understanding of CSR as philanthropy, the paper contends, despite a growing tendency to consider CSR as core to the company's own operations and supply chain (Meld. St. 10 [2008–9]: 8). Hence, in the following white paper on ownership (English version) the government aimed to "clarify and strengthen the expectations relating to corporate social responsibility" (Meld. St. 13 [2010–11]b: 6) beyond the nine core considerations that the previous white paper on ownership had explored.[9] Clarification meant listing expectations, including an expectation that companies with international operations and of certain size would adhere to the UN Global Compact and Global Reporting Initiative (Meld. St. 13 [2010–11]b: 61). These examples suggest that understandings and practices of responsibility move away from domestically established understandings to become more internationally oriented and standardized.

By 2009, all state-owned companies had developed ethical guidelines (Eierberetning 2009). The annual report also provides a list of what the Ministry of Trade and Industry did in order to follow up on the government's expectations to companies' work with *samfunnsansvar*. These expectations were later clarified and specified (Meld. St. 13 [2010–11]a), encouraging that work on *samfunnsansvar* become increasingly professionalized and corporatized. This is also apparent in the 2012 report, which presents a differentiation between general and specific state expectations to work on *samfunnsansvar* in addition to an overview of questions asked about each company's work on *samfunnsansvar* together with the answers each provided. This approach was further strengthened the following year, with state expectation that all companies comply regarding *samfunnsansvar*, and that potential deviations must be explained (the comply or explain principle) (Eierberetning 2013). In 2013, accounting law also demanded that large corporations report on *samfunnsansvar* to increase transparency (Meld. St. 27 [2013–14]). The materiality principle (*vesentlighetsprinsippet*) is added in the 2014 report, which means that companies "work with and report matters that are critical to the impact of companies on people, society, and the climate and environment" (Eierberetning 2014: 32). This principle stems from the Global Reporting Initiative (see introduction) and thus indicates, again, that Norwegian policy papers speak to an international discourse of CSR.

In the revised version of the ten principles on good corporate governance in 2014, companies are no longer expected to be aware of or recognize their *samfunnsansvar*. Rather, they "shall work systematically [*målrettet*] to safeguard their *samfunnsansvar*" (Meld. St. 27 [2013–14]: 67, translated by authors). This shift, we argue, reflects that successive governments increasingly moved away from the taken-for-granted cultural understandings of *samfunnsansvar* and toward adaptation of a global discourse of CSR, wherein work on *samfunnsansvar* has become professionalized[10] or corporatized. At the same time, the shared imagined idea of collective responsibility prevails in public discourse.

Beyond the state, public institutions, and private companies, the news articles indicate that all members of society are still expected to practice *samfunnsansvar*. The trade union LO has *samfunnsansvar* to not only secure jobs but also to consider climate and environment issues (e.g., Kallset 2016). Hegstad, Kvarme, and Sneltvedt (2013) claim that balancing tradition and renewal is a central question when defining the Church of Norway's *samfunnsansvar*. As examples, researchers practice *samfunnsansvar* through sharing knowledge in schools (e.g., Johnsen 2015); soccer clubs take *samfunnsansvar* through integration of refugees in sports (e.g., Hatlemark 2016). Individual citizens are also expected to take *samfunnsansvar*. Author and activist Sumaya Jirde Ali stated in an interview that "I am just a woman who takes her *samfunnsansvar* seriously" (Klassekampen 2017, translated by authors), referring to her participation in public debates about immigration and minority women's issues as well as the harassment that comes with such participation. Thus, over time, *samfunnsansvar* continues to have interpretive flexibility (Star and Griesemer 1989) since everyone—ministry, public institution, local soccer team, or an individual member of society—expect themselves and others to engage without reaching a consensus as to what *samfunnsansvar* means in practical terms. Businesses can, but do not necessarily have to, be included in these expectations. *Samfunnsansvar* as a duty (regardless of people fulfilling these expectations or not) is therefore still a normative part of the Norwegian social structure and imagined collective ideal. What emerges then is a tension between policy and commercial discourse versus public discourse.

While CSR and *samfunnsansvar* as competing responsibilities can in some contexts align, this tension shows how claims of responsibilities in other contexts can be conflicting (Trnka and Trundle 2017) yet, simultaneously, provide opportunities for strategic and rhetorical maneuvering.

The tension between CSR and *samfunnsansvar* is seemingly withering away as the term *bærekraft* (sustainability) is increasingly substituting CSR in policies nationally and internationally. The rhetorical shift in policy documents illustrates that Norwegian authorities have made further adaptions to an international discourse of responsibility. From the 2015 ownership report onward, there is an increased focus on *bærekraft*, and the reports state that sustainability should be integrated into business goals, strategies, and positioning alongside *samfunnsansvar*. This focus is likely related to the launch of the UN Sustainable Development Goals (SDGs), which were adopted by world leaders the same year. The SDGs were first mentioned explicitly in the 2017 report: "The best businesses integrate the United Nations' sustainable development goals in their external reporting" (Eierberetning 2017: 27). Although *samfunnsansvar* has been used alongside *bærekraft*[11] to varying degrees in ownership reports, the number of mentions of *bærekraft* is more pronounced from the 2017 report onward. *Bærekraft* first outnumbers *samfunnsansvar* in the 2019 report, a trend that continues into the following report. Compared to 2019 when *samfunnsansvar* is mentioned 70 times, the 2020 report demonstrates a substantial drop with only 10 mentions of *samfunnsansvar*. Meanwhile, *bærekraft* is mentioned 201 times in the same report.

Similar developments can be found in white papers on ownership. The white papers published in 2001, 2006, 2010, and 2013 mentioned *samfunnsansvar* 8, 40, 237, and 64 times, respectively. However, the most recently published white paper (Meld. St. 8 [2019–20]) mentions the term only once. Conversely, *bærekraft* is mentioned 179 times, the highest number in such white papers yet. This does not necessarily mean that the authorities are less preoccupied with businesses' responsibility. On the contrary, the government expects companies to conduct "responsible business" (*ansvarlig virksomhet*), which is in line with "the increasing pervasiveness of responsibility in contemporary discourse" (Trnka and Trundle 2017: 1). The move away from the societal (*samfunns-*) aspect, which was prevalent in previous white papers and is core in the Norwegian public understanding of responsibility, suggests a policy rupture with the established meanings of *samfunnsansvar*, aligning more with international relations and standards. Another aspect in the same white paper (Meld. St. 8 [2019–20]) is the prevalence of "sustainable value creation" compared to the previous white paper on ownership, which emphasized that practicing *samfunnsansvar* leads to long-term value creation. The move to sustainability illustrates a further push away from a local understanding of responsibility to an international arena, which focuses exclusively on responsible business.

Conclusion

This chapter points to challenges of translation and the importance of contextualizing and localizing international trends. We demonstrated how the originally Anglo-American concept traveled differently in public and policy discourse in Norway, thus supporting our argument that *samfunnsansvar* is not CSR. When CSR was first introduced in Norwegian newspapers and in companies, it was domesticated into *samfunnsansvar*. Although both CSR and *samfunnsansvar* are expected to be enacted on a voluntary basis, CSR is intended to hold companies accountable for their actions and contribute to value creation, while *samfunnsansvar* is an ethical compass that is ideally practiced with equal participation for the common good of society without expectation of financial gain. It is a boundary object (Star and Griesemer 1989) with interpretive flexibility that provides moral guidance to all actors regardless of their social and economic standing, where the corporate sector is just one among many actors in an interdependent sociopolitical landscape that characterizes Norwegian society. Yet, there is a pronounced expectation that the state should be a leading example in taking *samfunnsansvar*, without reaching a consensus of what such responsibility entails.

Despite that CSR traveled into public discourse, the cultural resonance engrained in *samfunnsansvar* prevails, which indicates that it is still a valued ideal in Norwegian society. In policy discourse, however, there was a shift from an undisputed understanding of responsibility in line with national "values and attitudes" (Meld. St. 61 [1996–97]) toward a business-oriented understanding in which *samfunnsansvar* also means financial value creation for stakeholders. Furthermore, *samfunnsansvar* has recently been adapted to an international rhetoric of sustainability and incorporation of the SDGs. The strengthened professionalization and report-driven approach to responsibilities also entails a move to a more standardized language that is arguably context independent. These shifts show the continuous influence of international trends and Norway's positioning as an international actor, as well as how different and competing understandings of responsibility can coexist.

By expecting companies to operate according to soft standardized frameworks instead of a national framework that is hard and highly regulated, the government allows Norwegian corporations to operate within an ambiguous and dynamic space where *samfunnsansvar* and CSR exist simultaneously. Because *samfunnsansvar* is arguably more elusive in the sense that it is not assessed according to standardized indicators, corporations are then likely to flexibly and strategically maneuver responsibility terms to fit specific economic, social, and political agendas without necessarily reaching consensus of what such responsibility entails. In chapter 4, Ståle Knudsen illustrates this maneuvering with Norsk Hydro's self-presentation and the flexible handling of its responsibility in dealings with the Alunorte scandal in Brazil. If collaboration is taken to be a particular Norwegian value, then Siri Lange's case, as seen in chapter 8, may be a testimony of how "traces of *samfunnsansvar*" inform the messy and diversified work with CSR, which is otherwise communicated as standardized and business oriented. The interpretive flexibility may further be applied rhetorically to support the prevalent idea that Norwegian corporations are particularly good at work with CSR. This may be done by, for instance, promoting Norsk Hydro as a model to be followed when Norwegian companies practice CSR abroad, as seen in chapter 4. But this strategic maneuvering may also provoke reactions and raise questions from the Norwegian public should corporations be found to not comply with the Norwegian values embedded in *samfunnsansvar*, especially if the company in question is fully or partly state owned. In sum, allowing companies to play at the margins of hard and soft frameworks as well as Norwegian and international understandings of responsibility may complicate the ability of governmental bodies— and the public at home—to hold Norwegian corporations operating abroad accountable. The arms-length governance of corporations can further serve as a free pass for state actors, which makes it challenging for the public to hold the state accountable for its investments both abroad and at home. While *samfunnsansvar* may be claimed to be in the genes (Ihlen 2011) or DNA of Norwegian corporations, there is no guarantee that such Norwegian values will make them more responsible than any other transnational corporation.

Acknowledgments

Research for this chapter has been conducted within the frames of the project Energethics (2015–19), funded by a FRIPRO grant from the Research Council of Norway (grant no. 240617). We are grateful to Ståle Knudsen for his extensive comments and valuable feedback during the development of this chapter.

Oda Eiken Maraire was a research assistant for the Energethics project. She is currently a PhD candidate in the Department of Social Anthropology, University of Bergen, Norway, and part of the research project, "Urban Enclaving Futures." With a focus on the real estate industry, her doctoral project explores imaginaries of future urban living and homemaking practices in affluent areas of Johannesburg, South Africa.

Isabelle Hugøy was a research assistant for the Energethics project, and since 2020 she has been a doctoral fellow in the Department of Social Anthropology, University of Bergen, Norway. Her doctoral project deals with human-soil relations and explores how soil is actualized across different knowledge registers in the context of efforts to decarbonize agricultural sectors in Norway and Costa Rica.

Notes

Both authors have contributed equally.

1. The material is collected from the electronic database Atekst owned by Retriever AS Norway—the most comprehensive database for local and national newspapers in Norway from 1945 onward. We have focused on printed publications in the timeframe 1 January 1945–31 December 2020.
2. We focus on white papers on ownership (*eierskapsmeldinger*) and CSR as well as annual ownership reports (*eierberetninger*). We focus particularly on the Norwegian versions to show how the wording shifts over time. The white papers on ownership outline the overall ownership policy. Annual ownership reports summarize results and value creation in companies in which the state has full or partial ownership.
3. Limitations of Atekst include: (1) several versions of the same article can be accessed with no information about which articles are actually published (Srebrowska 2005); (2) contract-based agreements limit access—in 2017, *Dagens Næringsliv*, Norway's largest business-oriented newspaper, did not renew their contract, thus *DN* articles are not available (Åm 2017); (3) the coverage of, in this case, *samfunnsansvar*, is influenced by power relations and the social, cultural, and economic structures in which journalists operate. As an example, most news published about the Norwegian oil industry up until 2000 originated from a group of journalists who had privileged

access to the industry and therefore did not criticize it per se (Sæther 2017). Sæther (2017) claims that actors with oil interests have greater access to the media and receive better coverage compared to, for example, environmental organizations. The close ties between politicians, bureaucrats, and the oil industry as well as the internationalization of companies has increased the distance between journalists and companies and can make it arduous for journalists to ask critical questions (Baumberger and Slaatta 2011: 55–56).

4. One influence of such shifts could be the report and associated policy agenda *Our Common Future* (also known as the "Brundtland Report"), published in 1987, which promoted the need for sustainable development (Ditlev-Simonsen, Hoivik, and Ihlen 2015: 177).
5. A revision of the OECD Principles of Corporate Governance was published in 2004 to include guidelines for corporate governance of state-owned enterprises. The work was partially financed by Norway (Meld. St. 22 [2001–2]).
6. In total, 2,175 articles contain both *samfunnsansvar* and *bevisst* from 1945 to 2020.
7. Retrieved 7 October 2021 from https://app.retriever-info.com/services/archive?searchString=samfunnsansvar.
8. The numbers include all conjugations of *samfunnsansvar*, *næringslivets samfunnsansvar*, and *bedriftenes samfunnsansvar* in news articles in printed publications between 1 January 1945 and 31 December 2020.
9. That is, restructuring, research, development and competency building, the environment, health, safety and the working environment, ethics, combating corruption, gender equality, integration and career opportunities for other groups, and civil protection (Meld. St. 13 [2006–7]: 56–63).
10. Throughout the years, white papers on ownership have argued for professionalizing state ownership and ownership policy. The establishment of the Ownership Department within the Ministry of Industry and Trade in 2002, together with the establishment of ten principles on good corporate governance and the publishing of different types of reports related to state ownership (thus becoming transparent), are examples of steps toward professionalizing state ownership.
11. This includes all conjugations of *bærekraft*.

References

Abel, Morten Erik. 1990. "Etikkdebatt nødvendig" [An ethics debate is necessary]. *Aftenposten*, 23 February, 15. Retrieved 25 January 2021 from Atekst database.

Aftenposten. 1984. "La oss diskutere saken" [Let us discuss the matter]. *Aftenposten*, 12 June, 2. Retrieved 17 December 2020 from Atekst database.

Andersen, Harald. 1985. "Gråtekoner i skolen" [Mourners in school]. *Aftenposten*, 2 December, 4. Retrieved 17 December 2020 from Atekst database.

Auld, Graeme, Steven Bernstein, and Benjamin Cashore. 2008. "The New Corporate Social Responsibility." *Annual Review of Environment and Resources* 33: 413–35.

Baumberger, B. E. and T. Slaatta. 2011. "Norsk oljejournalistikk—Statoils utenlandsvirksomhet som transnasjonalt nyhetsbeite" [Norwegian oil journalism—Statoil's operations abroad as a transnational news field]. *Norsk medietidsskrift* 18(1): 41–59.

Bowen, Howard R, and F. Ernest Johnson. 2013. *Social Responsibility of the Businessman.* Iowa City: University of Iowa Press.

Dahlsrud, Alexander. 2006. "How Corporate Social Responsibility Is Defined: An Analysis of 37 Definitions." *Corporate Social Responsibility and Environmental Management* 15: 1–13.

Ditlev-Simonsen, Caroline D., Heidi von Weltzien Hoivik, and Øyvind Ihlen. 2015. "The Historical Development of Corporate Social Responsibility in Norway." In *Corporate Social Responsibility in Europe: CSR, Sustainability, Ethics & Governance*, edited by S. Idowu, R. Schmidpeter, and Matthias Fifka, 177–96. Cham: Springer.

Dolan, Catherine, and Dinah Rajak. 2016. *The Anthropology of Corporate Social Responsibility*. New York: Berghahn Books.

Egeland, Erik. 1989. "Bedriftenes ansvar blir større" [Corporate responsibility grows]. *Aftenposten*, 23 November, 13. Retrieved 11 February 2021 from Atekst database.

Eierberetning. 2003. *Ownership Report from Ministry of Trade and Industry*. Government of Norway.

———. 2004. *Ownership Report from Ministry of Trade and Industry*. Government of Norway.

———. 2007. *Ownership Report from Ministry of Trade and Industry*. Government of Norway.

———. 2009. *Ownership Report from Ministry of Trade and Industry*. Government of Norway.

———. 2013. *Ownership Report from Ministry of Trade, Industry, and Fisheries*. Government of Norway.

———. 2014. *Ownership Report from Ministry of Trade, Industry, and Fisheries*. Government of Norway.

———. 2017. *Ownership Report from Ministry of Trade, Industry, and Fisheries*. Government of Norway.

Engelstad, Ingeri, Marianne Heske, Cecilie Mosli, Silje Larsen Borgan, and Kristine Jørgensen. 2017. "*Etterlyser grundigere kritikk*" [Calls for more thorough reviews]. *Klassekampen*, 25 November, 63. Retrieved 8 February 2021 from Atekst database.

Financial Stability, Financial Services, and Capital Markets Union. 2020. "Commission Action Plan on Financing Sustainable Growth." European Union. Retrieved 25 February 2021 from https://ec.europa.eu/info/publications/sustainable-finance-renewed-strategy_en.

Folkvord, Martin, and Martin Lægland. 2021. "Lege etter vaksinering av stortingspolitikere: —Ordentlig sint" [Doctor after vaccination of politicians at the Storting: Really angry]. *Verdens Gang*, 23 May. Retrieved 22 June 2021 from Atekst database.

Føllesdal, Andreas. 1997. "Hva skal vi med etikk-kurs?" [Why do we need ethics classes?]. 16 March, 9. Retrieved 1 February 2021 from Atekst database.

Gjølberg, Maria. 2010. "Varieties of Corporate Social Responsibility (CSR): CSR Meets the 'Nordic Model.'" *Regulation & Governance* 4: 203–29.

Habisch, André, Jan Jonker, Martina Wegner, and René Schmidpeter. 2005. *Corporate Social Responsibility across Europe*. Springer Berlin.

Haslund, Ebba. 1984. "Kvinner i menns samfunn" [Women in a men's world]. *Aftenposten*, 4 September, 6. Retrieved 11 February 2021 from Atekst database.

Hatlemark, Olav. 2016. "Tek samfunnsansvar" [Take societal responsibility]. *Firdaposten*, 19 June, 7. Retrieved 11 February 2021 from Atekst database.

Hegstad, Harald, Ole Chr. Kvarme, and Torunn Sneltvedt. 2013. "Kirken tar utfordringen" [The church takes the challenge]. *Aftenposten*, 28 December, 5. Retrieved 8 February 2021 from Atekst database.

Hellebust, Henning A. 1998. "Få bedrifter med miljømål" [Few companies with environmental goals]. *Aftenposten*, 27 February, 25. Retrieved 25 January 2021 from Atekst database.

Holtet, Einar Kr. 1986. "Sosial bevissthet rød tråd i mønsterplanen" [Social awareness as recurrent theme in national curriculum]. *Aftenposten*, 3 January, 3. Retrieved 17 December 2020 from Atekst database.

Hveem, Helge. 2009. "Norske utenlandsinvesteringer og norsk (utenriks) politikk: Dårlig forbindelse?" [Norwegian foreign direct investments and Norwegian (foreign) policy: poor connection?]. *Internasjonal Politikk* [International politics] 67(3): 381–412.

Hålien, Einar. 1998. "*Munnkurv og styrt informasjon*" [Muzzle and controlled information]. *Bergens Tidende*, 5 May, 26. Retrieved 25 January 2021 from Atekst database.

Ihlen, Øyvind. 2007. *Petroleumsparadiset: Norsk oljeindustris strategiske kommunikasjon og omdømmebygging* [Petroleum Paradise: Norwegian oil industry's strategic communication and reputation management]. Oslo: Unipub.
———. 2011. *Samfunnsansvar på norsk: Tradisjon og kommunikasjon* [CSR in Norwegian: Tradition and communication]. Bergen: Fagbokforlaget.
Ihlen, Øyvind, and Heidi von Weltzien Hoivik. 2015. "Ye Olde CSR: The Historic Roots of Corporate Social Responsibility in Norway." *Journal of Business Ethics* 127: 109–20.
Jaklin, Asbjørn. 1993. "Søkelys Fredag" [Limelight Friday]. *Nordlys*, 14 May, 2. Retrieved 1 February 2021 from Atekst database.
Johnsen, Morten Gisle. 2015. "Forskerne inn i skolen" [Researchers in the schools]. *Budstikka*, 2 September, 4. Retrieved 8 February 2021 from Atekst database.
Kallset, Kjell-Erik N. 2016. "LO-striden" [The LO feud]. *Klassekampen*, 2 November, 2. Retrieved 11 February 2021 from Atekst database.
Klassekampen. 2017. "Sumaya Jirde Ali," *Klassekampen*, 30 December, 32. Retrieved 8 February 2021 from Atekst database.
Knudsen, Ståle. 2015. "Corporate Social Responsibility in Local Context: International Capital, Charitable Giving and the Politics of Education in Turkey." *Southeast European and Black Sea Studies* 15(3): 369–90.
Knutzen, Thomas. 1999. "Menneskerettigheter i Orissa" [Human rights in Orissa]. *Aftenposten*, 16 July, 7. Retrieved 25 January 2021 from Atekst database.
Linden, Julie L. 2016. "Bekymret for feriedrikking" [Worried about vacation drinking]. *Drammens Tidende*, 20 July, 4–5. Retrieved 1 February 2021 from Atekst database.
Louche, Celine, Samuel O. Idowu, and Walter Leal Filho, eds. 2017. *Innovative CSR: From Risk Management to Value Creation*. New York: Routledge.
Luthen, Siri. 2009. "Bedrifters samfunnsansvar og statlig eierskap: Regjeringens implementering av bedrifters samfunnsansvar i statlig eide selskaper" [Corporate social responsibility and state ownership: The government's implementation of corporate social responsibility in state-owned companies]. Master's thesis, University of Oslo.
May, Steven K., George Cheney, and Juliet Roper. 2007. *The Debate over Corporate Social Responsibility*. Oxford: Oxford University Press.
Meld. St. 61. 1996–97. *Om eierskap i næringslivet* [About ownership in the business world]. White paper from Ministry of Trade and Industry, Government of Norway.
Meld. St. 22. 2001–2. *Et mindre og bedre statlig eierskap* [A smaller and better state ownership]. White paper from Ministry of Trade and Industry, Government of Norway.
Meld. St. 13. 2006–7. *Et aktivt og langsiktig eierskap* [An active and long-term state ownership]. White paper from Ministry of Trade and Industry, Government of Norway.
Meld. St. 10. 2008–9. *Næringslivets samfunnsansvar i en global økonomi* [Corporate social responsibility in a global economy]. White paper from Ministry of Foreign Affairs, Government of Norway.
Meld. St. 13. 2010–11a. *Aktivt eierskap—norsk statlig eierskap i en global økonomi* [Active ownership—Norwegian state ownership in a global economy]. White paper from Ministry of Trade and Industry, Government of Norway.
———. 2010–11b. Active ownership—Norwegian state ownership in a global economy. Report to the Storting (white paper) Summary. Ministry of Trade and Industry, Government of Norway.
Meld. St. 27. 2013–14. *Et mangfoldig og verdiskapende eierskap* [Diverse and value-creating ownership]. White paper from Ministry of Trade, Industry and Fisheries, Government of Norway.
Meld. St. 8. 2019–20. *Statens direkte eierskap i selskaper: Bærekraftig verdiskaping* [The state's direct ownership of companies: Sustainable value creation]. White paper from Ministry of Trade, Industry and Fisheries, Government of Norway.

Morsing, Mete, Atle Midttun, and Karl Palmås 2007. "Corporate Social Responsibility in Scandinavia: A Turn toward the Business Case." In *The Debate over Corporate Social Responsibility*, edited by Steven K. May, George Cheney, and Juliet Roper, 87–104. Oxford: Oxford University Press.

Moura-Leite, Rosamaria C., and Robert C. Padgett. 2011. "Historical Background of Corporate Social Responsibility." *Social Responsibility Journal* 7: 528–39.

Ness, Jan Gunnar, Erik Johnsrud, and Christian Lundin. 2002. "Forsikringsselskapenes oppgjørsetikk?" [Insurance companies' settlement ethics?]. *Aftenposten*, 7 December, 12. Retrieved 1 February 2021 from Atekst database.

Nordhaug, Odd, and Jørn Bue Olsen. 2010. *Etikk, ledelse og samfunnsansvar* [Ethics, leadership and societal responsibility]. Oslo: Forlag1.

Olsen, Jørn Bue. 2001. "Er SAS et ansvarlig flyselskap?" [Is SAS a responsible airline?]. *Aftenposten*, 8 August, 8. Retrieved 11 February 2021 from Atekst database.

Rabben, Bjarne. 1945. "Soldatane våre må få opplæring til det sivile livet" [Our soldiers must be trained for civilian life]. *Verdens Gang*, 8 November, 5. Retrieved 17 December 2020 from Atekst database.

Raumnes. 1983. "Opplysningskampanje for valget 1983: Flere kvinner inn i kommunestyrene" [Information campaign for the 1983 election: More women into municipal councils]. *Raumnes lokalblad*, 8 January, 2. Retrieved 17 December 2020 from Atekst database.

Reese, S. D. 2007. "The Framing Project: A Bridging Model for Media Research Revisited." *Journal of Communication* 57(1): 148–54.

Simonsen, Marie. 2007. "Snekker uten hammer" [Carpenter without a hammer]. *Dagbladet*, 14 June, 3. Retrieved 11 February 2021 from Atekst database.

Simon, Carsta, and Hilde Mobekk. 2019. "*Dugnad*: A Fact and a Narrative of Norwegian Prosocial Behavior." *Perspectives on Behavior Science* 42(4): 815–34.

Smith, Jessica 2021. *Extracting Accountability: Engineers and Corporate Social Responsibility*. Cambridge, MA: MIT Press.

Srebrowska, Urszula. 2005. "ATEKST kan lede på villspor" [ATEKST can lead to a wild goose chase]. *Norsk medietidsskrift* 12: 40–43.

Star, Susan Leigh, and J. R. Griesemer. 1989. "Institutional Ecology, 'Translations' and Boundary Objects: Amateurs and Professionals in Berkeley's Museum of Vertebrate Zoology, 1907–39." *Social Studies of Science* 19(3): 387–420.

Star, Susan Leigh 2010. "This Is Not a Boundary Object: Reflections on the Origin of a Concept." *Science, Technology, and Human Values* 35(5): 601–17. https://doi.org/10.1177/0162243910377624.

Sæther, Anne Karin. 2017. *De beste intensjoner: Oljelandet i klimakampen* [The best of intentions: The oil country in the climate struggle]. Oslo: Cappelen Damm AS.

Trnka, Susanna, and Catherine Trundle. 2017. "Competing Responsibilities: Reckoning Personal Responsibility, Care for the Other, and the Social Contract in Contemporary Life." In *Competing Responsibilities: The Ethics and Politics of Contemporary Life*, edited by Susanna Trnka and Catherine Trundle, 1–24. Durham, NC: Duke University Press.

Vike, Halvard. 2018. "The Protestant Ethic and the Spirit of Political Resistance: Notes on the Political Roots of Egalitarianism in Scandinavia." In *Egalitarianism in Scandinavia: Historical and Contemporary Perspectives*, edited by Mary Bente Bringslid Synnøve Bendixsen and Halvard Vike, 111–34. Cham: Palgrave Macmillan.

VG. 1948. "Kvinner krever sin andel i styre og stell" [Women demand their place in management]. *Verdens Gang*, 8 May, 14. Retrieved 17 December 2020 from Atekst database.

———. 1955. "Staten må utvide sin bankdrift" [The state must expand its bank operations]. *Verdens Gang*, 16 June, 2. Retrieved 17 December 2020 from Atekst database.

———. 1968. "Kjør, var svaret da sjåfør påpekte feil" [Drive, was the response when driver pointed out flaws]. *Verdens Gang*, 15 July, 6. Retrieved 17 December 2020 from Atekst database.

———.1969. "UH vil beordre leger og tannleger" [UH wants to command doctors and dentists]. *Verdens Gang*, 5 November, 3. Retrieved 17 December 2020 from Atekst database.

Welker, Marina. 2014. *Enacting the Corporation: An American Mining Firm in Post-authoritarian Indonesia*. Berkeley: University of California Press.

Østberg, Kristian. 1925. *Dugnad*. Oslo: Grøndahls & Søns Boktrykkeri. Retrieved 8 February 2021 from https://www.nb.no/items/URN:NBN:no-nb_digibok_2017032748101percent20?page=1

Åm, Ingrid Grønli. 2017. "*DN* går ut av mediearkiv" [*DN* departs media archive]. *Klassekampen*, 2 September, 53. Retrieved 11 February 2021 from Atekst database.

— Chapter 3 —

DYNAMICS OF LOCALIZED SOCIAL RESPONSIBILITY
A Case from Agder, Norway
Eldar Bråten

This anthology is concerned with the mutual imbrications of corporate social responsibility, capitalist dynamics, and state regimes. One might as well add a fourth dimension: the cultural representations by which this nexus is communicated and, possibly, forged—not least the common conviction that, in the Nordic context, corporate social responsibility is fashioned through the embrace of a peculiarly "Nordic model" based in values of egalitarianism and compromise. Rather than accentuating cultural values per se, the contributors draw attention to the variegated and complex institutional trajectories in which these values are embedded (see introduction). In other words, immediately, we enter into basic questions about morphogenesis (Archer 1995) (i.e., the dynamics of social formation): How should we understand the emergence of firms' social responsibility as practice and concept? Analytically, what kind of phenomenon is actually corporate social responsibility, Nordic or otherwise, when viewed in relation to the sociomaterial context out of which it arises? How best to frame this phenomenon theoretically: as essentially a question of economic tactics, political accommodations, cultural valuations, or institutional spinoffs?

In this chapter, I attempt to throw light on these central issues by way of a partly contrastive case, as it were. Like the other contributions, my ethnographic example concerns Norwegian energy production—a hydroelectric power plant—but not in an international context; the plant is located in Norway and supplies industries in its immediate vicinity (see Dale, chapter 9, for another Norwegian case).[1] Secondly, the company's social responsibility has been directed at the most local of sites—the residents living in the vicinity of the power plant and their specific needs. The case thus exemplifies aspects of community responsibility, a central dimension of the celebrated "Hydro model" discussed in chapter 4, while it also, empirically, details historical precursors to Norsk Hydro and Sam Eyde's industrial empire.

Thirdly, I focus on the company/community's historical formation—from approximately the 1920s to the late 1960s—rather than the contemporary situation. This I do to accentuate a situation where corporate social responsibility was not yet thematized as Corporate Social Responsibility—I am interested in responsible praxis prior to its branding, so to speak (see Matten and Moon 2008). During this phase, responsibility was an integral part of the fabric of a particular Norwegian political economy (see also chapter 4) rather than an explicit cultural ideal (Norwegian egalitarianism, etc.) to be exported. This also means that I am concerned with developments prior to the neoliberal shift in capitalism with which the concept of CSR is so intertwined (Rajak 2011: 9, 16–17, 238–39; Welker 2014: 12–18; Djelic and Etchanchu 2017). Drawing on Polanyi and MacIver (1944) and Granovetter (1985), I prefer the term "embedded" to denote unthematized imbrications of economic activity and ethical import (see Bråten 2013: 1–6), and I take the distinction between embedded and disembedded forms to be important for our analyses of corporate social responsibility more generally. In the following, I mark this distinction stylistically by using quotation marks when referring to CSR *discourses*, as opposed to implicit responsible practices.

Fourthly, this is a publicly traded corporation where shares are overwhelmingly controlled by private capital (see also Bendixsen, chapter 11). The firm—Arendals Fossekompani (AFK; lit. Arendal's Waterfall Company)—was established prior to the law about public reversion (*hjemfallsretten*; see Maraire and Hugøy, chapter 2) and still enjoys full legal rights over its energy resources. The case thus illuminates nonstate forms of CSR in the Norwegian energy sector. Certainly, the company is embedded in the wider societal context of Norway and bound by official laws and regulations. If not directly affected by *hjemfallsretten*, it has, nevertheless, operated in a public environment infused by ideals of political control over natural resources. Moreover, it emerged from the state/capital dynamic that forged large-scale, and rather high-risk, industrial ventures at the beginning of the twentieth century. However, I argue that at local levels the company has largely run its own course throughout the period discussed here, in relative insulation from state interference. Arguably, the community that developed around the power plant can be understood as a company affair.

My ambition is to explore what CSR entailed in this situation in which a private venture had to engage not only employees but also their families and the aspirations and activities of the community that, over time, took shape around the power plant. Moreover, as a clear-cut example of socially embedded responsibility, the case allows a somewhat different take on the more general questions raised in this anthology, concerning complexity and driving forces in CSR. Since my example evinces pre-thematized forms of social engagement, I cannot take recourse in the figure of "CSR": the empirical context does not provide me with a delineated object of study. Rather, I must tease out what can be considered as socially responsible about AFK practices from the ground in which its activities were enfolded. The case at hand, then, suggests a distinction between CSR as thematic object and as analytical concept.[2] While this distinction evokes Matten and Moon's (2008) analysis of "explicit" versus "implicit" forms of CSR in terms of their institutional embedding (in liberal market versus state economies, respectively), my argument here is instead epistemological: how, analytically, we can conceive of and identify CSR in *any* context of investigation.

In the following, I first account for the company's history and its practices of social responsibility, then interpret the local history in terms of Reidar Grønhaug's theory of social fields—a perspective that I believe enhances our grasp of CSR dynamics—before returning to some analytical implications of the distinction I make between CSR as figure and as ground.

Company History

Arendals Fossekompani (AFK) was established toward the end of the nineteenth century when, gradually, perceptive industrialists recognized hydroelectric power as a new and potentially profitable energy resource.[3] The firm arose in a rather peculiar regional context, that of Agder in the very south of Norway. Arendal was the leading maritime center and the wealthiest city in Norway until the Arendal bust of 1886, when the local economy virtually collapsed.[4] In the struggle to reestablish viable post-shipping businesses, three local figures took center stage: engineer-cum-capitalist Sam Eyde, the legendary founder of Elkem and Norsk Hydro (see Knudsen, chapter 4); Ragnvald Blakstad, another adventurous engineer and industrialist (Norman and Aanby 1996); and the shipowner, engineer, and politician, Gunnar Knudsen, later to become prime minister of Norway.[5]

However, when Arendals Fossekompani was established in 1896, investors were out to accumulate waterfall rights for profitable resale. It was only when this cash-generating ambition proved futile that hydroelectric energy became coupled to industrial ventures.[6] Knudsen clearly recognized the potentials of the new energy source and founded the country's first power plant for public supply of electricity in Skien, Telemark, in 1885, while Blakstad, who was among the founders of Arendals Fossekompani, struggled to shift the company's focus from trade to industrial production. Finally, when Sam Eyde entered the stage and backed up efforts, the reorientation succeeded.

At first, local resources were drawn into Eyde and Kristian Birkeland's ambitious plans for a Norwegian nitrogen industry (see Knudsen, chapter 4). In 1904, some of their first experiments with nitrogen oxide extraction took place at Evenstad, a minor fall in the Arendal riverways purchased by Blakstad's private company. However, when Norsk Hydro arose out of Elektrokemisk, now Elkem (Det Norske Aktieselskab for Elektrokemisk Industri) in 1905, this venture shifted elsewhere, while Elkem was refashioned to explore other potentials in hydroelectric power (Sogner 2014: 11–13). Elkem already owned parts of Arendals Fossekompani, and in 1907 they purchased enough shares to take control (Dannevig 1960: 20–22). Now, the stage was set for rapid development of Bøylefoss, the largest waterfall in the river as well as some upstream falls.

AFK's original ambitions were closely attuned to local conditions: Eyde sought to substitute tree coal with hydroelectric power to reinvigorate the considerable iron smelting industry in the region.[7] Actually, the industrialists started to develop waterfalls and production sites even before the technology was in place, while another of Eyde and Blakstad's industrial sites—Tyssedal in Hardanger, Western Norway—ran experiments (Dannevig 1960: 23–25, 29). As it turned out, the technology was not sufficiently effective to make iron production profitable given the prevailing market conditions, but Blakstad and Eyde soon found other niches in the smelting industries. The plants in Staksnes—soon to be renamed Eydehavn (lit. Eyde's harbor) to honor its local son-cum-founder—became a major center for production of silicon carbide and aluminum.

Structurally, the stage was now—around 1913—set, both companywise and in terms of infrastructure requirements. As I will try to show, this stabilization also precipitated core premises of community formation around the power plant. In Eydehavn on the coast, Arendal Smelteverk was in charge of carbide production, Det Norske Nitridaktieselskap (called Nitriden) ran aluminum smelting, while approximately sixteen kilometers inland Arendals Fossekompani committed to supply steady electricity to the plants' furnaces. The company chose not to locate its headquarters at Bøylefoss, however, but in the city of Arendal. Sam Eyde had considerable interests in all companies and served on the board of Arendals Fossekompani, while Gunnar Knudsen (prime minister of Norway from 1908 to 1910 and from 1913 to 1920), was head of its supervisory board, a position he held from 1911 until his death in 1928.

The prime minister's personal interest in developments—to the extent of serving as head supervisor in a local company such as Arendals Fossekompani—is evidence of the complex intertwining of state, politics, and private capital during this stage of Norwegian industrialization. It falls outside the scope of the chapter to analyze these macro developments, but we note that, while bolstering AFK with his personal name and presence, Knudsen was also a leading architect behind the concession laws of 1909 that *constrained* private speculation in the energy sector.[8] On the other hand, simultaneously, the state greatly facilitated corporate industrial development through the expansion of general infrastructure—roads, railroads, postal and telegram services, telephone lines, and the like.

We should also note that the state bank (Norges Bank) provided financial inputs to the formation of local industries, for example, through a loan of 1 million Norwegian kroner to AFK in the company's establishment phase (approximately a quarter of the company's value at the time) (Dannevig 1960: 32–33). Nevertheless, in general, capital stemmed from private—and foreign—investors, not state coffers. According to an official report in 1906, as much as 77 percent of the capital invested in the largest Norwegian waterfalls at the time originated abroad (Furre 1976: 18–19), and it is well-known that strong backing from the Swedish Wallenberg family and the French bank, BNP Paribas, was essential in launching Eyde's industrial empire. However, in the case of Elkem, Eyde managed to buy out foreign investors so that, in 1910, it was a full-scale Norwegian company; hence, the power plant at Bøylefoss also came about through Norwegian capital (Dannevig 1960: 18, 52–53).

At the regional level, the state, in the form of local municipalities, proved important first and foremost as a customer, although this had never been the intention. Since publicly owned energy projects could not keep up with the increasing demands for electricity within the local population, AFK profited from energy sale to the public grid when industrial demands ebbed. The municipality of Arendal was an especially important safety net in the company's economy throughout the period discussed in this chapter (Dannevig 1960: 58–59, 61–62, 69–71, 76–80). On the other hand, as public energy production gradually got off the ground, new tensions emerged concerning water management at the regional level. Since they provided electricity to industries, AFK preferred a constant water supply throughout the year, while the local state plants, which supplied public consumers, sought higher production during the winter season when demand was higher.[9] Another major state input to the realization of AFK's ventures was the regional railroad, Arendalsbanen. The line was built concomitantly with developments of local waterfalls and passed by Bøylefoss. Undoubtedly, the railroad facilitated the construction of the power plant and its consequent operations.

In other words, in the early 1910s, we enter the phase during which the industry is being localized—where abstract and sometimes rather lofty visions of profit become realized in terms of specific waterfalls, power stations, dams, power lines, melting plants, and localized communities. As regards the power production at Bøylefoss, we can divide the following century into three phases: (1) the construction phase from 1911 to 1913, when necessary facilities were put in place—to a large extent by way of temporary, nonlocal laborers; (2) the production phase from 1913 onward, which entailed a steady and largely profitable energy production as well as, increasingly, a permanent, stable, and locally recruited workforce; and (3) the automatization phase from the late 1960s, which resulted in a much smaller workforce. This latter transition largely coincided with a restructuring of ownership in Arendals Fossekompani, a profound diversification of activities (see Røed 2021) and, we must assume, a refashioning of relations between company and local community as well.[10]

Since my ambition is to investigate social responsibility at the interface of corporate activity and local community, I focus on the second phase here. During this period, AFK was, indeed, a highly localized affair, and I aim to discern the core dynamics that forged the company's CSR in this context. It will become apparent that AFK's engagement in community welfare was considerable during this period.

CSR Prior to Branding

I should note that the following account is based primarily on local people's narratives about the company and its surrounding community. I have not carried out research in company archives, and the three published company histories (Dannevig 1960; Folkman 1996; Røed 2021) are rather sketchy regarding local forms of social responsibility.[11] Further research would provide nuance to my historical account, but it would not detract from the fact that, in general, locals have had a very positive view of the company's operations.

First and foremost, people point to the fact that AFK managed to provide stable, permanent (overwhelmingly male) employment throughout the twentieth century, even during periods of national crisis (especially, the depression of the 1930s and the tribulations of World War II). Moreover, wages were decent from the outset. Employees at Bøylefoss were thus seen as—and felt—privileged; jobs at AFK guaranteed long-term economic security during volatile times. Hence, the company offered the core attractions associated with state employment at the time: lifelong financial safety that allowed long-term planning, savings, and investments in family life—housing, education for children, eventually a car, improvement in living standards, and so forth.

Moreover, one partly deliberate effect of this stability was lifelong learning among workers. In order to enhance the workforce, AFK supported adult technical education for employees with proven manual skills; perhaps even more important was the work culture that developed onsite. This culture was partly an effect of infrastructural constraints that created a degree of geographical and institutional insulation. As noted, the plant was located inland, away from urban facilities, and was connected to the center by a railroad with limited traffic, not a proper road. This hampered the utilization of formal, technical competence from outside when need arose.

Moreover, it was critical to have workers nearby to handle crises swiftly. Smelting furnaces on the coast needed a constant supply of energy; even short power outages would destroy extremely expensive equipment. In other words, both the power plant itself and the vulnerable power lines required continual attendance and rapid response during emergencies (e.g., floods, turbine problems, or heavy snowfalls, falling trees, etc., that took down the lines). These requirements necessitated *boplikt*: workers were obliged to reside on plant premises or immediately nearby and to respond unconditionally when the company called them in. Moreover, *boplikt* occasioned a degree of labor surplus in the company's operations. There were unavoidably slack periods on the premises between extraordinary situations in which labor could be directed at tasks beyond the day-to-day operations for which they were recruited.

These factors combined to bolster the relative insulation of the plant: most technical tasks and problems were solved onsite through a kind of social contract that accorded employees a degree of autonomy with respect to job content. Often, workers were only confronted with the problem at hand and had to work out the pragmatics of solutions themselves. This instituted a jack-of-all-trades culture in which workers learned from each other through practical problem-solving and, we must assume, where they saved AFK from significant expenses while augmenting their own competence. Even the tools and equipment needed to handle various practical tasks were manufactured onsite by workers with limited or no formal education. When external specialists were required, workers served as onsite assistants in order to pick up knowledge and practical tricks.

Crucially, this dynamic played into the formation of local community as well. The wide-ranging exchange of skills and services that characterized work life meant, also, that there was little need for external specialists to solve practical tasks in the neighborhood. Housing is a focal point in this respect, and we may discern two phases as regards people's living accommodations. Up to the late 1950s, AFK provided housing for workers and their families on plant premises. Due to large numbers of children, living conditions were crowded but modern relative to the standards of the time, certainly in comparison with the cottar households from which many workers were recruited. Then, in the early 1960s, workers channeled personal competences and their nonspecialized cooperative work style into the construction of private housing (*selvbygging*), partly on plant premises, partly in the adjacent area. This villa phase must be seen as a direct spinoff of AFK's labor regime; it realized accumulated skills generated over decades in the workspace. The company facilitated the transition in other ways as well, allowing workers to borrow tools and equipment needed for house building and, occasionally, providing surplus material from the plant. Moreover, to the extent houses were built onsite or nearby, they were integrated into the company's infrastructure; land plots were fitted with electricity supply, water and sewage, and, in some cases, telephone lines. The overall effect of these inputs was up-to-date and highly affordable private housing in the local community.

We note that AFK thus contributed significantly to the fulfilment of two basic needs among dependent laborers seeking to gain a foothold during the tribulations of the first half of the century: steady income, sufficient to support a nuclear family, and one's own place to live. These are, of course, essential economic vectors in a context of poverty and precariousness, but in the Norwegian setting they also attain meaning in terms of culturally valued notions of autonomy (see Vike 2012): steady income and private housing ensure much appreciated social independence.

AFK was also imbricated in other aspects of people's communal life. There is only space to discuss these involvements cursorily here, but it is apparent that, as is often the case (Welker 2014: 12–18), the company fulfilled state functions. For one, leading a family life involves schooling for children, and AFK established and subsidized its own primary school on the premises as soon as production got going. Simultaneously, the local municipality expanded its public school system, and after some discussion, the company school integrated with public schools in 1920. The school building of the adjacent community of farmers and cottars was relocated to the exact midpoint between what was regarded as the centers in the two communities—thus equally awkward for children in both localities.

Moreover, AFK established a health building (*sykestua*) on the premises, stacked with essential supplies and medicines. This was intended to keep the workforce going and, given the geographical distances, to deal with emergencies until patients could be brought to better medical facilities. So, primarily, *sykestua* targeted workers but in due course also served family members. Furthermore, two onsite grocery stores sponsored by the company answered to people's daily needs; the local post office—established by the company—took care of postal services; AFK employed a station master to serve at the public railroad; it opened plant buildings for all kinds of family celebrations in the community and later built a separate community hall for this purpose; it supported communal activities as well, such as sport and leisure and the activities of voluntary politicoreligious organizations; and it built a seaside cottage that could be rented by employees.

There are examples of AFK providing a kind of social assistance to unfortunate locals. In 1936, when one of the workers died at a young age, the widow was provided with a pension and allowed to stay in company housing with her eight children until they were grown. In another case, AFK took care of a local farmer who had sold land and waterfall rights to the company during its establishment; when his farm went bankrupt, the company provided him with a job at the site. The company also paid child allowance (*barnetrygd*), and youth were drawn into the productive core in that they got their first job experiences at the site during summer holidays (*sommerjobber*).

Unfortunately, my data are presently too weak to draw clear conclusions about wages, worktime, work security, and other labor rights that are, typically, outcomes of formal negotiation processes. It has proven difficult to trace these accommodations between capital and labor through local narratives about past events. Despite the somewhat rosy accounts provided by local residents, we must assume that such deliberations were frequent and not always unproblematic. It is interesting, in this context, to note that company and workers sought to avoid local bickering altogether when the latter organized at the company's behest in the early 1960s and a new labor contract was agreed on: simply to adhere to the results of wage negotiations in Hafslund, a leading industrial concern. It seems that this was the first real instance of formalized union activity on the premises.

Summing up, this account substantiates prevailing views in CRS studies: firstly, social responsibility qua corporate practice precedes by far the current objectification of corporate initiatives as "CSR." Present-day discourses have important precursors in managerial trusteeship, philanthropy, and paternalistic concerns for workers and community (see Rajak 2011: 9–10; Djelic and Etchanchu 2017). Secondly, there are clear-cut examples of socially responsible practices outside of state-owned enterprises. In the local arena, AFK was not only, proverbially, a state in the state but also, to a certain extent, a welfare provider within the emerging welfare state. Evidently, as Djelic and Etchanchu (2017) emphasize, the border between polity and economy is not always clear-cut; private businesses are capable of substituting for state functions, and perhaps also, in the context of contemporary transnationalism, marginalizing and reworking established state arrangements (Rajak 2011: 232; Welker 2014: 14–15; Matten and Crane 2005: 171). Essentials of capitalism, then, such as private ownership, dependent labor, and profit-oriented production, do not rule out quite comprehensive forms of social responsibility, even prior to the current situation where "CSR" can be seen as part of corporate branding.

Thirdly, AFK is evidence of welfare substitution even in the special Norwegian context of comprehensive state involvement in society. Again, this is not unique: Ihlen (2011: 38–41) cites several examples of "paternalistic" capitalism in Norway; Fossåskaret (2009) discusses a case of localized industrialization (that of Bjølvefossen in Ålvik) that resembles the AFK case; and, as noted in chapter 4, the community of Rjukan is paradigmatic in the idealized Hydro model. What is surprising is the time span of AFK's local forms of CSR—its engagement extends well into the historical phase when state welfare took root.

Certainly, throughout the century, and in particular toward the end of the period discussed here, state structures grew in importance. As noted, AFK's school gave way to public education as early as the 1920s, improved public healthcare reduced the need for onsite medical facilities, state schemes for economic compensation during sickness and old age (fully realized with *Folketrygden* in 1967) made people less dependent on AFK's private pension insurances, and, importantly, better roads increased people's geographical mobility. Further, by the mid-1960s, local workers had sufficient means to acquire cars, so they started to shop for daily necessities in the urban centers rather than locally. Hence, the last onsite grocery store closed its doors in the late 1990s. The central state also affected the local work culture through formal regulations of work life. Gradually, professionalization of work tasks and concerns for security undercut the jack-of-all-trades approach, both at the plant and in the community. Nevertheless, up until the late 1960s, much of what went on in the community was intimately linked to AFK's presence and its particular practices of social responsibility.

Social Fields, Scales, and Proper Dynamics

The question of why AFK engaged so comprehensively with the local community is, however, not answered by the simple observation that capitalism is compatible with socially responsible forms of production. Evidently, it would be fallacious to argue, in a converse manner, that social responsibility is somehow a necessary upshot of capitalism, or more pointedly given the thematic of this anthology, Norwegian or Nordic forms of capitalism. As they border on ideological rather than analytical arguments, both positions are equally wanting, and this anthology attempts to get past such charged debates by calling for a more nuanced approach in which CSR is seen as emergent from complex interchanges among diverse, and possibly contradictory, dynamics (see introduction).

Now, to analyze CSR as an outcome of dynamic complexity is not an altogether straightforward task; it requires a perspective on the nature of complexity itself, and in the following I rely on Reidar Grønhaug's theory of social fields (1974, 1978), which is geared precisely to this challenge: the empirical investigation of constitutive dynamics in social formations. Grønhaug's core analytical concepts are (1) social field, (2) scale, (3) proper dynamics, and (4) dominance.[12]

Social fields are essentially the patterns of interaction that form around specific tasks—the social networks that come about as people act purposefully with respect to certain objectives (e.g., to produce hydroelectric power, to generate profit, to take social responsibility, to improve one's life conditions, to negotiate labor rights, etc.). Evidently, the interactional patterns that form around such specific purposes are embroiled in each other in complex ways, engendering sub- and supra-fields. In other words, social fields are nested: separate relative to the purposes that define them but interconnected in terms of the overall social forms that they generate.

Scale is simultaneously an ontological proposition and a methodological device in Grønhaug's approach. On the one hand, social fields *have* scale (i.e., objective extensions in space and time). On the other hand, the ethnographer *varies* scale methodologically (i.e., by systematic modulation of the number of roles, persons, networks, etc., included in one's inquiry) in order to discover the objective extensions of social fields. The methodological issues need not concern us here; the important point is that societal configurations are made up of social fields with real extension in time and space. For instance, it is possible to delineate three different AFKs, as it were, relative to the different historical phases I have outlined above. Qua social field, present-day AFK has significantly different purposes and much greater scale than it had in the localized phase I discuss in this chapter (see Røed 2021).

Proper dynamics is a less straightforward concept, but we appreciate Grønhaug's basic point that all social fields, emergent from specific objectives as they are, sustain a certain logic or dynamic appropriate to the requirements of the tasks or purposes at hand. They have a kind of operational rationale that influences their form and impacts. For instance, I argue the specific purpose of energy production *for smelting industries* set in motion a proper dynamic that forged AFK's overall form. Crucially, the requirement of steady supply to furnaces entailed specific demands on the labor force; notably residence duties.[13] While my analysis details the operational interrelating of task requirements in a rather specific setting, we might as well expand Grønhaug's perspective to discern more general forms of proper dynamics (e.g., a governance dynamic of political fields, a profit-generating dynamics of corporate fields, etc.) (see introduction).

Crucially, when adopting this tripartite scheme (social field, scale, and proper dynamics) we need not assume coherence across social fields. On the contrary, we presume ontological multiplicity: different tasks or purposes engender different operational logics, and the interchange among fields varies as well, resulting in dissimilar societal forms. Given this perspective, we should not be surprised to find divergent and possibly contradictory dynamics within field conglomerates that we regularly reify as entities—as when we, for instance, think about Arendals Fossekompani, Statkraft, or Equinor as individual, corporate units.

My main point is that CSR varies in this respect, too. We cannot presume that corporate social responsibility is a uniform phenomenon across the many social fields that make up a capitalist venture. We must recognize CSR's variability, even contradictory character, within companies and businesses (see Knudsen, Müftüoğlu, and Hugøy, chapter 10; Welker 2014). Its precise shape is a matter to be discovered in each and every case, not something that can be assumed a priori by way of our preferred perspective or definitions. Some of the fields in which CSR emerges may then turn out to have a cultural proper dynamic; others are better seen as economic or political. In other words, we may indeed find cultural ideals (e.g., adherence to "Norwegian" or "Nordic" values) to be both prominent and formative in certain fields—say, in formulations of "CSR" policy—while economistic logics might characterize other fields; perhaps during implementation of "CSR" where abstract ideals are put to test in the context of material interests of various sorts. The one does not necessarily exclude the other.

Driving Forces in CSR: Field Interchanges and Relative Dominance

This call for analytical precision, then, is a way to ensure that our theoretical perspectives, or for that matter ideological preferences, do not overdetermine analysis. But the challenge is more profound since, inevitably, our reasoning is based on the social ontology that we embrace (i.e., how we conceive of social constitution)—in this case, the interrelationships of the diverse social fields in which corporate social responsibility is being forged. How do we conceive of interchanges among social fields in the constitution of overall societal forms, and is it possible within this complex mutuality to discern a principal dynamic that has especially formative powers? Can we, as it were, reduce CSR to an ultimate or last-instance source?

Grønhaug's fourth principle (dominant social fields) is concerned with these questions of mutuality and relative impact. Evidently, the perspective bars any straightforward reduction of manifest CSR practices and conceptions to singular or universal dynamics; the socially responsible configurations we encounter in specific corporations must be seen as emergent from highly specific (i.e., empirically variable) forms of complex mutuality. They are never general, as it were; analytically, we need to deconstruct CSR and "CSR" in terms of the particular fields, dynamics, and interchanges that engender them. It follows, then, that empirical forms of corporate social responsibility cannot be derived *directly* from a materialist logic, from requirements of capitalist production alone. The precise impacts of these requirements must be identified and assessed relative to bearings from other social fields.

In the case of AFK, I maintain that infrastructural prerequisites of production were crucial in the firm's involvement with community. The chain of requirements entailed by energy production for smelting industries (steady power supply that demanded *boplikt*) can even be viewed as causally efficacious in community formation. Nevertheless, once established, community engendered a reality that transcended AFK's production logic—a range of social fields (taskscapes) with their own proper dynamics and forms of impact. It is important to note that analyses along these lines may bring us far beyond what we regularly view as business domains. When granting community the power of formative force, we need to take seriously the apparently "nonproductive" social fields of which it consists (see Bråten 2013). This entails tracing how formations of, for example, personhood, kinship, neighborhood, and religion may impact the operation of business ventures.

These are emphatically not trivial dimensions. In the case of AFK, community dynamics were part and parcel of securing steady production (thus profitability) while also establishing the sociocultural context out of which AFK's responsible practices grew. Community had reverse formative impacts on the company's operations, as it were. The critical period seems to be the late 1920s and early 1930s. As mentioned, we see a shift in the organization of production during this stage: from the use of temporary and dispensable labor (a large number of mobile construction workers in the 1910s) to a stock of permanent, resident workers in the late 1920s. The rather stable accommodation between capital and labor that formed in this period turned out to have a Christian flavor; it was rooted in interchanges with low church Protestant revivalism.

I surmise that, here, we witness a religious rather than a material proper dynamics. For one, Christian orientations and values preceded the foundation of AFK. Local evangelicals formed the first mission association in the municipality of Froland in 1868, and ambulating emissaries inspired a series of religious revivals (*vekkelser*) around the turn of the century. The area around Bøylefoss was no exception. There was a notable *vekkelse* here in 1903, and subsequently, several families engaged in local evangelicalism, domestic religious gatherings, mission associations, and the construction of prayer houses (*bedehus*). Hence AFK started to operate in a predisposed "value context": a setting that provided certain constraints and affordances with respect to the formation of CSR.

This interchange among relatively autonomous social fields is worthy of more detailed analysis; here, it suffices to note three forms of mutual impact between firm and community. Firstly, since AFK recruited labor locally, a significant part of the stable workforce on which production relied were fervent Christians. While labor is an empty input when seen from the abstract, economistic perspective of profit generation, in the real world of localized ventures, workers are, rather, social persons who come with specific values and orientations (see also Welker 2014; Bråten 2013). In AFK's case, these pre-givens became all the more important with the requirement of *boplikt*, which extended the social contract beyond the workers into fields of family and community. Secondly, chief machinists during the formative phase were active Christians themselves, so we witness a kind of alliance *in the religious field* between laborers and onsite management. Again, we need to view social actors, here company supervisors, as social persons rather than production inputs. Thirdly, as community matured, local families started to intermarry, instigating yet other forms of interconnectedness. *Kinship* came to play a significant role in consolidating community, but since, to a degree, people married across class distinctions, this dynamic also affected fields of production. Arguably, intermarriage between the children of laborers and management blurred divides within the production regime and strengthened the Christian-flavored capitalist contract further. This inter-dynamic, while crucial for AFK's formation and success, cannot easily be reduced to the firm's logic of production.

In a broader analysis, we may well discern formative impacts in the organizational structure of AFK. The company had a relatively dispersed form of ownership, and CEOs were engineers rather than economists (Helge Røed, personal communication; see also Røed 2021). This situation may have engendered a degree of shared culture among managers and workers around technical proficiency, and since the onsite leaders were machinists rather than (theoretical) engineers, they were even closer to employees in this sense. We thus see the contours of a relatively democratic structure in which onsite managers at Bøylefoss had great leeway in daily operations and, essentially, shared work orientation with their subordinates. Both were primarily geared toward the practical challenges of running the plant securely and efficiently; profitability was, so to speak, a side effect of technical proficiency and ingenuity rather than an explicit concern in and of itself.

As noted, this complex situation renders dubious any axiomatic attribution of AFK's social responsibility to capitalist dynamics per se. Conversely, it would be equally simplistic to view CSR as a direct manifestation of extra-productive dynamics (e.g., cultural, normative, or religious precepts). Even though the region of Agder is famous as a Bible Belt of distinctly conservative flavor (Røed 2010), one cannot deduce specific local forms from general cultural orientations. These are, perhaps, obvious points, but the analytical challenge is no less demanding; if so, our task is to trace how diverse social fields and dynamics become imbricated in the forging of corporate social responsibility in specific settings.

For instance, while scholars (e.g., Thorkildsen 1997) underline the populist and political force of revivalism in Norwegian Christianity, it is important to keep in mind that evangelicalism inspired quite divergent orientations in practice. The movement was certainly driven from below by laypeople (small-scale farmers, dependent cottars, housewives, lumberjacks, mine workers, etc.), and there is no reason to doubt its democratizing effects. Through evangelical fervor, people enhanced their skills in reading, writing, and collective organizing and developed a critical faculty through opposition to official theology and priesthood.[14] This empowerment of lower classes facilitated subsequent labor organizing, while, in other contexts, it sustained a conservative pietism: a thoroughly bourgeoisie attitude (*borgerlighet*) that, no doubt, undergirded capitalist expansion. The case I discuss tends strongly toward the latter, but it is not difficult to find counter cases, even in the local vicinity, where tensions within production regimes occasioned worker radicalization and class struggle. Eydehavn at the other end of the power lines is a case in point (see Røed 2013). The smelting plants on the coast went through conflicts and strikes during the same period that the "bourgeoisie contract" was forged inland.

What we witness around the power station, then, was a mutually reinforcing dynamics among disparate social fields; *boplikt*, low-church Christianity, intermarriage, and practices of CSR had unidirectional effects on both firm and community. One core analytical question remains, however; is it possible, given this complex mutuality, to discern the *most dominant dynamics* in local formations? Here, it is crucial to note a theoretical implication of Grønhaug's perspective: to acknowledge complexity does not entail a symmetrical social ontology in which all social mechanisms must be deemed equally important in producing a given outcome. Quite to the contrary, it would be analytically defensive to refrain from discerning the relative impact of diverse mechanisms in the forging of, for example, specific forms of corporate social responsibility.

Pursuing this deeper analysis, I surmise that we need to retain a focus on the sociomaterial relations of production. In this particular case at least, it is pertinent to argue that capitalist dynamics—the never-ending quest for profit—was the *overriding* force in community formation and in AFK's socially responsible engagements. Profit drive did not determine local forms, but it was this dynamic that—literally—created the very beneficiary of AFK's corporate social responsibility in the first place (the local community), and it was this drive that generated the economic surplus required to sustain AFK's local engagements. The infrastructural chain of preconditions that forged this localized phase of AFK has been detailed above: smelting furnaces on the coast required uninterrupted energy supply, which further necessitated localized and committed labor that could maintain dams, turbines, and power lines; hence, workers were obliged to live onsite, which in turn entailed a community-oriented form of CSR. Combined with its relative geographical isolation and insularity from state interference, I believe we can argue confidently that AFK was the community's dominant social field. Furthermore, as a private capitalist venture, profit drive was the most dominant force in the forging of the company itself. Again, a counterfactual question may be illustrative: what if AFK were not as profitable as it proved to be; what if its forms of local engagement threatened its bottom line financially?[15] I dare to argue that we would have seen quite a different form of corporate social responsibility with perhaps no local community to engage with at all.

Conclusion

Evidently, the AFK case corroborates a core argument in this anthology: there is no one capitalism (or neoliberal capitalism). At the *empirical* level, we encounter complex and varying socioeconomic formations that are emergent from a multiplicity of forces, and, obviously, this pertains to the social responsibility that corporations forge as well. Hence, analytically, we need to pay attention to the interchanges of capitalist proper dynamics with extra-core—geographical, structural, cultural, agentive, interactional—impacts, some of which may enhance capitalist objectives, some of which may hamper them. In the case of the community that grew around AFK's power station, we witness interchanges that consolidated a rather nonantagonistic social contract between labor and capital.

One upshot of this social contract is apparent: it engendered a flexible, dependable, and diligent workforce that greatly enhanced capitalist production. We note, then, that AFK's nonarticulated forms of CSR (i.e., social responsibility as embedded practices rather than stated ideals) may have had the same dampening effect on worker organizing (unions, class struggles, strikes, etc.) that, presently, explicit "CSR" policies are claimed to have (see e.g., Rajak 2011). The company's engagement of persons and community (rather than laborers in a narrow, technical sense) was integral and crucial to this contract. In contrast, at the other end of the power lines in Eydehavn, it seems that interchanges among social fields engendered more antagonistic and conflictual accommodations between labor and capital.

More generally, I believe the case suggests that, analytically, corporate social responsibility ought to be seen as a *derivative* phenomenon. Firstly, it is derivative in the formal sense that I alluded to in the introduction when differentiating between CSR as figure and as ground. As figure, social responsibility is a thematic field defined by explicit discourses about "CSR" (i.e., the concept has clearly delineated empirical reference points). As ground, however, social responsibility pertains to unthematized ethical dimensions that are embedded in corporate practices; lacking clear empirical signposts, the concept inevitably takes on analytical import. The socially responsible is not prerecognized, as it were, but must be delineated through our *perspectives* on social responsibility. In contexts without explicit "CSR" discourses, then, CSR is derivative in the sense of having to be deduced analytically. For instance, above, I have identified certain welfare provisions as evidence of AFK's social responsibility.

Secondly, we note that this formal distinction is not altogether abstract but has empirical anchoring in the fact that practices of CSR *predate* discourses about "CSR." In my case and more generally (see Matten and Moon 2008), "CSR" as a special kind of reflexive orientation is derivative in the sense of being a historical emergent: something arising out of something else. It resonates with corporate practices that already had, or could be adjusted or reformulated to project, ethical dimensions. Acknowledging this temporal dimension hopefully guards against an unduly constricted approach to CSR (see also Djelic and Etchanchu 2017). We would be foundationally critical of the "CSR" figures propounded in various contexts (e.g., in specific corporations, business fields, state bodies, UN institutions, and perhaps also in some academic discourse) as they inevitably are narrower than and often conceal the ground from which they stand out. Exploring CSR to its fullest extent entails paying attention to the shadow side of "CSR" discourse as well (i.e., unthematized ethical dimensions of corporate activity): the ethical principles that fall outside the purview of explicit "CSR" discourses and the ethical challenges that remain unengaged in real-life corporate practices.

Thirdly, CSR is derivative with regard to social constitution since we must assume an asymmetrical relation between preconditions (for CSR) and emergent forms (of CSR). More pointedly, it is more reasonable to claim that CSR (as practice and discourse) ebbs and flows with the prime conditions for its emergence than the opposite—that CSR's preconditions could somehow fluctuate with manifestations of CSR. This abstract argument becomes clearer when we, with Grønhaug, recognize that social fields depend on specific (not general) forms of dynamic. The fact that we discuss *corporate* social responsibility ties CSR inextricably to the proper dynamics of corporations. Despite its variegated surface forms, I take CSR to be ontologically rooted in (thus logically secondary to) the proper dynamic of capitalist production: profit drive generates the very practices that demand ethical considerations in the first place while also impacting significantly on the specific forms of CSR that emerge. In state-run corporations, other concerns and goals may be enfolded into the productive dynamics as well, but as is evident from other case studies in this anthology, political and societal objectives are increasingly being disentangled from capitalist motivations, even in Norwegian state corporations. Current policies seek to insulate or protect the core dynamic of profitability from other considerations. This is, arguably, further evidence of the derivative nature of CSR; ethical aspects of corporate activity cannot but be rooted in economistic concerns as these are corporations' proper dynamics, their very raison d'être.

Finally, it is worth repeating that the derivative character of CSR does not rule out socially responsible practices or a genuine ethical concern among owners and management about the societal effects of company activity (presently codified as "CRS" or "ESG"). It does not in principle rule out the possibility of "corporate virtue" or "compassionate capitalism" (Rajak 2011: 2). The point is that a company's accommodation to specific sociomaterial and cultural settings is driven, ultimately, by a proper dynamics of profitability that, we must assume, overrule other concerns when contradictions become too problematic. The case of AFK is illustrative in this respect as well: we deal with a highly profitable venture where investments in corporate social responsibility never threatened financial survival.

Eldar Bråten is professor in the Department of Social Anthropology, University of Bergen, Norway. His research has focused on several topics based on fieldwork in Central Java, Indonesia: Islamization, concepts of self and person, cultural heritage, entrepreneurship, and state decentralization. Bråten has also carried out research on historical transformations of social inequality in Norwegian rural communities and is now largely publishing on theoretical issues.

Notes

1. To be precise, subsequent to the company's considerable expansion and diversification in the 1970s, it is now a transnational actor, engaging in businesses far beyond local energy production (see Røed 2021).
2. Welker (2014) interrogates another core concept in discourses on CSR in a similar manner: "the corporation."
3. A special thanks to my key informant who provided invaluable insights into the local history, and to Helge Røed for analytical inputs.
4. The whereabouts of the crash are disputed. Received narratives point to cultural conservatism and structural impediments that hampered a necessary adjustment from sail to steam in shipping technology (Slettan 1998: 416–18; Hagemann 2005: 183–87; Røed 2010: 173), but there are also strong contributing factors at the level of social agency (Torstveit 2012; Røed 2021: 31–32). Through collusion and deliberate concealment, local elites in control of the commercial bank in the city (Arendals Privatbank) managed to run fraudulent financial schemes over an extended period, and when the bubble collapsed in 1886, total outstanding debts were 12.5 million kroner—a sum amounting to close to US$1.3 billion in 2011 value (calculated from Torstveit 2012: 195). The crisis precipitated a series of bankruptcies in Agder, mass unemployment, and largescale emigration to America, and it contributed to the establishment of Arbeiderpartiet (the Labor Party), which was founded in Arendal in 1887 (Hagemann 2005: 134–36).
5. Eyde and Knudsen grew up here; Blakstad was from Asker, close to Oslo, but moved to and established a woodworking industry in Arendal in the 1880s.
6. The company first offered waterfalls to the central and local state, and when these attempts failed, it courted foreign capital; in particular, Siemens and other German interests (Dannevig 1960: 16–20).
7. The rich iron ore resources in Agder were developed from as early as the sixteenth century, with two notable plants in the immediate vicinity to Arendal: Nes Verk and Froland Verk (established during the seventeenth and eighteenth century, respectively).

8. As noted above, *hjemfallsretten* does not apply to AFK. Although the *power plant* was built after 1909, the company could draw on the fact that waterfall rights were purchased as far back as 1896. It has been argued that, gradually, the three industrialists took quite divergent positions with respect to Norwegian energy policy: Knudsen saw hydroelectric power as a common national resource and argued for state control, while the capitalists favored private, corporate utilization, with Eyde emphasizing export-oriented production and Blakstad a broader use of the resource (Norman and Aanby 1996).
9. These tensions were handled through Brukseierforeningen, an association for all land and waterfall owners in the riverways.
10. While the regular workforce was thirty to forty persons up to the late 1960s—all connected to the power plant at Bøylefoss—AFK now has an amazing twenty-two hundred employees in twenty-seven different countries (https://arendalsfossekompani.no/).
11. Presently, AFK has its own division for CSR, but the contemporary context is extremely different from the historical phase discussed in this chapter. Now, ambitions are guided by the UN discourse on sustainability (with special emphasis on goal no 7, "green energy for all," and no 9, "innovation and infrastructure") rather than particularities of onsite community (Arendals Fossekompani 2019; see also Røed 2021).
12. I believe Grønhaug's approach allows more realistic and powerful analyses of corporations and their social responsibility than what is possible through the analytical lens of "becoming" so characteristic of current enactment perspectives. The latter approach typically accentuates the motility of phenomena—that they are "inherently unstable and indeterminate, multiply authored, always in flux, and comprising both material and immaterial parts" (Welker 2014: 4). In contrast, Grønhaug's perspective is directed at the sociomaterial formations that, after all, result from such enactments—their degree of extension, continuity, and impact. While Djelic and Etchanchu (2017), through their comparative, historical approach, share this ambition to scrutinize the manifest societal configurations of which CSR is part, Grønhaug's generative approach takes our understanding beyond the "ideal types" that inform their analyses.
13. Over time, technological developments (automatization, improvements in transportation, and more reliable turbines and power lines) decreased the need for *boplikt*.
14. To a large extent, these low church orientations came to suffuse the official state church in Norway, engendering a less antagonistic relation than in Sweden (Thorkildsen 1997).
15. As Taraldsen (1999: 88) puts it: "In financial circles Arendals Fossekompani AS is known as the 'money machine.'"

References

Archer, Margaret Scotford. 1995. *Realist Social Theory: The Morphogenetic Approach*. Cambridge: Cambridge University Press.
Arendals Fossekompani. 2019. *Arendals Fossekompani: Samfunnsansvar og bærekraft 2019*. [Arendals Fossekompani: Social responsibility and sustainability 2019]. Report. Retrieved 13 May 2022 from https://arendalsfossekompani.no/wp-content/uploads/1_AFK_Baerekraftsrapport_FINAL.pdf.
Bråten, Eldar. 2013. "Introduction: Cultural Embedding." In *Embedded Entrepreneurship: Market, Culture, and Micro-business in Insular Southeast Asia*, edited by Eldar Bråten, 1–28. Boston: Brill.

Dannevig, Birger. 1960. *Aktieselskabet Arendals Fossekompani 1896–1911–1961*. [The joint stock company Arendals Fossekompani 1896–1911–1961] Arendal: Akjseselskapet Arendals Fossekompani.
Djelic, Marie-Laure, and Helen Etchanchu. 2017. "Contextualizing Corporate Political Responsibilities: Neoliberal CSR in Historical Perspective." *Journal of Business Ethics* 142(4): 641–61.
Folkman, Kristian, ed. 1996. *A/S Arendals Fossekompani: Kraft og børs 1896–1996* [A/S Arendals Fossekompani: Energy and stock market 1896–1996]. Kristiansand: A/S Arendals Fossekompani.
Fossåskaret, Erik. 2009. "'… Må jeg få lov å henvende mig til Dem …': Paternalistiske direktørar som lokalpolitiske aktørar" ['… May I ask thee …': Paternalistic directors as local political actors]. *Arr—Idehistorisk tidsskrift* 20: 81–93.
Furre, Berge. 1976. *Norsk historie 1905–1940* [Norwegian history 1905–1940]. Oslo: Det Norske Samlaget.
Granovetter, Mark. 1985. "Economic Action and Social Structure: The Problem of Embeddedness." *American Journal of Sociology* 91: 481–510.
Grønhaug, Reidar. 1974. "Micro-Macro Relations: Social Organization in Antalya, Southern Turkey." PhD dissertation, Bergen, Norway: Department of Social Anthropology, University of Bergen.
———. 1978. "Scale as a Variable in Analysis: Field in Social Organization in Herat, Northwest Afghanistan." In *Scale and Social Organization*, edited by Fredrik Barth, 78–121. Oslo: Universitetsforlaget.
Hagemann, Gro. 2005. *1870–1905: Det moderne gjennombrudd* [1870–1905: The modern breakthrough]. Oslo: Aschehoug.
Ihlen, Øyvind. 2011. *Samfunnsansvar på Norsk: Tradisjon og kommunikasjon* [Social responsibility in Norwegian: Tradition and communication]. Bergen: Fagbokforlaget Vigmostad & Bjørke AS.
Matten, Dirk, and Andrew Crane. 2005. "Corporate Citizenship: Toward an Extended Theoretical Conceptualization." *Academy of Management Review* 30(1): 166–79.
Matten, Dirk, and Jeremy Moon. 2008. "'Implicit' and 'Explicit' CSR: A Conceptual Framework for a Comparative Understanding of Corporate Social Responsibility." *Academy of Management Review* 33(2): 404–24.
Norman, Victor D., and Anne-Tone Aanby. 1996. "Ragnvald Blakstad—markedspioner i Norsk krafthistorie" [Ragnvald Blakstad—market pioneer in Norwegian energy history]. In *A/S Arendals Fossekompani: Kraft og Børs 1896–1996*, edited by Kristian Folkman, 17–35. Kristiansand: A/S Arendals Fossekompani.
Polanyi, Karl, and Robert Morrison MacIver. 1944. *The Great Transformation*. Boston: Beacon Press.
Rajak, Dinah. 2011. *In Good Company: An Anatomy of Corporate Social Responsibility*. Stanford, CA: Stanford University Press.
Røed, Helge. 2010. "Sørlandet—et politisk 'annerledesland'" [Sørlandet—a land of "political alterity"]. In *Sørlandsk Kultur: Mangfoldet og Motsetningene* [The culture of Sørlandet: Plurality and contradictions], edited by Berit Eide Johnsen, 146–97. Kristiansand: Høyskoleforlaget.
———. 2013. *Eydehavn: Fortellinger om et Industristed* [Eydehavn: Tales of an industriral locality]. Tvedestrand: Bokbyen Forlag.
———. 2021. *Kraft og bærekraft: Arendals Fossekompani 125 år* [Power and sustainability: Arendals Fossekompani 125 years]. Oslo: Gyldendal.
Slettan, Bjørn. 1998. *Agders historie 1840–1920: Ansikt mot sjøen, grunnfeste i jorda*. [The history of Agder 1840–1920: Face turned to the sea, rooted in the soil]. Kristiansand: Agder Historielag.
Sogner, Knut. 2014. *Creative Power: Elkem 110 years, 1904–2014*. Oslo: Elkem.

Taraldsen, Kristen. 1999. *An Adventure in Industry: From Iron Ore to High Technology*. Gjøvik: Wigestrand Forlag.
Thorkildsen, Dag. 1997. "Religious Identity and Nordic Identity." In *The Cultural Construction of Norden*, edited by Øystein Sørensen and Bo Stråth, 138–60. Oslo, Stockholm, Copenhagen, Oxford, Boston: Scandinavian University Press.
Torstveit, Johs. G. 2012. *Storsvindel, bankkrakk og nytt politisk parti: Arendal 1886–88* [Major fraud, bank bust and a new political party: Arendal 1886–88]. Arendal: Arendals Tidende.
Vike, Halvard. 2012. "Varianter av Vest-Europeiske statsformasjoner—utkast til en historisk antropologi" [Varieties of West European state transformations—draft for a historical anthropology]. *Norsk Antropologisk Tidsskrift* 23: 126–42.
Welker, Marina. 2014. *Enacting the Corporation: An American Mining Firm in Post-authoritarian Indonesia*. Berkeley: University of California Press.

— Chapter 4 —

MODEL OF A MODEL
Norsk Hydro at Home and Abroad
Ståle Knudsen

In 2015, I attended a seminar on "Understanding Culture in an International Workplace" at the Norwegian University of Science and Technology in Trondheim. The keynote was given by Norsk Hydro's CEO Svein Brandtzæg. He underlined how the corporation had succeeded in the remote Norwegian township Rjukan one hundred years previously because they had taken social responsibility (*samfunnsansvar*), how an agreement with the union in 1967 made the corporation a pioneer for the Norwegian Work Environment Act (Arbeidsmiljøvernloven, 1977) and how they now enact the Hydro model in Brazil, especially by cooperating with their employees. "What we are doing in Brazil now is very similar to what we did in Rjukan one hundred years ago, for example by supporting education and taking care of remote villages."

Three years later, Hydro was embroiled in scandals related to their alumina refinery in Alunorte, Brazil. It seemed that their CSR, sustainability, and community work had not been all that responsible after all—which brought the largest owner, the Norwegian state, into question for its passivity.

Currently one of the world's largest aluminum producers, Norsk Hydro has also been a core corporation in the development of industrialism in Norway (see table 0.1 in the introduction). Whereas until fifteen to twenty years ago it was engaged in a range of activities, including oil and gas production, Norsk Hydro has consolidated its activities around the processing of aluminum and aluminum products. Their primary source of raw materials is their own extraction and processing of alumina in Brazil. Thus, when we first designed the Energethics project from which this book emerges, Norsk Hydro was not included since it is not involved in energy production outside of Norway. However, when pursuing our research from 2015 through 2019, we repeatedly came across references to Norsk Hydro as model, reference point, and example. It pressed itself upon us through informants' statements, in academic texts, in media coverage and opinion pieces, in parliamentary debates, and by journalists addressing questions to us concerning Norsk Hydro. Norsk Hydro seeped into the project from everywhere. This ubiquity convinced us that the story about how the state and the Nordic model influence the way Norwegian corporations handle responsibility when they operate abroad cannot be satisfactorily told without including Norsk Hydro.

Thus, by telling the story of Norsk Hydro, I will show in this chapter the importance of the example set by or granted to Hydro for the development of state policies and corporate strategies related to responsibilities of Norwegian capital abroad. The story of Norsk Hydro is indicative of general developments in the relation between corporations, industrial capital, the state, and the Nordic model in Norway. Zooming in on Norsk Hydro will also help us highlight many of the main dynamics, dilemmas, challenges, and tensions involved when taking Norwegian (state) capital and/or the Nordic model abroad. As such, this chapter provides a backdrop to the other chapters in the book and can fruitfully be read as a companion chapter to the introduction in that it develops many of the same themes. It does so by relating the story about one particular corporation that has often been considered a model for so many things in Norway. The Hydro model, in many respects, became a model for how capitalism could thrive within a social democratic polity, and, as Emil Røyrvik argues in his chapter in this volume, "Hydro is an exemplary company in the sense of both co-constituting and instantiating the Nordic/Norwegian model" (see also Røyrvik 2011: 182).

Norsk Hydro has been articulated as a reference point and model in many different areas, by various actors, and in manifold ways. We can broadly distinguish between:

(1) an academic-political discourse that centers on Norsk Hydro as a model for state ownership and state-corporation relations;

(2) references to Norsk Hydro as model for CSR either (a) in relation to communities and unions, articulated by Norsk Hydro itself or representatives of other corporations or unions, or (b) as a model for sustainability, as articulated primarily by academicians; and

(3) Norsk Hydro as a model for the embeddedness of capital in society, exemplified especially by the alignment of "corporate values" with "Norwegian values."

Before discussing each of these varieties of the model, this chapter first provides a brief outline of the history of the corporation and its role in the political economy of Norway. The last section takes a closer look at Norsk Hydro in Brazil and discusses how and to what extent the varieties of the Hydro model came into play and were challenged and negotiated when the corporation recently experienced several incidents/scandals related to its operations there.

Norsk Hydro in the Political Economy of Norway and Beyond

Norsk Hydro has arguably been the most important corporation in Norwegian industrial history and remained by far the largest industrial conglomerate in Norway up until the early 2000s. In many respects, Norsk Hydro exemplifies and symbolizes major trends in Norwegian political economy. The pre-1940 history of Norsk Hydro is characterized by early industrialization fostered by foreign capital. It was established in 1905 by Norwegian entrepreneur Sam Eyde, Norwegian chemist Kristian Birkeland, and Swedish investor Marcus Wallenberg.[1] Supported by Swedish and French capital, Norsk Hydro initially experienced great success producing synthetic fertilizers. Although Norsk Hydro is known for its cooperation with local communities and unions during this period, it also saw fierce confrontations with workers and their unions, most dramatically displayed in the infamous Menstad battle where police and military personnel were mobilized (by then Minister of the Interior Vidkun Quisling), in an understanding with corporate management, to quell a large incident of worker unrest (Lie, Myklebust, and Norvik 2014: 50–51). The narrative about cooperation with unions and communities in Hydro's early history is obviously a curated or selective narrative, retrospectively allocating identity, continuity, and values to the corporation.

Norsk Hydro was largely taken over by the Nazi regime during World War II, with the German shares falling into the hands of the Norwegian state after the war. The state became a majority owner of Norsk Hydro, but it was a reluctant owner. The previously revolutionary leaders of the Labor Party now underlined that there were limits to the state's engagement in the corporation (Lie et al. 2014: 51). Yet, during the next decades, Norsk Hydro also experienced strong pressure for aligning with the social democratic project, becoming one of the important arenas for the development of the tripartite model, all while the state refrained from involvement in business operations. Industrial crises involving fully state-owned corporations during the 1970s and 1980s became a major drain on state finances and resulted in increased legitimacy of the hands-off approach the state had taken with Norsk Hydro. In the ensuing restructuring, ÅSV—a major state-owned industrial corporation—was taken over by Norsk Hydro.

Although the leading social democrats considered the way in which the state enacted its ownership of Norsk Hydro to be wise and were generally pleased with the corporation's activities, their stance was more reluctant when it became clear that Norway was to embark on the development of significant offshore oil and gas fields. The Conservative Party wanted to make Hydro the major instrument for developing the resources, while the Labor Party preferred to establish a new, 100 percent state-owned corporation. With the establishment of Statoil in 1972, it was the latter view that prevailed. Still, Norsk Hydro remained an important actor in the oil and gas sector. Hydro was Statoil's (later Equinor's) main domestic competitor and was often considered the more dynamic and effective of the two.

The corporation developed and diversified into a holding corporation with far-flung interests in production of metal, fertilizers, oil and gas, as well as other produce. From the 1970s onward it invested in Brazil and elsewhere. Despite a tendency toward corporatization and privatization in Norwegian policies since the 1980s, the state retained more than one-third of the shares in Norsk Hydro, and there was a great deal of continuity in the way governments related to the corporation. Starting around 1990, Hydro embarked on a more conscious strategy for internationalization and, from the end of the 1990s, reformulated—in accordance with international trends—its purpose toward creating shareholder value. This shift from industrial to financial capital had effects on the ways Norsk Hydro relates to Norwegian institutional mechanisms and articulates responsibility.

The corporation also changed strategy from being a broad-based industrial conglomerate to concentrating on aluminum production, selling off other aspects of production—including fertilizer production (which was incorporated as a new independent company, Yara). The oil and gas division of Norsk Hydro was merged with and in effect taken over by Statoil in 2008. Norsk Hydro is now a transnational corporation specializing in aluminum. It has—according to its own website—operations in forty countries, engaging thirty-five thousand workers involved in all stages of the production of aluminum and aluminum products. Headquartered in Oslo, the corporation's activity in Norway is typically centered on research and development and high-end aluminum production in small communities where Norsk Hydro is the dominating employer. It was only during this last period—from approximately 1990—that Norsk Hydro emerged as an explicit model.

The First Model: State Ownership

While the Norwegian state has been and is a major owner of large Norwegian corporations (see introduction), its ownership of Norsk Hydro since after World War II is seen as particularly successful in that the distance the state has kept has been combined with commercial success. As such, the way state ownership of Norsk Hydro has been enacted is often talked about as the "Hydro model," which comes with positive connotations, with the designation "model" signifying an ideal to be followed in the way in which the state enacts its ownership in other major corporations. While policy papers (e.g., green and white papers) do not explicitly refer to a Hydro model, the concept is widely used in public debates,[2] including in (business) scholars' contributions in the public domain,[3] and by think tanks (Gitmark 2014; Storsletten 2019).

Scholars consider that the Hydro model of state ownership was replicated and spread in Norway from the early 1990s onward (Lie et al. 2014: 64) and that the Hydro model constituted a template for more explicit and consistent policies for state ownership from the late 1990s when former state agencies were corporatized and partly privatized (see introduction). The following quote nicely summarizes what the Hydro model is usually taken to mean:

the so-called Hydro model ... entails that the state is *one* among several owners, and that the company is listed [on a stock exchange]. It has been a core principle that the state behaves as any other owner and respects the company's integrity as a listed company, and that the state as the dominant owner does not discriminate against minority shareholders. That means that the state respects common rules for good corporate governance of ownership (*eierskapsstyring*). That means in practice that the state does not send governance signals (*styringssignaler*) outside of the formal channels that the ownership affords. (Christensen 2015: 4, my translation)

One major reason it developed into a model for state ownership was that Norsk Hydro, unlike corporations that the state owned fully and which ran into a suite of political and financial problems during the 1970s and 1980s (Lie 2016; Lie et al. 2014: 62), continued to be a commercially successful corporation. It has been argued that it was successful precisely because the state kept a distance. "Through the larger part of the 60 years that the state has had the majority or 'near majority' [of the shares], the state has not 'governed' [*styrt*] Hydro — or tried to govern Hydro — through its ownership. ... The state has been a passive owner" (Grønlie 2006: 160, my translation).

While this hands-off policy on the part of the state is commonly considered to have facilitated the commercial success of Norsk Hydro, state ownership has also been seen as a factor in securing stability and promoting long-term strategic thinking (Lie et al. 2014: 62). In practice, governance of listed companies with state ownership has, since the 1980s, gravitated in the direction of the Hydro model. Rather than being the result of a conscious strategy by governments, this emerged as a political consensus when state agencies were corporatized and state corporations partly privatized. It has been and continues to be a reference point for managing state ownership when reforming (partly) state-owned corporations. For instance, when discussing the potential partial privatization of Statkraft, one scholar suggested that "partial privatization in accordance with the so-called Hydro model would be a good solution for Statkraft."[4]

The Second Model: CSR and Sustainability

While reference to the Hydro model will usually denote the model for (distanced/inactive) state ownership, it is common to refer to Norsk Hydro as a model in other respects also, more closely connected to the diffuse field of CSR, corporate responsibility, or sustainability. This is less articulated in public discourse but is regularly invoked by people working on corporations' relation to unions, communities, and the environment, who will then often consider the way Norsk Hydro does things to be a good example of the Norwegian Way.

An Equinor manager with extensive international experience stated in a workshop organized by the Energethics project that "CSR is there to create the foundation for the business we are going to have. That is very important. It is embedded in the Norwegian DNA." Here, he referred to Norsk Hydro at Rjukan and stressed that Norsk Hydro cared about not only the environment but the whole community. Similarly, a union representative, who was involved in the establishment of a union to interact with Equinor in Tanzania (see Lange's chapter in this volume), stressed how Norsk Hydro had one hundred years of experience with industrial workers and had learned how important cooperation is to avoid in-house unions (*husforeninger*). She considered that, contrary to Statoil (later Equinor), they managed this well on the Norwegian shelf. She praised their way of doing things in a tidy and orderly manner (*ryddig og ordentlig*) and said that "this is what one envisioned down there [in Tanzania] as well. It is much better to have one [union]. We tried to have a kind of Norwegian model."[5]

It is important to note here that not only corporate management but also union representatives consider Norsk Hydro to be a model for how to handle CSR and relate to the environment and local communities. LO, the major industrial union in Norway, embraces Norsk Hydro as a model of the Norwegian model. A team from the union visited the Hydro operations in Brazil and reported, in an article in a magazine published by the union, that there was close cooperation between the corporation and its employees. The Norwegian government and LO had been pushing for such cooperation. They noted that there was some conflict concerning what issues should be included in the work of the local union (education, politics?), but, overall, they relayed that "the Hydro model is puttering along, also in Brazil" (*hydro-modellen putrer og går, også i Brasil*) (LO 2011).

Norsk Hydro's self-presentation—as exemplified in the vignette—as well as references to Norsk Hydro as a model tend to focus on its history and experience of dealing with communities and unions. Until the 1990s, this was not articulated as being CSR (or *samfunnsansvar*; see chapter in this volume by Maraire and Hugøy). However, toward the end of the 1990s, "CSR was put on the agenda in a new way, as a matter of self-driven, strategic initiatives," with Hydro hosting an international seminar on CSR (Carson, Hagen, and Sethi 2013: 26) and appointing an executive vice president of CSR (Røyrvik, this collection) in 1999. This was, notably, the same year that the board decided to adapt to the financialization of the global economy and let shareholder value be the primary yardstick for their operations (Røyrvik 2011: 150). Local resistance against Hydro's Utkal project in India, and the corporation's subsequent backing out from the project in 2001, was instrumental when the Hydro management decided to heed the advice of Norwegian Church Aid and embed a dedicated strategy for CSR in corporate governance (Hveem 2009: 394).

Scholars who have surveyed the adoption of CSR by corporations in Norway, or focused on Norsk Hydro itself, have also conveyed this narrative of Hydro being an early adopter of CSR. This includes sustainability: "Norsk Hydro is a representative example of the sustainability frontrunners among the largest and most influential companies in Norway" (Ditlev-Simonsen, Weltzien, and Ihlen 2015: 178). This literature stresses that Norsk Hydro had a central role in the formation, in the early 1990s, of the World Business Council for Sustainable Development (Weltzien, and Ihlen 2015: 178) and that Norsk Hydro was among the first to publish a sustainability report (in 1989/90; Brun and Thornam 2013: 91). Rather than being a model for the Nordic/Norwegian way of doing things, these moves toward sustainability may indicate that Norsk Hydro is emerging as a model for sustainability/CSR in a globalized business environment.

The Third Model: Embeddedness

The self-presentation of Norsk Hydro not only portrays the corporation as a model for handling relations with communities and unions (as illustrated by the vignette) but also subtly aligns corporate values with widespread understandings of Norwegian values. For instance, an article on Norsk Hydro's website profiles their former CEO (or "general director") Johan B. Holte, stressing how he

> got rid of the class symbols in the company. The red carpets that paid homage to former managing directors were removed. So were the sleekest cars in the garage. Holte drove his own Volkswagen when he needed to go to Notodden or Rjukan. This was noticed. The distance between top management and the workers lessened, just as the managing director intended.[6]

While this may be read as an independent initiative on Norsk Hydro's side to be more egalitarian, a more comprehensive analysis demonstrates that Norsk Hydro was also induced or pressed to adapt to reigning social-democratic policies in post–World War II Norway.

The Norwegian Industrial Democracy Program from 1962 focused on areas of work-life relation and workplace democracy, which Norsk Hydro came to pioneer from the late 1960s (see Røyrvik's elaboration in his chapter; also Røyrvik 2011: 156), and constituted core pillars of the Norwegian tripartite model. Thus, the way Norsk Hydro related to unions and workers, and labor overall, came to be considered not only the way Norsk Hydro did things but the Norwegian way, of which Norsk Hydro is considered an exemplar.

Scholars and politicians, focusing on Norsk Hydro's cooperation with unions and communities as well as on the way state ownership is exercised, tend to emphasize the institutional dynamics of the Hydro model. This is largely congruent with academic approaches that consider institutional mechanisms as core to the Nordic model (see introduction). However, it has also been argued that the legitimacy of the Hydro model may be based on a more comprehensive and wider model concerning how the corporation is thoroughly embedded in and intertwined with Norwegian society through an informal implicit contract between the corporation, society, and the state based on "a multitude of attitudes, perceptions and expectations more or less mutually held" (Grønlie 2006: 160).

Diverting from the formal as well as informal institutional embeddedness described by scholars, the management of Norsk Hydro—along with employees and unions—tends to emphasize values as core to the way Norsk Hydro does business. In current business parlance, this is articulated in their "Purpose" to foster a "more viable society," or what they call the Hydro Way.[7] During the presentation mentioned in the vignette, CEO Brandtzæg stated that "the Hydro Way is about putting a name on the culture of the corporation. It is about the values we take with us to all countries in which we operate."

While corporate leadership could rhetorically anchor their approach to responsibility in a history of care for communities, in practice this was not seen as sufficient or comprehensive enough when going global, both because the legal and regulatory framework was often weaker and because the corporations were less familiar with and embedded within the social and political landscape. With the internationalization of the corporation and, especially, the turn to shareholder value, the embeddedness dimension of the Norsk Hydro model is less convincing. The values that Norsk Hydro claims to take with it abroad are not explicitly articulated as being Norwegian values. Rather, the corporate values presented are very generic it is typical speak by management in transnational corporations. At the seminar mentioned in the vignette, a veteran Hydro manager reflected that "the Nordic model has something to do with our view on humanity" and described how an employee representative had come with tears in his eyes and thanked him after Norsk Hydro had implemented the Norwegian model in a foreign company Hydro had bought. Thus, undoubtedly, the particular history and embeddedness of Hydro in Norwegian society does give it a capacity to mobilize egalitarian and transparent management forms when expedient, as the case study by Røyrvik demonstrates. Røyrvik argues that in practice Hydro operates with dynamic and hybrid management forms.

However, the corporate culture's Norwegian character is partly reemployed by the corporate management by repeated reference to company history. The corporation's particular (Norwegian) history of "Care, Collaboration, and Courage" (keywords in the Hydro Way) subtly aligns the corporate values with Norwegian values, as was expressed in the Equinor manager's earlier comment concerning CSR as embedded in the Norwegian DNA. The Hydro culture fostered through more than one hundred years of history, embedded from the very start in both the local community and wider society, is thus often referred to when discussing the responsible business conduct of Norwegian corporations abroad. However much the corporation has become internationalized, it remains convenient to refer to the Norwegian background to foster and articulate an identity and a culture.

Norsk Hydro in Brazil: Business, Scandals, and Politics

This section explores how the Norsk Hydro model is challenged, negotiated, and defended—both at home and abroad. Since the Hydro management obviously thinks that Brazil is a good place to look to see how the corporation pursues responsible business abroad based on their history in Norway, Brazil will also be my focus here. Norsk Hydro's long history of engagement in Brazil, their reliance on their processed raw materials from Brazil, as well as some recent controversies relating to their operations there makes this focus particularly appropriate.[8]

Norsk Hydro has been active internationally since around 1970 and made their first investment in Brazil during the mid-1970s. The investment in Brazil was important in order to have some control of the extraction and first processing of raw materials for aluminum production. However, this early investment in Brazil became controversial, partly because Brazil was then a brutal military dictatorship but especially since their bauxite-extraction activities in Trombetas had severe, negative impacts on indigenous populations and the environment (Akerø et al. 1979; Leira 2020). The scandal resulted in the Norwegian state pulling the fully owned ÅSV out of the Brazilian consortium in which both ÅSV and Norsk Hydro were partners. But Norsk Hydro waited it out, retained their shares, and eventually so expanded their activities in Brazil that more than 50 percent of all of Norsk Hydro's workforce is now located in Brazil, and Brazil counts for almost half of Norsk Hydro's industrial activity. In 2010, Norsk Hydro bought most of the Brazilian bauxite producer, Vale. The price tag—4.6 billion USD—meant that this was (by then) the largest Norwegian investment abroad. This takeover of the larger part of Vale meant that Hydro secured access to bauxite in a "100-years perspective" (Leira 2020: 116).

In 2018, Norsk Hydro operations in Brazil faced two challenges to the image of Hydro being particularly responsible and ethical: the first concerning toxic spills, the second relating to corruption.

Following heavy rain in February 2018, local residents in the Barcarena municipality and Brazilian authorities accused Hydro of allowing toxic spills from the alumina refinery, Alunorte, which were polluting rivers and posing a threat to local populations. Brazilian authorities fined Hydro 50 million Norwegian crowns and required production to be halved while investigations took place. Alunorte is the world's largest aluminum refinery with two thousand employees, and the partial closure had severe consequences for Hydro since the company depends on the Alunorte production of raw material for further processing in Norway and elsewhere. While the Brazilian authorities' experts documented toxic spills, the external consultants hired by Norsk Hydro found "no environmental damage." The incident received a lot of attention in Brazilian media, and Norsk Hydro faced the combined trouble of reputational loss and severely reduced production capacity. In this context, CEO Brandtzæg stressed that they would "strengthen our societal engagement to ensure that we contribute to sustainable development in Barcarena in line with Hydro's strategy for CSR."[9] In a primetime interview on NRK, the major state TV channel in Norway, the same day, he stressed that his major concern was the well-being of the local population (Leira 2020: 94). This aligned well with their announcement to the Oslo stock exchange the day before that Norsk Hydro would invest 250 million Norwegian crowns in a Sustainable Barcarena Initiative, which would address the local communities surrounding the Alunorte facilities.[10]

Thus, the frame of reference for Hydro's handling of its responsibility initially was not the Norwegian model or Norwegian values but the international business language of CSR and sustainability, which was mobilized here as it would have been by any other large TNC faced by scandal that threatened their bottom line. They needed to rebuild trust and find ways to get the Brazilian authorities to revoke the instruction to operate at half capacity. This was their major concern, as this cut inflicted a loss in earnings amounting to more than 400 million Norwegian crowns per month. The value of Norsk Hydro shares plummeted 15 percent in the first month after the incident (Leira 2020: 93). Writing about Norwegian business interests in Brazil, Torkjell Leira shows that it was only when the business implications of the incident dawned on the management that they took action: "Hydro did not define the situation as a 'crisis' before the sanctions from the Brazilian environmental authorities came, in other words not until it had serious consequences for the corporation's bottom line" (Leira 2020: 95, my translation). Thus, it was not Hydro's values relating to communities and responsibility but the effect the incident had on shareholder value that directed the way Hydro responded.

The second critique against Norsk Hydro's activities in Brazil came in December 2018 when NRK released a documentary about them. Contrary to political discourse, which focused only on the event of alleged toxic spills, the documentary portrayed a much more complex picture of Hydro's presence in the state of Pará. It told the story of contested land rights between Hydro and the Tauá people living at the outskirts of the Hydro Alunorte property, an area defined as "traditional land area" according to a contract signed in 1982 by the Brazilian company Vale, which purchased land from the state. Norsk Hydro, on the other hand, stated that the contract had expired and that the Tauá people who had returned should once again be dislocated. In 2016, the mayor of Barcarena presented a new regulation plan that redefined the area to fit industrial purposes. The redefinition served the interests of not only Hydro but also the mayor, who by then had already benefitted economically from the expansion of the refinery through contracts with Hydro worth 141 million Norwegian crowns. Although Hydro terminated their relationship with the mayor three years after he took office, Transparency International Norway claims that the collaboration should have ended when the mayor was elected in 2012 due to strong conflicts of interest.

This critique did not have the same impact on the corporation as the critique of the alleged toxic spill earlier the same year, perhaps because it did not have immediate effects on profits or perhaps because Hydro's image was already tainted. This scandal seems not to have received the same attention in Brazil as the previous one. It was more complex and not only about bad foreign capital but also about a corrupt local leader. The incident discussed earlier concerning rainwater spill, however, attracted considerable media attention first in Brazil and later in Norway. In this context, a Brazilian journalist came across the website for our Energethics project and contacted us to request an interview. Although I did not have particular insight into the Brazilian case, she insisted that it was relevant to talk to me. The journalist had one major question: given that the Norwegian state is a major owner of Norsk Hydro, does it put pressure on the corporation, and if not, why? She saw this in the context of the Norwegian state wealth fund recently having (allegedly) divested from hydrocarbon extraction (oil, gas, and coal) as a move to support energy transition. Thus, while the Norwegian state made such ethical choices concerning its investments in the wealth fund, why did it not intervene in Norsk Hydro's unsustainable activities in Brazil?[11]

The Norwegian media coverage of the Hydro troubles in Brazil did not initially touch on the role of the Norwegian state. It was seen purely as the corporation's own responsibility, and the focus in reports and commentaries was on the way in which the corporate leadership handled the challenge, including the engagement of external consultants to assess whether there had actually been overflows and pollution. It was leftist parliamentarians who eventually brought attention to the role of the state. The minister of trade, industry, and fisheries was challenged to explain in the Norwegian Parliament, Stortinget, how the government had responded to the incident.[12] Said ministry is formally the owner of the state's shares in Norsk Hydro, and Minister Torbjørn Røe Isaksen thus represented the state's role and responsibility. Isaksen was criticized for reproducing Hydro's narrative by treating their investigations as facts while dismissing Brazilian environmental authorities' investigations as allegations. Further, his ministry was criticized for not having conducted independent evaluations to assess whether Hydro acted according to the state's expectations on CSR.

Isaksen asserted that the ministry would conduct independent assessments but stressed that it would not be done in a manner whereby the ministry would override the company's board. Rather, he referred to the ownership dialogue they had with Norsk Hydro as any large shareowner would have and further noted that "when it comes to CSR (*samfunnsansvar*) and sustainability there are formulated clear expectations in the White Paper on state ownership which the Stortinget collectively supports. We have clearly expressed these expectations to Norsk Hydro and other corporations, and we have repeated these expectations concretely in relation to the situation at Alunorte."[13] He reiterated the government's hands-off ownership policy: "It is important to remember that the state as owner does not have other rights than other shareholders ... The Ministry does not operate this company. The board operates and is responsible for it [the company]."[14]

So, herein lies the answer to the Brazilian journalist's question: the way the right-of-center government interpreted the state ownership policy, embedded in the Stortinget, meant in practice that the state should keep an arm's-length relationship with Norsk Hydro. Ownership should be professional, and politics and business must not be mixed. This is based on and articulates a widespread conception concerning limited liability public companies: that ownership and management should largely be separate, that owners should not interfere in daily operations and only exert influence though the board and at the general assembly. This is an ideal and practice that has emerged with the modern corporation (Micklethwait and Wooldridge 2003). The Conservative Party in Norway in particular, generally supportive of business, is ideologically committed to this ideal and therefore ends up with the policy articulated by Isaksen in Stortinget.

However, large corporations often have shared interests with the states of their respective home country, and the two can be intertwined in a multitude of ways. An odd twist to the story of the Alunorte scandal shows how that applies in this case. Half a year before the Alunorte scandal/incident, Norwegian minister for climate and environment Vidar Helgesen sent an unusually sharp and critical letter to his Brazilian counterpart. Norway and Brazil had cooperated on issues, such as the environment and indigenous populations, for many years, and Norway is a major contributor to REDD+. The minister now expressed concern about issues, such as accelerating deforestation and environmentally unfriendly decisions by President Michel Temer's government. Soon after this, Temer met Norwegian prime minister Erna Solberg in Oslo, where he was again confronted by the critique and had to face both demonstrators and a humiliating press conference. According to Leira (2020: 57–60), this incident was one of the main reasons that the Alunorte spill became such an important incident. This was explicitly acknowledged in Brazilian media. It was Helgesen's counterpart in Brazil, Minister Sarney Filho, who instructed IBAMA (Brazilian Institute of Environment and Renewable Natural Resources) to fine Norsk Hydro and halve their production. It was payback time. During an interview with one of the larger TV channels in Brazil, Filho stressed that the Norwegian state is a major owner in Norsk Hydro and should therefore be held responsible, especially in Amazonas. This resulted in widespread attention in Brazilian media on the role of the Norwegian state in the Alunorte case, and it is likely that when the Brazilian journalist contacted me approximately a week following the interview with the minister, her questions were informed by his claims.

So, Norsk Hydro became part of the politics of interstate relations whether it wanted to or not. However much the Norwegian state tries to distance itself from corporations in which it has significant ownership interests, it cannot avoid those corporations becoming implicated. In this case it was a reaction to the humanitarian approach of the Norwegian state. Inactive state ownership is no guarantee that corporations do not become implicated in politics. Moreover, corporations themselves often seek alliances with governments, and governments often promote abroad businesses that are based in their own countries. Statkraft's involvement in Turkey was secured by the intense involvement of Norwegian ministers (and even the Norwegian king), especially by tending relations with the minister of energy in Turkey. And this applies, of course, not only to state-owned corporations. When BP wanted to get a foothold in Azerbaijan when the Soviet Union was about to break up, they managed to mobilize UK prime minister Margaret Thatcher to work for their case; she even attended the signing of an MoU in Baku. "It was the perfect illustration of the use of the British foreign policy machinery by a private oil corporation" (Marriot and Minio-Paluello 2013: 57).

This brief review of the unfolding of Norsk Hydro's activities in Brazil and the controversies surrounding them indicates that the Nordic model and state ownership may be of relatively little importance for the corporation's operations abroad (but see Røyrvik's chapter in this volume). It is not a Nordic way of doing things or Hydro's Norwegian tradition for relating to communities and unions or state ownership that shapes its policies in Brazil. However, back home in Norway, Norsk Hydro is still held to account by the public and media, which consider Norsk Hydro a primary exemplar of the Nordic Model. While most of the conservative dailies in Norway primarily reported on the Norsk Hydro problems in Brazil, several left-leaning publications as well as the main business newspaper, *Dagens Næringsliv*, carried critical articles and opinion pieces concerning Hydro's activities in Brazil. One opinion piece typically claims that the Hydro problems in Brazil affect the reputation of Norway.[15] The documentary produced by NRK about the corruption case, the state

TV channel's critical questions to the CEO concerning the spills, and Leira's book further testify to how much Norsk Hydro is exposed to the critical attention of the Norwegian public. State ownership comes with expectations among the public and politicians, although the meaning and content of state ownership obviously is negotiable and has undergone change. According to Hugøy and Maraire's chapter in this collection there is, among the Norwegian public, a strong expectation that the state should stay out ahead and be a good example of social responsibility, and by extension that corporations in which the state is a major owner should be particularly responsible.

Conclusion

We argued in the introduction that to meaningfully study the Nordic model one should distinguish between academic approaches to the model and its use as a political-rhetorical tool in social interaction. While the first accentuates the tripartite model, the welfare state, and egalitarianism, the second is increasingly sliding toward emphasizing some idealized Nordic—or rather Norwegian—values. Yet, there is obviously a dialectic between these two levels. Emil Røyrvik (2011) claims that Hydro drastically transformed when it adapted to the shift from industrial capital to financial capital during the late 1990s, resulting in corporation management thinking that the corporation's primary responsibility is shareholder value. He argues "that a partial dismantling, or at least a major transformation of the social democratic state and the Norwegian model of democratic capitalism (Sejersted 1993), has in effect been a partial result of the active political process of neoliberalization in Norway" (Røyrvik 2011: 179).

This results in ambivalences, contradictions, and tensions that are, in Norway, especially articulated in debates about active/passive state ownership. Norsk Hydro was once an integral part and totally intertwined in the fabric of a particular Norwegian political economy. By increasingly playing along with the rules, premises, and languages of globalized capital—including a shift to shareholder value and the adoption of the language of CSR—Norsk Hydro has untangled itself from the shackles of the Norwegian political economy, and the expectations (*forventninger*) (see introduction) that the state expresses for the corporation's responsible conduct is but a thin disguise of this fact. Thus, as was seen in the case of Brazil above, the way state ownership is enacted at arm's length gives Norsk Hydro license to function as any other TNC when operating abroad, focusing on shareholder values and mending problems by invoking the internationally acknowledged tool and language of CSR.

This case thus indicates that the ideals that come with the analytical Nordic model—state guidance, dialogue with unions, responsible interaction with local communities—are difficult to uphold for large Norwegian corporations when internationalizing. The expectations the Norwegian state expresses do not in any way substitute for the "implicit common understanding" (*underforståtte fellesforståelse*) (Grønlie 2006: 164) that the Hydro model once implied. Yet, Norsk Hydro considers the Nordic/Norwegian background to be capital, which they can mobilize in managing their public image. They dis-embed the model from any particular Nordic institutional arrangements and rewrite it so that it attaches to and represents their particular Norwegian history and experience, and, supposedly, also Norwegian values. And here again, Norsk Hydro can be considered a model: the other corporations we have studied have followed Norsk Hydro and made the same maneuver: when going global, it is not Nordic institutional mechanisms but rather "Norwegian values" that are hinted at in their self-presentation.

Acknowledgments

Research on which this chapter rests has been conducted within the frames of the project Energethics (2015–19), funded by a FRIPRO grant from the Research Council of Norway (grant no. 240617).

Ståle Knudsen is professor in the Department of Social Anthropology, University of Bergen, Norway. He was leader of the project Energethics (2015–19) from which this book emerges. Knudsen has, since the early 1990s, done ethnographic fieldwork in Turkey, and his publications include the monograph *Fisheries in Modernizing Turkey* (Berghahn, 2009).

Notes

1. Bråten outlines in detail in chapter 3 the history of Sam Eyde's first industrial investment in Norway and the way in which social responsibility was handled in a remote industrial community.
2. See, e.g., https://www.dagbladet.no/kultur/farvel-til-hydro—modellen/66290463, https://www.aftenposten.no/meninger/kronikk/i/347RM/statens-aktive-eierskap, both retrieved 20 July 2020.

3. Retrieved 20 July 2020 from https://www.magma.no/liberale-verdier-og-statlig-eierskap, https://www.bi.no/forskning/business-review/articles/2015/01/kongsberg modellen/.
4. Retrieved 10 July 2020 from https://www.europower-energi.no/public/hydro-modellen-god-for-statkraft-privatisering/1-2-185613.
5. I am grateful to Siri Lange who allowed me to use this piece of information from her fieldwork.
6. Retrieved 10 May 2021 from https://www.hydro.com/en-NO/about-hydro/company-history/1946—-1977/1967-a-dynamic-and-visionary-leader/.
7. Retrieved 10 December 2020 https://www.hydro.com/Document/Index?name= The percent20Hydro percent20Way percent20 percent28EN percent29&id=3399.
8. This section leans heavily on Torkjell Leira's book (2020) *Kampen om regnskogen — sannheten om Norge i Brasil* (The fight for the rainforest—the truth about Norway in Brazil).
9. Norsk Hydro Press Conference, Oslo, 9 April 2018.
10. Dagens Næringsliv, 10 April 2018: 4–7.
11. Retrieved 12 April 2018 from https://exame.com/brasil/da-noruega-ao-para-as-contradicoes-da-hydro-alunorte/.
12. https://www.stortinget.no/globalassets/pdf/referater/stortinget/2017-2018/refs-201718-06-14.pdf.
13. https://www.stortinget.no/globalassets/pdf/referater/stortinget/2017-2018/refs-201718-06-07.pdf, p. 4838.
14. https://www.stortinget.no/globalassets/pdf/referater/stortinget/2017-2018/refs-201718-06-07.pdf, p. 4838.
15. "Hydro og norsk omdømme" ("Hydro and Norwegian reputation"), Eirin Heddeland, *Dagsavisen*, 26 March 2018, 37.

References

Akerø, Dan B., Dag V. Poleszynski, Helge Hveem, and Per Erik Borge. 1979. *Norge i Brasil: Militærdiktatur, folkemord og norsk aluminium* [Norway in Brasil: Military dictatorship, genocide, and the Norwegian aluminum industry]. Oslo: H. Aschehoug & Co.

Brun, Pål, and Hanne Thornam. 2013. "Corporate Sustainability Reporting." In *CSR and Beyond*, edited by Atle Midttun, 88–116. Oslo: Cappelen Damm.

Carson, Siri G., Oivind Hagen, and S. Prakash Sethi. 2013. "From Implicit to Explicit CSR in a Scandinavian Context: The Cases of HÅG and Hydro." *Journal of Business Ethics* 127: 17–31.

Christensen, Sverre A. 2015. "Liberale verdier og statlig eierskap" [Liberal values and state ownership]. *Magma: Econas Tidsskrift for økonomi og ledelse* 4.

Ditlev-Simonsen, Caroline D., Heidi von Weltzien Koivik, and Øyvind Ihlen. 2015. "The Historical Development of Corporate Social Responsibility in Norway." In *Corporate Social Responsibility in Europe*, edited by S. Idowu, R. Schmidpeter, and M. Fifka. CSR, Sustainability, Ethics & Governance, 177-196. Cham: Springer.

Gitmark, Hanne. 2014. *Statlig eierskap* [State ownership]. Oslo: Tankesmien Agenda.

Grønlie, Tore. 2006. "Hydro-modellen" [The Hydro model]. *Nytt Norsk Tidsskrift* 23(2): 159–64.

Hveem, Helge. 2009. "Norske utenlandsinvesteringer og norsk (utenriks)politikk: Dårlig forbindelse?" [Norwegian foreign direct investments and Norwegian (foreign) policy: Poor connection?]. *Internasjonal Politikk* 67(3): 381–412. https://www.idunn.no/ip/2009/03/art01.

Leira, Torkjell. 2020. *Kampen om regnskogen: Sannheten om Norge i Brasil* [The fight for the rainforest - The truth about Norway in Brazil]. Oslo: Res Publica.

Lie, Einar. 2016. "Context and Contingency: Explaining State Ownership in Norway." *Enterprise and Society* 17(4): 904–30.

Lie, Einar, Egil Myklebust, and Harald Norvik. 2014. *Staten som kapitalist: Rikdom og eierskap for det 21. århundre* [The State as a capitalist: Wealth and ownership of the 21st century]. Oslo: Pax forlag A/S.

LO. 2011. *Aktuell bakgrunn: Hydro in Brasil* [Relevant background: Hydro in Brazil]. Oslo: LO Norway International Department.

Marriott, James, and Mika Minio-Paluello. 2013. *The Oil Road: Journeys from the Caspian Sea to the City of London*. London: Verso.

Micklethwait, J., and A. Wooldridge. 2003. *The Company: A Short History of a Revolutionary Idea*. New York: Modern Library.

Røyrvik, Emil A. 2011. *The Allure of Capitalism: An Ethnography of Management and the Global Economy in Crisis*. New York: Berghahn Books.

Sejersted, Francis. 1993. *Demokratisk kapitalisme* [Democratic capitalism]. Oslo: Universitetsforlaget.

Storsletten, Aslak V. 2019. *Et mindre og bedre statlig eierskap* [Smaller and better state ownership]. Civita-note 24 (2019). Civita.

— Part II —

Ethnographies of Norwegian Corporations' Engagement with CSR

— Chapter 5 —

TRAVELING, TRANSLATION, TRANSFORMATION
On Social Responsibility and the Nordic Model in China

Emil A. Røyrvik

Is it possible to identify a Nordic or Norwegian model of organization, work, and management when globalized Norwegian companies establish and run businesses abroad? The existing literature on the so-called "export" of the Nordic model asserts that the Nordic model is left behind at home (e.g., Løken, Falkenberg, and Kvinge 2008; Børve and Kvande 2018; Knudsen et al. 2020). The studies argue empirically that, when Norwegian companies internationalize, the Nordic model is not brought along in their new countries of operation, and they run their businesses as any global company or TNC. This is probably a fair assessment as far as it goes. This chapter problematizes this common understanding of a lack of "export" of the Nordic model, based on an understanding that cultural models are not "exported" and transferred like commodities but rather travel, are translated, transformed, and co-constructed anew in entangled cultural encounters.

 The argument is based on extensive multisited ethnographic (partly collaborative) work during an eight-year period (2001–9) with the globalized aluminum corporation, Norsk Hydro, forming the basis of an ethnographic extended case study using Hydro as the ethnographic point of departure for a cultural critique of globalized capitalism (Røyrvik 2013a). The chapter investigates how core ideas and practices that can be associated with the Nordic model play out in their foreign operations in the authoritarian state of China, focusing on issues related to workplace democratic ideals and socially responsible operations. The chapter highlights the translations and hybridity in the adoption and transformation of (aspects of) the Nordic model in China and suggests that several key notions, values, and principles attributed to the Nordic model indeed were enrolled and mobilized in Hydro's international ventures in China and, furthermore, were culturally translated and reassembled together with other internationally traveling concepts and trends as well as with local practices and knowledge traditions. The new local co-construction and reassemblage of aspects of the Norwegian model were enacted and materialized through cultural encounters in hybrid forms, and the chapter shows in particular how Hydro translated its Nordic model tradition of implicit CSR.

The chapter thematizes the Hydro model of state-corporation interaction and governance characteristic of state ownership in the Norwegian (Nordic) model. Hydro has 31,000 employees in 40 countries; as of 2021, the Norwegian state owned 34.26 percent of Hydro shares. Yet the prevailing logic of (partial) state ownership by the Norwegian state, developed arguably first in its relationship with Hydro and thus labeled "the Hydro model" (see chapter 4), is to refrain from direct intervention and active management of its shareholder position in a corporation. The logic is that the state cannot act as private owner (shareholder) because it is *not* a private owner (Lie 2005: 201). A strong confirmation of the Hydro model was established in the late 1980s (Lie 2005: 201), and this policy is followed to ensure financial markets and other stakeholders in the globalized market society of corporate independence from the state. To partially remedy the problem this model creates related to democratic control over (partially) state-owned companies, the Norwegian state rather governs and influences large corporations' international operations through signals and expectations of socially responsible behavior, communicated both publicly through, for example, actively promoting international CSR initiatives and more directly in frequent dialogue with top management.

Building on and contributing to theories of CSR and the Nordic model, the chapter argues that the existing literature on the international "export" of the Nordic model fails to take into account the dynamic social practices of travels and translations documented in the case, partly because the Nordic model is to some extent treated as a rationalized myth, reified as a static object/model, thus to some extent removed from the organizational realities and fields of practice, and partly because of the theoretical shortcomings in conceptualizing cultural "export" of phenomena such as the Nordic/Norwegian model. In the ethnographic case, however, we find that core ideas, values, and practices of the Norwegian model—in particular, the Nordic tradition of implicit CSR—function dynamically as a hybrid, living reality co-constructed in translocal cultural encounters. In this way, the chapter also contributes to long-standing yet somewhat disparate theoretical traditions focusing on cultural travel and translation, such as the anthropology of globalization, cultural encounters, and translation (e.g., Clifford and Marcus 1986; Clifford 1997; Larsen 2009), the anthropology of "traveling models" (Reyna 2007; Behrends, Park, and Rottenburg 2014), and actor-network-theory (ANT) of translation (e.g., Latour 1984; Callon 1984).

First, the chapter describes the discussions and struggles over the definition and role of corporations in society particularly in terms of social responsibilities. What follows is a section detailing the ethnographic context of Norsk Hydro, its highly significant role as an industrial locomotive in the developing Norwegian industrial society and economy, and, in particular, its key role in developing and promoting the Nordic model of work life and organization, as well as the place of CSR in this picture. Third, the chapter details the case of Hydro's arguable "export" and translation of the Nordic model and social responsibility to their new venture in Xi'an, China.

The Struggle over the Corporation

While the larger surge in the specific focus on the concept of corporate social responsibility emerged during the 1990s, the history of the concept is much longer, as is the practice of "implicit CSR" (see below and chapter 3). Not incidentally, we can at least trace the scholarly discourse back to management guru Peter Drucker's book, *The Concept of the Corporation* (1993 [1946]). With the creation of limited liability joint stock companies and the rise of big business bureaucracies, the large corporations realized early that they had inherent reputation and legitimacy challenges. During the crises and depression of the 1930s, the critique against big business became overwhelming and instigated both new laws, regulations, and institutions as well as business-branding campaigns to posit business firms as socially responsible (Bakan 2004). It was also Drucker who popularized the term "management by objectives" in his 1954 *The Practice of Management* and thus galvanized the now dominant notion that the institution of management is first and foremost management by objectives.

Both management by objectives and CSR can today be considered part of the dominant corporate governance package associated with neoliberalism, where variants of American management (by objectives), including new public management (NPM), are its concrete, technical materialization. Critics have labeled CSR a neoliberal construct devised largely to allow corporations to dodge their inherent social and ethical commitments as important social actors and institutions while simultaneously posing as socially responsible actors. In this perspective, the CSR concept is similar to the well-known family of neoliberal constructs that perverts the original and everyday meaning of the terms it parasitizes (Lorenz 2012). Examples are notions such as quality control, transparency, and accountability—ideas that are hardly problematic in everyday usages of the terms. The neoliberal hijacking of the terms, however, transforms and often more or less flips their meanings.

The CSR trend from the 1990s might also fruitfully be perceived in this perspective. With the widespread fall of the perception of the corporation as a social actor with broad social responsibilities and the triumph, to a greater or lesser extent depending on national contexts, of a more myopic understanding of the corporation as a profit-maximizing vehicle where its only, or at least its primary, mission is the increase of shareholder value, we have simultaneously witnessed the creation and widespread rise of CSR as a cultural construct. The economist Milton Friedman is the emblematic voice of the tradition conceptualizing corporations as profit machines, denouncing, in a famous 1970 *New York Times* essay, social responsibility as socialism. The title of the piece says it all: "A Friedman Doctrine—the Social Responsibility of Business Is to Increase Its Profit" (Friedman 1970). Later often referred to as "the Friedman doctrine," it states that a company has no social responsibility to the public or society, only to its shareholders. He justifies this by arguing that shareholders are the owners of a company and that corporate executives are the employees of the owners of the business. He considers the corporate executive employees to be the agents of the owners with their only responsibility being toward the desires of the owners—which translates into maximizing profits—while playing by the rules of the game—which include laws, regulations, and ethics.

While Bower and Paine (2017) dissect the flaws in this argument related to the view of shareholders as the owners of the company (they are owners/holders of shares, not owners of the company) and managers as their agents, this doctrine nevertheless developed into both principal-agent theory and the surge of shareholder value that during the last forty years of neoliberalization has become dominant and has transformed the purposes of business to a large extent in line with the Friedman doctrine (Ho 2009; Røyrvik 2013a; Bower and Paine 2017).

It is in this broader context that we must situate the revival and new emergence of CSR since the late 1990s with more nuanced perspectives on CSR and related concepts—such as corporate citizenship (Matten, Crane, and Chapple 2003), sustainability, and business ethics—and consider in particular the notion of CSR in the context of the Nordic model (e.g., Gjølberg 2010; Ihlen 2011; Knudsen et al. 2020). The revival of CSR is thus premised upon the preceding descent of the corporation as a societal institution. Broadly, we might divide the recent academic debate on CSR into three main perspectives (Marrewijk 2003): (1) the shareholder perspective associated with the Friedman doctrine; (2) the stakeholder perspective associated with Freeman (1984), arguing that the company has responsibility toward all parties affected by its operations; and (3) the societal perspective, arguing that the company operates legally and morally on the basis of a social contract and that they are an integral, constitutive part of society and thus responsible to all of society. I argue below that Hydro's approach to social responsibility in China, despite the company's massive turn to value for the shareholder from 1999, also illustrates perspectives two and three.

In the context of the Nordic model, the societal perspective on corporations has arguably had a comparatively stronger presence than in many other countries and regions of the world. This is one main reason why, while in many other countries CSR has been used by corporations to bypass the state, in the Nordic countries "the states have taken the lead role in promoting CSR and sustainability and expect Norwegian-based TNCs to act responsibly when 'going global'" (Knudsen et al. 2020: 2). Official Norwegian CSR policies have mainly been devised in light of a perceived governance gap in the global economy and have especially targeted Norwegian-based business operations abroad (Carson and Nilsen 2021).

The case of Norsk Hydro, to which we now turn, exemplifies this particular Nordic approach to CSR. And as I have elaborated upon extensively elsewhere (Røyrvik 2013a), Hydro also exemplifies the major struggle, duality, and ambivalence between the two opposing conceptualizations of the corporation as an inherently societal actor versus the shareholder-value view. Norsk Hydro was created in 1905, the same year that Norway gained its independence, and has arguably been the most important locomotive in the development of Norway as an industrial nation. While being a cornerstone in the Norwegian social democratic industrial state, from 1999 Hydro turned seriously toward a shareholder-value orientation (Lie 2005: 424–33) and transformed into what I describe (Røyrvik 2013a) as a hybrid organization, positioned ambivalently but with considerable balancing capacity, with one foot in each of the two opposing paradigms conceptualizing the corporation.

Hydro, the Nordic Model, and CSR

As an industrial force in developing the modern Norwegian economy, state, and society, Hydro was significantly also a key actor in the development and institutionalization of the Nordic model in Norway both at the macro level of the tripartite collaborative arrangements and, not least, at the company level of collaborative and democratic arrangements between management on the one hand and workers and unions on the other.

Inspired by the human relations tradition and the early sociotechnical research on coal mining in Britain (Trist and Bamforth 1951), the so-called work-life collaboration trials were introduced in Norway in the 1960s by a joint British-Norwegian team headed by Einar Thorsrud (Thorsrud and Emery 1970; Emery and Thorsrud 1976). The major initiative from 1962 was labeled the Norwegian Industrial Democracy Program, because the ideology behind it was to enhance democracy at the workplace and in industry. Thorsrud was appalled by the alienation and meaninglessness experienced by workers in the Taylorist scientific management regime, treating people solely as manual labor and essentially machines. He wanted to turn Herbert Marcuse's (2002 [1964]) "one-dimensional man" on its head and employ the whole human at work (Sørhaug 1996). However, increased productivity for the companies was always central. To cajole the companies into participation, Thorsrud said he would "eat his hat" if productivity did not rise in tandem with democratizing work relations (Sørhaug 1996).

In collaboration between employer and employee unions as well as between management and workers/unions, a series of concrete trials of increased democratic organization at several industrial plants and companies were brought to life. Norsk Hydro was a key partner in these trials and has since identified with these trials and the resulting Norwegian model of democratic work-life relations. A national strategy for the humanization of work came out of these initiatives, and the model has in successive stages been heavily institutionalized in both Norwegian state laws—such as the law of employee representation on organization boards and, not least, the unique law on working environment—and particularly in comprehensive agreements between the work-life partners.

However, far from all major Norwegian business enterprises took part in the trials; on the contrary, major industrial and financial actors in the Norwegian system were formed in a much stronger sense (than in, for example, Norsk Hydro) by the American management tradition. This tradition was represented, in particular, by the management consultant George Kenning and what became the Kenning school in Norwegian business life, a more authoritarian ideology, top-down organization, which advocated the principles of "loyalty" and "following orders" (Sørhaug 1996). Thus, the contemporary Norwegian model in actual practice contains a continuing struggle over the main and opposing representations of what constitutes a company, its internal relations, and its role in society.

Norsk Hydro was a pioneer in the Norwegian industrial democracy program (Mumford 1997: 310), which contained a series of main principles and events: the first was creating improved representative systems of joint consultation, involving the establishment of "worker managers." Furthermore, the program focused on workplace democracy, with employees importantly gaining both the resources and the power to be able to change their own work organization when and where they judged it was necessary and appropriate (Mumford 2006).

Some of the results from the program became law and formal agreements, for example, giving workers the right to demand jobs conforming to certain sociotechnical and psychological principles and requirements, such as variety of work, personal decision-making power, learning opportunities and organizational support, a desirable future, and social recognition. Subsequently, a program initiated by Kristen Nygaard, the inventor of object-oriented software programming, emerged for increasing trade union competence in information technology and thereby, implicitly, trade union power (Mumford 1997). Important concepts that emerged out of the Norwegian Industrial Democracy Program were, for example, the ideas of sharing of responsibilities, worker participation and codetermination, autonomous work groups, or semiautonomous work groups, forerunners of concepts such as self-managing and self-directed work teams. Importantly, the core idea and value of the program, and arguably of the Nordic/Norwegian model, is democratization.

It was General Director (CEO) Johan B. Holte who took the initiative to involve Hydro in the industrial democracy program. Together with shop steward Tor Halvorsen, chairman of the labor union at Hydro's facilities at Herøya, Norway, Hydro put all its weight into the program (Lie 2005: 302–15). Holte said, for example, as Hydro communicates on their website:

> The most important is not the immediate increase in productivity and economic advantages, but that the human being and human values are put center stage ... It is a democratization of the work situation through a higher level of knowledge and through improved collaborative relationships. (My translation)[1]

We see again that humanization and democratization at work go hand in hand with productivity and economic gain. Hydro has thus maintained a long tradition of social responsibility, and their strong focus on HSE (health, safety, and environment) emerged in tandem with their commitment to the Norwegian model (Lie 2005); furthermore, this focus is an integral part of their own culture-building efforts and communicated purpose ("a more viable society") and values, summed up in their comprehensive company platform, the Hydro Way (Røyrvik 2013b).[2]

Drawing on the distinction between *explicit* and *implicit* forms and traditions of CSR (Matten and Moon 2008)—that is, explicitly codified and formulated corporate CSR policies versus CSR as implicitly assumed institutional frameworks in the companies—writers on CSR in the Nordic context highlight how the Nordic welfare regime and the Nordic model of tripartite agreements, partnerships, and social democratic political culture have also formed a Nordic tradition of implicit CSR and an implicit culture of CSR in Norwegian companies (e.g., Gjølberg 2010; Carson and Nilsen 2021). In this tradition, a consensus emerged that explicit CSR is redundant in the domestic context while increasingly necessary in international operations due to the perceived governance gap abroad.

Hydro was also, however, an early Norwegian industrial actor in formally adopting CSR as corporate policy, as evidenced by the 1996 employment of anthropologist Rolf Lunheim as a director to investigate the social and cultural implications of Hydro's controversial bauxite project in Utkal, India, where the local indigenous people engaged in civil disobedience to stop the project.[3] Hydro eventually pulled out of the project. Hydro's commitment to CSR was not least signaled by appointing an executive vice president of corporate social responsibility in 1999. CSR has since been a continuous area of responsibility for one of the executive vice presidents and part of the corporate management group. According to a 2002 article in the popular Norwegian engineering magazine *Teknisk Ukeblad*: "Hydro is one out of few Norwegian corporations actively working with CSR." The magazine interviews director Lunheim, who states: "Industry is a social matter where society and company have reciprocal economic interests that transcend cultural and religious differences. Hydro has since [its inception, with] its establishment at Rjukan [in Norway in 1905,] been in close contact with the local community and handled the challenges that emerge between industry and society" (my translation).[4]

In 2015, the title of one of the executive vice president positions was "CSR and General Counsel,"[5] which was changed in 2019 to "Legal, CSR, and Compliance."[6] In December 2019, a major reorganization created a new executive vice president position for "Corporate Development," in which one big area of responsibility is that of "Sustainability" (organized in "Group Sustainability"), which now incorporates social responsibility, the environment, a climate office, and extrafinancial reporting. According to Hydro, they perceive many advantages to gathering these areas of responsibility in one group, for example, to further develop their systems and routines for managing risk in their supply chain related to sustainability and human rights.[7] The reorganization may have been instigated by the severe environmental and social responsibility problems and critique of Hydro's operations at the Alunorte facility in Brazil (see chapter 4).[8] It would be safe to assume that CSR, like HSE, is now being considered an integral part of the way Hydro conducts its operations everywhere, and furthermore, that CSR is, in line with the broader trend, increasingly being subsumed under the heading "Sustainability" and formalized as explicit CSR policies, as for example in the Hydro Way corporate value-based management and identity platform.

Created in a thorough organizational brand process aided by the New York–based consultancy Siegal+Gale, which conducted interviews and surveys throughout the organization in 2003, the resulting comprehensive report was the foundation upon which the Hydro Way was launched in 2004 (Røyrvik 2013b). It highlighted Hydro's "mission, talents, and core values." Interestingly, in the Siegal+Gale report, three underlying external forces are highlighted as drivers of the need for Hydro to reorient and rebrand itself: a "more demanding shareholder," the "trend to internationalize," and a "growing sustainability imperative" (Røyrvik 2013b). A few quotes from the report illustrate how employees and managers highlight the continuing tradition of social responsibility in Hydro:

> "Working at Hydro, you have an understanding that what you are doing is important. It makes a difference, every day, in the lives of millions of people."
> —Agri Employee

> "We see the world through one lens where there is no distinction between business performance and social contribution. They are mutually supportive." —Corporate Employee

> "I don't think we have the capacity to isolate business needs from social needs—not without a lot of trial and some pain." —Aluminum Executive

> "For better, for worse, we've used profit in ways that let us contribute more over time—not just to customers and shareholders, but to people generally."
> —O&E Employee

> "We helped build a country not just a company. It is in our blood to see the world of business through the lens of society." —Corporate Executive

> "The very premise of our existence was to help found a nation, not just make money." —O&E Employee

> (Røyrvik 2013b: 20–23)

The Hydro Way and Hydro's increasing commitment to explicit forms of CSR illustrate the rise of organizational signification, expressiveness, and the rising importance of branding and image building (Røyrvik 2013b; Røvik 2007). In its new China ventures, Hydro very actively used the Hydro Way material, which was well received by local managers and employees there, while in Norway the material was often considered superfluous and of little relevance (Røyrvik 2013b). A quote from Hydro's facilitator of the Hydro Way process illustrates some of these issues (Røyrvik 2013b: 21).

> Of course, introducing the Hydro Way in such a culture as ours, it was unfamiliar for many. For most of our staff what Hydro is doing is self-evidently important and beneficial to society. It does not need any form of "profiling" or "branding." You know what we say, that Hydro has "a very high level of its low profile." This is because what we do permeates society fundamentally.

The Chinese employees I talked with often praised the Hydro Way material, typically highlighting how they liked both the way the company emphasized respect for people and the environment and, not least, the mission of a more viable society.

Even though there have been several ups and downs in the Hydro management's commitment to the Norwegian model's ideals of democratization and humanization, there is no doubt that there have been very close relationships and tight collaboration between management and workers/unions in Hydro since Holte became CEO in 1967. After a relatively slow period, the collaborative arrangements were revitalized, beginning in 1986, and Hydro's relationship with the main labor union, LO, and with the Norwegian national Labor Party has consistently been close and on good terms. For example, Halvorsen moved on to become head of LO, and the chairman of LO (Tor Aspengren) was, for several years, a member of the Hydro board of directors (Lie 2005). In sum, Hydro is an exemplary company in the sense of both co-constituting and instantiating the Nordic/Norwegian model, which at the macro level has been described as "democratic capitalism" (Sejersted 1993), where democracy is considered to be the overarching system value of capitalism, and the core question is how the economic domain can contribute to enabling democratic participation and societal development (Slagstad 2001). Though it has come under increasing pressure during the last decades (e.g., Byrkjeflot et al. 2001)—not least due to the neoliberal transformations of society, including, as I argue elsewhere, the strong shareholder turn in Hydro (Røyrvik 2013a)—to varying degrees, Hydro continues to strive to bring aspects and elements of this tradition when establishing ventures abroad. As Knudsen summarizes (see chapter 4), Hydro has widely been considered a model in terms of state ownership and with respect to social responsibility related to community, unions, and sustainability, as well as for a particular model of capital's embeddedness in society "exemplified especially by the alignment of 'corporate values' with 'Norwegian values'" (p. 117). Knudsen argues that it has increasingly become CSR and "Norwegian values" rather than Nordic model institutional arrangements that are pronounced in Hydro's self-presentation.

Focusing on the Norwegian model of democracy at work and its embedded tradition of implicit social responsibility in the community, as we shall see, these cultural practices and views traveled and translated in interesting ways in China.

Traveling with the Nordic Model and CSR to China

In 2002, Hydro opened their first wholly owned industrial plant in China, a magnesium alloy facility, in the ancient city of Xi'an. The ethnographic story of the plant is described in detail elsewhere (Røyrvik 2013a); here I want to scrutinize the case in light of the arguable "export" of the Nordic model to Xi'an and of the related notion of social responsibility. The Nordic model "on the move" can be considered a "traveling model" (Reyna 2007; Behrends et al. 2014)—that is, cultural intentions and plans to move some human practices and cultural views from somewhere and implement them elsewhere. As exemplified by the Nordic model, not all models emerge from the United States (Peck and Theodore 2015); Reyna (2007) highlights that not all traveling models travel equally well and distinguishes between high- and low-fidelity models. Setting up a McDonald's franchise in Norway can be considered a high-fidelity operation because of the relatively few contradictions encountered and the relative ease in standardizing and "copying" such operations. "Exporting" Western democracy to the Middle East or "implementing" development programs in Africa are low-fidelity cases because they involve much more socially complex, contested, and abstract ideas, institutions, and practices and are more difficult to standardize while simultaneously necessitating higher levels of multilateral relations and interaction. The fidelity of a model, in Reyna's words, is to some extent due to "the intensity of contradiction between different structural actors within fields of power ..." (Reyna 2007: 79), and low fidelity is the case when the efforts to implement a traveling model are in greater contradiction with the interests and operations of the other actors in the field where the model is arriving. As shown in the research referred to in the beginning of the chapter, which documents that the Nordic model is not "exported," it clearly does not travel well and can be considered low fidelity.

Hydro corporate management in Oslo deliberated for many years before deciding on establishing their first wholly owned production plant in China, what eventually became the Xi'an plant. Hydro had been criticized for not showing social responsibility when, in 2001, management decided to close the magnesium alloy plant at Herøya, Norway.[9] The main reason for establishing the plant in Xi'an was to serve the automotive market in Japan and the car makers that had established manufacturing plants in China. Hydro's main concern about entering China was related to the perception of cultural differences and the popular belief in the international business community that, because of those differences, foreign companies had substantial difficulties succeeding in China. Thus, Hydro finally opted for a management and organization model in the Xi'an venture that, to a considerable extent, ran counter to commitments to the Nordic model. Based on knowledge gained during management's participation in cultural training courses, Hydro decided on a quite radical adaptive localization strategy. Based on popular notions of Chinese culture as a Confucian, top-down, hierarchical, and loyalty-based system,

Hydro determined that they had to abandon the ideals of the Nordic model and needed to establish and run what they perceived to be a "Chinese company," with only Chinese managers and employees. This did not go well in the first years. The plant performed poorly on all indicators, from productivity to quality of metal to HSE. Marketwise, Japanese customers did not want the products from Xi'an. Hydro tried in successive moves to remedy the situation, first by substituting the first general manager (CEO) with a Chinese professional trained in the American management tradition, who introduced detailed management systems at the plant, and, not least, later, by moving a Hydro-internal Western general manager to the plant to try to secure, more or less at all costs, that the plant complied with HSE standards.

In Røyrvik (2013a), I disclose one of the main premises of the failure of the plant in the early years. It turned out that the Chinese managers and employees who were hired by Hydro in Xi'an had extensive knowledge beforehand about Hydro and the Nordic model. Partly because foreign companies are established in dedicated industrial zones and there is considerable exchange of knowledge and personnel between companies from different countries, the Chinese workforce in these zones is highly knowledgeable about the diverse models of management, organization, and culture that the various international companies represent.[10] The managers and employees at Hydro's Xi'an plant were thus seriously surprised and disappointed when it turned out that the plant was run the way it was, and there was a high turnover at the plant. As one local manager noted: "I wanted to work for a Norwegian company, but it was not as I thought it would be." However, I call this cultural encounter between Hydro and the local context and workforce in Xi'an during the first years a "reverse culture crash" (Røyrvik 2013a). It was a spectacular failure of cultural translation, where Hydro's local organization had been constructed based on notions of what the Norwegian-dominated international project team believed constituted a Chinese company, while the local workforce (the entire workforce was local) expected and anticipated working for an exemplary Nordic model company. The employees responded, in the way industrial sociology and anthropology have extensively documented, by sabotaging through silent protest, slow and sloppy work, and generally low motivation and lack of compliance with corporate policies. But as I will show below, much more productive encounters and translations eventually emerged. This initial failure of cultural translation illustrates how translation processes are people- and context-dependent, fragile, and, not least, susceptible to failure if reciprocal relationships, especially in terms of cultural knowledge in this case, are lacking. The case illustrates how culture is on the move, largely constituted in a postcolonial world in motion (Clifford 1997), as both "transnational and translational" (Bhabha 1992: 438).

The Xi'an facility was on Hydro's list of underperforming plants that corporate management contemplated closing down when a general manager very dedicated to the Nordic/Norwegian model was hired as a final effort to try to salvage the plant. This last GM was a technical expert with management experience from Hydro's Herøya industrial complex, arguably the most important site in Hydro's participation in the industrial democracy collaboration trials and in their co-development of the Nordic/Norwegian model. He had a strong commitment to the Norwegian model and conceived of Hydro as standing firmly in this tradition. He had also participated in establishing the plant in Xi'an; during that process, he had developed a keen interest in and knowledge of contemporary, local Chinese cultural notions and practices. He turned out to be quite a para-ethnographer, and I've related elsewhere (Røyrvik 2013a) how he was responsible, together with his local team, for turning the plant around completely. From being an underperforming plant, the Xi'an facility, in just over a year, became best in class, producing the highest quality magnesium alloys in the Hydro system (and arguably in the world), with high productivity and recognition as the best plant on HSE in the Hydro system. The skeptical Japanese customers now *only* wanted products from the Xi'an plant. The plant expanded production by 50 percent by installing a new production line and simultaneously expanding the site facility. This expansion was solely designed and managed by local plant managers, employees, and the GM, who also hired contractors and other essential personnel, and did not involve the Hydro-wide professional project organization as is normal procedure in projects of this scale and scope. Similarly, the plant became highly innovative, for example, by developing production technology that other Hydro plants also came to want and that the main R&D center at Herøya became involved with. Furthermore, the plant was offered prestigious R&D projects for high-end customers. With these developments, the plant had arguably reached a new and hybrid form of "democratic innovation management" that Hernes (2007) labels the Nordic model's ideal relationship between an involvement-oriented management and union-organized employees that is constituted through broad participation and codetermination.

The new GM said he used management and organization principles from Herøya and the Norwegian model to unleash the energy, motivation, creativity, and diligence of the plant employees with the eagerness of his all-Chinese workforce to learn, develop, and progress. He said that "in several ways it is more fulfilling to work as GM in a Norwegian-model type-of-way here at the Xi'an plant than in Norway, because of the vitality and responsiveness I experience from the employees." Manager and employee involvement surged under his leadership. He got his managers to believe in and apply many of the values and principles of the Nordic model, not least through his example of leadership through dialogue, constant involvement, and delegating power, responsibility, resources, and autonomy. Importantly, he consciously adopted an explicit stance and demeanor toward exemplifying high tolerance and acceptance of failure. "You have to show them in practice, in the way you react, that it is ok to do something wrong. And you must show it again and again." He had learned that what he called "the Maoist culture of chopping off people's heads for doing wrong" was the major obstacle toward enabling a culture of learning and taking responsibility and initiative. Thus, he used every opportunity to signal and exemplify that it is perfectly normal to be mistaken and to make bad judgments, but he insisted upon reflecting over each episode in a respectful and trusting atmosphere. "Failure and mistakes are opportunities for learning rather than punishment," was one of his credos, and "when the employees came to trust that this was actually the reality," he said, "their engines for learning and individual progress turned to full throttle."

Furthermore, working together with the HSE and HR (human resource) managers, the management team made the production workers become much more involved and active in a Nordic model way of working. For example, the classic suggestion box on the shop floor had been empty for a long time, but now a steady flow of suggestions came in from the operators and shop-floor stewards. The HSE manager was responsible for facilitating this change. She said: "Earlier maybe the employees didn't think there was any point in putting suggestions in the box, but now they really have started to believe that their inputs are valued and taken seriously."

The GM was held in very high esteem among the employees and managers, and his gentle style of management was frequently noted; for example, the quality control manager stated that "his management style is very soft, but he always gets us to do our best." Likewise, his genuine interest in his employees and in understanding the Chinese ways of thinking were often noted by the Chinese employees. His technical expertise was also an important source of his status and authority among the staff. He knew magnesium production through and through, and his implementation of Nordic model principles was mostly done by way of practical processes related to production. The GM was, however, careful to point out that he never simply copied a Herøya-type Norwegian model and tried to implement it "as is" in Xi'an. "I use values, ideas, and principles of management and organization from the Norwegian model and adapt them to the situation, people, and culture here," he said.

Hybrid Collaboration and the Traveling Cafeteria

One example of this form of adaption is that the systematic collaboration between management and unions in the Nordic model, both directly and indirectly through employee representation, had necessarily to take another shape in the Chinese context—especially the formal, representative collaboration. Only one union is allowed, the Chinese Communist Party's All-China Federation of Trade Unions (ACFTU). As in all foreign companies, the Xi'an plant had employed one representative from the union; interestingly, the union representative was the HSE manager at the plant. This role appropriation would, in a Nordic context as well as in many other countries, be considered a complete undermining of the labor union. However, in the eyes of both the GM and employees, the union representative did much to further collaboration and employee involvement and to foster good working conditions at the plant. In addition, the union representative (HSE manager) and the HR manager arranged to help employees outside of the plant, for example with housing. This is in keeping with part of the mandate of the labor union in China. However, this type of social welfare is also quite dependent on the discretion of the employer and the work of the union representatives. At Hydro Xi'an, according to the GM as well as the HSE and HR managers, they wanted workers to influence their own situation both at and outside of work. This approach to translation illustrates one of the main dictums of translation in ANT, that instead of "transmission" it is a process of "continuous transformation" (Latour 1984: 268) that leads to a chain of context-dependent translations. In the context of formal organizations and institutions, this might be translated, as it were, to Czarniawska and Sevón's claim that "to set something in a new place is to construct it anew" (2005: 8). In ANT, "translation is the mechanism by which the social and the natural worlds progressively take form" (Callon 1984: 224), and it was indeed the construction of a new form of hybrid "Nordic-Xi'an model" at play.

Hydro had, like most international companies, also employed several so-called migrant workers, often considered unskilled, moving in from other Chinese provinces to work. In China, these workers have, in general, few social rights and are frequently exploited by employers, but at Hydro they were relatively well paid (three times more than they could expect, according to the GM), and the HSE and HR managers put in a lot of effort to help the workers in terms of what the workers themselves wanted. The workers were very satisfied with and expressed excitement about the kinds of support and training they received and the opportunities that were afforded. As one production worker emphasized: "I learn many new things and improve my skills." The managers also went out into the local community and supported workers outside of the plant by, for example, helping them enroll in courses to enhance professional skills and to learn English as well as with other socioeconomic and psychosocial issues. The HR manager emphasized this strongly and said: "We help many workers with their economic affairs so that they, for example, are able to acquire their own housing." According to managers and employees, this social responsibility helped improve both motivation and productivity at the plant, and the plant produced much more and of better quality than expected by anyone in the Hydro system. This extended, networked way of translating the Nordic model, both within the corporation and in the local community, and in collaboration between management and the Chinese "union," illustrates how cultural translation is not a unilateral sender-receiver type of communication or transfer logistics but rather, as Bachmann-Medick (2006) maintains, a dynamic process of transformation that takes shape in reciprocal forms of cultural encounters characterized by negotiation of cultural difference.

Some other important examples illustrate Hydro's approach to the Nordic model and social responsibility in their China venture. One early discussion on CSR in China was whether Hydro should acquire and own the Chinese supply companies providing the raw magnesium needed for the alloy plant. These suppliers had severe challenges in terms of HSE and issues of social responsibility. Should Hydro acquire some suppliers to secure stable and high-quality supplies of raw magnesium and simultaneously take responsibility to lift and develop these suppliers to Hydro standards? Hydro finally concluded that they could not take on such a total supply chain responsibility: it was too risky, and too much investment would be required. They opted for the route of trying to affect the suppliers in what they saw as a positive way by being a demanding customer that required certain standards of HSE in order to purchase from the suppliers. They established a group of suppliers that they worked in close collaboration with, both to improve quality of the metal and standards of HSE. The example highlights some of the ethical dilemmas of corporate social responsibility.

Another early and important event related to CSR ensued when Hydro, in the preparations of the construction site, was met with demonstrations by local farmers. Hydro had an agreement with the Xi'an municipality for use of the land for the plant and, before hiring a subcontractor to prepare the construction site, had been assured that everything was formally in order. The local farmers, however, occupied the site and managed to physically shut down the work. Hydro, at first, left the problem to be solved by the municipality, because formally the issue of the land was a question between the municipality and the farmers. But Hydro soon left this formalistic path and chose, with the indispensable aid of their own local Chinese consultants, to negotiate directly with the farmers. It turned out that the farmers felt they had not been compensated adequately for the land by the municipality. Hydro and the farmers came to an agreement by giving the farmers access to paid work in the preparation of the site; the local farmers, with shovels, crowbars, levers, and small machines, worked side by side with big bulldozers from the subcontractor. Some people from the local farming community were also later hired as production workers at the plant. In the aftermath of the resolved conflict, which had delayed the completion of the plant considerably, as one of Hydro's project managers explained: "We enjoyed an excellent relationship with the local farmers," who, in large numbers and in ceremonial costumes, ritually inaugurated the plant site. This exemplifies a practical kind of social responsibility Hydro undertook in the Xi'an project.

An important example related to the "traveling Nordic model" and linked with CSR was found in the discussions and negotiations related to the design of the infrastructure plant, especially as concerned the plant's cafeteria. In the planning and project phase, some of the important local Chinese advisors and consultants, either working for Hydro or hired on contractual basis by Hydro, wanted two separate cafeterias at the plant. The plant was designed by the project group, mostly Norwegian engineers, according to more or less standard Hydro principles and values, where an important symbolic idiom is *one* joint cafeteria for all staff, operators, office workers, and managers alike. This design instigated discussions in the project phase in China, where local representatives thought this would be alien in the Chinese context and argued for two cafeterias, one for production workers and one for managers and office staff. This would more appropriately reflect local cultural notions of authority and power chains, as well as each group's place in the organizational structure and hierarchy, they argued. The Norwegian-based project team refused and ultimately won the discussion, arguing that a joint cafeteria is part of the way Hydro works and would facilitate better collaboration, involvement, and relations at the plant. The project team had to negotiate this issue also because the chosen strategy was first to create a "Chinese company," but as this specific case shows, from the inception there were negotiations between the perceived need for radical local adaptation against Hydro and the Nordic model principles. The joint cafeteria was explicitly referred to by Hydro managers as reflecting the Norwegian model of close collaboration between management and production, and further it was to be a signal of equality, low hierarchies, and a short distance to power. It might be perceived as a concrete, *material metaphor*, instantiated in the plant design and building structure, of some of the ideals, values, and principles of the Norwegian model. Here we see that infrastructure design is an integral part of the traveling Nordic/Norwegian model as it was negotiated and translated in the local Chinese context.

Importantly, in ANT, translation is enacted through processes of *inscription*, "the result of translating one's interest into material form" (Callon 1991: 143). Referring to Reyna's (2007) distinction between high- and low-fidelity traveling models and the conceptual pair of inscription and translation in ANT, I suggest that in this case the infrastructure design was inscribed with aspects of the Nordic model in a way that helped a low-fidelity model travel. This inscription in plant design and its material infrastructure functioned as a material metaphor contributing to a partially successful translation of a low-fidelity model in China—a translation that came on most strongly, as we have seen, several years after the opening of the plant. The cafeteria case might furthermore be interpreted as Hydro taking on social responsibility of furthering democratic workplace ideals through their international operation, which is significant in the Chinese context.

From Export to Travel and Translation

If we summarize key characteristics of the Norwegian model and how it traveled and was translated at the Xi'an plant, an interesting picture emerges. Of formal representative roles and functions of the Norwegian model, only the safety representative was directly implemented, while neither employee representation on the board nor collective wage negotiations were adopted. Both of these deficits relate to the constraints placed on independent labor unions in the Chinese institutional context. The company had, however, a huge *collective* bonus system based on productivity, which (only) partly ameliorated the problem of the lack of collective wage negotiations. On the other hand, the main principles of organizational design (work roles, hierarchy, responsibility, plant infrastructure such as the cafeteria, etc.) were adopted. Fully developed autonomous work groups were not established, according to the GM, but there was continuous development in this direction.

In terms of the psychological job demands, so central in the Norwegian industrial democracy project and materialized in the Norwegian law on working environment, these demands were in practice translated in the local context. Meaningful work and a variety of tasks; having one's own decision-making power, learning opportunities, and organizational support; and social recognition for independent efforts as well as linking work with a desirable future were all issues that were part of the relationships and codetermination at the plant. According to the Xi'an GM and former Herøya technical expert and manager, the collaborative relationships between management and the union were in fact better in Xi'an than at Herøya—the cradle of the Hydro Norwegian model. In Xi'an, the GM maintained, both managers and employees were (more) genuinely concerned about improving the plant and making money and that the employees should have a good life both at work and outside of work.

Communication and collaboration between management and the union (and workers) was, as described above, very different in formal organization than in the Norwegian context, but at the same time, on a very high level in terms of participation and codetermination. The collaborative relationship, although labor was organized completely differently with the HSE manager as both union and communist party representative at the plant, involved everything from production and productivity, professional training and development, to R&D, innovation, and, not least, socioeconomic and psychosocial issues both inside and outside of the plant. At the most basic level, it is evident that Hydro eventually, after the failed attempt of establishing a so-called Chinese company in Xi'an, was to a large extent able to translate values and principles of democracy at work so vital in the constitution of the ideal (and idealized) Norwegian model of work, organization, and management.

As shown, the more practical and institutional materialization of the values and principles were, by both personal experience and preference (e.g., the Herøya GM) and necessity (e.g., Chinese constraints and different mandate of the "labor union"), as well as the complex transnational relationships mobilized, manifested in hybrid forms and emerged in dynamic cultural encounters that co-constructed cultural practices and models anew. In conclusion, we might appreciate that acts of social responsibility in Hydro's translations in the Xi'an venture eventually could be interpreted as a new hybrid international-localized version of the Nordic/Norwegian model so formative of the Hydro company. In line with Bachmann-Medick's (2006) claim, the case highlights how (cultural) translation has become a concept of generative relationships and movement, and transformation, or what Clifford (1997) theorized as "travel and translation." This translational conceptualization of culture transcends the "them-us" frame of classification in conventional ethnography (Marcus 1995) and the colonial imaginary. Rather, it establishes cultural relations and models as associations (Latour 1984, 1987) formed in multilateral encounters of negotiation and mobilization, including conflict, empathy, and power, over cultural differences and possibilities.

Hydro, in its Xi'an investment, chose at first an unusually strict strategy of an adaptive, decentralized, and domestic orientation (trying to become what they believed to be a completely "Chinese company"). This failed both in terms of productivity, quality measures, market situation and HSE, work environment, and motivation. It was an interesting failure of translation, in which Hydro constructed Chinese culture in a reified and static way, whereas local Chinese employees expected to work for a Nordic model company. After some trial and error to save a disastrous situation, Hydro eventually moved toward a much more explicit orientation focusing on adapting a Nordic/Norwegian-like model in Xi'an. The process became in reality a transnational and translational orientation where several practices of organization, management, and diverse cultural practices and traditions were translated and integrated in hybrid and "glocalized" (Robertson 1995) transformations. This included local practices and vernaculars as well as practices and systems from the American management tradition, but in the emerging new assemblage some of the core values, principles, and aspects of the Nordic/Norwegian model were highly present and visible. As we saw, for example, the Nordic and Hydro model tradition of responsibility in the community (see also chapter 4) met in new ways local Chinese notions and practices of communal responsibilities through the particular type of Chinese "union" ACFTU.

Interestingly, the Nordic tradition of implicit CSR was a notable part of the *project* of establishing the plant in Xi'an from day one. This has probably much to do with the fact that the nonlocal project team members were mostly experienced project managers and experts with long careers in Hydro Norway. The consequences of the decision to run an "all-Chinese" plant surfaced mostly when the project phase terminated and the plant went into the phase of daily operations. After almost being closed and with the subsequent turnaround, aspects of the Nordic model and its implicit CSR component surfaced again and were realized to a large extent at the plant in operation. Furthermore, we see that, when the Hydro Way material was launched, it was thoroughly introduced and well received at Hydro's Chinese plants; this success can be taken to exemplify and support the literature emphasizing the broad emergence of explicit CSR in Norwegian-based companies' international operations.

The chapter argues, in some opposition to the extant literature, that the Hydro case in Xi'an shows that some of the core aspects and practices of the Nordic model successfully traveled and translated to an authoritarian regime and that corporate social responsibility in this case can be read into the way the core values and principles of this model—democratization and humanization and all that these entail—are enacted at the workplace and beyond. In the translations demonstrated in the present case, we can also perceive of a particular case in Hydro's international engagements and approach to CSR as part of Hydro's tight history and relationship to the Norwegian state and its self-image as a "humanitarian superpower"—an active promoter and "exporter" of moral values of good, be it through peace building, humanitarian work, or, as in this case, democratization and broader social responsibilities of Norwegian-based TNCs. Reified, formulaic, and static ideas about the Nordic model, as well as theoretical concepts steeped in unilateral sender-receiver notions of "export" and "transfer," might stand in the way of discovering similar kinds of travels and translations in other cases and contexts.

Acknowledgments

I want to thank Norsk Hydro and its members for providing an open and interesting research environment and for extensive ethnographic collaborations during an eight-year period. I also want to thank the editor and two anonymous reviewers for good advice and feedback.

Emil A. Røyrvik is an anthropologist and professor in the Department of Sociology and Political Science, Norwegian University of Science and Technology (NTNU). Based broadly in sociocultural anthropology and interdisciplinary research, Røyrvik's work focuses on ethnography and theorizing in the context of moral and political economy, especially capitalism as a social system (including financialization and inequality), professional knowledge work, organizational, managerial and expert cultures, money and measurement, and economic and cultural globalization. His book *The Allure of Capitalism: An Ethnography of Management and the Global Economy in Crisis* (Berghahn Books, 2011) is based on extensive ethnographic research collaboration with Norsk Hydro.

Notes

1. "Det viktigste er ikke den øyeblikkelige økning av produktiviteten og økonomiske fordeler, men at mennesket og de menneskelige verdier blir satt i sentrum … Det er en demokratisering av arbeidssituasjonen gjennom et høyere kunnskapsnivå og gjennom forbedrede samarbeidsforhold." See https://www.hydro.com/no-NO/om-hydro/var-historie/1946-1977/1966-de-fant-tonen-og-formet-en-foregangsbedrift/ (retrieved 15 December 2020).
2. See 'the Hydro Way' material here: https://www.hydro.com/globalassets/08-about-hydro/the-hydro-way/hydro_brochures_a4_en.pdf (retrieved 20 January 2021).
3. See https://www.framtiden.no/199602014843/aktuelt/bedrifters-samfunnsansvar/sivil-ulydighet-mot-hydros-bauxitt-prosjekt.html (retrieved 20 January 2021).
4. Dordi Digre, "Mer etikk i bagasjen" [More ethics onboard], *Teknisk Ukeblad*, 10 January 2002, retrieved 20 January 2021 from https://www.tu.no/artikler/mer-etikk-i-bagasjen/219547.
5. See https://www.hydro.com/no-NO/media/news/2014/Endringer-i-Hydros-konsern ledelse/ (retrieved 23 January 2021).
6. See https://www.hydro.com/en-NO/media/news/2019/changes-in-hydros-corporate-management-board/ (retrieved 23 January 2021).
7. Source: Hydro Group Sustainability (personal communication).
8. See, for example, https://www.reuters.com/article/us-norsk-hydro-brazil-idUSKCN1SR2IK (retrieved 15 January 2021).
9. See, for example, https://www.nrk.no/okonomi/nedleggelse-pa-heroya-1.545103 (retrieved 8 April 2021).

10. The All-China Federation of Trade Unions (ACFTU), the Communist Party labor union, with its 130–280 million members, is also an important factor in terms of knowledge exchange among managers and employees. All foreign companies have a representative from the ACFTU on their staff, and information about the various foreign companies and their respective traditions travels through this network (more on the role of this type of labor union below).

References

Bachmann-Medick, Doris. 2006. "Meaning of Translation in Cultural Anthropology." In *Translating Others*, vol. 1, edited by Theo Hermans, 33–42. Manchester: St. Jerome.
Bakan, Joel. 2004. *The Corporation: The Pathological Pursuit of Profit and Power*. London: Constable.
Behrends, Andrea, Sung-Joon Park, and Richard Rottenburg, eds. 2014. *Travelling Models in African Conflict Management: Translating Technologies of Social Ordering*. Leiden: Brill.
Bhabha, Homi K. 1992. "Postcolonial Criticism." In *Redrawing the Boundaries: The Transformation of English and American Studies*, edited by Stephen Greenblatt and Giles Gunn, 473–65. New York: Modern Language Association of America.
Bower, Joseph L., and Lynn S. Paine. 2017. "The Error at the Heart of Corporate Leadership. Most CEOs and Boards Believe Their Main Duty Is to Maximize Shareholder Value. It's Not." *Harvard Business Review*, May–June. Retrieved 10 January 2021 from https://hbr.org/2017/05/the-error-at-the-heart-of-corporate-leadership?ab=seriesnav-spotlight.
Børve, Hege, and Elin Kvande. 2018. "Den norske samarbeidsmodellen: Egnet for eksport til USA?" [The Norwegian cooperation model: Suitable for export to the USA?]. *Tidsskrift for Samfunnsforskning* 59(1): 26–40. doi: 10.18261/ISSN.1504-291X-2018-01-02.
Byrkjeflot, Haldor, Sissel Myklebust, Christine Myrvang, and Francis Sejersted, eds. 2001. *The Democratic Challenge to Capitalism: Management and Democracy in the Nordic Countries*. Bergen: Fagbokforlaget.
Callon, Michel. 1984. "Some Elements of a Sociology of Translation: Domestication of the Scallops and the Fishermen of St. Brieuc Bay." *Sociological Review*, Supplement 32(1): 196–233. doi: 10.1111/j.1467-954x.1984.tb00113.x.
———. 1991. "Techno-economic Networks and Irreversibility." In *A Sociology of Monsters: Essays on Power, Technology and Domination*, edited by J. Law, 132–61. London: Routledge.
Carson, Siri G., and Heidi R. Nilsen. 2021. "CSR in the Norwegian Context." In *Sovereign Wealth Funds, Local Content Policies and CSR*, edited by Eduardo G. Pereira, Rochelle Spencer, and Jonathon W. Moses, 621–33. Cham: Springer.
Clifford, James. 1997. *Routes: Travel and Translation in the Late Twentieth Century*. Cambridge, MA: Harvard University Press.
Clifford, James, and George E. Marcus, eds. 1986. *Writing Culture: The Poetics and Politics of Ethnography*. Berkeley: University of California Press.
Czarniawska, Barbara, and G. Sevón. 2005. *Global Ideas: How Ideas, Objects and Practices Travel in the Global Economy*. Malmö: Liber.
Drucker, Peter F. 1993 [1946]. *The Concept of the Corporation*. New York: Routledge.
———. 2006 [1954]. *The Practice of Management*. New York: Harper Business.
Emery, Fred, and Einar Thorsrud. 1976. *Democracy at Work*. Leiden: Martinus Nijhoff.
Freeman, R. Edward. 1984. *Strategic Management: A Stakeholder Approach*. Boston: HarperCollins.
Friedman, Milton. 1970. "A Friedman Doctrine—The Social Responsibility of Business Is to Increase its Profit." *New York Times*, 13 September, Section SM, p. 7. Retrieved 12 January 2021 from https://www.nytimes.com/1970/09/13/archives/a-friedman-doctrine-the-social-responsibility-of-business-is-to.html.

Gjølberg, Maria. 2010. "Varieties of Corporate Social Responsibility (CSR): CSR Meets That 'Nordic Model.'" *Regulation and Governance* 3: 203–29.
Hernes, Gudmund. 2007. "Med på laget" [On the team]. *Fafo Report 09*. ISSN: 0801: 6143.
Ho, Karen. 2009. *Liquidated: An Ethnography of Wall Street*. Durham, NC: Duke University Press.
Ihlen, Øyvind. 2011. *Samfunnsansvar på Norsk: Tradisjon og kommunikasjon* [CSR in Norwegian: Tradition and communication]. Bergen: Fagbokforlaget.
Knudsen, Ståle, Dinah Rajak, Siri Lange, and Isabelle Hugøy. 2020. "Corporate Social Responsibility and the Paradoxes of State Capitalism." *Focaal—Journal of Global and Historical Ethnography* 88: 1–21.
Larsen, T. 2009. *Den globale samtalen* [The global conversation]. Oslo: Scandinavian Academic Press.
Latour, Bruno. 1984. "The Powers of Association." *Sociological Review*, Supplement 32(1): 264–80. doi: 10.1111/j.1467-954x.1984.tb00115.x
——. 1987. *Science in Action: How to Follow Scientists and Engineers through Society*. Cambridge, MA: Harvard University Press.
Lie, Einar. 2005. *Oljerikdommer og internasjonal ekspansjon: Hydro 1977–2005*. [Oil wealth and international expansion: Hydro 1977–2005]. Oslo: Pax Forlag.
Lorenz, Chris. 2012. "If You're So Smart, Why Are You Under Surveillance? Universities, Neoliberalism, and New Public Management." *Critical Inquiry* 38(3): 599–629.
Løken, Espen, Geir Falkenberg, and Torunn Kvinge. 2008. "Norsk arbeidslivsmodell—ikke for eksport?" ["Norwegian work-life model—not for export?"]. *Fafo-report*, no. 32.
Marcus, George E. 1995. "Ethnography in/of the World System: The Emergence of Multi-sited Ethnography." *Annual Review of Anthropology* 24: 95–117.
Marcuse, Herbert. 2002 [1964]. *One-Dimensional Man*. New York: Routledge.
Marrewijk, Marcel van. 2003. "Concepts and Definitions of CSR and Corporate Sustainability: Between Agency and Communion." *Journal of Business Ethics* 44(2/3): 95–105.
Matten, Dirk, Andrew Crane, and Wendy Chapple. 2003. "Behind the Mask: Revealing the True Face of Corporate Citizenship." *Journal of Business Ethics* 45 (1/2): 109–20.
Matten, Dirk, and Jeremy Moon. 2008. "'Implicit' and 'Explicit' CSR: A Conceptual Framework for a Comparative Understanding of Corporate Social Responsibility." *Academy of Management Review* 33(2): 404–24.
Mumford, E. 1997. "The Reality of Participative Systems Design: Contributing to Stability in a Rocking Boat." *Information Systems Journal* 7(4) (October): 309–22.
——. 2006. "The Story of Socio-technical Design: Reflections on Its Successes, Failures and Potential." *Information Systems Journal* 16(4) (October): 317–42.
Peck, Jamie, and Nik Theodore. 2015. *Fast Policy: Experimental Statecraft at the Thresholds of Neoliberalism*. Minneapolis: University of Minnesota Press.
Reyna, Stephen P. 2007. "The Traveling Model That Would Not Travel: Oil, Empire, and Patrimonialism in Contemporary Chad." *Social Analysis: The International Journal of Anthropology* 51(3): 78–102.
Robertson, Roland. 1995. "Glocalization: Time-Space and Homogeneity-Heterogeneity." In *Global Modernities*, edited by M. Featherstone, S. Lash, and R. Robertson, 25–44. London: Sage.
Røyrvik, Emil A. 2013a. *The Allure of Capitalism. An Ethnography of Management and the Global Economy in Crisis*. New York: Berghahn Books.
——. 2013b. "Incarnation Inc.: Managing Corporate Values." *Journal of Business Anthropology* 2(1): 9–32.
Røvik, Kjell A. 2007. *Trender og translasjoner: Ideer som former det 21. århundres organisasjon* [Trends and translations: Ideas shaping the 21st century's organization]. Oslo: Universitetsforlaget.
Sejersted, Francis. 1993. *Demokratisk kapitalisme* [Democratic capitalism]. Oslo: Universitetsforlaget.

Slagstad, Rune. 2001. *De nasjonale strateger* [The national strategists]. Oslo: Pax Forlag.
Sørhaug, Tian. 1996. *Om ledelse: Makt og tillit i moderne organisering* [On management: Power and trust in modern organizing]. Oslo: Universitetsforlaget.
Thorsrud, Einar, and Fred Emery. 1970. *Mot en ny bedriftsorganisasjon* [Toward a new company organization: Experiments in industrial democracy]. Oslo: Tanum.
Trist, Eric L., and Ken W. Bamforth. 1951. "Some Social and Psychological Consequences of the Longwall Method of Coal-Getting." *Human Relations* 4: 3–38.

— Chapter 6 —

BETWEEN SOCIAL FOOTPRINT AND COMPLIANCE, OR "WHAT IBAMA WANTS"

Equinor Brazil's Social Sustainability Policy

Iselin Åsedotter Strønen

In June 2018, a group of around twenty women gathered at a handicraft and agricultural fair in Campos dos Goytacazes, a northern coastal oil-hub city in the state of Rio de Janeiro, Brazil. The women were selling cakes and meat pies, straw mats, embroidered tablecloths and kitchen towels, figurines made of seashells, and other products typical of regional handicraft traditions. While other stalls at the fair identified the vendors as belonging to an agricultural cooperative or a *quilombo* (protected communities descending from African slaves), the women found shade under a somewhat differently decorated party tent, one bearing the logo of the Norwegian state oil company Statoil (now Equinor).

The women are part of a long-term environmental education project financed by Equinor, aimed at women making a (very meager) living in the processing chain of artisan fishery. The project, called PEA FOCO (Environmental Education Project Strengthening Community Organization/ Projeto de Educação Ambiental Fortalecimento da Organização Comunitária), provides education in environmental governance, civic and political rights, and gender issues, and seeks to enable the women to pursue alternative and supplementary livelihoods. Participating at the fair with homemade handicrafts is an example of the latter. The project is not a voluntary CSR (corporate social responsibility) project but a prerequisite of the Brazilian state for Equinor's operating license in the offshore Peregrino field in the Campos basin. Other foreign companies operating in the oil and gas sector are facing the same conditions. While the project itself—scheduled to last for as long as the Peregrino field is in operation[1]—is run by a contracted Brazilian consulting firm called TRANS FOR MAR, Equinor is the project owner. Equinor Brazil reports on the project to a federal agency, IBAMA (Brazilian Institute of the Environment and Renewable Natural Resources/Instituto Brasileiro do Meio Ambiente e dos Recursos Naturais Renováveis),[2] a subdivision of the Brazilian Ministry of the Environment. If IBAMA were to be unhappy with the project, it could lead to a potentially toilsome embroilment between Equinor and IBAMA and to delays in future licensing processes, and it could also, as a hypothetical worst-case scenario (though politically unlikely), jeopardize Equinor's current operating license.

The Peregrino field, Brazil's most developed offshore field, is located approximately seventy kilometers off the coast of the state of Rio de Janeiro (region Norte Fluminense). Equinor has been present in Brazil since 2001 and started up production in the Peregrino field in 2011 (Equinor 2020.[3] The Peregrino field is Equinor's largest operation outside Norway,[4] and the company has expanded its Brazilian portfolio substantially during recent years. In 2018, Equinor Brazil was singled out as a separate business area because the increasing scope and complexity of Equinor's Brazil operations required a more autonomous management structure.

The PEA FOCO project has been running since 2011. In 2016, it won Equinor's internal SSU (safety and sustainability) award as the best social sustainability project among all projects worldwide. PEA FOCO is also positively viewed by Brazilian authorities, which since 2011 have obliged oil companies to develop projects benefiting different disenfranchised social groups in impacted onshore communities. At the time of field research, the projects in the Campos basin (in addition to Equinor's project) included projects targeting fishermen (Petrobras), youth (Chevron), and *quilombola* communities (Shell), as well as an environmental observation laboratory (Petrorio).

This chapter seeks to understand the sociopolitical and socioterritorial context surrounding the PEA FOCO project, as well as the dynamics characterizing the relationship between Equinor and Brazilian authorities. This allows me to "resituate the state ... as central to our understanding of what CSR *does* both for companies themselves and its target publics" as aptly formulated in the introduction (emphasis in original) to this edited volume. To that end, I will address three main interrelated research questions: What are the main contextual characteristics of the region where the PEA FOCO project is embedded? How is the project conceptualized by the different actors involved: Equinor, IBAMA, the consultancy, and project participants? And how does the fact that PEA FOCO is a legal requirement impact the way in which it is operationalized and conceptualized within Equinor?

The chapter is based on four fieldwork trips to Rio de Janeiro and the Campos region in the period 2017–19, where I conducted participant observation and unstructured interviews with employees in Equinor's Rio office, in IBAMA, and with the women and consultants in the PEA FOCO project.

Analytical Facets of CSR

Approaching CSR practices and discourses through an ethnographic lens allows us to unpack how this policy field is discursively constituted, contextually conceptualized, and practically enacted under different circumstances and in different locations. CSR can best be seen as "an evolving and flexible and overlapping set of practices and discourses" (Dolan and Rajak 2016: 5) that are undercut by the assumption that corporations somehow stand in a relationship with and have a responsibility to society. What this relationship and responsibility consist of is, however, one of the core issues of discordance both within the research community and out in the "real world." The concept originated from the United States as a management model set in the particular American ideological, political and financial context, where the rationale was to align profit maximization with social expectations (Gjølberg 2010: 204), for example through philanthropy. During the past decades it has spread throughout the world and beyond the business community, and in the process been adapted to different political, cultural, and institutional contexts and ideas of governance (Gjølberg 2010).

Researchers have deployed a wide variety of perspectives to frame different subsets of CSR research, ranging from "the business perspective" on how CSR can contribute to securing "the bottom line," to a "societal perspective" that investigates CSR's role and effect. While the former perspective, that is, "the bottom line," dominated the first phase of CSR research, increasing focus has been placed on how it impacts communities and societies (Brejning 2012: 1, see, e.g., Rajak 2011; Welker 2014).

The literature on CSR has frequently considered the voluntary aspect—as opposed to mandatory—as one of its defining characteristics (Banerjee 2008: 60; Van Aaken, Splitter, and Seidl 2013: 352).

However, the flexibility of CSR as a concept and practice implies that it has also been taken to encompass other dimensions of business practice faced with externally defined parameters, such as labor regulations and environmental standards (Brejning 2012: 1). Moreover, the introduction of mandatory CSR provisions in several countries has prompted researchers to question the voluntary characteristic of the concept, and to call for theory development that encompasses both its voluntary and mandatory dimensions (Waagstein 2011; Gatti et al. 2017).

Noting that there is no precise definition of the CSR concept among academics, Gjølberg argues that "defining CSR is not just a technical exercise, but a normative and an ideological exercise as well" (Gjølberg 2010: 205). Researchers are thus faced with the fact that conceptual clarity of the concept presents itself as an issue on two levels: both as regards theoretical definition of CSR for the purpose of analysis, and what kind of actions, guidelines, and policies public authorities, corporations, CSR practitioners, and others define as CSR in any given empirical context. Comparative discussion thus requires "a working definition of the concept" (Waagstein 2011: 465). For the purpose of the analytical focus of this chapter, I apply a broad theoretical definition of CSR that encompasses both voluntary and mandatory initiatives and regulations that go beyond the corporation's core undertaking, and invoke and/or allude to the corporation's responsibility vis-à-vis society. This working definition allows me to situate this study within the CSR literature, at the same time as it allows for incorporating ethnographic findings that reveal diverse emic interpretations of whether the PEA FOCO project is regarded as CSR or not.

The reason for doing so is that the case presented here does represent a modality of CSR that goes beyond definitions of the concept as voluntary initiatives with an ostensible social- and community-oriented purpose, insofar as it is, firstly, compulsory and, secondly, emerging from the historical development of environmental licensing practices in Brazil. Within IBAMA there were some discordances as regards to whether these policies were conceptually defined as something different from CSR (e.g., as an evolving legal and institutional trajectory of environmental licensing processes) or whether these policies were framed and discussed as part of various modalities (including "orthodox" voluntary CSR) in which O&G companies engage with local communities. From an etic perspective, it thus makes sense to discuss this case in relation to the CSR literature exactly because it illustrates the heterogeneity and context specificity of business-state-society relations and regulations in practice, and of the malleability of the ethos that corporations have a commitment to society and adjacent communities. The case also illuminates how Equinor Brazil conceives of the project as a "hybrid," as regards both their "social footprint" (speaking to the idea of CSR) and "compliance" (speaking to the idea of complying with mandatory environmental licensing standards). Thus, even though the project is mandatory, it cannot be considered exterior to the "travelling idea" of CSR (Gjølberg 2010: 205), neither emically nor etically.

Dashwood and Puplampu argue that "when assessing a company's commitment to CSR principle it is important to 'unpack' the firm and analyze its internal dynamics" (2010: 192). The analysis reveals that Equinor Brazil's company structure and hierarchy harbors and engenders heterogeneous rationales and perceptions within the corporation regarding the role and importance of the PEA FOCO project. Inquiry into these dynamics reminds us that we must also unpack the dynamics between the corporation and the regulatory bodies it relates to. Studies of the dynamics between extractive companies and their host state reveal how this relationship is shaped by complexity and friction at various scales, encompassing global capitalism in the widest sense as well as the intimate workings of personal human relationships (see, e.g., Appel 2019 and Shever 2012 for the O&G sector; see Welker 2014 and Rajak 2012 for the mining sector). This study extends our understanding of the convoluted processes shaping energy politics, showing how internal and politicized dynamics in the host state influence how CSR policies are formulated and negotiated within the corporation. Such a multilayered and multiprocessual perspective allows us to take into account a broader panorama of factors that shape the field where CSR policies are crafted in a given locality and temporality.

CSR in Brazil

CSR and its implications for international development have since long been discussed and problematized (Blowfield and Frynas 2005). The inclusion or exclusion of particular groups and interests through the figure of "the stakeholder" (Blowfield and Frynas 2005: 508), ideological perceptions of the issues (e.g., "poverty") that CSR should ameliorate (2005: 510–11), and the question of whether CSR can compensate for or "improve" faulty governance in developing economies (2005: 50) are all questions that highlight CSR's far-reaching implications. Hilson (2012) argues that the encounter between extractive industries and developing countries is characterized by different factors than those of extractive industries operating in developed countries. Faulty state structures, weak judicial architecture, corruption, fragile civil societies, and the countries' weak economic strength vis-à-vis the companies they are hosting are among the factors that spur companies to set the terms for their own engagement (Hilson 2012). Therefore, CSR efforts made by O&G companies in developing countries have frequently been illusory or even deceiving. A major obstacle is the lack of national regulations and regulatory bodies, with the implication that citizens do not have institutions they can hold accountable (Hilson 2012: 133). Consequently, Hilson argues that "for CSR to be effective in any location, there must be a foundation of robust regulations and enforcement in place for it to *complement*" (2012: 136, emphasis in original). Assuming that Hilson here understands efficiency as equivalent to "complying with stated goals," CSR has to work in tandem with a state order; it cannot function efficiently in an institutional and judicial vacuum. That is not to say that CSR practices in so-called developed countries do not also raise questions of accountability and power, but a case can be made for there being additional layers of challenges present in so-called developing countries.

Several of the abovementioned issues hit the mark for Brazil. Corruption, large gaps between decision makers and civil society, enormous social inequalities, a judicial and political system saturated with elite and corporate power, and a long history of environmental destruction provide ample space for unaccountable corporate action. Concurrently, Brazil is one of the world's major emerging economies, which are often referred to as the BRIC countries.[5] It has a long history of O&G industry that has fostered the establishment of a national expertise, institutional and judicial norms and structures, and public attention to the extractive economy. While mainstream media is decidedly "business friendly," Brazil also has a long history of "counterforces" to corporate and elite power — social movements, civil society organizations, and progressive intellectuals. These are, however, unevenly distributed across Brazil's enormous and heterogeneous territory and are constantly fighting an uphill battle.

Brazil has a lengthy and bleak record of corporate space for loopholing social and environmental concerns. But the country also has a relatively established "CSR movement," as the Brazilian literature coins it, which grew out of the post-dictatorship and come-neoliberalism (and increasing poverty) era of the 1990s.[6] This CSR tradition has conventionally and predominantly been characterized by corporate philanthropy, emanating from the industry itself (de Oliveira 2010; Duarte 2010). But Brazil has also been at the forefront in the Latin American continent in adapting certification, accountability, and reporting practices associated with international CSR practices, such as the Global Reporting Initiative (GRI) (Duarte 2010: 356). Moon, citing the work of Sanchez-Rodriguez, lists a "CSR-timeline" in Brazil, consisting of "1960s–1970s: ethical approaches, limited impact, influenced by Christian values. 1980s: political approaches, influenced by re-democratization. 1990s: integrative approaches, concern with social problems. 2000s: instrumental approaches, growing adherence of companies to CSR practices" (Moon 2019: 5). Moon furthermore suggests that a new era can be added to the timeline: "2010s: values-based approaches, increasing recognition of the urgency of tackling the UN SDGs and the new mindsets required such as those of eco and social entrepreneurship" (Moon 2019: 25).

While the features indicated above reflect tendencies within industry-driven CSR, environmental licensing legislation, which the PEA FOCO project, analyzed in this chapter, is part of, has grown out from a process of policy development within the Brazilian state, influenced by national and international concerns with nature conservation and environmental protection.

In the 1970s, Environmental Impact Assessment (EIA) and environmental licensing had already been created in state laws in Rio de Janeiro, São Paulo, Minas Gerais, and Santa Catarina (Silva Dias, personal communication, March 2020). At the federal level, EIA was established in 1981 as part of National Environmental Policy (*Política Nacional do Meio Ambiente*), enabling Environmental Impact Assessments of industry- and infrastructure projects (Silva Dias 2017: 20). In 1990, a resolution was passed that specified the criteria for licensing processes tied to mineral extraction, and in 1994, an additional resolution was passed for the oil and gas industry (Silva Dias 2017: 276–77, footnote 52). In 1986, the National Environment Council (CONAMA) established a standard guide on how to do EIA (Silva Dias, personal communication, March 2020).

Enforcement of environmental licensing processes in the O&G sector were relatively slack up until Petrobras's monopoly ended in 1998. However, with the subsequent influx of foreign companies in the O&G sectors, the necessity to establish more clearly defined guidelines and procedures emerged (Silva Dias, personal communication, August 2019).

Moreover, in 1997, CONAMA Resolution 237 was established, which is the main norm that regulates environmental licensing in

Brazil until today. CONAMA 237 specified, for the first time, that the licensing of offshore oil and gas is the exclusive responsibility of IBAMA. This made it necessary to form technical teams at IBAMA specifically working with licensing the oil and gas industry.

Another important driver for these processes was the 1998 law on environmental crimes, which established that oil companies that did not have an environmental license could be prosecuted criminally. The combination of these three factors (the end of Petrobras's monopoly, CONAMA 237, and the law on environmental crimes) contributed to the advance of oil licensing in the late 1990s (Silva Dias, personal communication, March 2020).

An interesting feature of the present case is therefore that the current regulatory framework set by IBAMA is a piece of state legislation whereby a so-called developing country is attempting to regulate and concretize international O&G companies' responsibility toward their host communities and Brazilian society and to create a state-sanctioned system for regulating and monitoring how they manage this responsibility. As such, it can therefore be conceptualized as a part of what Matten and Moon (2008: 409) refer to as "implicit CSR," which they conceptualize as:

> ...corporations' role within the wider formal and informal institutions for society's interests and concerns. Implicit CSR normally consists of values, norms, and rules that result in (mandatory and customary) requirements for corporations to address stakeholder issues and that define proper obligations of corporate actors in collective rather than individual terms. (Emphasis in original)

Matten and Moon's elaboration of "implicit CSR" thus points toward a broader institutional and social landscape that corporations as a collective body of actors must engage with and respond to, as opposed to setting their own individual terms and conditions for appropriate corporate social policy. Concurrently, "implicit CSR" also points to a legitimization of society's right to levy social expectations and claims upon corporations through state institutions. This idea holds widely different traction in the various countries Norwegian energy companies are operating in abroad, as illuminated throughout this book. Arguably, Brazil is the country where such claims are the most pronounced. These claims and accompanying policies are, however, contingent upon deeply political processes and struggles inside the Brazilian state. Consequently, current legislation and enforcement capacities are vulnerable to political change and volatility. Indeed, as this chapter is written, current president Jair Bolsonaro is very vocal in his quest for removing environmentalist and social "obstacles" to corporate free reign. This includes underfunding and attacking state institutions responsible for regulating and overseeing such concerns, including IBAMA. But before we learn more about IBAMA's role in setting the agenda for environmental licensing processes, let us first get a fuller picture of the Campos region where these policies are unfolding.

Industrial Development in the Campos Region

Oil was first discovered in the Campos basin in 1974, and production started up in 1977. In 1997, extraction and production of oil was opened to foreign companies with the passing of Law no. 9.478/97, also known as the Oil Law. This ended the monopoly of Petrobras, the Brazilian state oil company, which had been in effect since the full nationalization (excluding distribution) of the Brazilian oil industry in 1953 (de Medeiros Costa et al. 2015: 5).[7]

The 1997 Oil Law introduced the payment of royalties and "special participation"[8] to municipalities near oil camps (Neto, Passos, and Silva Neto 2008: 184). The region, previously marginalized from capitalist investments in Brazil, suddenly received not only a large influx of revenue but also a disproportionate share (in relation to other regions) of private direct investment attracted to O&G activities and industrial development. This set off "a war between places" (*guerra de lugares*) as the different municipalities competed for additional industry-related investments from foreign and domestic capital (Neto et al. 2008). The result has been a fragmentation of the regional territory, as the different municipalities design their own development strategies to attract investments. The influx of royalties, rather than going to social development for the benefit of the general population, has to a large extent been channeled into infrastructure facilitating industrial development (Neto et al. 2008).

Industrial and extractive activities in the region have had multiple effects on local livelihoods. Fishers complain about the impacts of the oil fields in the form of encroachment on marine space, exclusion from safety zones, increased circulation of large vessels, and seismic activities (Petrobras 2014: 166). The habitat created by the oil platform pillars as well as waste from the platforms have drawn fish away from natural habitats. The safety zones, with a radius of five hundred meters, bar fishers from access to these new marine habitats. If they do enter the zones—and some do because of the potentially high reward—they run the risk of being boarded and fined by the Brazilian navy.

Fishers have an additional problem even closer to home: the Porto do Açu Industrial Complex in São João da Barra municipality. Covering 130 square kilometers, the complex constitutes the largest industrial investment in Latin America. The building phase of the port was marked by tense conflict, involving land appropriation, house demolitions, and violent forced removals. The port, now in operation, is still heavily contested because of the trail of broken promises of local employment and economic opportunity left in its wake, and because it has barred fishers from access to their best shrimp fishing grounds as well as the port traditionally used for rest, offloading, and refueling.

The Campos region has thus, since the turn of the millennium, become a space for far-reaching transformation as a consequence of diverse industrial development. It has experienced an investment and royalty "rush," but without political structures or political will to invest the money in social development. It has become a site of expectations and increasing frustrations, as traditional livelihoods are crowded out and increased opportunities for education and work fail to materialize.

Licensing O&G Activities

The impact area for the Peregrino field stretches from the city of Niterói north of Rio de Janeiro to the northern border between the state of Rio de Janeiro and the state of Espiritu Santo. As a condition for their licenses to explore and to operate, O&G companies must run projects in selected communities along the coastline. PCAP projects (Compensation Plan for Fishery Activities/ Plano de Compensação da Atividade Pesqueira) tied to the license to explore are short-term compensatory projects aimed at mitigating potential economic loss in fishing communities caused by exploration activities. PEA projects (Environmental Education Projects/Programa de Educação Ambiental) are tied to the license to operate. These are long-term environmental education projects, aimed at both teaching vulnerable citizen groups about the impacts of O&G activities and enabling them to participate in political and public decision-making processes. The companies are also to organize social communications projects informing coastal populations about their presence and activities.[9]

The legal underpinning for PEA and PCAP projects is the Nota Técnica CGPEG/DLIIC/IBAMA Nº 02/10; the Technical Note elaborated by IBAMA setting the guidelines for conditions tied to the licensing process. The rationale for the PEA projects is formulated as "the necessity to develop formative processes to aid qualified intervention of certain social groups in decision-making processes [related to] the costs/benefits emerging from the exploration of natural resources" (Art. 4.1.1, author's translation from Portuguese). In other words, the aim of PEA projects is to mobilize sociopolitically marginalized groups and enable them to engage with the direct and indirect consequences of O&G activities. Before we venture into the details of Equinor's PEA FOCO project, it is worthwhile to take a closer look at the institutional setting within the Brazilian state where these policies were conceived.

IBAMA's Contested Politics

IBAMA's main office is located in the capital city of Brasilia, but the technical division responsible for the oil and gas sector is located in Rio de Janeiro. The O&G division is the only subdivision located outside Brasilia. Many of the current generation of senior technicians entered IBAMA in a broad public servant recruitment process in 1999. Within the Brazilian academic and political landscape, a number had a progressive background with studies in social and environmental sciences during the years of conservationist struggle of the Amazonia, the murder of Chico Mendes,[10] and the 1992 Rio Declaration on Environment and Development.

In 2002, Luiz Inácio Lula da Silva won the presidential election for the Worker's Party (PPT). This coincided favorably with the ambitions of the incoming technical staff, who were eager to develop a more comprehensive and substantive framework for the environmental licensing process than had previously been the case. Under the first Lula government (2003–6), the Rio office was shielded from external pressure from the industry and from adversarial political interests. The directorate for IBAMA is politically appointed, which in a Latin American context means that political pressure and directives are filtered downward according to the ambitions and interests of the person in charge—as well as the ambitions and interests of those who put him or her there. Under the first Lula administration, the government appointed directors who shared the Rio office's ambitions for a renewed and strengthened environmental licensing procedure and who allowed them to develop their internal organization and knowledge base. Consequently, the Rio office consolidated itself as a highly knowledgeable and tightly knit division, with little overturn in personnel and close knowledge of the O&G industry.

With the second Lula government and the subsequent Dilma Rousseff government, internal political struggles hardened. On several occasions, new directors were appointed that had interests and ambitions adverse to the Rio office, and more political pressure was "filtered down." The Rio office had by then, however, consolidated sufficiently to manage to stand their ground, or as one senior technician formulated it: "Many times I thought that it was over, but we are still here." Nonetheless, the battle to maintain their space and leverage is ongoing. In 2017, the director's seat of the Rio office was moved to Brasilia, because the Brasilia main office thought that the Rio division was becoming too autonomous.

The Rio-based IBAMA team's strategic vision is founded in critical environmental education: an intellectual and ideological tradition that emerges from conservationist struggles in the past and the tradition of popular education (*educação popular*)—often associated with the Brazilian educator and philosopher Paulo Freire. In the first decade of the millennium, the Rio division started to develop and test politically how a new strategy for environmental licensing could be developed that incorporated these ideas into formal policy. Eventually, this strategy was formalized in the Technical Note referred to above.

The companies initially resisted IBAMA's new clout and strategy. However, as one IBAMA employee expressed, "It helps a lot to have legislation that is strong and not only on paper. [The O&G companies] started out with a lot of resistance, but now they have fallen into the fold." One of the analysts stated that the big difference between how O&G companies behave in Brazil and how they behave in other developing countries is the existence or not of state regulation. "If you do not have state regulation, the companies only do voluntary projects: ephemeral projects without a base. But IBAMA has the possibility to demand something that is sustainable in the long run."

Before IBAMA developed the current environmental licensing strategy, the companies were used to doing "things without criteria," as one technician put it. Moreover, Petrobras had a long history of dispensing "white elephants" and paternalistic gifts and trinkets to local communities,[11] and it was therefore of crucial importance for IBAMA that the companies did not reinforce this patronage model.

The Technical Note outlined that the companies had to communicate consistently that the projects were a legal requirement. All branding and promotional and educational material—written or audiovisual—was required to include the following phrase: "The realization of the [name of the project] is a means of (indemnization, mitigation, and/or compensation) required by the environmental licensing process, led by IBAMA" (Technical Note 7.1, translation from Portuguese by the author).[12]

The analysts agreed that, had state regulations not been in place, the companies would not have carried out projects of such scope and focus as they now had to. This was a matter of both will and capacity. "They have the money, but not the theoretical or methodological tools," one IBAMA employee commented. "They would rather do social responsibility projects." The companies thus had to be brought to heel with regards to following the theoretical and methodological guidelines of the strategy. It was not the companies themselves that developed the projects; rather, they made a public call inviting consultancies to submit projects in alignment with IBAMAs Technical Note. IBAMA participated in selecting the project, and the final project plan was developed in cooperation between the consultancy, the corporation, and IBAMA. Although IBAMA could not determine the size of the companies' budgets spent on PCAP and PEA projects, they could assess whether the budgets were realistic considering the projects' scope and ambitions. IBAMA also had close contact with the consultancy (and the corporations), and regularly visited the projects in the field.

Equinor was considered one of the better, if not best, O&G companies in terms of their handling of the environmental licensing process. Equinor worked "in alignment" (*alinhado*) with IBAMA instead of engaging in "posturing" as some of the larger companies did (with Petrobras being considered the most challenging company to work with, being bureaucratically sluggish and reluctant to submit to IBAMA's authority). PEA FOCO was also considered best practice in terms of ongoing PEA projects. One of the analysts qualified this statement, however, commenting that Equinor had been very lucky with the consultancy and that theirs was a rather small, cheap, and easy project to handle. In response to my attempt to tease out more details about their views on Equinor's performance, one technician was evidently reluctant to dispense praise, stating that the companies [in general] were "merely following the law." This comment illustrates IBAMA's eagerness to entrench the idea that these projects were legal obligations to the Brazilian state and society, and not contingent upon the companies' good will. One technician commented that the companies (without specifying which) were reluctant to start up the projects, but once they went well and were positively evaluated, they were very eager to "appropriate" the project, that is, to pass it off as "their brainchild." For that reason, as stated above, IBAMA was very cautious that the companies did not use the projects for corporate branding and publicity, neither toward the broader public nor vis-à-vis the local "stakeholders," e.g., the communities where the projects operated. This illustrates how the environmental education projects, albeit mandatory, reverberated with the practices and ideas associated with CSR, both within the corporations, the public, and the state, in spite of IBAMA's intention to draw a sharp conceptual line between legal requirement and voluntary CSR practices. It also shows how strongly CSR is associated with corporate branding. Theoretically, it serves as an example of the fruitfulness—and importance—of foregrounding the distinction between CSR as thematic object and analytical concept, as highlighted by Bråten in chapter 3 of this book.

The PEA FOCO Project

Equinor's PEA FOCO project covers nine different fisher communities: Atafona, Açu, and Quixaba in the municipality of São João da Barra; and Barra de Itabapoana, Barrinha, Gargaú, Guaxindiba, Lagoa Feia, and Sossego in the municipality of São Fransisco. In 2014, and at the behest of IBAMA's recommendation—or rather requirement—Equinor also integrated a PCAP project for a previous and unsuccessful exploration in the Juxia well (block BM-C-47[13]). In practice, that means that the PEA FOCO project (now also integrating the PCAP project) is scheduled to continue until production in the Peregrino field ends.

In 2014, the women formed a registered association called AMA PEA FOCO (Association of Women supported by PEA FOCO/ Associação de Mulheres Apoiadoras do PEA FOCO). The association's judicial status allows it to solicit representation in formal municipal consultative councils and to solicit audiences with political bodies. Through the association, they collectively discussed and voted for establishing two communal industrial kitchens in the two target municipalities. The kitchens are funded by Equinor as part of the project, but they formally belong to AMA PEA FOCO. The kitchens thus have multiple functions responding to the dual aims of PEA and PCAP: to function as organizational and mobilizing meeting spaces (in alignment with the purpose of collective empowerment of marginalized groups), and to enable the women to develop cooking and organizational skills toward strengthening their economic livelihoods (in alignment with the purpose of mitigating potential economic loss due to O&G activities).

PEA FOCO and Women in the Region

The PEA FOCO project has been developed and is run by a contracted environmental consultancy, TRANS FOR MAR, which specializes in sustainability projects in the coastal region. TRANS FOR MAR has three people employed as field staff with combined backgrounds from popular education, the arts, and environmental governance studies. The company also has one administrative coordinator and one didactic/pedagogic coordinator. All three are women.[14] Two local women from the project work as administrative assistants. The project also hires other professionals as needed (e.g., cooks to hold cooking classes).

The PEA FOCO project is neither couched nor conducted as a politically partisan project; rather, it is explicitly nonpartisan. However, its pedagogical design takes inspiration from the tradition of popular education and critical pedagogy in Brazil. A key tenet of this tradition is that marginalized subjects and populations must gain awareness of the structural conditions for their oppression and develop collective emancipatory strategies in order for transformation to occur.[15]

Women in the seafood-processing sector on the Norte Fluminense coastline are decidedly marginalized. Historically a sugar cane plantation region, the area is culturally conservative with patriarchal, racialized, and religious social ideologies marginalizing women of color and low socioeconomic status in particular. The political apparatus is dominated by elite family dynasties that thrive on patronage and clientelism. Corruption and unresponsive public institutions are, as in most of Brazil, the norm rather than the exception.

Labor in the seafood-processing industry has historically been regarded not as "proper work" but as women "helping out" their husbands alongside their household duties. These perceptions remain to a large extent.[16] Consequently, female fishery workers have not had any occupational class identity or any form of representation or social organization. They have no bargaining power vis-à-vis the owners of the processing facilities. Women's salaries are substantially lower than those of male fishers and, not least, the profits reaped by re-vendors. The officially recognized Fishermen's Colonies (Colônia de Pescadores), which organize and register male fishers in the public fishermen's registry, neither registered female fishery workers nor acknowledged them as such—until the PEA FOCO project started to push for it. Being on this list entitles fishers to economic compensation during the spawning period when fishing is forbidden,[17] as well as to pension and health coverage.

The spatial design of the area itself accentuates women's marginalization: villages are scattered over long distances, and public transportation is extremely neglected. Consequently, women are generally physically immobile and hindered from gaining access to public institutions, social arenas, and knowledge about the outside world. Female illiteracy is high, especially among elderly and middle-aged women. Many dropped out of school early either to work in the fishing industry to help sustain family or because of early marriage and/or early pregnancy (which still is prevalent). Public education in the area has also been, and to a certain extent still is, poor. Moreover, the absence of a regional tradition for popular social organization has further contributed to low political awareness and few arenas for collective mobilization.

PEA FOCO and Women's Lives

This panorama represents the context of as well as the justification for the PEA FOCO project. The comprehensiveness of female seafood workers' marginalization was not lost on Equinor's Brazilian SSU consultant, who referred to it as "modern slavery." In 2011, the PEA FOCO project started with a year of door-to-door mobilization in the nine project communities (conducted by the consultancy), aimed at identifying and recruiting women in the target group. Subsequent phases included the formation of village nucleus and popular educators in each of the target communities as well as the diffusion of the educational and pedagogical content of the project. In keeping with the tradition of popular education and popular mobilization in Brazil, TRANS FOR MAR staff has formed close social and personal ties with the women. In addition to regular workshops, meetings, and events both at community and municipal levels, as well as in the city of Campos, the project staff conducts regular house visits. The underlying rationale for this proximity is the need to be close to the women's social realities and life worlds; the project facilitators cannot act as distant come-and-go external consultants.

Throughout the years, several hundred women have participated in events organized by the project. At the moment, there is a "hard core" of around thirty-five to forty women who participate in events at the municipal level and many more who participate at the local "nucleus" level.

The project has had a transformative effect on many of the women's lives. It has provided them with a broad array of new knowledge and information and become an arena where they get social support for personal growth. One of the participants in her fifties, who makes a living from river fishing, filleting fish, and selling food products from her home, explains it like this:

> I got to know the project through a colleague, and we started to attend meetings together. I wanted to go and see what it was about, I knew that [the oil companies] are extracting our oil and gas, and I went to the meetings and understood more about it. Through the project I learned about my rights, and then I started to ask questions—my husband said that I had become a busybody. Through the project I get support and learn how to resolve things.

Although the project as such does not proselytize "gender equality," it has increased gender awareness and self-confidence as well as fomented occupational class identities. Many of the women said that they had never thought of themselves as workers before. Therefore, they had not contemplated that they deserved labor rights and social entitlements as well. Several of the women told stories of how they had experienced radical transformations in their lives, such as daring to speak up in a group for the first time, ceasing to follow conservative religious doctrines in the communities, and abandoning abusive labor relations. The current main coordinator in the field, a strong-willed, kind-hearted woman in her late fifties with a long history of engagement with popular sector communities, has become an important supportive figure for many whose lives are filled with the usual tragedies that befall women living in poverty: illness, death, domestic violence, severe economic problems, material deficits, children who fall into misfortune, and abuse and neglect by political and public institutions. As PEA has evolved into the association AMA PEA FOCO, TRANS FOR MAR has helped them to petition municipal authorities for better or missing public services as well as the Fishermen's Colonies and the Ministry of Fishery in order to be included on the Fishermen's Registries. The latter has been of particularly great symbolic importance for the women in addition to its economic significance.[18] Moreover, AMA PEA FOCO has been able to get elected for one seat and one deputy seat as representatives for civil society in two municipal councils (health and environment). While these minor victories are unlikely to have a significant impact upon political and gendered inequalities in the region and in the larger picture, for the women involved it does represent a politics of hope (Appadurai 2007) insofar as it has provided them with a space to collectively articulate grievances and formulate claims. There are, however, evidently also deep tensions between the significance that the project has for the women involved and the larger structural and political landscape that these policies form part of. This aspect will be further discussed toward the end of this chapter. For now, we will leave the dusty fishing villages in the Campos region, and return to Rio de Janeiro, where we will see that there are also tensions between different ways of perceiving and conceptualizing the project *within* Equinor.

Negotiating PEA FOCO

The 2016 SSU award that Equinor Brazil received for the PEA FOCO project is discreetly on display in the slick and shiny lobby of its Rio de Janeiro office building, located near Praia do Flamengo in the upscale Flamengo area. The staff is working diligently and quietly in large, spacious, and modern offices, with a stunning view of the Sugarloaf and the Rio de Janeiro bay. In all respects, this office space and the communities where the PEA FOCO project is unfolding are worlds apart.

The PEA FOCO project falls under the responsibility of the social performance consultant.[19] In 2015, this desk was downsized from three persons when the slump in oil prices caused Equinor's Oslo office to instruct the Brazil office to cut costs. In 2018, and at the time of this research, Equinor Brazil gained more autonomy as it was organized as a separate business area within Equinor's corporate structure. Consequently, the social performance officer reported to the head of sustainability, security and emergency response. That person in turn reported to the vice president of SSU (safety, security, and sustainability) in Brazil's autonomous country board, known as Development and Production Brazil (DPB). The head of SSU in turn reported to Equinor Brazil's CEO, who was part of Equinor's Corporate Executive Committee. During my last research stint, I was told by staff in the SSU department that Equinor Brazil was still trying to figure out exactly what this new management structure implied, but that they were nevertheless in close contact with Equinor's office in Oslo. Specifically, I was told that the head of the SSU department was in frequent contact with the Oslo-based head of sustainability for Equinor's international operations, especially about claims and complaints emerging directly from the communities. As of 1 June 2021, Equinor Brazil ceased being a separate business area and was put under the umbrella of Exploration and Production International (EPI), which manages operations in all six countries outside of Norway and the United States (Equinor 2021: 27).

The long-term presence of socially committed CSR staff with an acquired understanding of local issues is vital to ensure the long-term management of projects. Staff with a technical/managerial approach may not understand local complexities or have a sufficiently qualitative methodological understanding of how best to engage with local communities (Frynas 2005: 591). In that respect, Equinor Brazil has been lucky, or perhaps wise, when picking staff to handle their social performance portfolio. In the course of my field research, there have been two different persons in charge, Thomás and Sarah.[20] Both had previous experience from community consultancy and were commended both by TRANS FOR MAR staff and the women for having genuine understanding of and interest in the nitty-gritty details of developing a project embedded in such challenging and complex sociopolitical realities. As one TRANS FOR MAR employee said: "The difference between Equinor and other companies is that you can discuss process with them, not only result." Another positive trait mentioned was the level of trust between the company and consultancy, in stark contrast to Brazilian energy companies. Moreover, Equinor was more reasonable when negotiating contracts and budgets than other O&G companies and, in general, respected the consultancy's expertise and let them do their work.

Welker (2014) remarks that CSR officers are often viewed with suspicion by their coworkers. Constituting one of the "ameliorative disciplines" (alongside, e.g., environment, health, and HR), they often have to fight for their legitimacy and justify their existence more than those in technical and managerial areas (Welker 2014: 41). While I have no reason to believe that Equinor's SSU staff was viewed with suspicion, it was evident that they found themselves in a betwixt-and-between position where they had to mediate between "the project out there" and "corporate realities in here." A lot of "translation work" went into transforming the qualitative aspects of the project into corporate molds.

At our first meeting, Thomás told me that the SSU department had developed a new strategy after the 2015 budget cuts. At the time, they also had a project called Women of Gamboa, also working with female seafood workers. However, this project was voluntary, and the person sent from the Norway office to steer budget cuts had not agreed to keep it.[21] The CSR desk was downsized from three people to one person, and only the mandatory projects remained. "The others were not related to the company's corporate growth strategy," Thomás said.

The centrality of the trope and rationale of "the business case" in relation to CSR has been thoroughly explored in the literature (Trebeck 2008). Equinor's Brazil SSU department had over previous years worked deliberately to make "the business case" for their projects more visible to the board. Thomás's superior at the time commented that:

> When I got the position, I saw a [social sustainability] strategy without a direct connection to the company strategy. We had to make building blocks. And we also have to link it to Brazil Roadmap 2030 ... the company's ambition, the pillars, are to create value to communities and to act with transparency. That is the line of action that the social investment strategy should be linked to—everything should be connected.

Consequently, the SSU team elaborated a comprehensive document linking IBAMA's demands with Equinor's own guidelines, values, and strategies, featuring an elaborate flowchart showing how these synergized with the goals and purposes for PEA FOCO. Neat numerical tables summarized the achievements of the PEA FOCO project in the field.

Somewhat puzzling is the fact that the SSU department had to "justify" and enumerate a state-sanctioned mandatory project. I suggest that this reflects the hegemony of corporate cognitive models that requires "legibility" (Scott 1999) in the form of condensed numerical and schematic depictions of the world. Qualitative "stuff" becomes anomalies and empty signifiers once it reaches the boardroom; or, as one of the SSU staff formulated it:

> We have to make performance indicators for each project. We have a lot of good projects: what are the indicators for that; how can we show the leadership? We do not convince people [within Equinor] with perceptions, we have to present numbers: how many women trained; the kitchens; number of meetings. When you go there to see for yourself—see Thomás with the women, how they hug him and cry—you see that they are happy. But for those who are not in the field [e.g., the board], you need numbers.

I suggest that the necessity to make legible the synergies between Equinor's values and strategies and PEA FOCO's existence and achievement also reflects an organizational setup where each department has to justify and defend its budget in competition with other units. In that process, "the social area" has to defend their existence shoulder to shoulder with, for example, the unit in charge of "core activities," such as exploration and drilling. It then makes sense that for a corporate gaze searching for legibility, such a document represents a "truth claim" that makes the social budget more difficult to challenge. The strategy worked, as it were. In the 2018 budget, the SSU department got what it asked for from the board.

The Boundaries of Responsibility

In conversations with Equinor staff, PEA FOCO was discursively framed within vexing rationales. I was told that "we need to have a social footprint" and that they wanted to leave something with "lasting value," in contrast to assistentialist and philanthropic donations. I was also told that the project's rationales fit well with the two internal sustainability pillars: to create local value and to act with transparency. Because, it was explained, "when we do work in the communities, it creates local value [e.g., it leaves material and social resources in the communities]. And when the women go to public institutions with their demands, that creates transparency."

However, at other times, Equinor staff stated quite bluntly that the rationale was, above all, corporate not altruistic. Orthodox CSR speech was recurrent in our conversations; "to achieve the social license to operate," "compliance," "business strategy," and "mitigating expectations." One interlocutor commented:

> The purpose is to build trust, to build relationship. Of course, there is no such thing as a free lunch. We do this because we want to do good, but also because we hope that in the future, they do not challenge us. It opens doors, builds relationship, so in the future we can get their social license to operate.

The company was fearful of running into problems with local communities, and they had procedures in place for how to deal with any issue that might arise. For the company, public relations involve a constant boundary-making process (Appel 2012) where expectations are mitigated, claims kept in check, and social grievances averted. This is not to say that the individual staff's "moral orientation" (Trebeck 2008: 350) was not genuine or that the importance—or desire—of leaving a "social footprint" is not incorporated into Equinor's business philosophy. However, it points to the corporation's raison d'être—to keep doing business—which serves as a "metacode" (Rottenburg 2009) that triumphs and frames supplementary rationales.

Equinor's corporate self-understanding is founded upon self-reassurance about the possibility of doing business with a clean conscience. However, what it means to have a clean conscience evidently depends on what you consider your responsibility. Upon being asked where, in his opinion, a company's responsibility starts and ends, one of the managers responded that "the simple answer is that it starts with compliance. What you need to do. PEA and PCAP are compliance. And then you might want to do other things that are not compliance, other projects."

What the manager points to is the distinction between what in corporate lingo is referred to as "have to have" and "nice to have." Voluntary projects fall into the category of "nice to have." PEA FOCO, however, was defined as "compliance." It follows from the parameters of measuring compliance that the yardstick for the project's success was IBAMA's stamp of approval, though for the staff involved, it clearly also mattered that the project went well.

PEA FOCO's status as a matter of compliance was codified and condensed into the phrase often uttered by all parties involved: "what IBAMA wants." However, as we learned earlier, "what IBAMA wants" was part of a broad and contested political struggle that reveals the heterogeneity of the Brazilian state as well as IBAMA's fragile clout. These dynamics expose that as much as O&G companies try to pose as apolitical market actors in countries such as Brazil, they are nevertheless deeply engaged in vexing and contested power relations within the Brazilian state and society.

Conclusion: The Politics of Compliance

This chapter has explored the socioterritorial and sociopolitical context for the PEA FOCO project, a context that is also the justificative for IBAMA's ambition to force O&G companies to contribute toward the betterment of the social and human development along the Norte Fluminense coastline.

Per se, the PEA FOCO project has had significant personal importance for many of the women involved, and it has also contributed to rising the question of women's status as fishery laborers in their families and communities. Albeit modestly and with great difficulty, it has also provided the women with a venue for advocacy vis-à-vis local political bodies. In the larger picture, however, the project forms part of a broader context of deep structural inequalities shaping the encounter between the international oil and gas sector and marginalized fishing communities (Quist 2019). In such a perspective, the project can be read in light of Shever's (2010) highly critical account of how Shell in Argentina "used gendered practices and affective techniques both to quell opposition to the company's operations and to foster individual and collective—but not corporate—responsibility for human health and welfare" (Shever 2010: 28). It can also be read in light of Ottinger's (2013) work from New Orleans on how corporations attempt to foster "communication and cooperation rather than conflict" (Ottinger 2013: 4) through community-corporation partnerships, partial accommodations to community claims, and the invocation of neoliberal models for responsible citizenship. Furthermore, the project raises highly complex questions of how to conceive of the fact that O&G companies are mandated by one central state body to empower marginalized groups' ability to critically engage with the O&G companies themselves—as well as local political bodies and state institutions—yet in a context where all parties involved strive to appear apolitical and apartisan.

These questions are too broad to analyze in the context of this chapter, but it is worthwhile to note that IBAMA seemed aware of these paradoxes. However, IBAMA's point of departure appeared to be a pragmatic realization of the fact that the O&G companies were there to stay. It is thus preferable to nudge them into recognizing the larger socioterritorial context within which they are operating and to make them engage with the communities that are affected by their productive and economic presence. It is also preferable that the state is in charge of designing and coordinating strategies for mitigating some of these impacts instead of leaving it up to the corporations themselves. Through IBAMA's progressive-developmental gaze, it hence seemed sensible to make corporations contribute with a grain of sand to strengthen those groups who suffered the most from Brazil's democratic, social, and civic deficiencies.

Garsten and Jacobsson (2013) discuss CSR as a post-political form of governance. However, I suggest that IBAMA's environmental licensing process, as a modality of mandatory CSR policies, or what Matten and Moon (2008) referred to earlier as "implicit CSR," constitutes a tacit politization of CSR. However, the risk is of course that these projects serve as lightning rods for more critical discussions about O&G companies' direct and indirect role in reinforcing the very same problems that the projects are intended to mitigate. Such discussions are also beyond the scope of this chapter. But as we have seen, the tension between the PEA FOCO project's significance for the women involved, and the structural and political context within which it is embedded, is evidently deeply present.

It is pertinent to ask: does Equinor's "best practice" social performance in Brazil reflect something particular about the "Nordic model"? As discussed by Knudsen in chapter 4, the Nordic model is analytically conceived of as being informed by the ideals of state guidance, union collaboration (see chapter 8, this volume), and responsible interactions with local communities (chapter 4: 131). In my field research material, the Norwegian state was most notable by its absence. Indeed, the Norwegian state was never mentioned by anyone interviewed in the course of this fieldwork, unless explicitly brought up by the researcher. Rather, it was the Brazilian state's expectations and demands, directed toward all transnational energy companies operating in the sector, that was a constant point of reference in terms of who Equinor had to dialogue with and be accountable to. As in Knudsen's review of Norsk Hydro's endeavors in Brazil (see chapter 4), we may thus also conclude that as the Norwegian state's ownership was "enacted at an arm's length" (conclusion: 324), Equinor had a "license to function as any other TNC when operating abroad, focusing on shareholder values and mending problems by invoking the internationally acknowledged tool and language of CSR" (conclusion: 324) or, in the currently most dominant corporate lingo, sustainability. However, as the Hydro case discussed by Knudsen testifies to, the Norwegian state may very easily be put in the spotlight if something happens that attracts negative media attention. No wonder then that Equinor Brazil was certainly watchful of their public reputation.

As for the specific management of PEA FOCO within the corporate organization, it is difficult to make a conclusive argument about there being something particularly "Nordic" about Equinor Brazil's project management without having done comparative fieldwork in non-Nordic companies operating in the same business environment and being subjected to the same regulations. However, the research material indicates that Equinor Brazil has run the PEA FOCO project in a manner that reflects that the organization readily accepts the Brazilian state's regulations and comprehends its rationale. Moreover, research material also indicates that Equinor Brazil is trying to run the project in a conscientious manner, not only for the purpose of ticking a "compliance box."

However, the material also suggests that it is IBAMA's institutional, legal, and political clout that upholds PEA FOCO's space within Equinor's organization. As the termination of the Women of Gamboa project indicates, the corporate bottom line as well as criteria of legibility levied upon formulations of corporate strategies means that "nice to have" projects stand on unstable ground. The bottom-line rationale for the PEA FOCO project within the corporate matrix is thus its status as a mandatory project, individual CSR staff's personal engagements in the project notwithstanding.

The case also raises questions concerning the circumstances under which host states have maneuvering space for steering CSR policies of O&G companies operating in their country, and what is required to enforce these policies. As this case attests to, this space is contingent upon a host of contextual factors, actors involved, and political conjunctures. As I have shown, IBAMA engages in a two-front struggle: to nudge the companies into accepting their authority and demands, but also to maintain their space in the midst of political struggles for control of the state. This case thus illuminates the deeply political dimension of CSR as a relation of power both within the state and between the state and corporations. However, the present research suggests that corporations can, if sufficient institutional and political power is in place, be pushed into committing to long-term projects where the state has a say in defining objectives and methodologies (as opposed to voluntary "philanthropy"). However, the quality of the follow-up (as opposed to "ticking a box") evidently also depends on institutional setups and management inside the corporation. Equinor Brazil's SSU staff has worked closely with IBAMA to make sure that they are complying with "what IBAMA wants" in qualitative terms also. It remains to be seen what will happen with Brazil's environmental licensing process and the PEA FOCO project should IBAMA lose their clout in the future. That would be a litmus test for whether Equinor's stated desire to leave a social footprint, and their apparent concern for the women involved, stretches beyond the politics of compliance.

Acknowledgments

Research for this chapter has been conducted as part of the project Energethics: Norwegian Energy Companies Abroad; Expanding the Anthropological Understanding of Corporate Social Responsibility (2015–19), funded by a FRIPRO grant from the Research Council of Norway (grant no. 240617). This chapter is a revised version of the article "Between Social Footprint and Compliance, or 'What

IBAMA Wants'": Equinor Brazil's Social Sustainability Policy," which appeared in *Focaal* 88 (2020): 40–57. Thank you to *Focaal* for allowing me to reuse the text. The author would like to thank Equinor staff involved in this case study: you have been very forthcoming and hospitable. Thank you also to TRANS FOR MAR and IBAMA staff, who have generously given me their time and shared their experiences. Above all, gratitude is due to the admirable women in the PEA FOCO project for including me in their everyday activities with such warmth and generosity and for sharing their thoughts and life stories. Thank you also to the Energethics project group, led by Professor Ståle Knudsen, for your superb academic and collegial qualities. I am also grateful to the two anonymous reviewers at Berghahn Books as well as Ståle Knudsen for useful suggestions for how to revise the original text. And finally, thank you to my parents, Frode and Åse Karin Strønen, for indispensable childcare support when I have been away on fieldwork.

Iselin Åsedotter Strønen is associate professor in the Department for Social Anthropology, University of Bergen, Norway. She has conducted research on the multiple interfaces of the oil and gas economy, state building, social development, and inequality in Venezuela, Angola, and Brazil. Strønen is the author of the monograph *Grassroots Politics and Oil Culture in Venezuela: The Revolutionary Petro-State* (Palgrave McMillan, 2017), and the coeditor (with Margit Ystanes) of *The Social Life of Economic Inequalities in Contemporary Latin America: Decades of Change* (Palgrave McMillan, 2017). Her work has also appeared in *Focaal*, *History and Anthropology*, and *Ethnos* among other publications.

Notes

An earlier version of this text was published as: Strønen, Iselin. 2020. "Between Social Footprint and Compliance, or 'What IBAMA Wants': Equinor Brazil's Social Sustainability Policy." In Theme Section, "Corporate Social Responsibility and the Paradoxes of State Capitalism," ed. Ståle Knudsen and Dinah Rajak. *Focaal—Journal of Global and Historical Anthropology* 88: 40–57.

1. Until 2040 according to current estimates.
2. IBAMA manages environmental licensing processes for offshore projects and projects that extend across state borders. Oil and gas projects are handled by IBAMA's subsection the Directorate of Environmental Licensing/General Coordination for Environmental Licensing of Marine and Coastal Enterprises (Diretoria de Licenciamento

Ambiental/ Coordenação Geral de Licenciamento Ambiental de Empreendimentos Marinhos e Costeiros).
3. An overview of Equinor Brazil's operations can be found at https://www.equinor.com/where-we-are/brazil.
4. The Peregrino field is co-operated with the Chinese company Sinochem, but Equinor holds the operating license.
5. BRIC is an acronym for Brazil, Russia, India, and China.
6. I have not come across any other ethnographic studies of CSR and the oil and gas industries in Brazil, but see Pündrich, Aguilar Delgado, and Barin-Cruz (2021) for CSR in Petrobras and Hoelscher and Rustad (2019) for CSR in aluminum refineries Vale/Norsk Hydro in Brazil.
7. The oil and gas industry in Brazil is regulated by the National Regulatory Agency of Petroleum, Natural Gas and Biofuel (ANP) (Agência Nacional do Petróleo, Gás Natural e Biocombustíveis).
8. Special participation (*participação especial*) is a special payment deducted from the gross revenue of the extraction and production operation (Neto, Passos, and Silva Neto 2008: 184n67).
9. Equinor has a 24/7 "hotline" that community members can call with questions and concerns as well as a corporate email. I have been informed that these venues for contact are barely ever used. They also sporadically visit the Fishermen's Colonies and organize events for fishers, such as, e.g., skin cancer screening. In 2017, Equinor and Shell started up a joint voluntary CSR project called Mar Atento (Attentive Sea) in order to train fishermen in offshore emergency response, e.g., in case of oil spill accidents. I do not have qualitative data on this project.
10. Chico Mendes was a Brazilian rubber tapper, trade union leader, conservationist and human rights activist. He was assassinated by a rancher in 1988.
11. Petrobras has a long track record of spending money on corporate social responsibility in various configurations, also in different forms of long-term sponsorships. For example, they have financed the large-scale Tamar turtle conservation project since 1983. However, what was meant by "short-term philanthropy to communities" was exemplified to me as, e.g., donating a truck but not funds for maintenance and a driver.
12. Both Equinor and TRANS FOR MAR made constant references to IBAMA and "what IBAMA wanted" in their interaction with the women, and its logo was printed alongside that of Equinor on all material involved in the project.
13. See https://www.equinor.com/content/dam/statoil/documents/annual-reports/2014/Statoil-20-F-2014.pdf, p. 35.
14. The administrative coordinator, with a degree in social sciences, has a long history of consultancy, including for IBAMA and the United Nations Development Programme (UNDP). The didactic coordinator is a university professor with a PhD in environmental education.
15. See, however, Welker 2014, chapter 4, for a discussion of participatory approaches as diluted critical education.
16. Traditionally, women have not ventured out onto the open sea but have engaged in river fishing and collecting crabs in the mangroves; they are the backbone of the local processing industry through fileting fish and rinsing shrimps and crabs.
17. This period is set to three months for saltwater fishing and four months for river fishing. The compensation is the equivalent to a minimum salary per month.
18. These victories are also fragile, e.g., some of the women who were added onto the Fisherman's Registry suddenly disappeared from the list. It was not known if this was accidental or simply sabotage on the part of the Fishermen's Colony.

19. See https://www.equinor.com/where-we-are/brazil for additional voluntary projects and sponsorships in Equinor Brazil, which this person also is in charge of.
20. Pseudonyms.
21. The project took place in a community defined as part of the Peregrino impact area, but not in one of the target communities allocated to Equinor by IBAMA.

References

Appadurai, Arjun. 2007. "Hope and Democracy." *Public Culture* 19(1): 29–34. https://doi.org/10.1215/08992363-2006-023.

Appel, Hannah. 2012. "Offshore Work: Oil, Modularity, and the How of Capitalism in Equatorial Guinea." *American Ethnologist* 39(4): 692–709. https://doi.org/10.1111/j.1548-1425.2012.01389.

———. 2019. *Licit Life of Capitalism: US Oil in Equatorial Guinea*. Durham, NC: Duke University Press.

Brejning, Jeanette. 2012. *The Historical and Contemporary Role of CSR in the Mixed Economy of Welfare*. Farnham, Surrey: Ashgate.

Banerjee, Subhabrata. 2008. "Corporate Social Responsibility: The Good, the Bad and the Ugly." *Critical Sociology* 34(1): 51–79. https://doi.org/10.1177/0896920507084623.

Blowfield, Michael, and Jedrzej George Frynas. 2005. "Setting New Agendas: Critical Perspectives on Corporate Social Responsibility in the Developing World." *International Affairs* 81(3): 499–513. http://www.jstor.org/stable/3569630.

Dashwood, Hevina S., and Bill Buenar Puplampu. 2010. "Corporate Social Responsibility and Canadian Mining Companies in the Developing World: The Role of Organizational Leadership and Learning." *Canadian Journal of Development Studies* 30(1–2): 175–96. https://doi.org/10.1080/02255189.2010.9669287.

de Medeiros Costa, Hirdan K., Edmilson M. dos Santos, João P. L. Santos, and Rafael Puglieri. 2015. "The Technological and Economic Features of Brazilian Oil, Gas and Biofuel Industry." In *Energy Law in Brazil*, edited by Xavier Y. M. de Alencar, 3–13. Cham: Springer International Publishing.

de Oliveira, Luciana. 2010. "Idéias do presente, practicas do passado: Elites empresariais e a questão social no Brasil e na Argentina; estudo comparativo sobre discursos e práticas de Responsabilidade Social Empresarial" [Present ideas, past practices: Business elites and the social question in Brazil and Argentina; A comparative study on discourses and practices of Corporate Social Responsibility]. PhD dissertation, Universidade Federal de Minas Gerais, Brazil.

Dias, Julio Cesar Silva. 2017. "O manejo interinstitucional de 'degradação legítima': A burocratização subordinada da avaliação de impactos ambientais no planejamento territorial coordenado pela política energética brasileira" [The interinstitutional management of 'legitimate degradation': The subordinate bureaucracy of the assessment of environmental impacts in the territorial planning coordinated by Brazilian energy policy]. PhD dissertation, Universidade Federal do Rio de Janeiro, Brazil.

Dolan, Catherine, and Dinah Rajak. 2016. "Introduction: Towards the Anthropology of Corporate Social Responsibility." In *The Anthropology of Corporate Social Responsibility*, edited by Catherine Dolan and Dinah Rajak, 1–28. New York: Berghahn Books.

Duarte, Fernanda. 2010. "Working with Corporate Social Responsibility in Brazilian Companies: The Role of Managers' Values in the Maintenance of CSR Cultures." *Journal of Business Ethics* 96(3): 355–68. https://doi.org/10.1007/s10551-010-0470-9.

Equinor. 2021. *Annual Report and Form 20-F*. Oslo: Equinor

———. 2020. "Brazil." https://www.equinor.com/no/where-we-are/brazil.html# (accessed 1 August 2020).

Frynas, Jedrzej F. 2005. "The False Developmental Promise of Corporate Social Responsibility: Evidence from Multinational Oil Companies." *International Affairs* 81(3): 581–98. https://doi.org/10.1111/j.1468-2346.2005.00470.x.

Garsten, Christina, and Kerstin Jacobsson. 2013. "Post-political Regulation: Soft Power and Post-political Visions in Global Governance." *Critical Sociology* 39(3): 421–37. https://doi.org/10.1177/0896920511413942.

Gatti, Lucia, Babitha Vishwanath, Peter Seele, and Bertil Cottier. 2017. "Are We Moving Beyond Voluntary CSR? Exploring Theoretical and Managerial Implications of Mandatory CSR Resulting from the New Indian Companies Act." *Journal of Business Ethics.* https://doi.org/10.1007/s10551-018-3783-8.

Gjølberg, Maria. 2010. "Varieties of Corporate Social Responsibility (CSR): CSR Meets the 'Nordic Model.'" *Regulation and Governance* 4: 203–29. DOI: 10.1111/j.1748-5991.2010.01080.x.

Hilson, Gavin. 2012. "Corporate Social Responsibility in the Extractive Industries: Experiences from Developing Countries." *Resource Policy* 37: 131–37. https://doi.org/10.1016/j.resourpol.2012.01.002.

Hoelscher, Kristian, and Siri Aas Rustad. 2019. "CSR and Social Conflict in the Brazilian Extractive Sector." *Conflict, Security & Development* 19(1): 99–119. DOI: 10.1080/14678802.2019.1561633.

IBAMA (Instituto Brasileiro do Meio Ambiente e dos Recursos Naturais Renováveis). 2010. *Nota Técnica CGPEG/DLIIC/IBAMA Nº 02/10*. Ministerio do Meio Ambiente (MMA). [Technical Note CGPEG/DLIIC/IBAMA Nº 02/10. Ministry of the Environment (MMA)]. Rio de Janeiro, Brazil.

Matten, Dirk, and Jeremy Moon. 2008. "'Implicit' and 'Explicit' CSR: A Conceptual Framework for a Comparative Understanding of Corporate Social Responsibility." *Academy of Management Review* 33(2): 404–24. DOI:10.2307/20159405.

Moon, Christopher J. 2019. "'Rio+25,' The Global Compact in Brazil and Opportunities Presented by the UN Sustainable Development Goals." In *Corporate Social Responsibility in Brazil: CSR, Sustainability, Ethics & Governance*, edited by Christopher Stehr, Nina Dziatzko, and Franziska Struve, 3–28. Springer.

Neto, Jayme F. B., William do Souza Passos, and Romeou e Silva Neto. 2008. "O petróleo como grande financiador da 'Guerra de lugares': O caso dos municípios da Bacia de Campos-RJ" [Oil as a great financier of the "War of places": The case of the municipalities of the Basin of Campos-RJ]. X Seminario Internacional de la RII, Santiago de Querétaro, 20–23 May. Santiago de Querétaro, Mexico.

Ottinger, Gwen. 2013. *Refining Expertise: How Responsible Engineers Subvert Environmental Justice Challenges*. New York: NYU Press

Petrobras. 2014. *Diagnóstico Participativo do PEA-BC*. [Participatory diagnostic of PEA-BC]. September 2014.

Pündrich, Aline Pereira, Natalia Aguilar Delgado, and Luciano Barin-Cruz. 2021. "The Use of Corporate Social Responsibility in the Recovery Phase of Crisis Management: A Case Study in the Brazilian Company Petrobras." *Journal of Cleaner Production* 329: 1–9.

Quist, Liina-Maija. 2019. "Contested Sea: The Politics of Space, Seafaring and Extraction among Fishers and the Oil Industry in Mexico." PhD dissertation, University of Helsinki.

Rajak, Dinah. 2011. *In Good Company: An Anatomy of Corporate Social Responsibility*. Redwood City, CA: Stanford University Press.

Rottenburg, Richard. 2009. *Far-Fetched Facts: A Parable of Development Aid*. Cambridge, MA: MIT Press.

Scott, James. 1999. *Seeing like a State: How Certain Schemes to Improve the Human Condition Have Failed*. New Haven, CT: Yale University Press.
Shever, Elana. 2010. "Engendering the Company: Corporate Personhood and the 'Face' of an Oil Company in Metropolitan Buenos Aires." *Polar* 33(1): 26–46. DOI: https://doi.org/10.1111/j.1555-2934.2010.01091.
———. 2012. *Resources for Reform: Oil and Neoliberalism in Argentina*. Stanford, CA: Stanford University Press.
Trebeck, Katherine. 2008. "Exploring the Responsiveness of Companies: Corporate Social Responsibility to Stakeholders." *Social Responsibility Journal* 4(3): 349–65. https://doi.org/10.1108/17471110810892857.
van Aaken, Dominik, Violeta Splitter, and David Seidl. 2013. "Why Do Corporate Actors Engage in Pro-Social Behaviour? A Bourdieusian Perspective on Corporate Social Responsibility." *Organization* 20(3): 349–71. https://doi.org/10.1177/1350508413478312.
Waagstein, Patricia R. 2011. "The Mandatory Corporate Social Responsibility in Indonesia: Problems and Implications." *Journal of Business Ethics* 98(3): 455–66. https://doi.org/10.1007/s10551-010-0587-x.
Welker, Marina. 2014. *Enacting the Corporation: An American Mining Firm in Post-authoritarian Indonesia*. Oakland: University of California Press.

— Chapter 7 —

GENDER, REGULATION, AND CORPORATE SOCIAL RESPONSIBILITY
The Case of Equinor's Social Investments in Tanzania
Siri Lange and Victoria Wyndham

In April 2016, at one of Dar es Salaam's most posh hotels, Equinor, a Norwegian energy company, awarded prizes to the finalists in their business competition, Heroes of Tomorrow. The seven finalists on stage were all young men. After the winner had received his prize and been congratulated by his fellow contestants and the company representatives, Norway's female ambassador to Tanzania called on stage two of the young women who had participated in the competition. She hailed them for their efforts and awarded them token prizes.

Multinational corporations (MNCs) have been criticized for their rhetorical support to—as opposed to substantive engagement with—gender equality in their corporate social responsibility (CSR) activities in low-income countries. This chapter focuses on the factors that influence the gendered dimensions of CSR in the petroleum sector: host country regulations, perceptions of risk, and the company's profile in terms of gender equality. We use Equinor in Tanzania as a case study. Equinor is a private energy company focusing mainly on oil and gas, in which the Norwegian state owns 67 percent of the shares. We argue that national regulations in host countries, perceptions of risk, as well as the need to gain a social license to operate from host communities mean that the gendered dimensions of CSR in the petroleum sector differ in important ways from other sectors. The study also shows that company ownership by a state that profiles itself as a champion of gender equality does not in itself lead to gender-sensitive social investments. The main beneficiaries of Equinor's social investments in Tanzania in the period 2014–18 were men, but this fact is disguised by the use of gender-neutral language in CSR reporting.

Global development institutions, such as the UN and the World Bank, have invited business entities to play a central role as development partners, and several of the Sustainable Development Goals (SDGs) are linked to the private sector. Many corporations have embraced this new role as part of their corporate social responsibility (CSR) strategies. At the same time, the "gender equality as smart economics" agenda has won terrain. This agenda was initially introduced by the World Bank and later adopted by the UN, other development actors, and business. By claiming to empower women, corporations attempt to moralize their image in order to attract consumers and investors and to expand their markets (Calkin 2016: 164). The business case for empowering women is linked to women as consumers, women as beneficiaries of social investments, and women as employees, managers, and members of boards. Feminist researchers have criticized this instrumental engagement with gender equality for simply being window dressing and for disregarding the structural factors behind poverty and global inequality (Allison, Gregoratti, and Tornhill 2019; Calkin 2015b, 2017; Moeller 2013, 2018; Roberts 2015; Tornhill 2016). While some companies have appropriated the concept of women's empowerment for their own purposes, women as a group as well as women's perspectives and needs are still missing from many CSR initiatives (Grosser and McCarthy 2019: 1106; Kolk and Lenfant 2018:14). This is particularly true in the extractive sector.

CSR was for many years regarded as the voluntary contributions of corporations to society. Multinational corporations (MNCs) in the extractive sector have been heavily criticized for bypassing governments by territorial enclaving and for taking over the role of the state by offering social services and thus increasing their own power (Ferguson 2005; Rajak 2011, 2016a). Recent years have seen a trend by host countries to introduce laws and policies that regulate CSR and make corporate contributions mandatory (Hayk 2019; Jayaraman, D'souza, and Ghoshal 2018; Wanvik 2014). However, there has been limited research on the way in which such actors are involved in CSR decision-making and how they influence the processes and outcomes of CSR (Gilberthorpe and Rajak 2017; Welker 2014; Hayk 2019; Knudsen 2018; Scheyvens, Banks, and Hughes 2016; Strønen 2020; chapter 6 in this volume). In addition to the companies themselves, central and local governments, NGOs, consultancy firms, and various forms of community representatives, including traditional authorities, can be involved.

A number of authors have called for studies of the "institutional culture of actors in the corporatized gender-equality agenda" (Calkin 2015a: 305) and for "more field-based research on how corporations engage in gender and development" (Allison et al. 2019: 54). In this chapter, we look at the different factors that may influence the gendering of CSR, focusing on the following research question: Why, despite Norway's focus on gender equality, did Equinor not succeed in implementing a stronger gender focus in its Tanzanian operations?

Equinor is an interesting case for a study of the gendered aspects of CSR in the extractive sector for several reasons. First, it is an MNC from the Global North with large investments in the oil and gas sectors of several countries in the Global South. Second, Equinor is a national oil company in which the Norwegian state is the largest shareholder with 67 percent ownership. Norway is a country that has profiled itself as a champion of gender equality and, in its foreign policy, has stated explicitly that other countries can learn from its experience (Selbervik and Østebø 2013; Skjelsbæk and Tryggestad 2020).

There is a certain Anglo-American bias to the literature on CSR (Knudsen Rajak et al. 2020; introduction to this volume), focusing on private companies from the English-speaking world. But the ownership of the MNC—that is, whether the company is private or state owned—and the MNC's geopolitical background can potentially play a role when it comes to CSR (Frynas 2009). So far, few studies have investigated the link between the gendered dimensions of the CSR of state-owned companies and the gender policies of the states that own them.

Due to unresolved legal regulations within the petroleum sector in Tanzania, a final investment decision has yet to be made, but Equinor, together with other petroleum companies, plans to build a plant for liquified natural gas (LNG) in Southern Tanzania. In an effort to comply with national policies and laws and in order to secure a social licence to operate, Equinor has made a number of social investments.

A working hypothesis for this study was that Equinor's CSR in Tanzania would reflect Norway's self-proclaimed concern with gender equality. Our hypothesis proved to be only partially accurate. We argue that the company has adopted the business case for gender equality in terms of leadership and staff, but corporate guidelines do not focus on gender equality in social investments. In the four-year period 2014–18, Equinor's social investments at the local level in Tanzania almost exclusively benefited men. A comparison with Equinor's social investments in Brazil demonstrates the importance of regulations in the host country and the qualifications and profile of local partners (consultancy firms and NGOs).

Methods

This study is part of a larger multiyear research project titled Energethics: Norwegian Energy Companies Abroad; Expanding the Anthropological Understanding of Corporate Social Responsibility (see introduction to this volume). Data collection took place in Tanzania and Norway in the period January 2016 to December 2019 and focused on labor rights (chapter 8 and Lange 2020) and gender equality in social investments (this chapter and Lange and Wyndham 2021).[1] In 2018, the company changed its name from Statoil to Equinor. For simplicity, we will refer to the company as Equinor throughout this chapter.

We interviewed and had informal conversations with sustainability staff at various levels, board members, country managers, and community liaison officers as well as representatives of civil society organizations at both the national and local levels. We also examined the company's web pages and relevant Tanzanian and Norwegian policy documents. We have focused on projects that were set up specifically as social investments by Equinor and that were initiated before December 2018.[2]

The chapter is structured as follows: first, we present an overview of the literature on the promotion and regulation of CSR and the role of national institutions and perceptions of risk in the extractive sector. We then follow with a presentation of the role that the Norwegian state, as the majority owner of Equinor, takes in shaping the company's CSR. The main part of the chapter analyzes Equinor's self-presentation as a corporation, demonstrates the way in which its most costly social investments in Tanzania were put in place as a result of legal requirements in the host country, and examines how perceptions of risk and the efforts to achieve a social license to operate have shaped the social investments at community level. The conclusion summarizes the findings of the study and draws some parallels between Equinor's projects in Brazil and Tanzania, arguing that national regulations—and characteristics of the consultancy sector in the two countries—can partly explain the great discrepancy between the company's CSR projects in the two countries.

Regulating and Promoting CSR: Global and National Measures

The UN has called for the involvement of the private sector in development efforts, and the SDGs differ markedly from the Millennium Development Goals (MDGs) by explicitly giving business a role to play (Hayk 2019; United Nations 2020). In the early 2000s, many corporations started linking their CSR to sustainability (Dashwood 2012; Dolan and Rajak 2016), and several scholars have argued that MNCs, particularly those that operate in the Global South, have co-opted the discourse of sustainable development (Gilberthorpe and Banks 2012; Orock 2013: 46; Spencer 2018). One reason why MNCs may be inclined to link up to the SDGs is that the goals, in the words of Rochelle Spencer (2018: 79), "do not challenge the structural causes of poverty, the patterns of wealth distribution, and structural inequality."

Companies in the food/drinks and apparel sector—such as Coca-Cola and Nike—have, as a central part of their CSR, made a claim of empowering adolescent girls and women in an effort to "moralize the corporation" (Calkin 2016: 164). In the case of Nike, the focus on empowerment of adolescent girls came as a response to public critique of the company, which took the form of anti-sweatshop campaigns and the anti-globalization movement (Moeller 2014). Feminists have debated the difference between rhetorical and substantive "engagement with feminist aims" and to what degree feministic ideas and goals have been depoliticized by mainstream institutions (Calkin 2015a: 304; de Jong and Kimm 2017). While some feminists have argued that the co-optation of feminist aims has in fact served to "legitimize anti-feminist policy goals," others have argued that the visibility of gender in current development work reflects "the success of particular strands of (neo) liberal feminism" (Calkin 2015a). Adrienne Roberts (2015) has coined the term "transnational business feminism" (TBF) to describe the market-oriented approach to gender inequality, which holds that it makes sense economically to invest in women and to include them at all levels of decision-making.

In addition to linking their business activities to the MDGs and SDGs, many MNCs have signed voluntary global guidelines, including the UN Global Compact (UNGC), which was launched in 2000. The Global Compact presents itself as the "world's largest corporate sustainability initiative" (UN Global Compact 2020) but has been criticized for being merely symbolic, "legitimizing the business case for development" (Roberts and Soederberg 2012), and for allowing "member companies to enhance their reputation despite few mechanisms for accountability" (Welker 2014: 145). The UNGC lends not only authority to the MNCs that are signatories to it but also offers concepts and terms that the companies can reproduce in their image building and reporting on CSR (Rajak 2016b: 46). Daniel Berliner and Aseem Prakash (2015: 115) have introduced the term "bluewashing" to describe this effect of membership in UNGC. In an effort to link itself to gender equality agendas, the UNGC collaborated with UN Women in 2010 to formulate the seven Women's Empowerment Principles, but gender equality is not mentioned in the ten UNGC principles that companies sign on to.

Corporate social responsibility was for many years understood as the voluntary contributions to society that a company undertakes in order to enhance its public image and to secure a social license to operate. CSR, then, was an add-on to the taxes and royalties that companies were obliged to pay by law. Many states have failed to regulate the practices of multinational corporations (Dolan and Rajak 2011; Idemudia 2014; Spencer 2018). In the case of the extractive industries, limited regulation is linked to advice from the World Bank in the 1980s and 1990s, which recommended that countries in sub-Saharan Africa put in place investor-friendly laws and policies to attract investors (Hilson 2012; Lange 2011).

In recent years, a number of countries, including India, Indonesia, and Ghana, have enacted laws that regulate CSR and make it mandatory (Hayk 2019; Jayaraman et al. 2018; Pandey and Mukherjee 2019; Wanvik 2014). In Brazil, special requirements for the petroleum sector were introduced in 2011, mandating that oil and gas companies must by law implement community projects. The process is organized by a subdivision of the Brazilian Ministry of the Environment: the Brazilian Institute of the Environment and Renewable Natural Resources (IBAMA). IBAMA was set up under President Lula da Silva and is still staffed by people who are concerned about civic and political rights (as seen in chapter 6). The consultancies are invited to submit project proposals in line with IBAMA's guidelines, and the projects are then developed in cooperation between IBAMA, the consultancy, and the corporation. The consultancy firm that oversees Equinor's social investment in Brazil is inspired by "the tradition of popular education and critical pedagogy" in the country, where "subaltern groups must develop knowledge about the structural conditions for their marginalization, learn to think of themselves as political, acting subjects, and develop collective emancipatory strategies in order for social transformation to occur" (Strønen 2020: 49). In addition to helping women improve their economic status, including pension rights, the judicial status of the association "allows them to solicit representation in formal municipal consultative councils and to solicit audiences with political bodies" (Strønen 2020: 48). Through the project then, the women involved have managed to gain political representation. Strønen found that, when oil and gas prices plummeted in 2015, Equinor decided to stop financing some of their voluntary social investments in Brazil, but the project targeting poor women was continued because it was mandatory by law.

Like Exxon (Muñoz and Burnham 2016: 153), Equinor is very attentive to compliance. One reason is that corporations within the extractive sector have enormous up-front capital costs and are therefore quite concerned with risk. MNCs face risk from national governments, which may withdraw concessions in case of noncompliance or may change regulatory frameworks, including nationalization of the resources (Lange and Kinyondo 2016; Sørreime and Tronvoll 2020; Wilson 2015; and chapter 6 in this volume). MNCs also face risk from local communities in the form of social unrest (Dashwood 2012; Davis and Franks 2014: 32; Shapiro, Hobdari, and Oh 2018), and many are open about the fact that CSR is, first of all, a question of risk management and getting a social license to operate (Kirsch 2016; Wanvik 2016: 524). Calkin adds a twist and describes CSR as "a mechanism to minimize resistance" (Calkin 2016: 159). This is often done by sponsoring social services and infrastructure in collaboration with local stakeholders (Frynas 2009: 4; Visser 2006).

In the coming sections, we contribute to this field of research by analyzing the gendered aspects of Equinor's CSR: the role played by Equinor's majority owner, the Norwegian state; the way in which Equinor presents its CSR at the corporate level; host country regulations; and the social investments that the company has carried out at the national and local levels in Tanzania.

Equinor's CSR at Corporate Level: Limited Regulation by the Owner

Statoil was established in 1972 as a national oil company. It started operating abroad in the 1990s and is now present in more than thirty countries. Statoil was partly privatized in 2001, and in May 2018 the company changed its name to Equinor. The majority shareholder of Equinor is the Norwegian state, with 67 percent of the shares. Norway has a strong tradition for state-supported feminism, and there is largely a consensus for gender equality. Ingunn Skjelsbæk and Torunn Tryggestad (2020: 184) argue that, in Norway, gender equality has in fact "emerged as an identity marker of a core value that characterizes 'us.'" Gender equal, they write, "is a descriptive term for the national identity." In 2016, when the Norwegian foreign minister launched the new National Action Plan for Women's Rights and Gender Equality in Norway's Foreign and Development Policy (Ministry of Foreign Affairs 2016), he argued that Norway could become a "superpower" within the fields of pro-gender foreign policies (Skjelsbæk and Tryggestad 2020: 183).

While Norway flags gender equality in its aid programs, the Norwegian government has adopted a hands-off policy when it comes to state-owned MNCs, such as Equinor. Norway requires state-owned companies to sign on to the UNGC, apply the Global Reporting Initiative (GRI) standards, adhere to the OECD responsible business conduct recommendations, and "take up ILO's core conventions in their business" (Knudsen, Müftüoğlu, and Hugøy 2020: 61; and chapter 10). Apart from this, there is little interference in state-owned companies.

Equinor's Self-Presentation

The image of a young, smiling blond woman on an offshore platform adorns Equinor's web page on sustainability (Equinor 2020c). In terms of global CSR initiatives, Equinor's website refers to the company's adherence to the UNGC and eight other external voluntary codes (2020c). The company's sustainability report for 2019 links strategies, milestones, and performance directly to six different SDGs—"Decent work and economic growth, Life below water, Partnerships for the goals, Quality education, Affordable and clean energy, and Climate action" (Equinor 2020a: 11)—but not to SDG 5: "Achieve gender equality and empower all women and girls." For Equinor, the moralizing of the corporation is not tied to gender but to climate change and the efforts to brand itself as a climate-friendly corporation.

In the scholarship on business and gender, there has been concern with the limited number of women on most company boards and the fact that "women remain under-represented at the most senior corporate level" (Gutiérrez-Fernández and Fernández-Torres 2020). Equinor's sustainability reports demonstrate that the company gives high priority to informing the public about the gender profile of the staff. The report for 2019, for example, states that, in that year, 30 percent of the permanent employees were women and that Equinor submitted "employees' gender profile for inclusion in the Bloomberg Gender-Equality Index"[3] (Equinor 2020a: 55). The report also presents a graph showing more than one-third of leadership positions as being held by women. What is missing from the sustainability reports in the last few years, however, is reporting that shows how gender is considered in the company's social investment efforts.

The company's change of name from Statoil to Equinor in 2018 was a major exercise in corporate communication. In addition to numerous advertisements in newspapers and magazines, the company released a one-minute commercial titled "Equinor: This Is What Changed Us" (Equinor 2018b). One of the very first sequences of the film shows Norwegian women marching in the 1970s under the banner "Unity in the fight for women's emancipation."[4] In her analysis of this commercial, Emilie Hesselberg (2019: 36, 65) argues that Equinor uses women's liberation as a metonym for development and change and thus seeks to create a link between women's rights and Equinor's business activities. The reference to gender equality as national branding for Nordic countries is not uncommon (Jezierska and Towns 2018; Nickelsen 2019). It should be noted that the film also shows a gay couple with a baby and a wedding between a woman of color and a white man. The main message of the film is that Norwegian society has changed for the better and so has Statoil/Equinor, which has evolved from being an oil and gas company to a "broad energy company" and thus needs a new name that reflects this change (Equinor 2018b).

National Regulations in the Host Country: Tanzania

The discoveries of large natural gas deposits in Tanzania from 2012 onward spurred a heated debate as to how the resource could best benefit the country. Based on the negative experiences with MNCs' investment in the country's mining sector, politicians and local businessmen argued that it was important not only to secure fair revenues to the state but also to ensure that this sector created employment for Tanzanians. The National Natural Gas Policy of 2013 emphasizes skills development of Tanzanians in the sector (United Republic of Tanzania 2013: 14–15). The Petroleum Act of 2015 makes it mandatory for all companies within the sector to draft detailed plans for local content (United Republic of Tanzania 2015b), and there are strict restrictions on the number of foreign employees that a company operating in Tanzania is allowed to hire (Kinyondo and Villanger 2017; Lange and Kinyondo 2016: 1102; United Republic of Tanzania 2015b).

In direct response to the local content requirements, Equinor initiated a program to support higher education within the fields of geosciences and petroleum engineering through a collaboration between universities in Tanzania, Angola, and Norway (Statoil 2017b). In the period 2013 to 2017, Equinor spent US$2.3 million on the Angola Norway Tanzania Higher Education Initiative (ANTHEI) program.[5] In the batch of petroleum geoscience students who graduated from the ANTHEI program in December 2016, there were eight men and only one woman. The gender balance is better in the master's degree program in petroleum financing, where approximately 30 percent of the students are women.[6] However, there are no gender disaggregated data on the company's web pages or in the sustainability reports, just an overall total number of students.

Tanzania's Environmental Management Act (2004) mandates Environmental Impact Assessments, and the National Natural Gas Policy (2013) has a short section on CSR, but up to 2015 Tanzania had no laws, policies, or guidelines focused specifically on CSR. Equinor was therefore relatively free to design their social investments projects in line with their own corporate policies. In the coming section, we will present these policies and the social investments that were carried out at the local level in Southern Tanzania.

Equinor's CSR in Relation to Risk at Community Level and Achieving a Social License to Operate

An important part of Equinor's self-identification and image is to have high ethical standards. The company refers to its performance culture as "values-based" (Equinor 2018a: 22). The most central guideline in this regard is the *Equinor Book* (formerly the *Statoil Book*), a fifty-page document presenting, among other things, the vision, values, performance framework, and corporate toolbox of the company. Approximately half a page is dedicated to a section on "working with communities," where the main message is that Equinor will conduct its business in a manner consistent with the ten principles of UNGC and the United Nations Guiding Principles on Business and Human Rights (Equinor 2018a: 20). The book states that the company is "committed to equal opportunity," but it does not mention gender or women (Equinor 2018a: 24).

Since gender is absent from the company's main policy document at the global level, the incorporation of gender perspectives depends

Table 7.1. Overview of stakeholders and relevant policy documents. © Siri Lange

Stakeholders that Equinor relate to for their planned investment in Tanzania	Relevant policy documents	Mention of "women" or "gender"
The Norwegian state	white papers	No
The United Republic of Tanzania	National Natural Gas Policy, 2013	Yes
	The Petroleum Act, 2015	Yes
Host communities in Mtwara and Lindi	CSRE policy	No
	The Equinor Book	No
	Equinor's human rights policy	No

to a large degree on the national regulations in the host countries, the interests and qualifications of the sustainability staff at the various levels, and, possibly, perceptions about risk. In the coming sections, we will present the social investment projects that the company carried out in Tanzania in the period 2014–18.

The gigantic natural gas reserves in Tanzania are located off the coast in the southern part of the country outside the regions of Mtwara and Lindi. These regions fare very poorly in terms of socioeconomic indicators compared to Northern Tanzania. The overwhelmingly Muslim population is commonly stigmatized by outsiders for ostensibly lacking interest in development, while the southerners themselves feel that they have been neglected and marginalized from development (Ahearne and Childs 2018; Kamat et al. 2019). In 2013, the government decided that onshore gas that was extracted by a Chinese company in Mtwara should be piped to the industrial areas around Dar es Salaam rather than processed locally. Violence erupted in Mtwara, resulting in at least six deaths (Ahearne and Childs 2018; Must 2018; Poncian 2019). Although the violence was directed against the government and not the company, the situation was a clear sign to the petroleum companies that the local population was frustrated and that the companies could potentially be the next target. The great majority of the people who participated in the riots were young men (Kamat et al. 2019; Must and Rustad 2019).

Sponsoring Surgery for Lymphatic Filariasis

Equinor's main social investment in Southern Tanzania has been support to the treatment of lymphatic filariasis, a neglected tropical disease (NTD). The disease is caused by a species of filarial worms that are transmitted by mosquitoes; it can lead to the abnormal enlargement of body parts, such as the scrotal area (hydrocele), and cause immense pain, disfigurement, and social stigma (World Health Organization 2020). In Tanzania, lymphatic filariasis is associated with fishermen.

As mentioned above, the great majority who participated in the 2013 protests against the planned gas pipeline were men. A study from Indonesia found that "local governments were very sensitive to unrest, and companies were therefore inclined to carry out CSR projects that had the potential to curb social unrest" (Wanvik 2014: 288). Based on this, one can speculate whether the company's motivation to sponsor men's health was linked to the 2013 riots. When we aired this possibility for Equinor Tanzania, however, the staff argued strongly against this interpretation. They emphasized that their motivation for the project was that, while there were many projects addressing malaria and HIV in the region, none dealt with lymphatic filariasis, and Equinor wanted "to do something different," "something that could change peoples' lives," where "the outcome would be very visible." As one interviewee put it: "Those who receive the surgery will never forget Statoil!"

The top management of Equinor Tanzania expressed some ambivalence about carrying out this form of philanthropic social investment. In interviews, they said that local expectations and requests for community support were extremely high, that they tried to communicate that Equinor is not a development agency but a business venture, and that they had not yet had any return on their investments in Tanzania. However, as had other Norwegian state-owned companies operating abroad (see chapter 10), Equinor adapted to the local perceptions of CSR and trusted their local sustainability staff's advice when they said that a project helping patients suffering from lymphatic filariasis would be very well received locally and contribute to a social license to operate.

By 2018, a total of 640 men had had been treated for the disease. On its web page, Equinor uses the gender-neutral term "persons" when referring to this number with no indication that this is an illness that, situationally, only men suffer from. In addition to creating general goodwill among the local population and thus a social license to operate, the company states that the program "provides a platform where we can engage with the regional government and local stakeholders" (Equinor 2020d). A senior Equinor manager readily admitted that the company rides "the wave of goodwill" created by the surgeries.[7]

In 2014, when the treatment of lymphatic filariasis project was conceived, there were no government policies focusing specifically for CSR in Tanzania. However, in 2015, the Ministry of Energy and Minerals published "Guidelines for Corporate Social Responsibility and Empowerment in the Extractive Industry in Tanzania," which they state would act as "soft law." The policy states that the ministry and local authorities "have the responsibility to guide and supervise the implementation of the CSRE programs" (United Republic of Tanzania 2015a). The guidelines thus mandate that all CSRE projects must be planned together with local authorities. Referring to the guidelines, a senior female staff member with the regional authorities in Lindi told us that they had informed Equinor that they needed to support a health project for women in addition to the project on lymphatic filariasis. The two parties agreed that, from 2019, Equinor would start supporting fistula repair for women. Obstetric fistula is "an abnormal opening between a woman's genital tract and her urinary tract or rectum" and the condition is a result of obstructed labor (World Health Organization 2022). Like lymphatic filariasis, obstetric fistula is a condition that entails stigma and that the underresourced public health system in Southern Tanzania has been unable to handle adequately. This example indicates that a change in policy—making the role of local government in the planning of CSR projects mandatory—contributed to a process in which Equinor expanded its support in the health sector to include health services for women. Equinor has continued funding the public health system to carry out these two forms of surgery in the period 2019–22. In the following section we turn to Equinor's support to business training for youth.

Creating (Male) Heroes for the Future through Business Training

Neoliberalization and structural adjustment reduced job opportunities in the public sector in many countries in the Global South, and self-employment and entrepreneurship have been launched as one of the main measures against poverty. Business training and microfinance projects have been promoted by both corporations and NGOs, the great majority of which have targeted women based on the idea that entrepreneurship can lift women and their families out of poverty (Calkin 2015a; McCarthy 2017; Roberts 2015; Tornhill 2016). It is therefore somewhat surprising that Equinor's efforts to stimulate entrepreneurship in Southern Tanzania made no attempts at targeting women as a group. On the contrary, the project has benefitted men almost exclusively.

The business competition was a localized version of Equinor's branding tool Heroes of Tomorrow (HoT), which supports "talented young people in sport, culture and education, helping them to become the Heroes of Tomorrow" (Equinor 2020b). In Tanzania, Equinor adapted HoT to focus on entrepreneurship. One reason for this was a wish to link the program to Tanzania's emphasis on local content in the oil and gas industries. On the Equinor Tanzania web page, the program is presented in the following way:

> The programme was established in 2014 and by 2016 more than 250 youth in Mtwara and Lindi were trained on entrepreneurship through this initiative. The first round of the competition had five winners while the second round saw 10 youth from Mtwara and Lindi emerging as winners. By 2018, more than 15 new businesses have been established in Mtwara and Lindi thanks to this programme. (Equinor 2020d)

By referring to the gender-neutral term "youth," the company conveniently hides the fact that, in both 2014 and 2016, all of the finalists were male. Lack of gender balance in the competition appears to be the result of a lack of gender sensitivity both among the Equinor staff involved and in the consultancy firm that Equinor hired to organize the competition. The consultancy firm was given responsibility for advertising the competition, to perform the first round of selection, and to train the shortlisted candidates. From more than four hundred applications, the consultancy firm selected forty candidates who were offered a six-day business management training course to improve their proposals. We do not have the exact figures for the male-female ratio among the contestants, but a picture of the HoT training in 2015 published by the consultancy firm (Darecha 2020) shows that, out of the approximately forty-eight people present, only four appear to be female. A list of the forty candidates was handed over to a panel of male and female experts chosen by Equinor from local businesses and academia.

By outsourcing a central part of the project to a consultancy firm that apparently lacked adequate knowledge of the local context and ways to involve women,[8] Equinor repeated the mistakes that some of the MNCs in the mining sector of Tanzania had made (Selmier, Newenham-Kahindi, and Oh 2015). However, rather than reflecting critically about what could have been done differently in order to involve more women, some of the Equinor staff blamed women's limited participation on cultural aspects in Southern Tanzania:

> There are some cultural aspects that make women feel that they should not go in front and show their abilities. This was the main problem in Mtwara and Lindi where girls are forced to get married at a younger age, so very few were able to "fight" in the competition where men were in big numbers. Very few women signed up for the competition and therefore their chance to win was already minimized.[9]

The argument made by the Equinor staff that cultural factors make involving women difficult is not uncommon. When women struggle to succeed for whatever reason (for example, due to poor markets) after having attended economic empowerment programs, blame is placed on cultural restraints "rather than material conditions" (Tornhill 2016). However, two other actors in the region have demonstrated that it is possible to design projects that benefit girls or involve women. In a project that aims to improve local communities' capacities to hold local authorities to account for the revenues from gas, Oxfam Tanzania has involved the same number of women as men by recruiting animators through the Village Assembly and by setting as a criterion that at least half of the participants must be female.[10] And Songas, a company processing onshore gas in the Lindi region, has earmarked two out of three scholarships for girls (Mwakyambiki, Sikira, and Massawe 2020). These two examples show that it was not characteristics of the local communities that hindered the inclusion of women in HoT: it was poor design. The examples also demonstrate the importance of working with the right partners.

The managers of Equinor Tanzania were uncomfortable with the fact that no women have been among the fifteen finalists during the two rounds of competitions. They explained to us that for the next round, they would introduce a system of female role models to inspire more women to participate. The role model idea was introduced at the award ceremony in 2016, where two young women, who had competed but were not among the top finalists, were presented with token awards by Norway's female ambassador to Tanzania. The ambassador held a speech in which she encouraged the two women to carry out their business ideas. The event was covered by local television channels and other news media. Improving image is one postulate for corporate engagement in CSR and branding (Aluchna

2017:16). Since journalists were covering the awards ceremony and a promotional video was produced,[11] the special awards to women probably served not only to present women as role models but also to improve the gender balance on stage and thus the company's visual imaginary. At the same time, the Equinor management, both at the headquarters level and at the country level, appeared to be genuinely concerned about the lack of gender balance in Heroes of Tomorrow. After the two first rounds, the competition has not been organized again.

Much of the criticism that feminist scholars have directed toward the so-called economic empowerment programs of MNCs, such as Coca-Cola and Nike, are relevant for Equinor's business training as well (Calkin 2015b; McCarthy 2017; Tornhill 2016). Equinor presented entrepreneurism as a solution for young, jobless people, but there are limited markets in Mtwara, particularly now that the offshore gas investments have been postponed. Moreover, the great majority of the participants in the two rounds of business training and contests were students at Stella Maris University, many of whom had come to Mtwara to study.[12] Not only did this project benefit almost exclusively men, but to a large degree it also benefited men from the more privileged parts of the country. There is great frustration in Mtwara and Lindi that the few job and business opportunities in the region are seized by "outsiders" (often Christians from the northern parts of the country).

The male-dominated business training in Tanzania stands in great contrast to the way that social investments are talked about at the headquarters level of Equinor in Norway, where we were told that the company pays "a high attention to gender issues," gives "extra attention to vulnerable groups," and asks "how women and men will be impacted." The manager at HQ level described these strategies as "affirmative action, making sure that women's voices are heard," and linked the company's concern with gender directly to Norwegian ownership: "Coming from Norway and being a Norwegian company helps."[13] To substantiate and illustrate this point, Equinor's project in Brazil—which targets poor women—was given as an example of Equinor's focus on women, despite the fact that Equinor did not design the project. The project in Brazil won Equinor's internal award for best safety and sustainability project globally in 2016 (Statoil 2017a). As seen in chapter 6, there is reason to believe that the project's success is closely linked to the fact that it is designed and implemented by a consultancy firm that is very professional and staffed by women who genuinely care about the women whom they are hired to help.

Table 7.2. Overview of Equinor's social investments in Tanzania 2014–18. © Siri Lange

Regulation/ motivation	Project investment	Partner(s)	Direct beneficiaries
Local content requirements (National Natural Gas Policy of 2013 and the Petroleum Act of 2015)	Higher education in geosciences and petroleum engineering (national level)	Norwegian and Tanzanian universities	Men (70–90 percent)
Social license to operate, mitigate risk	Treatment of lymphatic filariasis (local level)	Ministry of Health Regional hospitals	Men
	Business training for youth (local level)	Consultancy firm, Stella Maris University, Mtwara Regional Library	Men (approximately 90 percent)

As can been seen from table 7.2, Equinor's social investments in the period 2014-18 benefited first and foremost men. However, in Equinor Tanzania's information brochures from the same period (distributed in Tanzania in 2016 and 2017), women are overrepresented. For example, the brochure *Tanzania Gas Project—From Discovery to Gas Sales* has a front page showing Tanzanian schoolgirls wearing T-shirts with the company's logo. In the brochure, there are pictures of fifteen Tanzanian females and eight males. Another brochure, titled *Sustainability* in English and *Sisi na jamii* (We and the society) in Swahili, has a smiling African woman wearing a helmet with the company logo on the front page. This brochure has pictures of eight women and five men. The picture representations indicate that Equinor, just like many other corporations and organizations, seeks to showcase women as the beneficiaries of the company's social investments.

Conclusion

This chapter has unpacked the gendered aspects of Equinor's CSR as it is presented at the corporate level and enacted through the company's social investments in Tanzania. Feminist research has criticized global corporations' rhetorical support to gender equality for their own gain (Calkin 2015a). Our findings demonstrate that companies in the oil and gas sector differ in important ways from the kind of companies that feminist research has focused on up to now: global companies that manufacture products for markets in the Global North.

Equinor anchors its CSR in the term *sustainability*, and the company states that its ambition is to "contribute to sustainable development."[14] This is a bold ambition for an oil and gas company in an era of intense public focus on climate change. The company's sustainability reports and web pages have therefore focused on rebranding itself as a climate-friendly energy company. In contrast to companies like Nike and Coca-Cola, which have designed their CSR to appeal to consumers in the Global North and claimed to empower women and girls in the economically disadvantaged parts of the world (Calkin 2017; Moeller 2014; Roberts 2015; Tornhill 2016), the main stakeholders for companies operating in the extractive sector—those who have the power to make an investment profitable or in the worst case a gigantic loss—are government authorities and project-affected communities. Considerations of risk are therefore central to all decisions that the company makes.

One of the main interests of this chapter was to investigate the ways in which guidelines and regulations at global and national levels influence the CSR of oil and gas companies. It has been argued that state ownership of an MNC can have important consequences for its CSR (Frynas 2009) and that companies' strategic decisions, "such as CSR and gender issues reporting, are clearly influenced by the institutional context of the country in which the company is located" (García-Sánchez, Oliveira, and Martínez-Ferrero 2020:370). Based on this, our hypothesis was that Equinor, the majority of which is owned by a state that has gender equality as one of its main trademarks, would be concerned with gender equality in its social investments. However, as seen in the introduction to this volume, state ownership plays a limited role since the Norwegian state does not formulate its own regulations for state-owned companies operating abroad but requires companies to comply with international frameworks. Gender equality is not central in the global CSR initiatives that the company has signed on to nor is it anchored in the company's documents and policies on sustainability.

Each country office is given complete autonomy when it comes to designing community investments, but in line with Equinor's focus on compliance, they do so in accordance with legal regulations. As seen in chapter 6, Iselin Strønen's findings from Equinor's social investments in Brazil offer important lessons on the role of national laws and guidelines when compared to our findings from Tanzania. Brazilian law requires petroleum companies to have projects that support marginalized groups in host communities. A government body monitors the projects, while the projects are designed and implemented by consultancy firms in collaboration with the funders. In Tanzania, by contrast, there is no governmental body to oversee CSR in the extractive sector and no law that requires oil and gas companies to support local communities. The only legislation that regulates the companies' CSR is the Petroleum Act, which requires companies to hire and train local staff. Equinor's main social investment is directly linked to this legislation, and since engineering is a field dominated by males, the majority of the beneficiaries have been men. Our study also indicates that Tanzania's soft law on CSRE (the CSRE policy) helped local authorities secure support for a project that targeted women's health. Future research is important to help us examine the ways in which host governments can alter the power asymmetries between transnational companies and themselves (Hayk 2019; Scheyvens et al. 2016).

In this study, we were also interested in the role of local partners in the design and implementation of social investments. Again, a comparison with Equinor's project in Brazil is relevant. As seen in chapter 6, in Brazil, progressive intellectuals, civil society organizations, and social movements constitute a historical counterforce to corporate and elite power. The consultancy firm that implements Equinor's award-winning project is inspired by "the tradition of popular education and critical pedagogy" in the country, and Strønen concludes that the project has indeed had "a transformative effect on many of the women's lives" (Strønen 2020: 50). In Tanzania, Equinor carried out business training in collaboration with a local consultancy firm that appears to have been completely gender blind, resulting in a situation where very few women participated in the training and no women were among the top fifteen finalists. Women's organizations at the national level in Tanzania have been skeptical of collaboration with petroleum companies because they fear the reputational risk (Wyndham and Lange 2019). A national law on CSR and a national regulative body, as in Brazil, could perhaps have contributed toward making such collaboration less risky for the CSOs and could have contributed to a more equal power balance between them and the corporations.

In line with the ideals of transnational business feminism (Roberts 2015), Equinor's sustainability reports present gender-disaggregated data as recommended by international CSR frameworks, such as the gender balance among staff and in leadership, but the reports do not emphasize gender equality in its social investments. Although the company links its activities to the SDGs, it does not present itself as a development actor, a development expert, or an expert on gender equality and empowerment, as some other MNCs have (Roberts 2015: 224). However, Equinor has in common with many other MNCs (Calkin 2015a) the tendency to use women and girls as its public face. By using a gender-neutral language in their reporting on social investments in Tanzania, referring to the male beneficiaries as "persons" and "youth" and by overrepresenting girls and women in their visual communication, Equinor—which is owned by a country that has gender equality as one of its trademarks—manages to a certain degree to disguise the fact that in the period 2014–18, the company's main beneficiaries in Tanzania were male. As of November 2022, Equinor had yet to make its final investment decision, and social investments at the local level have therefore been kept to a minimum in recent years. However, based on the discomfort that Equinor managers revealed to us when discussing the lack of gender balance in their local projects, there is reason to believe that the company will make efforts to redesign its social investments to benefit women as well as men if the plan to build an onshore plant for liquefied natural gas (LNG) is carried out.

Acknowledgments

This book chapter is a revised version of an article published in 2021: "Gender, Regulation, and Corporate Social Responsibility in the Extractive Sector: The Case of Equinor's Social Investments in Tanzania." *Women's Studies International Forum* 84: 102434. The study was funded by a FRIPRO grant from the Research Council of Norway (grant no. 240617). Ethical clearance was granted from Tanzania Commission for Science and Technology (COSTECH, permit number 2019–190–NA 2016–30). The authors have not received any financial support from the company during the course of the study and have no personal ties to any of its staff. We wish to thank Equinor for letting us interview staff members at its headquarters in Norway and at their Tanzania branch. We are grateful to all of the individuals who shared their viewpoints and experiences with us as well as the anonymous reviewers for their very constructive comments. We also wish to thank Haldis Haukanes, Ståle Knudsen, Liv Tønnessen, Iselin

Strønen, Vibeke Wang, and the members of the Rights and Gender Cluster at CMI for commenting on earlier drafts of this chapter.

Siri Lange holds a PhD in social anthropology and is a professor in the Department of Health Promotion and Development (HEMIL) at the University of Bergen, Norway. Prior to joining HEMIL, Lange was a senior researcher at the Chr. Michelsen Institute (CMI) in Bergen (2002–17). Lange has published extensively on social, economic, and political issues in Tanzania.

Victoria Wyndham holds a master's degree in global development from the University of Bergen, Norway. She currently works at the British Institute of International and Comparative Law.

Notes

An earlier version of this chapter was published as: Lange, Siri, and Victoria Wyndham. 2021. "Gender, Regulation, and Corporate Social Responsibility in the Extractive Sector: The Case of Equinor's Social Investments in Tanzania." *Women's Studies International Forum* 84: 102434.

1. The first author carried out eight field visits to Tanzania (Dar es Salaam, Lindi, Mtwara, and Mwanza) and visited three different Equinor branches in Norway (Bergen, Oslo, and Stavanger). Interviews were conducted in English, Norwegian, and Swahili. As part of her master's thesis (Wyndham 2018), the second author conducted interviews in Dar es Salaam and Stavanger in October and November 2017 together with the first author. All interviewees have been granted anonymity.
2. Since we focus on projects that were set up specifically as social investments, we exclude Equinor's sponsorship of the 2015 annual meeting of one of the umbrella organizations for CSOs in Mtwara. We also exclude a project on safety training for fishermen that was a requirement linked to an environmental impact assessment (EIA) as well as projects that the company has sponsored as part of their former consortium with Shell.
3. "The reporting framework provides a comprehensive, standardized format for companies to voluntarily disclose information on how they promote gender equality across four distinct areas: company statistics, policies, community engagement and products and services" (https://www.bloomberg.com/company/press/2019-bloomberg-gender-equality-index/).
4. *Enhet i kampen for kvinnenes frigjøring.*
5. A substantial part of the budget goes directly to Norwegian universities to pay for the salaries and travel expenses of the Norwegian professors.
6. Lange, observations in class and interviews with lecturers, December 2018.
7. Lange, interview in Dar es Salaam, 14 October 2016.
8. The owner and head of the "social enterprise firm" Darecha hails from and grew up in Dar es Salaam; http://www.africanleadershipacademy.org/staffuly/young-leaders/julius-shirima-tanzania/.
9. Lange and Wyndham, interview in Dar es Salaam, 24 November 2017.

10. Lange, interview in Lindi with representative for Lindi Region Association for NGOs (LANGO), 6 December 2019, and in Dar es Salaam with representative for Oxfam Tanzania, 11 December 2019.
11. The award ceremony can be watched approximately forty-three minutes into the forty-seven-minute-long promotional video for HoT in Tanzania: https://www.youtube.com/watch?time_continue=3andv=sWTmTBNTEfYandfeature=emb_logo.
12. Lange, interview in Mtwara with headmaster and lecturers at Stella Maris, 28 November 2019.
13. Lange and Wyndham, interview, 13 September 2017.
14. https://www.equinor.com/en/how-and-why/sustainability/recognition-and-awards.html.

References

Ahearne, R., and J. Childs. 2018. "'National Resources?' The Fragmented Citizenship of Gas Extraction in Tanzania." *Journal of Eastern African Studies* 12(4): 696–715.
Allison, K., C. Gregoratti, and S. Tornhill. 2019. "From the Academy to the Boardroom: Methodological Challenges and Insights on Transnational Business Feminism." *Feminist Review* 121(1): 53–65.
Aluchna, M. 2017. "Is Corporate Social Responsibility Sustainable? A Critical Approach." In *The Dynamics of Corporate Social Responsibility: A Critical Approach to Theory and Practice*, edited by S. Idowu and M. Aluchna. Cham: Springer.
Berliner, D., and A. Prakash. 2015. "'Bluewashing' the Firm? Voluntary Regulations, Program Design, and Member Compliance with the United Nations Global Compact." *Policy Studies Journal* 43(1): 115–38.
Calkin, S. 2015a. "Feminism, Interrupted? Gender and Development in the Era of 'Smart Economics.'" *Progress in Development Studies* 15(4): 295–307.
———. 2015b. "Post-feminist Spectatorship and the Girl Effect: 'Go Ahead, Really Imagine Her.'" *Third World Quarterly* 36(4): 654–69.
———. 2016. "Globalizing 'Girl Power': Corporate Social Responsibility and Transnational Business Initiatives for Gender Equality." *Globalizations* 13(2): 158–72.
———. 2017. "Disrupting Disempowerment: Feminism, Co-optation, and the Privatised Governance of Gender and Development." *New Formations* 91(18): 69–86.
Darecha. 2020. "Social Investment Project Management Services." Retrieved 24 May 2020 from https://darecha.org/services/csr-project-management-services/.
Dashwood, H. S. 2012. "CSR Norms and Organizational Learning in the Mining Sector." *Corporate Governance: The International Journal of Business in Society* 12(1): 118–38.
Davis, R., and D. Franks. 2014. *Costs of Company-Community Conflict in the Extractive Sector Corporate Social Responsibility Initiative*. Report No. 66. Cambridge, MA: Harvard Kennedy School.
de Jong, S., and S. Kimm. 2017. "The Co-optation of Feminisms: A Research Agenda." *International Feminist Journal of Politics* 19(2): 185–200.
Dolan, C., and D. Rajak. 2011. "Introduction: Ethnographies of Corporate Ethicizing." *Focaal—Journal of Global and Historical Anthropology* 60: 3–8.
———. 2016. "Toward the Anthropology of Corporate Social Anthropology." In *The Anthropology of Corporate Social Anthropology*, edited by C. Dolan and D. Rajak, 1–28. New York: Berghahn Books.
Equinor. 2018a. *The Equinor Book: Version 1.0*. Oslo: Equinor.
———. 2018b. *Equinor: This Is What Changed Us*. Film. 2020, from https://www.youtube.com/watch?v=Ec3N64De1tk.

———. 2020a. *2019 Sustainability Report*. Retrieved 24 May 2020 from https://www.equinor.com/en/how-and-why/sustainability.html.
———. 2020b. "About Us: Equinor Sponsorships." Retrieved 24 May 2020 from https://www.equinor.com/en/about-us.html#sponsorship.
———. 2020c. "Sustainability at Equinor." Retrieved 24 May 2020 from https://www.equinor.com/en/how-and-why/sustainability.html.
———. 2020d. "Tanzania." Retrieved 24 May 2020 from https://www.equinor.com/en/where-we-are/tanzania.
Ferguson, J. 2005. "Seeing Like an Oil Company: Space, Security, and Global Capital in Neoliberal Africa." *American Anthropologist* 107(3): 377–82.
Frynas, J. G. 2009. *Beyond Corporate Social Responsibility: Oil Multinationals and Social Challenges*. Cambridge: Cambridge University Press.
García-Sánchez, I.-M., M. C. Oliveira, and J. Martínez-Ferrero. 2020. "Female Directors and Gender Issues Reporting: The Impact of Stakeholder Engagement at Country Level." *Corporate Social Responsibility and Environmental Management* 27(1): 369–82.
Gilberthorpe, E., and G. Banks. 2012. "Development on Whose Terms? CSR Discourse and Social Realities in Papua New Guinea's Extractive Industries Sector." *Resources Policy* 37(2): 185–93.
Gilberthorpe, E., and D. Rajak. 2017. "The Anthropology of Extraction: Critical Perspectives on the Resource Curse." *Journal of Development Studies* 53(2): 186–204.
Grosser, K., and L. McCarthy. 2019. "Imagining New Feminist Futures: How Feminist Social Movements Contest the Neoliberalization of Feminism in an Increasingly Corporate-Dominated World." *Gender, Work and Organization* 26(8): 1100–1116.
Gutiérrez-Fernández, M., and Y. Fernández-Torres. 2020. "Does Gender Diversity Influence Business Efficiency? An Analysis from the Social Perspective of CSR." *Sustainability* 12(9).
Hayk, A. C. 2019. "Enabling Locally-Embedded Corporate Social Responsibility: A Constructivist Perspective on International Oil Companies Delivering Healthcare in Rural Ghana." *Extractive Industries and Society* 6(4): 1224–33.
Hesselberg, E. 2019. "Et naturlig navnevalg? En kritisk diskursanalyse av kommunikasjonen av navneendringen fra Statoil til Equinor" [A natural choice for a new name? A critical discourse analysis of the communication related to the change of name from Statoil to Equinor]. Master's thesis in social communication, University of Agder, Kristiansand, Norway.
Hilson, G. 2012. "Corporate Social Responsibility in the Extractive Industries: Experiences from Developing Countries." *Resources Policy* 37(2): 131–37.
Idemudia, U. 2014. "Corporate-Community Engagement Strategies in the Niger Delta: Some Critical Reflections." *Extractive Industries and Society* 1(2): 154–62.
Jayaraman, A., V. D'souza, and T. Ghoshal. 2018. "NGO-Business Collaboration Following the Indian CSR Bill 2013: Trust-Building Collaborative Social Sector Partnerships." *Development in Practice* 28(6): 831–41.
Jezierska, K., and A. Towns. 2018. "Taming Feminism? The Place of Gender Equality in the 'Progressive Sweden' Brand." *Place Branding and Public Diplomacy* 14(1): 55–63.
Kamat, V. R., P. Le Billon, R. Mwaipopo, and J. Raycraft. 2019. "Natural Gas Extraction and Community Development in Tanzania: Documenting the Gaps Between Rhetoric and Reality." *Extractive Industries and Society* 6(3): 968–76.
Kinyondo, A., and E. Villanger. 2017. "Local Content Requirements in the Petroleum Sector in Tanzania: A Thorny Road from Inception to Implementation?" *Extractive Industries and Society* 4(2): 371–84.
Kirsch, S. 2016. "Virtuous Language in Industry and the Academy." In *The Anthropology of Corporate Social Responsibility*, edited by C. Dolan and D. Rajak. New York: Berghahn Books.

Knudsen, S. 2018. "Is Corporate Social Responsibility Oiling the Neoliberal Carbon Economy?" *Ethnos* 83(3): 505–20.
Knudsen, S., I. B. Müftüoğlu, and I. Hugøy. 2020. "Standardizing Responsibility through the Stakeholder Figure: Norwegian Hydropower in Turkey." *Focaal: Journal of Global and Historical Anthropology* 88: 58–75.
Knudsen, S., D. Rajak, S. Lange, and I. Hugøy. 2020. "Bringing the State Back In: Corporate Social Responsibility and the Paradoxes of Norwegian State Capitalism in the International Energy Sector." *Focaal: Journal of Global and Historical Anthropology* 88: 1–21.
Kolk, A., and F. Lenfant. 2018. "Responsible Business under Adverse Conditions: Dilemmas Regarding Company Contributions to Local Development." *Business Strategy and Development* 1(1): 8–16.
Lange, S. 2011. "Gold and Governance: Legal Injustices and Lost Opportunities in Tanzania." *African Affairs* 110(439): 233–52.
———. 2020. "Doing Global Investments the Nordic Way: The 'Business Case' for Equinor's Support to Union Work among Its Employees in Tanzania." *Focaal — Journal of Global and Historical Anthropology* 88: 22–39.
Lange, S., and A. Kinyondo. 2016. "Resource Nationalism and Local Content in Tanzania: Experiences from Mining and Consequences for the Petroleum Sector." *Extractive Industries and Society* 3(4): 1095–104.
Lange, S., and V. Wyndham. 2021. "Gender, Regulation, and Corporate Social Responsibility in the Extractive Sector: The Case of Equinor's Social Investments in Tanzania." *Women's Studies International Forum* 84: 102–434.
McCarthy, L. 2017. "Empowering Women through Corporate Social Responsibility: A Feminist Foucauldian Critique." *Business Ethics Quarterly* 27(4): 603–31.
Ministry of Foreign Affairs. 2016. *Freedom, Empowerment and Opportunities: Action Plan for Women's Rights and Gender Equality in Foreign and Development Policy 2016–2020*. Retrieved 22.11.2022 from: https://www.regjeringen.no/globalassets/departementene/ud/vedlegg/fn/womens_rights.pdf.
Moeller, K. 2013. "Proving 'the Girl Effect': Corporate Knowledge Production and Educational Intervention." *International Journal of Educational Development* 33(6): 612–21.
———. 2014. "Searching for Adolescent Girls in Brazil: The Transnational Politics of Poverty in 'the Girl Effect.'" *Feminist Studies* 40(3): 575–601.
———. 2018. *The Gender Effect: Capitalism, Feminism, and the Corporate Politics of Development*. Oakland: University of California Press.
Muñoz, J.-M., and P. Burnham. 2016. "Subcontracting as Corporate Social Responsibility in the Chad-Cameroon Pipeline Project." In *The Anthropology of Corporate Social Responsibility*, edited by C. Dolan and D. Rajak. New York: Berghahn Books.
Must, E. 2018. "Structural Inequality, Natural Resources and Mobilization in Southern Tanzania." *African Affairs* 117(466): 83–108.
Must, E., and S. A. Rustad. 2019. "'Mtwara will be the New Dubai': Dashed Expectations, Grievances, and Civil Unrest in Tanzania." *International Interactions* 45(3): 500–31.
Mwakyambiki, S. E., A. N. Sikira, and F. A. Massawe. 2020. "Gendered Access to Indirect Benefits from Natural Gas Extraction in Kilwa District, Tanzania." *International Journal of Social Sciences and Humanities* 4(1): 1–2.
Nickelsen, T. 2019. "Merkevaren Norden" [Nordic branding]. *Apollon* 2: 34–39.
Orock, R. T. E. 2013. "Less-Told Stories about Corporate Globalization: Transnational Corporations and CSR as the Politics of (ir)Responsibility in Africa." *Dialectical Anthropology* 37(1): 27–50.
Pandey, R., and A. Mukherjee. 2019. "Towards Anthropology of Corporate Social Responsibility in India." *Oriental Anthropologist: A Bi-annual International Journal of the Science of Man* 18(2): 223–44.
Poncian, J. 2019. "Extractive Resource Ownership and the Subnational Resource Curse: Insights from Tanzania." *Extractive Industries and Society* 6(2): 332–42.

Rajak, D. 2011. *In Good Company: An Anatomy of Corporate Social Responsibility*. Stanford, CA: Stanford University Press.

———. 2016a. "Expectations of Paternalism: Welfare, Corporate Responsibility, and HIV at South Africa's Mines." *South Atlantic Quarterly* 115(1): 33–59.

———. 2016b. "Theatres of Virtue: Collaboration, Consensus, and the Social Life of Corporate Social Responsibility." In *The Anthropology of Corporate Social Responsibility*, edited by C. Dolan and D. Rajak. New York: Berghahn Books.

Roberts, A. 2015. "The Political Economy of 'Transnational Business Feminism': Problematising the Corporate-Led Gender Equality Agenda." *International Feminist Journal of Politics* 17(2): 209–31.

Roberts, A., and S. Soederberg. 2012. "Gender Equality as Smart Economics? A Critique of the 2012 World Development Report." *Third World Quarterly* 33(5): 949–68.

Scheyvens, R., G. Banks, and E. Hughes. 2016. "The Private Sector and the SDGs: The Need to Move beyond 'Business as Usual.'" *Sustainable Development* 24(6): 371–82.

Selbervik, H., and M. T. Østebø. 2013. "Gender Equality in International Aid: What Has Norwegian Gender Politics Got to Do with It?" *Gender, Technology and Development* 17(2): 205–28.

Selmier, W. T., A. Newenham-Kahindi, and C. H. Oh. 2015. "'Understanding the Words of Relationships': Language as an Essential Tool to Manage CSR in Communities of Place." *Journal of International Business Studies* 46(2): 153–79.

Shapiro, D., B. Hobdari, and C. H. Oh. 2018. "Natural Resources, Multinational Enterprises and Sustainable Development." *Journal of World Business* 53(1): 1–14.

Skjelsbæk, I., and T. L. Tryggestad. 2020. "Pro-gender Norms in Norwegian Peace Engagement: Balancing Experiences, Values, and Interests." *Foreign Policy Analysis* 16(2): 181–98.

Spencer, R. 2018. "CSR for Sustainable Development and Poverty Reduction? Critical Perspectives from the Anthropology of Development." In *Disciplining the Undisciplined? Perspectives from Business, Society and Politics on Responsible Citizenship, Corporate Social Responsibility and Sustainability*, edited by M. Brueckner, R. Spencer, and M. Paull. Cham: Springer.

Statoil. 2017a. *2016 Sustainability Report*. Retrieved 24 May 2020 from https://www.equinor.com/en/how-and-why/sustainability/sustainability-reports.html.

———. 2017b. "Where We Are: Tanzania." Retrieved 2 March 2018 from https://www.statoil.com/en/where-we-are.html.

Strønen, I. Å. 2020. "Between Social Footprint and Compliance, or 'What IBAMA Wants': Equinor Brazil's Social Sustainability Policy." *Focaal. Journal of Global and Historical Anthropology* 88.

Sørreime, H. B., and K. Tronvoll. 2020. "Performing Accountability in Petroleum Resource Governance in a Shrinking Democratic Space: The Case of Tanzania." *Extractive Industries and Society* 7(4): 1490–97.

Tornhill, S. 2016. "'A Bulletin Board of Dreams': Corporate Empowerment Promotion and Feminist Implications." *International Feminist Journal of Politics* 18(4): 528–43.

United Nations. 2020. "Sustainable Development." Retrieved 4 September 2020 from https://sdgs.un.org/goals.

UN Global Compact. 2020. "The World's Largest Corporate Sustainability Initiative." Retrieved 24 May 2020 from https://www.unglobalcompact.org/what-is-gc.

United Republic of Tanzania. 2013. *The National Natural Gas Policy of Tanzania*. Dodoma: Ministry of Energy and Minerals.

———. 2015a. *Guidelines for Corporate Social Responsibility and Empowerment in the Extractive Industry in Tanzania*. Dodoma: Ministry of Energy and Minerals in collaboration with Extractive Interstakeholders Forum.

———. 2015b. *The Petroleum Act 2015*. Gazette of the United Republic of Tanzania, 96(38) dated 18 September. Dodoma: United Republic of Tanzania (URT).

Visser, W. 2006. "Revisiting Carroll's CSR Pyramid: An African Persepctive." In *Corporate Citizenship in Developing Countries: New Partnership Perspectives*, edited by E. R. Pedersen and M. Huniche. Copenhagen: Copenhagen Business School Press.

Wanvik, T. I. 2014. "Encountering a Multidimensional Assemblage: The Case of Norwegian Corporate Social Responsibility Activities in Indonesia." *Norsk Geografisk Tidsskrift— Norwegian Journal of Geography* 68(5): 282–90.

———. 2016. "Governance Transformed into Corporate Social Responsibility (CSR): New Governance Innovations in the Canadian Oil Sands." *Extractive Industries and Society* 3(2): 517–26.

Welker, M. A. 2014. *Enacting the Corporation: An American Mining Firm in Post-authoritarian Indonesia*. Berkeley: University of California Press.

Wilson, J. D. 2015. "Understanding Resource Nationalism: Economic Dynamics and Political Institutions." *Contemporary Politics* 21(4): 399–416.

World Health Organization. 2020. "Lymphatic Filariasis." Retrieved 24 May 2020 from http://www.who.int/mediacentre/factsheets/fs102/en/.

———. 2022. "Obstetric Fistula." Retrieved 1 June 2022 from https://www.who.int/news-room/facts-in-pictures/detail/10-facts-on-obstetric-fistula.

Wyndham, V. 2018. "Gendered Perspectives in the CSR Policies of a State-Owned Petroleum Company Investing Abroad: Integrated or Irrelevant? Evidence from Tanzania." Master's thesis, Global Development Theory and Practice, Department of Health Promotion and Development (HEMIL), University of Bergen.

Wyndham, V., and S. Lange. 2019. "Making Sense of CSO's (In)action in Tanzania's Petroleum Sector: Where Is Gender?" In *Governing Petroleum Resources Prospects and Challenges for Tanzania*, edited by O.-H. Fjeldstad, D. Mmari and K. Depuy. Dar es Salaam and Bergen: REPOA and Chr. Michelsen Institute (CMI).

— Chapter 8 —

EXPORTING THE NORWEGIAN MODEL THROUGH THE "CAPACITY BUILDING" OF A LOCAL UNION BRANCH
The Case of Equinor in Tanzania
Siri Lange

This chapter focuses on the case of Equinor, a multinational corporation (MNC) that originated as a Norwegian national oil company, and their efforts in collaboration with a Norwegian union to support union work among its employees in Tanzania. These efforts were inspired by the Nordic tradition of social dialogue between corporations and strong, independent unions. Corporate managers and union representatives tend to refer to this social dialogue as "the Norwegian model," but this is a narrow conceptualization of the model that disregards the role of the state in the tripartite system. The tripartite system can be described as the formalized and strictly regulated interaction between corporations, trade unions, and the government. As seen in the introduction to this book, the tripartite system is often referred to as the Nordic model, and the defining characteristic of the model is the "influence that the labor movement has on capital and the state" (see also Knudsen et al. 2020). This is a result of specific economic and political developments that took place in the interwar period.

The Nordic countries share some characteristics, including egalitarian traditions, the welfare state, and "labour market politics and regulations" (Ervasti et al. 2008: 3). The "Nordic model" and the "Norwegian model" are terms that are often used interchangeably by scholars who study Norwegian industrial relations. Espen Løken and Freitas Barbosa (2008: 13) have identified six characteristics that are often emphasized when the Nordic or Norwegian model is described: "[1] universal welfare arrangements and a large public sector; [2] high employment, among both men and women; [3] small wage differences and a large degree of social mobility; [4] strong collective actors—both centrally coordinated wage formation and local bargaining at company level; [5] close cooperation between the government, employers' associations, and trade unions; and [6] strong codetermination and participation at the company level."

In contrast to most other countries, trade unions in Norway have certain mandatory and codified rights and therefore a strong legitimate status (Løken and Barbosa 2008; Rees, Preuss, and Gold 2014: 12). The relationship between Equinor and the Norwegian union where the majority of the employees are organized, Industri Energi, is very close, and the Union branch in Equinor Norway has a more influential role than is commonly found in MNCs; for example, the union is represented on the board. In this chapter, I explore the process whereby the Norwegian union branch acted as a mediator in the process of establishment of a union branch in Tanzania. I demonstrate that both the Norwegian management of Equinor and the Norwegian union and branch representatives tend to emphasize a very narrow aspect of what scholars and many politicians alike consider to be the Nordic model. Corporation managers and union representatives tend to equate what they refer to as the "Norwegian model" with a close relationship between managers and staff based on cooperation and dialogue (related to the sixth point on the list above), and they apparently disregard the other characteristics.

There is considerable diversity in trade unionism, both within and between countries (Harvey, Hodder, and Brammer 2017: 45; Tran, Bair, and Werner 2017). It is therefore important to understand labor struggles and unions "within their political and historical context" (Neve 2008: 214). Whereas radical unions see "their role as part of a larger class alliance in conflict with the state and capitalist system," reformist unions "emphasise social dialogue mechanisms" (Houeland 2018: 106). I show how Tanzanian labor history, combined with the extremely asymmetrical relationship both between the Norwegian and the Tanzanian union and between the management and staff at the Equinor office in Tanzania, influenced the local union branch and how a radical and confrontational union leadership was replaced by a union leadership that adopted the idea of close collaboration with the management.

The chapter is based on ten shorter field trips in Norway (Oslo, Stavanger, and Bergen) and eight in Tanzania (Dar es Salaam, Lindi,

Mtwara, and Mwanza) over a period of four years (January 2016 to December 2019). My research interests were twofold. As seen in chapter 7, I was interested in the gendered dimensions of Equinor's CSR and found that despite Equinor's profile as a company that is concerned with gender equality, the main beneficiaries of the projects at the local level are men. In terms of labor relations, which is the focus of this chapter, I wanted to understand the interrelationship between different levels/strands of the company both horizontally (between workers or union representatives in Norway and Tanzania) and vertically (between company leadership and union representatives in both countries).

I visited Equinor offices in Norway and Tanzania, union headquarters, civil society organizations, and the proposed site for a liquefied natural gas (LNG) plant. I held meetings and/or interviews in English, Norwegian, or Swahili with a large number of Equinor staff and branch and union leaders in Norway and Tanzania, including two Equinor board members, three different country managers of Equinor Tanzania, and top union leaders in both countries.[1] The corporate context restricted the degree of participant observation as Equinor offices are under strict surveillance in both Norway and Tanzania. One can only enter the premises by invitation, entrance requires digital registration, and one must keep a visitor's tag visible at all times. Employees at the Oslo offices, somewhat embarrassedly, admitted that they had been instructed to restrict visitors from leaving meeting rooms alone and, if required, to escort visitors to the bathroom and wait outside. Since I did multisited ethnography, I did not attempt to carry out participant observation with Norwegian or Tanzanian unions. Thus, I have limited ethnography of the day-to-day work within the corporation and the unions. Unstructured interviews, documents that branch leaders have shared with me, as well as follow-up conversations via email and phone/Skype are therefore the main sources of information for this chapter.

The chapter is organized as follows: The first part comprises a literature review of transnational labor activism and background information about Equinor and its relationship to labor. The second part presents Equinor Tanzania and background information about trade unions in Tanzania. The third part describes in depth the process of building up a local union branch at Equinor Tanzania using a "traveling model," the transformation that the branch went through, and how the "business case" for supporting union work gradually lost momentum. Finally, I show how the efforts to establish a Global Work Council have stalled, demonstrating that there is a clear limit to Equinor's willingness to cooperate with labor. In the concluding remarks, I argue that the traveling model that was presented to the Tanzanian staff was an ahistorical version of Norwegian industrial relations. While the model was born through conflict and is closely tied to the tripartite system and the welfare state, the Norwegian union Industri Energi,[2] which organizes most of the "blue-collar" workers in the oil and gas sector in Norway, presents a message to their "partners" in the Global South that close cooperation is a win-win for both parties.

Transnational Labor Activism

Multinational corporations (MNCs) engaged in resource extraction in the Global South have been heavily criticized; one response by the MNCs has been to formulate corporate social responsibility (CSR) strategies (Rajak 2011a; Welker 2009: Gilberthorpe and Rajak 2017). A relatively large body of literature looks at how various stakeholders, including NGOs, pressure companies to adopt specific policies (Gold, Preuss, and Rees 2020: 136; Dolan and Rajak 2011: 2; Spencer 2018; Welker, Partridge, and Hardin 2011), but there has been less focus on the role of trade unions.

In many European countries, workers are represented on company boards, and unions can therefore potentially influence companies' CSR policies and their relationship to labor abroad (Gold et al. 2020; Scholz and Vitols 2019). In Germany, workers' representation on boards is referred to as "shared governance" or "codetermination" (Jäger, Schoefer, and Heining 2019), and one study found that union representation on boards positively aligns with substantive CSR, such as "emissions reduction, the publication of a CSR report and commitment to employment security," but not with symbolic CSR, such as being a signatory to the UN Global Compact (Scholz and Vitols 2019: 244). This study did not look specifically at ways in which codetermination affects how the companies relate to labor abroad.

In Norway, employees were given the right to be represented on corporative boards by a 1972 amendment of the Companies Act (Heiret 2012: 52). In 1980, the principle of *bedriftsdemokrati* (corporate democracy) was included in the Norwegian Constitution. As a result of the increasing internationalization of Norwegian corporations in the 1990s and 2000s, the Norwegian confederation of trade unions (LO-Norway/Landsorganisasjonen i Norge) set up a network for union representatives at the corporate level (*konserntillitsvalgte*). The confederation also published a book that aims to give Norwegian union representatives in multinational companies some tools to handle CSR in their own corporations (Granden 2009). However, Nordic Union representatives are generally skeptical of the concept of CSR and push for formal global framework agreements (GFAs) rather than voluntary and informal CSR.

In contrast to NGOs, which may spread negative information about companies, many unions in Europe are concerned about protecting jobs and therefore do not wish to undermine corporate reputations (Rees et al. 2014: 12). In order to understand the role of trade unions in relation to labor abroad then, we must acknowledge that they are simultaneously internal and external stakeholders (Harvey et al. 2017: 45). This may explain why a review of the literature on how transnational advocacy networks support domestic struggles found that trade unions are "no longer viewed as a central player" (Zajak, Egels-Zandén, and Piper 2017: 903, 916). The authors also found that, although international labor rights organizations aim at strengthening local trade unions, they sometimes disempower "more radical and independent unions" and thereby delegitimize radical strategies (2017: 908, 911). It has been argued that partnership and social dialogue may work in coordinated market economies, such as the Nordic countries and Germany, but is far more problematic in liberal market economies (Gold et al. 2020). My case study shows that the union branch at Equinor Tanzania initially represented a radical union model but, in the end, adopted the social dialogue model that the union branch at Equinor Norway presented to them. The following sections present the relationship between Equinor and labor in Norway as well as in some of the other countries where Equinor operates.

Equinor: Background and the Relationship to Labor

National oil companies control 80 percent of the global oil resources (ILO 2009), but until now, the majority of studies of oil and gas companies and their conduct abroad have looked to privately owned companies (Frynas 2009). There is therefore a need to expand the study of MNCs that are engaged in resource extraction to include national oil companies. Statoil was established by the Norwegian Parliament as a national oil company (NOC) in 1972. The national oil company has been described as the Labor Party's (*Arbeiderpartiet*) "baby." In the early years of Statoil, both the CEO and the chairman of the board were labor politicians (Sæther 2017: 23, 313). Although many countries started reducing state ownership during the 1980s, this did not start in Norway until the 1990s (see introduction). Statoil remained entirely state owned until 2001 when parliament approved the privatization of a third of the Equinor shares (Sæther 2017: 293).

In May 2018, Statoil changed its name to Equinor. According to the company, "Equi" refers to "equal" and "equality" and is linked to the company's Norwegian heritage (Equinor 2018a). Equinor currently has operations in more than thirty countries and production in approximately twelve, including Angola, Brazil, and Nigeria (Equinor 2018b). Equinor publishes annual sustainability reports that cover environmental concerns, gender balance among its staff, its "social investment projects" in host countries, and human rights—including labor rights—for its own employees as well as those in the supply chain (Equinor 2020a).

Equinor's relations with their employees abroad are regulated by a number of framework agreements. One of the union representatives on the Equinor board argued in an interview that the company is "genuinely concerned about having strong guidelines. It is a trademark, a reputation brand (*omdømmemerke*), even if we are not so big." In the late 1990s, Equinor was among the first companies in the world to have a global framework agreement (GFA) with what is now the global federation IndustriAll[3] (ILO 2009: 70). According to one of my interlocutors in the Equinor branch of Industri Energi, other oil and gas companies, such as Shell and Esso, "are totally against such agreements—they are allergic to them." The agreement has been renewed a number of times, and states that it is the "right of every employee to be represented by a union of his or her choice and the basic trade union rights as defined by ILO conventions 87 and 98" (Industri Energi/IndustriAll Global Union and Statoil 2012).

A high-ranking Industri Energi representative explained that the agreement "is worth gold," since it enables the union to force Equinor "to meet the unions wherever they are." Another top-level representative of the Industri Energi union, who had also been the employee representative on the Statoil board for two periods, gave the Statoil leadership credit for the GFA with IndustriAll: "We had people in the Statoil leadership who saw that we would internationalize. They saw that if we were to be able to succeed with the Norwegian model, to bring it with us abroad, we needed that [framework agreement]." The representative emphasized health, environment, and safety (HES) and argued that, because Equinor is state owned, it has a particular responsibility: "When Statoil was to go abroad on behalf of the state, we needed help to get things in order." While this interlocutor emphasized HES, when asked what the Norwegian model implies, the response was as follows:

> A model similar to the one that we have here: to have dialogue, not conflict only ... it means to have a meeting place to address challenges within a set framework. Not all cultures have that—a place where you can meet the management face-to-face. In many places there are two to three levels between the employees and the top management. We want to have the kind of dialogue that we have found so useful here at home. The culture varies—some places they say: Wow, are they actually *talking* with the management? We have a meeting point, a place for discussion, a place to have a dialogue. And we believe that this gives the best results.

This language reflects a common understanding of industrial relations in Norway: the focus on dialogue, negotiation, mutual recognition, cooperation, and compromise (Ihlen and Hoivik 2013; see also the introduction in this volume). However, this interpretation of the Norwegian model is problematic in two ways, particularly when it is used to argue for a transfer of the model to other countries. First, the emphasis on dialogue and cooperation between managers and employees is presented as isolated from its historical background—the labor conflicts in the interwar period (Ihlen and Hoivik 2013; see also the introduction in this volume). Second and relatedly, by isolating the employer-employee relationship from the other characteristics of the model that academics see as central (Ervasti et al. 2008; Løken and Barbosa 2008), the role of the state is ignored.

The human resources department of Equinor[4] told me that "interaction and cooperation with the employees is part of our leadership culture" but that the corporation follows the labor regulations in the countries where they operate. Currently, among the countries in the Global South where Equinor operates, salaries are only negotiated through unions in Brazil and Nigeria. In the case of Brazil, most unions are progressive and militant (Houeland 2018) and reportedly trust neither the companies nor the authorities. According to one of the Norwegian union representatives on the Equinor board, "the kind of cooperation that they have had in Tanzania would not have been possible in Brazil." In 2017, a Brazilian union leader heavily criticized Equinor in a public hearing for referring to its social democratic traditions when securing licenses, only later to behave as any other oil company and earn money on people's misery (Borchgrevink 2019: 380).

In the case of Nigeria, where oil workers' unions have played a critical role in the struggle for democracy (Houeland 2018), there has been no cooperation with Norwegian unions. My interlocutors in the Industri Energi union say that in the late 1990s, union branch representatives traveled to meet the employees, but they failed to establish a platform for cooperation. Since then, there has been very limited collaboration with Industri Energi. A study of union work among oil workers in Nigeria found that the union steward at Statoil Nigeria had no knowledge of the GFA between Statoil and IndustriAll (Houeland 2017: 65).

According to one of the leaders of Industri Energi, some foreign unions see Norwegian union leaders and union representatives as collaborators and untrustworthy since they not only emphasize social dialogue but are also paid by the company to fulfill their role. This interlocutor gave two examples. In Angola, union leaders claimed that the Norwegian union leaders were corrupt since their airline tickets were paid for by Equinor (then Statoil), and therefore the Angolans refused to meet them. In the United States, union leaders are very skeptical of close collaboration with the employers and have similarly been reluctant to collaborate with Industri Energi.

Equinor in Tanzania

Equinor has been in Tanzania since 2007 (Equinor 2020b). In 2012 and 2013, the company made enormous gas discoveries in the deep sea—the largest abroad in the company's history. The company plans to build a liquefied natural gas (LNG) plant onshore but has yet to make the final investment decision. The delay in the decision is partly because of changes in Tanzania's regulatory framework, including the passing of the Sovereignty Act in 2017, which says that the parliament can ask to have contracts renegotiated without international arbitration (Sørreime 2019: 559). As of 2020, Equinor Tanzania only had twenty employees, but in 2014, the management envisaged having at least one thousand employees within a few years, and the company invested heavily to support a newly established union branch at its office.

Trade Unions in Tanzania: Co-option, Suppression, and Misuse of Money

In common with those in Vietnam and postsocialist countries in Eastern Europe, the labor regime in Tanzania has changed dramatically over the past fifty years. Unions played a central role in the struggle for independence, but during the one-party era (1977–92), all unions were co-opted by the ruling party Chama Cha Mapinduzi (CCM; Party of the Revolution). The Trade Union Act no. 10 of 1998 formally made trade unions independent of the government, and many independent unions have been formed. However, union density is low and there is little trust in unions. The Trade Union Congress of Tanzania (TUCTA) has a poor history in terms of accountability—in both 2009 and 2019, the secretary generals were suspended, accused of embezzlement (Babeiya 2011: 128; The Guardian 2019). In the early 2000s, foreign investment in the country's mining sector boomed (Lange 2011). In 2007, at least a thousand workers, some of them trade union leaders, were reportedly fired from a mining company after striking to protest the wage differences between foreigners and Tanzanians (Rugeiyamu, Kashonda, and Mohamed 2018). However, the state has also suppressed workers' rights. In both 2010 and 2015, civil servants organized under the TUCTA were told by the president that they would lose their jobs if they engaged in strikes (Rugeiyamu et al. 2018: 46). Labor rights are not mentioned in Tanzania's guidelines for CSR in the extractive industry (URT 2015), in contrast to Ghana's Mineral Commission's guideline for CSR, which includes workplace and labor standards (Jiao 2019).

Despite playing key roles in other African countries, such as Nigeria, South Africa, and Zambia (Atabaki, Bini, and Ehsani 2018; Houeland 2018; Webster 2018; Larmer 2006), unions have not played a significant political role in Tanzania since the late 1970s. There is lack of "solidarity and partnership" among the country's trade unions, and opposition parties and trade unions blame each other for the lack of interest and unwillingness to cooperate (Babeiya 2011: 127, 128).

This context is an important backdrop for understanding why the staff of Equinor Tanzania have changed their stance on unionization on several occasions. In the following sections, I present five main arguments. First, I show that the role that unions have in Norway, as *members of company boards*, can indeed influence a company's labor relations abroad. Following the advice of the board's Norwegian union representative, the Equinor Tanzania staff decided to unionize. Second, I demonstrate that the attempt by the Norwegian union branch to *export their reformist union model* initially failed, since the company management and the Tanzanian workforce had very different expectations as to the outcome of the wage negotiations. This is partly linked to the fact that the Norwegian management and union representatives isolated one aspect — *close collaboration* — from what they referred to as the Norwegian model — and did not acknowledge the central role of the welfare system in Norway for securing the model's success. Third, I demonstrate that, in their efforts to make the Tanzanian branch union leadership adopt the model, Equinor used a system that was well established in Tanzania by donors in development "partnerships": so-called *capacity building*. With time, and most likely linked to the extreme power asymmetries, the union branch in Tanzania gave up their radical stance and adopted a reformist union approach. Fourth, I argue that the Equinor management's attitudes toward unionization is closely linked to what they see as *beneficial for business* at any given point. Lastly, I point to the fact that Equinor has resisted establishing an *international organizational structure* that would facilitate interaction between their employees in different countries. This is the main barrier to the full involvement of unions in the company's operations outside of Norway.

Company Board Membership

In 2014, Equinor Tanzania was seen as a very promising project. The staff was small, consisting of thirty to forty office workers, but the company envisaged having thousands of employees within five years or so. Envisaged to be the corporation's largest investment abroad in history, the board decided to make a visit. The union representatives on the board asked the local staff whether they were unionized. The answer was no, but they were interested to learn from their Norwegian colleagues.

A year before the board's visit, the National Union of Mine and Energy Workers of Tanzania (NUMET) had contacted the Equinor management and asked for a meeting with the local staff. The Equinor management organized a meeting where NUMET representatives presented themselves to the local staff and encouraged them to join the union, but the response from Equinor employees was lukewarm. In interviews, the employees referred to the history of unions in the country and the misuse of members' money as reasons for why they were not interested in joining. However, after the board's visit, some of the Tanzanian staff contacted NUMET and asked for a new meeting.

What made the employees change their minds about unionization? First, witnessing the role the Norwegian union representatives played on the Equinor board made it clear to the Tanzanian staff that unions in Norway held a very different position from unions in Tanzania. Second, there is a long history of aid to Tanzania, and Norway has historically been one of the main development

Figure 8.1. Equinor's office building outside Oslo. The "capacity building" of the NUMET union branch leadership took place partly at the Equinor offices in Oslo, partly at the headquarters of the Norwegian union Industri Energi. The guests from Tanzania also visited the Confederation of Norwegian Enterprise. © Siri Lange.

partners, meaning that many Tanzanians associate Norway with aid. "Partnership," both between governmental bodies and between civil society organizations in the Global South and Global North, and "capacity building" have been central to development cooperation. This history partly explains why the employees in Tanzania were so receptive to the suggestion from the union representative from the Industri Energi Equinor branch. One of the Norwegian union board members recalls what they talked about with the Tanzanian staff: "They wanted advice and tips, and they knew little about the Norwegian culture, how we are organized. ... They had no experience with unions, but we explained to them: 'Make a meeting place with the management, and don't address the most difficult issues first.'" The union branch representatives in the board clearly recommended a nonconfrontational approach.

A Traveling Model

A NUMET branch at Equinor Tanzania was established in 2014, and twenty-three of the twenty-six employees in attendance joined the trade union. By the end of the year, a recognition agreement with Equinor was signed. However, the first wage negotiations after unionization showed that the parties held vastly different views. The Norwegian members of the Equinor Tanzania management described it as a "catastrophe." The union demanded a 150 percent wage increase but ended up with just 3 percent. The local understanding and reception of the wage negotiation model was substantially different from the Norwegian original, where, at least over the last twenty years, a demand for a 150 percent wage increase would be unheard of. As Behrends, Park, and Rottenburg (2014) have pointed out, those who support or sponsor a traveling model often advocate for "responsible" handling of the traveling model, but models often come "to be used in ways other than intended" (see also Lange 2008).

One does get the impression that the management of Equinor Tanzania did not consider that, in Norway, wage negotiations are part of the "income-political settlements" (*inntektspolitiske oppgjør*) where the deals include "not only salaries but also comprehensive adjustments of the welfare system, pensions," and more (see introduction). In Tanzania, there is a very limited welfare system, and public services are generally of poor quality. In interviews, branch union leadership explained that they were very content with the medical insurance that Equinor offered, but they felt that the Norwegian management did not fully understand the economic burden of private education in the country. Support for education is more attractive in Tanzania than a general pay raise because of expectations from the extended family. It may be hard for a worker to send his/her children to a good, private school and not do the same for one's nephews or nieces whose parents are less fortunate. When school fees are covered directly by the company, the employees escape such moral dilemmas. At the same time, companies that enter such agreements do, to some extent, take over the role of state, and thereby increase their influence and power in the societies where they operate (Ferguson 2005; Rajak 2016). In interviews, the Equinor management was very clear that their role as a company in Tanzania should not be confused with aid or replacing government authorities.

Capacity Building

After the first unsuccessful wage negotiation between Equinor Tanzania and the NUMET branch, the management decided that it was important to increase the Tanzanian staff's knowledge of

Figure 8.2. The office of the National Union of Mine and Energy Workers in Tanzania (NUMET). The staff at Equinor Tanzania established a union branch under NUMET. The branch leadership were taken to Norway for "capacity building." © Siri Lange.

industrial relations in Norway. As one of the Norway-based human resources (HR)[5] staff members diplomatically put it: "They had a slightly different way of working, that's why they were invited here." Equinor Tanzania asked Industri Energi to act as a mediator of the traveling model and invited the four members of the branch leadership together with Equinor's HR manager in Tanzania to Norway for a weeks-long visit in September 2015. The trip was paid for by Equinor but organized in cooperation with Industri Energi, who said that all "agreed that there was a need to build a culture of cooperation." Industry Energi's support to the NUMET branch was funded by the union's international solidarity fund.

During the visit, the NUMET Equinor branch leadership held meetings with the branch leadership at Equinor. The PowerPoint presentation was titled "Tanzania Visiting Statoil: Union Meeting, Discussion and Capacity Building," reflecting the perception that a transfer of knowledge from Norway to Tanzania was central to the process. To many Tanzanians, this is a well-known format. Through decades of development cooperation, civil society organizations and government entities from the Global North have offered countless capacity-building programs and seminars to Tanzanian institutions, organizations, and individuals.

The main themes presented included the tripartite collaboration model, the Industrial Democracy law of 1973 that gives "the employees representation in company steering bodies," membership and organization of the union, and the global framework agreement of 1998 (Industri Energi Statoil 2015). The guests had meetings with several central actors in Norway, including the Confederation of Norwegian Enterprise (Næringslivets Hovedorganisasjon, NHO). According to the Equinor HR representative, the union representatives "gained a better understanding of the fact that this is interaction (*samhandling*)."

Having invested in building knowledge and understanding among the branch leadership, the Equinor Tanzania management decided it was time to initiate a closer relationship with NUMETs central office. Therefore, in November 2015, a delegation of ten persons from Equinor Tanzania, including the Norwegian Country Manager and the Norwegian HR manager, traveled by plane to Mwanza (1,110 kilometers from Dar es Salaam) to meet with the NUMET national leadership.

The great majority of NUMETs members work at large-scale mines owned by multinational corporations. Several of these companies and their suppliers have actively engaged in union crushing. In an informal conversation, an expat manager of a drilling company shared with me his strategies for keeping membership in NUMET at a minimum. He explained that NUMET had managed to get 40 percent of his workers to join the union at the beginning of 2017. Under Tanzanian law, the unions have the right to collective bargaining when they have 50 percent membership. He started efforts to reduce union activities[6] and succeeded in getting the membership rate down to zero by the end of the year. Winding up his success story, he concluded triumphantly: "I got rid of them!"

In light of such experiences, Equinor's visit was a very special event for the NUMET leadership. In the words of one of the Norwegians: "To them, it was like having the king visit!" NUMET decided to make the most of this unusual visit and invited four television broadcasters and five newspapers to report on the visit. They also hired a professional filmmaker to record the events—the resulting film is similar to the usual genre the company produces: wedding videos. Accompanied by romantic music, we see the NUMET and Equinor staff visiting one of the few tourist attractions in the city, a small island in Lake Victoria with a zoo. We later see them in more "corporate" surroundings, in the meeting room inside the hotel.

As a splinter union, NUMET competes with the much stronger Tanzania Mines, Energy, Construction, and Allied Workers' Union (TAMICO). TAMICO is a member of the federation TUCTA, which is aligned with the ruling party. In all countries, but particularly in one of the world's poorest countries, prospective union members may be attracted to the union that appears to have good alliances and support from abroad (Zajak et al. 2017: 908). To NUMET, it was therefore important to showcase their cooperation with Equinor as broadly as possible to attract new members and to come through to Equinor as a reliable, nonconfrontational partner.

From a Radical to a Reformist Union

Despite the capacity-building efforts by the Norwegian Union branch and the Norwegian Confederation, the union leadership of the NUMET branch at Equinor Tanzania was perceived by many of the staff members as being too conflict oriented, "fighting with the management." The majority of branch members were in favor of opening dialogue rather than taking a combative stance, and they wanted a reformist style of unionism. In February 2016, the branch leadership was overthrown by the members, and a new leader, who was described as "calm" (*mpole*) and who collaborated well with the management, was elected.

News of the conflict reached the Industri Energi union in Norway, which asked for an update on behalf of the International Affairs section of the Federal Union (LO-Norway).[7] The new NUMET branch leadership put together a brief report where they introduced themselves and their backgrounds and reported that only ten of twenty-two local staff were members, which meant that they did not qualify for a collective bargaining agreement under Tanzanian law. The report lists six priority areas of the branch. The first item on the list is to ensure "good cooperation at all times with DPI TAN [Development and Production International Tanzania] in supporting TGP [the Tanzania Gas Project]"[8] (NUMET Tanzania Statoil Branch 2016). The employees in Tanzania have, to a large degree, adopted a model of close collaboration between management and the union branch; in other words, a reformist union model.

In the small and simple offices that house the NUMET headquarters in Mwanza, large gold-framed photos of the visit by the Equinor delegation hold a prominent place. In an interview, the general secretary admitted that the union has not achieved very much in their collaboration with Equinor but emphasized the need for balance: "There are so many trade unions; if you frustrate the employer, they can call any other trade union." His statement clearly illustrates the unequal power relationship between corporations and unions in Tanzania and that in his experience it is often the company that determines which union the employees are members of. He stresses that unions in other countries have "contributed to improving performance and benefits to the employees *and* the investors" and that ideally, unions and companies should be "business partners." This statement stands in clear contrast to NUMET's web presentation where NUMET presents itself as a radical union: "The history of the National Union of Mine and Energy Workers of Tanzania (NUMET) is a history of class struggle. This struggle is embedded in the inherent contradictions that exist between capital and labor but also the struggle against colonialism" (NUMET 2020).

In their ethnographic studies of labor politics in Kazakhstan and India, Eeva Keskülä and Andrew Sanchez (2019: 112) found that union leaders tend to make "emotive appeals to languages of struggle that they are usually unable to fulfil in their daily activities." In the case of NUMET, this gap between ideal and practice may be the pragmatic compromise of a poor and marginalized union that receives economic support from some of the larger corporations (including Equinor) but does not have any ties to the national federation TUCTA.

Since the heydays, the unionization efforts at Equinor Tanzania have lost momentum. The union branch is far from reaching its original goal of a collective bargaining agreement since it lost many members, partly due to the turmoil, partly due to the downsizing of the office in Tanzania.

The "Business Case" for Support of Unions

Seeing the unionization process over time demonstrates that the Equinor management's attitudes shifted as the final investment decision kept being postponed. According to the former HR manager at Equinor Tanzania, the visit to NUMET's headquarters was a strategic decision by the company because the management expected the number of employees to grow significantly. "We leaned on the same experience and philosophy as in Norway," he explained. An Equinor union representative based in Norway, who met the NUMET representatives during their visit to Norway, similarly emphasized the Norwegian experiences as a central factor for their work with unions abroad: "In the early years of the oil industry in Norway, there were many in-house unions (*husforeninger*), and they went on strike heedlessly." She explained how Hydro (established in 1905) had experience with industrial workers for more than a hundred years and therefore avoided such in-house unions (see chapter 4). "Things were tidy and orderly," she argued, "this is what we envisage down there as well — it so much better to have *one* union only — so we tried to follow the Norwegian model." Again, we see how some actors refer to the close collaboration between industry management and trade unions as "the Norwegian model" and appear to disregard the more common, wide conceptualizations of the Nordic/Norwegian model that see the state as central (Ervasti et al. 2008; Løken and Barbosa 2008).

For Equinor Tanzania, which expected to have thousands of employees, the prospect of collaborating with one union rather than several smaller ones was attractive. An additional factor that may have spurred Equinor Tanzania to make efforts to establish a good relationship with NUMET is fear of negative attention from the media as well as civil society organizations in Norway and Tanzania. Some MNCs in Tanzania have a bad reputation regarding labor relations, and foreign company abuse of workers' rights has attracted "considerable criticism from NGOs, trade unions and the media" (Lauwo and Otusanya 2014: 96, 101). If Equinor invests in Tanzania, a serious labor conflict would probably be addressed by Tanzanian civil society organizations (CSOs), as well as by Tanzanian and Norwegian media. Equinor's investment in the union branch must be seen in this context as well.

However, when the investment in Tanzania became less certain, the HR manager at Equinor Tanzania admitted that the company's engagement for getting the staff unionized had been reduced. As he put it, "there is no longer a business case" for securing the long-term rights of the employees. The Oslo-based Norwegian HR leader, who works closely with the Tanzanian HR leader in the same leadership group, argued along the same lines: Equinor will commit itself as little as possible as long as the final investment decision has not been taken. These statements demonstrate that, although Equinor has committed itself to international agreements and although many Norwegian employees talk of exporting what they refer to as the "Norwegian model," there is a limit to the commitment that Equinor Tanzania is willing to make.

The Missing Link: A Global Work Council

Within the EU, any company that has more than 1,000 employees of which 150 or more work in two different EU member states is mandated to have a European Works Council (EWC). The councils enable the employees to contribute to the "decision-making process in transnational issues" (ILO 2009: 77). Inspired by the role of European Works Councils, three initiatives have been taken to establish a Global Works Council for Equinor. First, LO-Norway has requested Norad (the Norwegian Directorate for Development Cooperation) to provide pilot funds to start a Global Works Council for Equinor staff in the different countries where the company operates. Although Equinor has operations in several developing countries, the initiative was not granted support.[9] Second, Industri Energi has sought to integrate the idea of a Global Work Council in their global framework agreement (GFA) with Equinor, but Equinor has refused to do so. Third, the three union representatives of the Equinor board have raised the issue of a Global Work Council in board meetings but have not succeeded in getting support for this initiative. Therefore, as there is no Global Work Council for Equinor, the NUMET branch's ties to the Equinor branch of Industri Energi (Oslo) are informal.

Internationalization of employment tends to fragment worker representation. As Robert Scholz and Sigurt Vitols (2019: 236) have pointed out, the "lower the proportion of employees in the 'home' country of a multinational, the more difficult it is to organize workers' voice, given the diversity of national industrial relations." A Global Work Council for Equinor employees would have given the Tanzanian representatives a platform for learning from unions that are more like themselves than Industri Energi, and it would have given them a very different form of bargaining power across borders. However, the company was quite resistant to this idea; therefore, the union representatives no longer see it as a realistic goal, indicating that, although Equinor has signed a global framework agreement with IndustriAll, there are clear limits to how much the corporation is willing to cooperate with unions in their global operations.

This is possibly related to Equinor's assessment of risk, where "labor strikes" are listed among the operational risks that the company may face.[10] In Norway, there were a number of strikes in the oil sector in the 1970s and 1980s, including a shutdown of production. In 2012, when seven hundred oil workers went on strike over pension rights, the government decided to force the parties to compulsory arbitration. The ILO was very critical of this (IndustriAll

2012). This case illustrates how the Norwegian tripartite system enables the state to intervene in labor conflicts that are perceived to threaten broader societal interests. It also shows that presenting the "Norwegian model" as a question of cooperation and dialogue between corporations and trade unions only—as many of the Norwegian Equinor staff and union representatives did when talking of a transfer of the model to Tanzania—represents a very narrow understanding, since it omits the role of the state, which is central to how the tripartite system functions in Norway (Ervasti et al. 2008; Løken and Barbosa 2008).

Conclusion

This chapter has analyzed the way the Norwegian energy company Equinor actively supported the establishment of a union branch at its office in Tanzania. During this process, close cooperation and dialogue between company management and union branches (and upward to unions and federations) was referred to as the "Norwegian model." The case study is an example of a "traveling rationality," where the goal is to transfer a social mode from one context to another, but where only the "objectified model" travels (Behrends et al. 2014: 2; Craig and Porter 2006).

Norwegian union representatives at federal and company levels as well as representatives for Equinor HR talked warmly of the "Norwegian model" and how beneficial it is for both the company and its employees. The objectified model they referred to emphasizes trust and cooperation between employers and employees, while the scholarly and political conceptions of the Nordic/Norwegian model—which focus on the central role of the state in this cooperation through the "income-political settlements" (*inntektspolitiske oppgjør*) and the state's role in securing universal welfare—were under communicated.

Tanzanians have ample experience with traveling models. By 2012, Tanzania was the country in sub-Saharan Africa that had historically received the second largest amount of aid, surpassed only by Ethiopia (Tripp 2012). To the Tanzanian staff then, the idea of capacity building and learning from Norway was a well-known scenario. It was also attractive, first because they hoped that unionization would secure them substantially higher wages and possibly other benefits, such as support for education for their children, but also because the trips to Norway were attractive on both economic and social terms.

At the time of data collection, the view that cooperation and dialogue is beneficial to both workers and the corporation appeared to be hegemonic among my interlocutors both in Industri Energi and the Norwegian section of the MNC. I argue that through their support for union work in Tanzania, Equinor, in close collaboration with Industri Energi, has managed to transfer this norm quite successfully. After some turmoil, the local union branch was transformed from radical to transformist, and the branch members listed "good cooperation at all times" with the management as their main priority. Trade unions do discipline workers (Houeland 2018). Up to now, Equinor appears to have benefited from their support for the establishment of a local union branch, and if the company decides to invest in Tanzania, it will certainly be an advantage for the company to have a union branch in place that sees cooperation with the management as central to its mandate. To what degree the unionized workers have benefited is an open question. The members have not succeeded in their goal of having a collective bargaining agreement, and a system of social dialogue that includes the Tanzanian state is not realistic because the union that the Tanzanian staff are members of, NUMET, is a split union that has no ties upward. It should be noted that over the years that Equinor has been in Tanzania, the Norwegian management has shifted several times. In 2019, I discussed the issue of unionization with one of the top managers who strongly disagreed with the idea that the "Norwegian model" could be exported to Tanzania.

The oil sector is generally characterized by contractors and contingent work (Atabaki et al. 2018), and the present and future employees of Equinor Tanzania are in a better position being organized than not. Equinor's willingness and efforts to support the establishment of a union branch in Tanzania is laudable, but as I have shown, it is closely connected to Norwegian corporate democracy and Equinor's close ties with Industri Energi, to which it is accountable. A pivotal point in the process was the Equinor board's visit to Tanzania, where the union representatives contacted the Tanzanian staff. Without this visit, the local staff of Equinor Tanzania might have remained unorganized. Equinor's support for unionization was probably a result of several factors, including Equinor's CSR policies, which include labor rights, an assessment that unionization of its Tanzanian staff would be beneficial for the company, as well as codetermination and the company's accountability to the Norwegian union, Industri Energi. This case demonstrates that a Norwegian MNC may do things quite differently from other MNCs. However, the degree to which this happens is partly contingent on coincidences—such as where the board happens to pay a visit at a specific time—and local characteristics—such as whether the local union culture is reformist, emphasizing social dialogue, as in Norway, or radical and dismissive of the "Norwegian way."

Acknowledgments

This chapter is a revised version of an article that was published in 2020: "Doing Global Investments the Nordic Way: The 'Business Case' for Equinor's Support to Union Work among Its Employees in Tanzania." *Focaal: Journal of Global and Historical Anthropology* 88: 22–39. The study is part of the research project Energethics: Norwegian Energy Companies Abroad; Expanding the Anthropological Understanding of Corporate Social Responsibility (2015–19), funded by a FRIPRO grant from the Research Council of Norway (grant no. 240617). The author has not received any financial support from the company under study and has no personal ties to any of its staff. I wish to thank Equinor for letting me interview staff members at its headquarters in Norway and at their branch in Tanzania. I also wish to thank Camilla Houeland, Isabel Hugøy, Ståle Knudsen, Dinah Rajak, as well as the anonymous reviewers for their constructive comments to earlier drafts. I am sincerely grateful to all the people who shared their viewpoints and experiences with me.

Siri Lange holds a PhD in social anthropology and is a professor in the Department of Health Promotion and Development (HEMIL) at the University of Bergen, Norway. Prior to joining HEMIL, Lange was a senior researcher at the Chr. Michelsen Institute (CMI) in Bergen (2002–17). Lange has published extensively on social, economic, and political issues in Tanzania.

Notes

1. Some of the interviews were recorded (with consent), but for the great majority I took handwritten notes, therefore the quotes may not be verbatim in the strict sense.
2. The union has sixty thousand members and a history of negotiating very good conditions for its members working offshore.
3. IndustriAll Global Union, 2018, retrieved 25 July 2020 from http://www.industriall-union.org/.
4. The Corporate People and Leadership Department. For Equinor's organization chart, see https://www.equinor.com/en/about-us/organisation.html.
5. Corporate People and Leadership (PL)

6. The employer explained that he organized English-language training for the local staff. "Doing small things like that keeps them away from the union." In addition to free language training, he offered them good pay raises and told the workers that they could not hold union meetings on work premises.
7. Email correspondence made available to the author.
8. This is followed by: "Competence development using Statoil experience working with the unions; continue to build skills in union management within Statoil environment; establish cooperation with Statoil corporate union leadership; continue promoting better employer/employee relations; continue promoting/initiating cultural bridging programs" (NUMET Tanzania Statoil Branch 2016).
9. Camilla Houeland, personal communication, 13 March 2020.
10. Ståle Knudsen, personal communication, 12 March 2019.

References

Anner, M. 2017. "Monitoring Workers' Rights: The Limits of Voluntary Social Compliance Initiatives in Labor Repressive Regimes." *Global Policy* 8(S3): 56–65.
Atabaki, T., E. Bini, and K. Ehsani. 2018. "Introduction." In *Working for Oil: Comparative Social Histories of Labor in the Global Oil Industry*, edited by T. Atabaki, E. Bini, and K. Ehsani. Cham, Switzerland: Palgrave Macmillan.
Babeiya, E. 2011. "Trade Unions and Democratization in Tanzania: End of an Era." *Journal of Politics and Law* (1): 123–31.
Behrends, A., S.-J. Park, and R. Rottenburg. 2014a. "Travelling Models: Introducing an Analytical Concept to Globalisation Studies." In *Travelling Models in African Conflict Management: Translating Technologies of Social Ordering*, edited by A. Behrends, S.-J. Park, and R. Rottenburg. Boston: Brill.
Borchgrevink, A. S. 2019. *Giganten: Fra Statoil til Equinor; Historien om selskapet som forandret Norge* [The giant: From Statoil to Equinor; The story of the corporation that changed Norway]. Oslo: Kagge.
Christensen, S. H. 2011. *Hydro i Brasil* [Hydro in Brazil]. Oslo: LO Norway International Department (with economic support from Norad).
Craig, D. A., and D. Porter. 2006. *Development beyond Neoliberalism? Governance, Poverty Reduction and Political Economy*. New York: Routledge.
Dashwood, H. S. 2012. "CSR Norms and Organizational Learning in the Mining Sector." *Corporate Governance: The International Journal of Business in Society* 12(1): 118–38.
Dolan, C., and D. Rajak. 2011. "Introduction: Ethnographies of Corporate Ethicizing." *Focaal: Journal of Global and Historical Anthropology* 60: 3–8.
Equinor. 2018a. "About our Name Change." Retrieved 29 May 2020 from https://www.equinor.com/no/about-us/about-our-name-change.html.
———. 2018b. "Where we are." Retrieved 5 June 2019 from https://www.equinor.com/en/where-we-are.
———. 2020a. "2019 Sustainability Report." Retrieved 24 May 2020 from https://www.equinor.com/en/how-and-why/sustainability.html.
———. 2020b. "Tanzania." Retrieved 24 May 2020 from https://www.equinor.com/en/where-we-are.
Ervasti, H., T. Fridberg, M. Hjerm, O. Kangas, and K. Ringdal. 2008. "The Nordic Model." In *Nordic Social Attitudes in a European Perspective*, edited by H. Ervasti, T. Fridberg, M. Hjerm, and K. Ringdal, 1–20. Cheltenham: Edward Elgar.
Ferguson, J. 2005. "Seeing like an Oil Company: Space, Security, and Global Capital in Neoliberal Africa." *American Anthropologist* 107(3): 377–82.

Frynas, J. G. 2009. *Beyond Corporate Social Responsibility: Oil Multinationals and Social Challenges*. Cambridge: Cambridge University Press.

Gilberthorpe, E., and D. Rajak. 2017. "The Anthropology of Extraction: Critical Perspectives on the Resource Curse." *Journal of Development Studies* 53(2): 186–204.

Gold, M., L. Preuss, and C. Rees. 2020. "Moving out of the Comfort Zone? Trade Union Revitalisation and Corporate Social Responsibility." *Journal of Industrial Relations* 62(1): 132–55.

Granden, G. 2009. *Samfunnsansvar—hva kan tillitsvalgte gjøre?* [Corporate social responsibility—what can shop stewards do?]. Oslo: Cappelen Damm.

Harvey, G., A. Hodder, and S. Brammer. 2017. "Trade Union Participation in CSR Deliberation: An Evaluation." *Industrial Relations Journal* 48(1): 42–55.

Heiret, J. 2012. "Three Norwegian Varieties of a Nordic Model—A Historical Perspective on Working Life Relations." *Nordic Journal of Working Life Studies* 2(4): 45–66.

Houeland, C. 2017. *Punching above Their Weight: Nigerian Trade Unions in the Political Economy of Oil*. PhD thesis. Ås: University of Life Sciences (NMBU).

———. 2018. "Between the Street and Aso Rock*: The Role of Nigerian Trade Unions in Popular Protests." *Journal of Contemporary African Studies* 36(1): 103–20.

Ihlen, Ø., and H. v. W. Hoivik. 2013. "Ye Olde CSR: The Historic Roots of Corporate Social Responsibility in Norway." *Journal of Business Ethics* 127(1): 109–20.

ILO. 2009. *Social Dialogue and Industrial Relations Issues in the Oil Industry*. Geneva: ILO.

Industri Energi/IndustriAll Global Union, and Statoil. 2012. *The Exchange of Information and the Development of Good Working Practice within Statoil Worldwide Operations*. Geneve: Industri Energi/IndustriAll Global Union, Statoil.

Industri Energi Statoil. 2015. *Tanzania Visiting Statoil*. Unpublished report. Oslo: Industri Energi Statoil.

IndustriAll. 2012. "Norwegian Government Enforces Compulsory Arbitration in Oil and Gas Dispute." Retrieved 8 June 2022 from https://www.industriall-union.org/norwegian-government-enforces-compulsory-arbitration-in-oil-and-gas-dispute.

Jiao, Y. 2019. "Flexible Corporate Social Responsibility: Evidence from a Chinese Company in Africa." *International Journal of Business Anthropology* 8(2).

Jäger, S., B. Schoefer, and J. Heining. 2019. *Labor in the Boardroom*. Cambridge, MA: National Bureau of Economic Research.

Kesküla, E., and A. Sanchez. 2019. "Everyday Barricades: Bureaucracy and the Affect of Struggle in Trade Unions." *Dialectical Anthropology* 43(1): 109–25.

Knudsen, S., D. Rajak, S. Lange, and I. Hugøy. 2020. "Bringing the State Back In: Corporate Social Responsibility and the Paradoxes of Norwegian State Capitalism in the International Energy Sector." *Focaal: Journal of Global and Historical Anthropology* 88: 1–21.

Lange, S. 2008. "The Depoliticisation of Development and the Democratisation of Politics in Tanzania: Parallel Structures as Obstacles to Delivering Services to the Poor." *Journal of Development Studies* 44(8): 1122–44.

———. 2011. "Gold and Governance: Legal Injustices and Lost Opportunities in Tanzania." *African Affairs* 110(439): 233–52.

———. 2020. "Doing Global Investments the Nordic Way. The 'Business Case' for Equinor's Support to Union Work among Its Employees in Tanzania." *Focaal: Journal of Global and Historical Anthropology* 88: 22–39.

Lange, S., and V. Wyndham. 2021. "Gender, Regulation, and Corporate Social Responsibility in the Extractive Sector: The Case of Equinor's Social Investments in Tanzania." *Women's Studies International Forum* 84: 102434.

Larmer, M. 2006. "'The Hour Has Come at the Pit': The Mineworkers' Union of Zambia and the Movement for Multi-party Democracy 1982–1991." *Journal of Southern African Studies* 32(2).

Lauwo, S., and O.J. Otusanya. 2014. "Corporate Accountability and Human Rights Disclosures: A Case Study of Barrick Gold Mine in Tanzania." *Accounting Forum* 38(2): 91–108.

Løken, E. 2014. "LOs engasjement: Anstendig arbeid i oljesektoren" [LO's engagement: Proper work in the oil sector]. In *Anstendig arbeid i oljesektoren: Ghana og Nigeria* [Proper work in the oil sector: Ghana and Nigeria], edited by C. Houeland. Oslo: LO Norway International Department.

Løken, E., and F. Barbosa. 2008. *Industrial Bacalao? Industrial Relations in Norway and Brazil and within Norwegian Companies in Brazil: Fafo-report 2008:04*. Oslo: Fafo.

Neve, G. D. 2008. "Global Garment Chains, Local Labour Activism: New Challenges to Trade Union and NGO Activism in the Tiruppur Garment Cluster, South India." In *Hidden Hands in the Market: Ethnographies of Fair Trade, Ethical Consumption, and Corporate Social Responsibility*, edited by G. D. Neve, P. Luetchford, J. Pratt and D. C. Wood, 213–40. Bingley: Emerald.

NUMET. 2020. "About Numet." Retrieved 29 May 2020 from numet.co.tz.

NUMET Tanzania Statoil Branch. 2016. "Updates on the Union (NUMET)." Unpublished PowerPoint presentation. 11 April.

Rajak, D. 2011a. *In Good Company: An Anatomy of Corporate Social Responsibility*. Stanford, CA: Stanford University Press.

———. 2011b. "Theatres of Virtue: Collaboration, Consensus, and the Social Life of Corporate Social Responsibility." *Focaal: Journal of Global and Historical Anthropology* 2011(60): 9.

———. 2016. "Expectations of Paternalism: Welfare, Corporate Responsibility, and HIV at South Africa's Mines." *South Atlantic Quarterly* 115(1): 33–59.

Rees, C., L. Preuss, and M. Gold. 2014. "European Trade Unions and CSR: Common Dilemmas, Different Responses." In *Corporate Social Responsibility and Trade Unions: Perspectives across Europe*, edited by L. Preuss, M. Gold and C. Rees, 202–22. Abingdon, NY: Routledge.

Rugeiyamu, R., E. Kashonda, and B. Mohamed. 2018. "The Major Milestones for Development of Trade Unions in Tanzania: Is the Environment for the Operation Conducive?" *European Journal of Business and Management* 10(24).

Ryggvik, H. 2012. "Norwegian Oil Workers: From Rebels to Partners in the Tripartite System." In *Working for Oil: Comparative Social Histories of Labor in the Global Oil Industry*, edited by T. Atabaki, E. Bini, and K. Ehsani. Cham: Palgrave Macmillan.

Sabaratnam, M. 2017. *Decolonising Intervention: International Statebuilding in Mozambique*. New York: Rowman and Littlefield International.

Scholz, R., and S. Vitols. 2019. "Board-Level Codetermination: A Driving Force for Corporate Social Responsibility in German Companies?" *European Journal of Industrial Relations* 25(3): 233–46.

Spencer, R. 2018. "CSR for Sustainable Development and Poverty Reduction? Critical Perspectives from the Anthropology of Development." In *Disciplining the Undisciplined? Perspectives from Business, Society and Politics on Responsible Citizenship, Corporate Social Responsibility and Sustainability*, edited by M. Brueckner, R. Spencer, and M. Paull. Cham: Springer.

Sæther, A. K. 2017. *De beste intensjoner: Oljelandet i klimakampen* [The best of intentions: The oil nation in the climate struggle]. Oslo: Cappelen Damm.

Sørreime, H. B. 2019. "The Shaping and Changing of Petroleum Resource Governance: Discourses of Natural Gas in Tanzania." *Forum for Development Studies* 46(3): 547–68.

The Guardian. 2019. "TUCTA Suspends Msigwa, Deputy for 'Abuse of Office.'" Retrieved 15 March 2020 from https://www.ippmedia.com/en/node/70134.

Tran, A. N., J. Bair, and M. Werner. 2017. "Forcing Change from the Outside? The Role of Trade-Labour Linkages in Transforming Vietnam's Labour Regime." *Competition and Change* 21(5): 397–416.

Tripp, A. M. 2012. *Donor Assistance and Political Reform in Tanzania*. Working paper No. 2012/37. Helsinki: UNU-WIDER.

URT. 2015. *Guidelines for Corporate Social Responsibility and Empowerment in the Extractive Industry in Tanzania*. Dodoma: Ministry of Energy and Minerals in collaboration with Extractive inter-stakeholders' forum. United Republic of Tanzania.

Webster, E. 2018. "Culture and Working Life: Ari Sitas and the Transformation of Labour Studies in South Africa." *Journal of Contemporary African Studies* 36(2): 163–74.

Welker, M., D. J. Partridge, and R. Hardin. 2011. "Corporate Lives: New Perspectives on the Social Life of the Corporate Form; An Introduction to Supplement 3." *Current Anthropology* 52(3): 3–16.

Welker, M. A. 2009. "'Corporate Security Begins in the Community': Mining, the Corporate Social Responsibility Industry, and Environmental Advocacy in Indonesia." *Cultural Anthropology* 24(1): 142–79.

Zajak, S., N. Egels-Zandén, and N. Piper. 2017. "Networks of Labour Activism: Collective Action across Asia and Beyond; An Introduction to the Debate." *Development and Change* 48(5): 899–921.

— Chapter 9 —

STAGING MUTUAL DEPENDENCIES
Energy Infrastructure and CSR in a Norwegian Petroleum Town
Ragnhild Freng Dale

In 2017, the Norwegian company Equinor staged a concert in Hammerfest in Northern Norway, a town of about ten thousand inhabitants, and invited the entire town to the festivities. The occasion was a celebration of the first petroleum field established in the Norwegian Barents Sea, the Snøhvit project, which also is the first and only field for liquefied natural gas (LNG) production in Norway. The development of the field was approved by the Norwegian Parliament (Stortinget) in 2002, more than three decades after the North Sea and other parts of the Norwegian continental shelf were developed. The plans were saturated with a series of expectations about local investments and responsible resource management, but the field was also fraught with environmental controversies and cost overruns during the construction period that continued after production started in 2007.

This chapter examines how Equinor enacted their responsibilities within the local community when they entered Hammerfest in Finnmark, a region sometimes described as Norway's "extreme northern periphery."[1] In both the construction and operation phases, Equinor has enacted the company's social responsibility toward the town and to the regulatory authorities through physical infrastructure, employment, impact assessments, and public events, thus entwining the Snøhvit operations with the life of the town. This development has in different ways fulfilled, exceeded, and fallen short of local expectations as the industry has developed over the years.

While many of the activities Equinor engages in or initiates in Hammerfest do not fit the traditional understanding of CSR per se, juxtaposing Equinor's position and way of interacting with a local community in a peripheral region of Norway to the international examples in this book provides a comparative view of the evolving language of CSR and societal responsibility, or *samfunnsansvar* (see chapter 2). Equinor engages differently in the north than in larger cities where the headquarters are located, and this regional focus highlights how material and political particularities of the region come to shape the perception of the company at other scales also (cf. Rogers 2012). Throughout this chapter, I will make three main points on the nature of CSR as practiced domestically: firstly, the relation between the company and the town must be seen in relation to the intertwinement of Equinor's ownership history (as the formerly fully state-controlled company Statoil); secondly, infrastructure and taxation play a crucial role in the community's gain and thereby their willingness to be a host municipality for petroleum; and thirdly, trust and the changing nature of trust are important as both the ownership structure and corporate communication structures change.

My material is based on fieldwork carried out in Hammerfest in the period 2015–17, participant observation; semistructured interviews with industry representatives, politicians, and residents of Hammerfest; as well as document analysis and media monitoring. After a fire broke out at Equinor's facilities in 2020, the material has been gathered through live-streamed public meetings and conversations with interlocutors in Hammerfest, which all took place online due to the COVID-19 pandemic.

Showcasing Good Times in an Arctic Petroleum Town

The Snøhvit project was the first petroleum project to be approved in the Barents Sea. Equinor marked its ten-year anniversary in 2017 with a celebration for the city to thank them for their hospitality and cooperation. The event was advertised in local newspapers, on social media, and by posters spread around the city. Heavy rain started falling the day before the event, making preparations difficult for the stage crew, but the weather started clearing a few hours before the concerts began. Volunteers, many of them local youth, wore rain jackets underneath light blue T-shirts provided by Equinor. The logo of the company and its partners were printed on the back, and the words "Hammerfest LNG celebrates ten years of production" in Nor-

Figure 9.1. Audience members gathered for Equinor's Snøhvit anniversary in Hammerfest, August 2017. (At the time the company still operated under the former name "Statoil.") © Ragnhild Freng Dale

wegian on the front. Cake was served inside a white festival tent from midday, but the crowd was relatively sparse before the program started three hours later. Throughout the afternoon, local catering businesses also sold food, much of it based on local fish and reindeer. Equinor's local industry coordinator was in the audience, beaming and greeting people in the crowd, accepting congratulatory remarks, and making small talk during the breaks between concerts.

At 3:00 P.M., the show host took the stage and introduced the plant manager of the gas plant at Melkøya at the time, Unni Fjær. She started her speech by saying that they had been planning this event for almost a year, seeing it as an opportunity to thank the whole town for great cooperation through the years. She emphasized that she meant not only the municipality but also its inhabitants, that the LNG plant was mutually beneficial both for Equinor and for them. Highlighting how important Equinor was for jobs in the region, she remarked that half of the people who live in Hammerfest have either worked at Melkøya or have a family member who has worked there. Her final words concerned the property tax paid to the municipality each year, a sum that amounted to nearly two billion Norwegian crowns over the ten-year period. Someone in the crowd gasped, as if this number was totally new or unprecedented. Someone else clapped, but the applause remained modest: the crowd was not yet big enough to sustain a longer round of spontaneous applause. Equinor's representative continued by emphasizing that she was not a fan of property tax per se but was "impressed" with what the municipality had done with the money, how they had used it to create prosperity and a town where people want to live. It was obvious, she said, that they had to invite the whole town to celebrate Melkøya's tenth anniversary and use the celebration as a platform to showcase young local talent.[2]

The next speech was by the then mayor of Hammerfest, Alf. E. Jakobsen, who spoke in his characteristically straightforward and humorous manner: "I can understand that she loves property tax," he started, jokingly stating the amount the company pays in taxes and how it has made them "Siamese twins" of sorts—when things go well for Hammerfest, they go well for Equinor, too. "And for the town," he continued, "it is no secret that if you hadn't come, we would be in deep shit." There had been a period with bad times in the fishing industry, and Hammerfest had been placed on the ROBEK list for municipalities, which requires the state to approve any loans a local authority wants to make because they are not deemed able to repay. "And if there is one thing we don't like," he continued, "it's the state meddling in the size of our loans." He proudly declared that now their loans were so large that property tax would probably be needed forever—a joke that carries a large degree of truth, as Hammerfest's investments in anticipation of Snøhvit's arrival had made them a heavily indebted municipality, fully dependent on property tax income to keep their economy afloat. He praised Equinor for throwing a party for the whole town and reminded everyone that the collaboration between Equinor and Hammerfest stretched all the way back to 1981, when the company first started looking for petroleum in the region. At the end of his speech, he presented a gift to Equinor's production manager, a work of art called *Vannpoesi* (water poetry). "What this symbolizes to me," he said, "is that when you have gas that will be produced until 2055, maybe longer, then it's good times for Hammerfest also."

The event continued with mini concerts and other performances, including youth bands from the local area, a few more known young artists, and a show by the local gymnastics club. According to the evening's host, the gymnastic routine was inspired by the gas pipelines at Melkøya, the young gymnasts illustrating the flow with their bodies and movements. After the concerts, people quickly disappeared from the city center, families went home, and the town remained relatively quiet for a Saturday night. Equinor had thrown a family-friendly party, and though performed for a sparse crowd, it seemed to be well received in the town.

A New Region at Home

Finnmark is the northernmost county in Norway, some fifteen hundred kilometers north of Norway's petroleum capital of Stavanger and the North Sea where Norway's petroleum activities started in the 1970s. It is also a region with a less diverse economy than other parts of Norway (Arbo 2010). Petroleum exploration began in the Barents Sea in the 1980s, and Equinor discovered Snøhvit in 1984. A lack of infrastructure combined with political concerns for a vulnerable Arctic environment kept further development at bay for nearly two decades (Ryggvik and Smith-Solbakken 1997; Thesen and Leknes 2010). The distance from the Barents Sea to the rest of the Norwegian continental shelf meant that gas in this area could not easily be connected to pipes to the continent. Its materiality demanded a different solution: an LNG plant that could convert the gas to a liquid state transportable on tanker ships.

The project was contested when the Plan for Development and Operation (PDO) was approved by the Storting in 2002 (St.prp. no. 35 [2001–2002]). Other potential projects in the Barents Sea were on hold as an integrated management plan for the northernmost ocean areas was due within a few years, while the gas field, Snøhvit, was exempted from this process. Opponents saw Snøhvit as preempting further development, creating a path dependency toward oil in the future.[3] Concerns over a vulnerable Arctic environment were also high, as they had been in previous decades (Thesen and Leknes 2010). Thirdly, the economy in the project was disputed, and the Petroleum Act had to be changed to make the project viable. The changes were pushed through the necessary instances of government and parliament led by the minister of finance from the Labor Party,[4] and some of the committee members handling the case noted that the pace of this process was almost too fast. This was, in particular, related to the emissions from the gas facility, which risked undermining Norway's efforts after the Kyoto Protocol (Innst. S. no. 100 [2001–2002]: 8). The final approval of Snøhvit therefore came with a caveat that Equinor should make a plan for reducing emissions from the field. The committee and the parliamentary debate also made

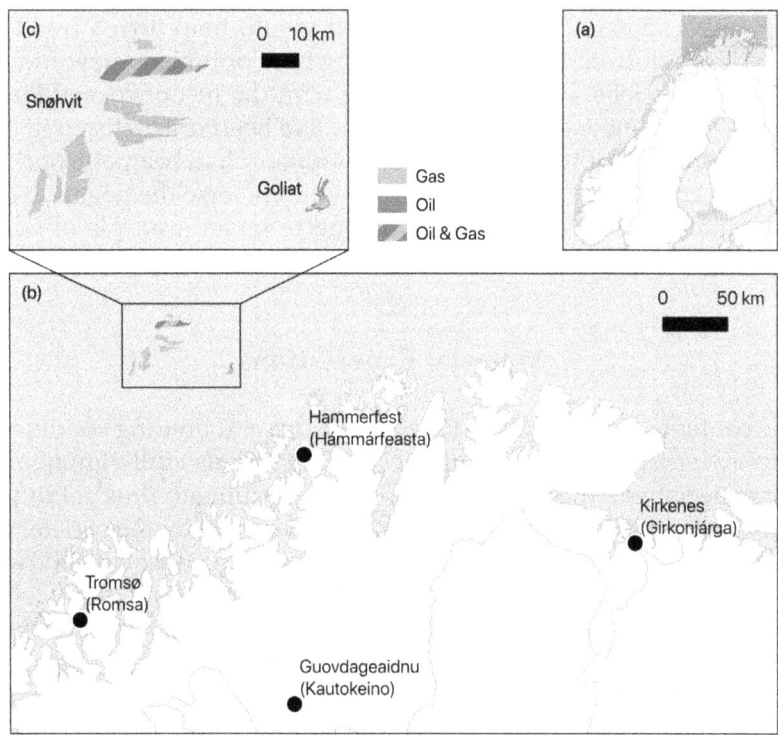

Map 9.1. Map showing the location of the two currently producing fields operated from Hammerfest: Snøhvit (Equinor) and Goliat (Vår Energi). Illustration: Tom Chudley

clear that jobs and ripple effects were expected from this development, particularly as Snøhvit was the biggest industrial development ever seen in Finnmark.

The expectations of active local job creation reflected the fact that Snøhvit was developed at a time when the industrial and political landscape was vastly different from the early years of Norwegian petroleum development. Companies and the supply industry were by now mainly located in the south and west of Norway. Furthermore, Equinor was registered on the stock exchange in 2001, an outcome of an internationalization and restructuring of governmentally owned firms that was started during the Conservative Party's rule in the 1980s. Bearing these changes in mind, the committee handling the PDO remarked that the project should set a minimum standard for further construction and production in the north[5] and thereby placed this responsibility on Equinor as the operator in charge. They also expressed an expectation that Snøhvit would help turn a trend of outmigration from the region, bringing new optimism, new industry, and new jobs. Hammerfest, along with the rest of coastal Finnmark, needed new jobs, as the fisheries had been restructured in the 1990s and most of the fish-processing industry had been outsourced to other countries. Snøhvit was expected to reverse the negative development and population decline and to be an example of what petroleum can come to mean for the north.

Material Expectations

The contents of the PDO are the foundations and binding conditions for the operator of a petroleum field. PDOs are also full of nonbinding expectations that are written into the document, thus solidified into a form that is not easily broken. Here lies much of the societal responsibility vested in Equinor: not from the company's own goodwill but the outcome of hearings, negotiations, legislation, and parliamentary debate. Snøhvit, with its "long and stable" period of operation, was expected to be positive for the town of the West-Finnmark region over the long term and bring both competence, investments, and ripple effects. When the broad majority in Stortinget approved the PDO for Snøhvit in 2002, the document included statements to ensure that the project would bring development, jobs, and economic opportunities to the region. The municipality of Hammerfest had been in close dialogue with Equinor throughout the process and entered into an agreement with the company that would pay for some of the necessary upgrades to infrastructure and establish a local industry coordinator in Hammerfest, who would be a point of contact for the local community, local business, and the municipality (St.prp. no. 35 [2001–2002]).

Equinor, on its side, exerted pressure by committing costs ahead of the decision; it signed contracts for gas sales with a specific start date for deliveries such that delays to the production start would be costly for the company and thus jeopardize the project altogether (Tveiterås 2010). Equinor's main problem was that taxation rules at the time did not allow them to manage costs the way they wanted, as the depreciation period was too long to be profitable in the short term. The change to the Petroleum Act reduced the depreciation period for new, large-scale LNG plants in Norway, and Equinor was allowed to write off the costs for the project over a shorter time period than normal: three years instead of six. To keep income for the state high, the whole LNG facility was classified as "offshore" rather than a normal onshore facility, meaning that the tax payments from the company to the Norwegian state would be greater.[6] Furthermore, the plant's location onshore within Hammerfest municipality meant that the municipality could claim property tax from the facilities—the property tax to which the mayor referred during the 2017 celebrations.

During an interview, one of Equinor's representatives called this a "win-win" for all parties, as Equinor, the Norwegian state, and Hammerfest municipality all gained from the outcome. The environmental NGO Bellona filed a complaint about these changes to the European Free Trade Association (EFTA), claiming that this was an illegal state subsidy of a polluting project. The Department of Finance defended the decision in a letter to the EFTA Surveillance Authority, emphasizing that the change was necessary to make petroleum viable in Norway's "extreme northern periphery" (Department of Finance 2002). Both the tax change and the project were eventually approved, and a construction period of five years followed before the field was ready to go into production. The delays increased total costs far beyond what the company expected but also created more work to be done locally during the construction phase—though the construction phase depended heavily on workers from outside Finnmark. In total, twenty-three thousand people worked on Melkøya for shorter or longer time periods (Eikeland et al. 2009).[7]

A Cornerstone of the Town

"I won't say it's meant everything, but it has certainly been very, very important," one of Hammerfest's politicians said to me in an interview, explaining how Equinor's Snøhvit and the start of the petroleum era was a boost after a long period of decline in the fisheries. The municipality made their plans on account of the promises and plans presented by both state and company, which predicted a growth in income, population, and jobs that would follow from the income of the gas facility, reflected in impact assessments and plans (Asplan Viak/Barlindhaug Consult 2001; Hammerfest Kommune 2001). With a guarantee of income from the property tax, the municipality could borrow money to invest in infrastructure for a petroleum town—but also to invest it so that inhabitants could see the benefits: schools, kindergartens, a landmark cultural center, and jobs that their youth would stay for.

The construction period turned Hammerfest into a booming town for five years. Locals still describe it as a "Klondike" mood, a surge of energy and activity, when several thousand construction workers descended on the small town. Interestingly, the flurry of activity was mostly seen as positive, and research on the impacts of Snøhvit during and directly after the construction years showed renewed optimism in both Hammerfest and the nearby town of Alta, with a great number wanting to stay in the region to work (Eikeland et al. 2009). Indeed, the title of the concluding report of the follow-on research opens with a reference to a newspaper article where a local teacher points to the new school she works in and says: "This is Snøhvit" (Eikeland et al. 2009). Ripple effects detailed in the report include a growing population, new optimism, and youth returning home. Such reports are part of the conditions in the PDO, financed by the companies but carried out by independent research institutes. The follow-on research enacts the assessment of whether the company meets the conditions and predictions made in the PDO and the impact assessments, thus already shaping what kinds of variables are to be measured and what experiences are discussed. Framing determines what matters or not (Beck 1992; Callon 1998), and as such, reports guide the gaze toward measurable effects of petroleum development. The choice to use a local teacher's statement as the opening narrative and title of the report strengthens this notion: Snøhvit's significance verified as all-encompassing by independent research reports, thus amplifying and strengthening the narrative of Snøhvit as a revitalization for the town that prepared the ground for more petroleum activity.

Another frequently narrated example is a collaboration between Equinor and the local high school, which was showcased in an industry report by KonKraft.[8] Across a full page in the report, the rector of the local high school says that the collaboration with Equinor and Melkøya had led to more motivated students and fewer absences in all subjects as well as a good dialogue with Equinor on what both parties want from each other (KonKraft 2016: 81).

Yet, even as these examples of the youth's positivity were listed in other industry reports, the trend had shifted when I conducted fieldwork in 2015 and 2016 in the aftermath of the global oil price crisis. The reports of ripple effects had indeed hinted at this, as the popularity of the petroleum sector started falling at the end of Snøhvit's construction period when fewer jobs were available (Eikeland et al. 2009: 99–100). The drop in applications to the high school program was more dramatic in the years following the drop in global oil prices, from long waiting lists to just four applicants in 2016. Two years later, just one applicant had chemistry and processing as their top priority. Industry representatives and the deputy mayor expressed concern to the media, as they wanted local, skilled petroleum workers who would be needed for future development of the Barents Sea (Reginiussen 2018).

The ten-year anniversary, then, should be seen as both a past- and future-oriented performance: both as an affirmation of the positive effects of Equinor's operations in the Barents Sea, and an attempt to create enthusiasm for the petroleum industry among the young generations of Hammerfest. A common trope in Hammerfest is that after Snøhvit, people "started painting their garden fences" again rather than letting them fall into disrepair. The gas production has become a synonym for stability and a future for the town.

CSR or *Samfunnsansvar*?

As discussed in the introduction to this volume, the term CSR does not easily resonate within Norway. The closest equivalent is the term *samfunnsansvar*, which translates more closely as social or societal responsibility as Maraire and Hugøy point out in chapter 2. None of these phrases are commonly used in Hammerfest, though people have clear expectations that the petroleum companies should create positive ripple effects and in particular contribute to job creation (Loe and Kelman 2016: 29). There is awareness in the local community of job opportunities in the wake of petroleum development, of sponsorships of festivals, art, and music, and of contributions to Hammerfest as an attractive place to live even for those who don't work in the industry, which people also expressed to me during my fieldwork.

To document these effects, reports become significant tools to verify the industry's importance by an independent party and as a basis for discussion of what petroleum development has meant and will mean for the region. This was also a narrative that Equinor's spokespeople liked to tell whenever they said something about the Snøhvit project. In an interview with Fredrik, a former industry coordinator in Hammerfest, he opened our conversation by asking if I had read these reports. In his opinion, they gave a very good idea of what Snøhvit meant regionally and what ripple effects had been created from their operations in the past decade. When I could confirm that I did indeed know their content, he was at ease and would gladly continue answering questions, even those that probed more deeply about their relationship with the town, the region, and the indigenous population.[9] As this had been verified by a third party in the research report, the implicitly communicated message was that I did not have to take his word for it. He also explained that this research had been important to the company during the construction phase: a way to monitor their effects as they went along.

Fredrik talked with enthusiasm about the good terms enjoyed between the municipality and the company, in particular investments in infrastructure and how Equinor had helped both start and develop vocational training and apprenticeships through the local high school. This was beneficial both for the town and for the company, he said, as it contributed to a stable workforce—most would be able to enter straight into well-paid jobs at a young age. Securing a local workforce would help strengthen the ties between the town and the industry, but it also meant better stability for Equinor as workers living locally are more likely to continue than those who commute from the south. In addition, the local jobs were among the most important themes in the PDO and thus an obligation Equinor would have to fulfill to remain credible in the region. This was not only an economic question, according to Fredrik. It was also one of *samfunnsansvar*, societal responsibility.

When discussing Equinor's role in the community, Fredrik told me that it was important for Equinor locally to *not* take a role as gift-giver, to fund all things large and small in the town, but rather to help fund activity and infrastructure that would also be beneficial to company activity and to stay out of other local affairs. "We provide money for the state [through taxes]," he said, "and then the politicians will have to judge what they want to do with it." In other words, the industry itself also frames their activities mainly as those of a good corporate citizen, where CSR activities are backgrounded and *samfunnsansvar* more important. Equinor participates in regional industrial energy projects and networks, employs locals and commuters who bring activity to the service industries, and participates in various sponsorship activities, which all entwine them in the material culture of the town. Yet, in line with Fredrik's words, one cannot understand Hammerfest's relationship to gas without understanding the importance of taxation.

The Importance of Taxation

I began this chapter with an ethnographic episode of speeches and gift-giving during Hammerfest LNG's ten-year anniversary celebration. Anthropological approaches to gift exchange stress that they not only serve as an exchange of things but also express the donor's and the recipient's perspectives on each other (Cross 2014: 123; Strathern 1999). The ceremony in Hammerfest—and the joking tone between representatives from local government and company—shows how Equinor's *samfunnsansvar* is both different from and exceeds the activities easily labeled as CSR activities. As the mayor made evident with his offer of a symbolic return gift to Equinor, it is not the gift-like parts of Equinor's display of societal responsibility that matter for the municipality and its inhabitants. Hammerfest is not in a relationship of indebtedness, such as those Dinah Rajak (2011) investigates in the international CSR performances, nor is this about reinforcing existing hierarchies between donor and recipient (Cross 2014). On the contrary; Norwegian society sees itself as an egalitarian society (Gullestad 1989). The gift exchange between the mayor and Equinor performed an equality between the parties that simultaneously underplayed and underlined their differences and obligations. As the north of Norway is more marked by gift economies than other parts of Norwegian society (cf. Kramvig 2005; Lien 2001), such exchanges have a wider symbolic significance than those of hospitality and ceremony alone. The mayor's return gift reminds Equinor that they are not giving money to Hammerfest out of goodwill but paying taxes as all businesses are required to. Equinor's obligatory social responsibility is thereby put on display by the gift, a social responsibility entwined with the company's relationship to the state and Norwegian law.

Equinor's representative played along with this joking and informal tone during the gift exchange, but if Equinor could choose, they would rather not pay this property tax. When the conservative government proposed a law that would remove property tax for municipalities in 2015, Equinor's leadership expressed support for such a change. The company proclaimed contributions to local ripple effects, growth, and jobs as important, but also argued that their competitiveness in the international arena would improve if the property tax were removed (Statoil 2015). Hammerfest and a range of other municipalities hosting petroleum installations were of the opposing view and expressed so in vocal terms both in the media and in the public hearing. To them, the tax income was crucial for economic survival.

Though the proposal was eventually scrapped, the response from Equinor shows a clear difference between company interest and municipal interest, which the mayor also marked during his stage appearance at the ten-year anniversary. Equinor will continue production in the community for at least thirty-five to forty years, and Hammerfest expects the yearly tax income to continue. The property tax ensures them a better economy than similarly sized municipalities without an LNG gas facility, a rare stability in a region otherwise dependent on the public sector and seasonal, often fluctuating, sectors, and the municipal budget is dependent on the continuation of that money flow.

Promise and Disappointment

The entwinement of social responsibility and legal requirements has been a key factor in the good relations built in Equinor's first Barents Sea petroleum project. But this relation between Equinor's local organization, Hammerfest LNG, and the town of Hammerfest has not become the standard for the company's operations in the north. The municipality of Nordkapp has been heavily disappointed by the development of the oil field Johan Castberg, where they were first led to expect an onshore terminal, as both political signals and Equinor's own rhetoric pointed in this direction. In 2013, Equinor invited the press to the potential landing site for an onshore terminal and popped a bottle of (nonalcoholic) champagne in front of media with the mayor of Nordkapp present. Subsequently, the company found less oil than they expected, oil prices dropped, and Equinor started quietly backtracking from their promise. In 2015, they presented plans for a floating production ship that would function independently of an onshore solution, and in 2017 they settled on this idea as their final concept solution. The terminal remained on the drawing board, possible if and only if the other companies exploring nearby decided to also develop their fields within the next few years.

The final decision to locate the operations farther south in Harstad and not bring the oil onshore at Veidnes was made in 2017. Politicians in Finnmark and particularly Nordkapp were disappointed by Equinor's U-turn, going forward with developing the field without the guarantee of local content that comes with onshore infrastructure. Labor Party politician Ingalill Olsen expressed that if there were no local content (for *their part* of Finnmark), then the oil might as well stay in the ground. After waiting patiently for Equinor to fulfill their promise that oil development at Castberg would bring a boost to the Nordkapp municipality in the form of jobs and other spinoffs, she changed her mind in a newspaper chronicle in March 2018 (Olsen 2018): the argument about jobs has disappeared, the people of Finnmark feel fooled, and without these local spin-offs, it just is not worth the risk to the local environment. It is then, similar to what Bråten shows in chapter 3, the embeddedness of the company that obligates it to the activities deemed as important locally: jobs, taxation, and ripple effects rather than sponsorship and other "typical" CSR activities.

When asked about the Castberg project in this same period, both Fredrik and other representatives at Equinor described their own company's handling of the local community's expectations as "unfortunate." They had acted too soon and instilled expectations that were unrealistic before they learned more about the field and the possibilities. Researchers Trond Nilsen and Stig Karlstad (2017) commented on the situation in the regional newspaper, noting that the "informal and unwritten relationship of trust" between Equinor and important political and industrial actors in the north had been solidly scarred by failing to bring oil onshore or at the very least to locate activity near the field. They concluded that Equinor can no longer count on the same support from Finnmark. On a local level, then, this is a demand for the company to be embedded in the places closest to petroleum activities; the experiences from Snøhvit show that local activity clusters around the host municipality, and though some jobs will fall to Hammerfest, people in Nordkapp see the company's *samfunnsansvar* as fulfilled if and only if they also see the company embedded within *their* municipality. The different fates of Snøhvit and Castberg also highlight how local expectations interweave with the materiality of the infrastructure necessary to extract it (cf. Barry 2013; Weszkalnys 2014).

What, then, about the state's role? When the PDO for Castberg was approved in 2018, it contained clear expectations that Equinor would consider a terminal and reach a decision later, but there was no demand save in the remarks of a few politicians from the opposition. Rather, the company was expected to make the soundest socioeconomic decision themselves (Prop. 80 S [2017–2018]). In early 2020, the new minister of petroleum and energy, Sylvi Listhaug, responded to a written question about the lack of an onshore terminal. She gave a long explanation of how "every stone [had] been turned" to make the onshore terminal profitable but emphasized that it was neither socioeconomically profitable nor profitable for the companies to build such a terminal.[10] Furthermore, she cited calculations by the companies of how many jobs the development of Equinor's field with the offshore solution would mean for the north both during construction and afterward. "If the companies had not found a profitable way to develop the field," she wrote, "then these big ripple effects [in the north] would not exist."

Her response underlines the national economy as aligned with the company's own judgments of economic viability. As pointed out in the introduction to this volume, when companies operate abroad, the state needs to show a professionalism in not instructing the companies in their operations. In Norway, responsibility is enacted within a different socioeconomic ensemble than in many places where Equinor operates abroad. The Norwegian government's hands-off approach concerning Castberg is indicative of a move away from the established social contract that local activity will mean local jobs. Though the state is the majority owner in Equinor, this is a passive ownership where the state does not see it as their responsibility to interfere in commercial decisions. As with the Hydro model (chapter 4), the state enacts its ownership in a passive manner. This also reflects what Maraire and Hugøy discuss in chapter 2: that the state is more concerned with a noninterfering ownership and the revenue produced by the company than with directly using its ownership to instruct companies. Though some political parties have protested this way of handling the Castberg project for relocating local benefits outside the region, the consensus in Stortinget has been not to instruct the company. The PDO may have insisted that Equinor spend time evaluating alternatives for making a terminal cost-efficient, but they trusted the company to make the most economically sound decision.

This ownership model was nearly overturned during the COVID-19 pandemic. Concerns for Norwegian jobs were high, and a corona crisis package was introduced to keep up the activity level in the petroleum industry. As part of this, Stortinget made the terminal at Veidnes a condition for the Castberg field. The state would foot most of the bill for the terminal to secure activity in the Norwegian petroleum sector through the crisis. Finnmark's politicians were overjoyed, but their hope was short-lived. A few months later, the government decided that this terminal was impossible after all. Unlike the early 2000s when taxation was adjusted for the Snøhvit project, the minister of petroleum and energy in 2020 saw it as politically, economically, and legally impossible to pursue (Johnsen 2020). This also reflects a shift in the planning level and the relationship between the state and the municipal level, which is governed more by market thinking now than before (Vike 2018). A company that was created to ensure that Norwegian oil would benefit the Norwegian population has, after changes to both Norwegian policy and the company's internationalization, withdrawn from these responsibilities in the local region with their change of plans for the Castberg field. On the local level, their retreat is understood not just as Equinor's decision but also the state's lack of disciplining the company. With insufficient instructions in the PDO, the infrastructure that would guarantee societal benefits is not a priority for the company.[11]

Handling Emergencies

Having covered the state-company entwinement and the taxation structure as critical points in the relationship between Equinor and their host municipality in the Snøhvit project, a third and important point must be made about how emergencies and incidents are handled by Equinor locally. The first such critical moment incurred when the gas plant began operations in 2007 and a thin, fine layer of black soot from the gas burner unexpectedly spread over town. The company's guarantee that the substance was not dangerous was met with skepticism from many inhabitants, a situation made worse by the fact that the instruments for measuring local air pollution were malfunctioning at the time. Equinor subsequently ordered an independent report from the University of Tromsø and paid for cleaning people's cars, homes, and windows. This process was overseen by their local industry coordinator at the time, who later remarked to me that not everyone had trusted the report (as it was paid for by the company) but that the incident gradually faded into the background as people became more accustomed to the presence of the LNG plant and the problem of the gas burner was solved.

The following autumn, Equinor reached out to the city for approval by holding their first concert for Hammerfest. The second concert took place in 2010 to celebrate Snøhvit's successful operation. Both concerts featured more famous bands and hosts than the 2017 event, with an atmosphere of a people's celebration aimed more at the population as a whole than the children and youth who are now Equinor's campaign focus nationally.[12] Such sponsorship is in part aimed at tamping down critique (Rogers 2012), and Equinor's gifting of the concerts certainly took place at a time when the company needed goodwill. The newspapers reported the first of these concerts as a successful event that had been welcomed by people in the town. Some shorter text messages to the editor[13] expressed that "some people had complained" about the concert and Equinor but praised the company for both the concert, the free food, and the good atmosphere on a cold autumn day with the flame of Melkøya shining in the background. "Where would Hammerfest be without Snøhvit?" one of them wrote. Another wrote that without the gas, there would be "no cultural house and no newly refurbished schools or the many jobs Snøhvit has given us." (Finnmark Dagblad 2008, my translation).

While not everyone was convinced, there was no public opposition, the narrative of Hammerfest's entwinement with the gas and oil so taken for granted that silence is more common than criticism. The knowledge of the chemicals sometimes surfaces in casual conversations, as does the fact that Snøhvit was mentioned in 2007 by the chief of defense as a possible terrorist target of strategic importance, which caused some worry in Hammerfest (NTB 2007). At the time of writing, a new hospital is under construction in Hammerfest, located closer to the sea and to Melkøya — a localization that has also led to debates about safety. These concerns have mostly been dismissed with reference to the legally required safety zones, which are in place to ensure incidents will not threaten the town or critical infrastructure.

Melkøya on Fire: Performing Local Accountability

The safety debates flared up again in September 2020 when a fire started at Equinor's gas facility at Melkøya. The flames were visible to everyone in the city, and the boats in emergency preparedness worked for eight hours to put out the fire with the aid of some larger ships that happened to be nearby. The incident was broadcast in real time by local news outlets, but neither they nor inhabitants of Hammerfest received any information about what had happened or what they should do. Some wondered if they needed to flee the city (and a few started doing so); others stayed inside out of fear of a potential explosion, while many went outside to look at the flames and black smoke. Personnel on Melkøya were evacuated, and the company communicated closely with the emergency services and the municipality, but little of this information reached inhabitants until much later on (Saue 2020). On the national news that same evening, standing on the shore looking out at the now-no-longer burning LNG plant, the plant manager said that they did not know why the fire had started.

The Petroleum Safety Authority (PSA) have criticized the safety culture at the installation on several occasions, including following an inspection they had conducted the year before. In the days following the event, a spokesperson for the PSA characterized the event as one of the most serious in Norwegian petroleum history and for which they would conduct a full investigation (NTB 2020). This was further confirmed by the PSA's investigation of the incident, which found several breaches of safety procedures and notes of concern that Equinor had not followed (PSA 2021).

Equinor on their side decided not to disclose any information about why the fire started until their internal investigations were finished. Nevertheless, to try and calm matters in town, they invited inhabitants to a public meeting a few days after the fire. Due to the ongoing COVID-19 pandemic, the meeting took place through Equinor's internal corporate communication platform on Microsoft Teams. In this session, the then plant manager, Andreas Sandvik, explained as much as could be said at the time, emphasizing that there were safety zones and separations of different parts of the facilities, so there was never a threat to the town or its inhabitants. Around his neck hung an Equinor key card, with the corporate slogans "I AM SAFETY" along with "Accountable, visible, and engaged" printed on the lanyard. This was clearly visible as he discussed the incident, avoiding clear conclusions as investigations were ongoing and the project team established to deal with the damage was only just set up.

Along with the plant manager was the then mayor of Hammerfest, Marianne Sivertsen Næss. She answered questions about the communication between the company, the municipality, and the emergency services, which she classified as excellent and a result of training for such unexpected scenarios. Participants could ask questions in the chat box, which were read by the head of communications for Melkøya. In the short hour the meeting lasted, participants also discussed improvements if such an incident were to occur again; for example, by sending an SMS to inhabitants or ensure they had information earlier. They emphasized the safety zones, which are a requirement by Norwegian law and verified by independent third parties. This evoked a sense of security, that the town and its inhabitants were safe even when such a serious incident occurred, and asserted their expert authority over the speculations that had flourished while the fire was ongoing.

Whether this meeting reassured people was impossible to gauge in this online format; there was no interaction save the chat box to ask questions, and only Equinor and the mayor appeared on camera. The format of communication and the nature of the dialogues were clearly in company control, where "expert knowledge … became information to be communicated but not a subject to be discussed" (Ottinger 2013: 100), their credibility backed up by the presence of the mayor. Equinor did not say much to the press in the following weeks but sent a brochure in the mail to inhabitants in the municipality, which described how Equinor was working to keep "zero damage to humans, environment and material, zero accidents and loss" (Equinor, 2021).[14] Some of my interlocutors were outraged by this—they had heard nothing about reasons for the fire at all, and now they received a brochure that proclaimed in glossy corporate language how responsible the company was in ensuring no damage or spills from their operations. The intent may have been to inform inhabitants and calm matters down, but the zero-damage claim after the fire gave the impression that the company had something to hide. To maintain an image as a dependable and trustworthy company under pressure, Equinor is working to restore that image in a way that is reactive rather than systematic (cf. Dolan and Rajak 2011).

Simultaneously, Equinor's reactions happened in a format that responded to the Norwegian society's demand for openness and information. Since the fire, Hammerfest LNG's plant manager has appeared before the municipal board several times to explain the current status of Melkøya and what it means for the local community. This, as he said during his explanation at one such meeting, was a channel to inform the population and the town. During a question-and-answer session afterward, questions were brought up that show how concerns for safety and for local jobs continue to be entwined. Two politicians asked about consequences for local jobs, and Equinor made assurances of constant efforts in recruitment, that all of them would keep their jobs, and that more than 300 of their 350 employees at Melkøya had Hammerfest as their home. Whether in normal circumstances or during this crisis, the care shown between the company and the municipality was one of mutual dependence, displaying both goodwill and recognition of the legal requirements for operation.

Conclusion: A Matter of Different Perspectives

To understand how Equinor enact their social responsibility in Hammerfest and the Finnmark region, then, several factors should be kept in mind. The geographic location in the Barents Sea and the materiality of the resource as gas and not oil has been key to the specific development of an LNG facility, which was contingent on new legislation and political priorities. The (mostly) positive experiences in Hammerfest and the disappointments in Nordkapp over the Castberg field underline the importance of what is written into the PDO, but also how the embeddedness of the company is related to the idea of *samfunnsansvar*. Equinor is accessible and responsive to the local community in Hammerfest, where the company is a cornerstone of the economy, whereas the Nordkapp municipality, where no activity was established, have found the company distant and irresponsive.

As the ethnographic material shows, local expectations are not directed solely at the company but also toward the state to make the company choose certain types of infrastructure over others. This reflects both an intertwinement of different levels of governance and the contradictory role of the state as both legislator and a passive majority shareholder in Equinor. Though the government could use their ownership to steer the company, they withhold from doing so and rather express their expectations and demands in documents such as the PDO. Expectations of local content is clear, but the question of *how* is mostly left to the company itself. Simultaneously, as reflected in the Castberg debates, Equinor's behavior in Finnmark is debated, restated, and reshaped continuously in the press, in debates in Stortinget, and elsewhere in the public sphere. This is also what marks the Norwegian case as different from the cases abroad; that their activities are read through the lens of *samfunnsansvar* both at the local and the national level.

The local celebration in Hammerfest should be seen as part of this process, as it took place not only on the ten-year anniversary of the field's start of production but also in parallel to the process of the Castberg field and further petroleum exploration in the Barents Sea. With the concert, Equinor displayed their tight and friendly relationship with their host municipality in the north, which circumvents the bad press around the Castberg project in Finnmark. Locals may come to a concert when one is offered, but as emphasized by the mayor during his speech, the relationship is built not on gifts to the community but on the binding commitments of the infrastructure and property tax.

The recent fire at Melkøya reveals both a fragility and robustness in this relationship. Though dialogue with the municipality was immediate, inhabitants did not get full information until many weeks after the event. The dissatisfaction with flashy brochures reflects a desire for security, to know operations in future will be safe and beneficial to the community. For local politicians, their relationship of mutual dependency and benefit with Equinor is contingent on the national political level and how legal requirements and tax arrangements are shaped. For the company, it is a matter of complying with

Norwegian law and political expectations, though the company's own judgment of profitability is increasingly trusted by the government. It is not that CSR does not at all exist on the national level but that the regulated and expected ripple effects such as jobs and taxation are what is deemed as *samfunnsansvar* proper in the Norwegian context.

Acknowledgments

The research has been supported by a Gates Cambridge Scholarship at the University of Cambridge and by the project Energethics (2015–19), funded by a FRIPRO grant from the Research Council of Norway (grant no. 240617). Additional research and writing have been funded by the FME NTRANS (grant no. 296205).

Ragnhild Freng Dale is a social anthropologist and senior researcher with the Western Norway Research Institute (Vestlandsforsking). Her research interests include energy infrastructure, petroleum, climate transitions, and community impacts, predominantly in Norway and Sápmi. She holds a PhD from the Scott Polar Research Institute at the University of Cambridge and is a member of the Young Academy of Norway.

Notes

1. Quotation from the Norwegian Department of Finance, who described the location to the European Free Trade Association when taxation rules were under discussion (Department of Finance 2002).
2. Such a focus harmonizes well with Equinor's main focus in their CSR activities nationally, where their "Heroes of Tomorrow" initiative targets young talents in sports, the sciences, and the arts (though the latter in particular has been disputed).
3. This was also correct: though only one other field is in operation today (the Goliat field, operated by Vår Energi), two are in the construction and planning phase (both operated by Equinor), and licenses for exploration in new areas have been awarded numerous times since the Barents Sea South East was opened in 2016.
4. The minister was the Finnmark-born Karl Eirik Schjøtt-Pedersen, who later became the director general of the Norwegian Oil and Gas association, an employer and industry organization for companies with activities on the Norwegian Continental Shelf (mainly the petroleum majors). They recently changed their name to Offshore Norway.
5. The remark was made by a political majority in the committee recommendation on the PDO for Snøhvit (Innst. S. no. 100 [2001–2002]).
6. Offshore operations are taxed at 78 percent in Norway, while taxation of onshore facilities amount to 28 percent.

7. In comparison, the whole of Finnmark has a population of approximately seventy-five thousand people.
8. KonKraft describe themselves as "a collaboration arena between NOROG, the Federation of Norwegian Industries, the Norwegian Shipowners Association and the Norwegian Confederation of Trade Unions (LO), with LO members Fellesforbundet og [sic] Industri Energi. It serves as an agenda-setter for national strategies in the petroleum sector, and works to maintain the competitiveness of the Norwegian continental shelf (NCS), so that Norway remains an attractive area for investment by the Norwegian and international oil and gas industry—including suppliers and the maritime sector" (KonKraft 2016).
9. As discussed in chapter 1 (Müftüoğlu et al., 45), such demonstrations of prior knowledge are important to secure access—even though I had reached Fredrik through other contacts within the company, it was important for him to check that I knew the "basics" before we started the interview.
10. https://www.stortinget.no/no/Saker-og-publikasjoner/Sporsmal/Skriftlige-sporsmal-og-svar/Skriftlig-sporsmal/?qid=78262.
11. Nordkapp's disappointment resembles Hasvik's experiences with the Goliat field, which is operated by Vår Energi (formerly Eni Norge) from Hammerfest. Hasvik, a municipality on the Sørøya island just fifty kilometers from the field, had been the potential landing site for an oil terminal until the company decided not to bring oil from the Goliat field to an onshore terminal. Hasvik, a fishing-based community, had been left with a high risk in the event of an oil spill, while Hammerfest gained most of the local ripple effects (Dale 2018). In both of these cases, a combination of the company and the state was blamed: the company for caring only for costs, and the government for not using their power to secure local content.
12. Aiming the event at children aligns with the "Heroes of Tomorrow" campaigns of Equinor, which are mostly directed at developing young talent in sports, the sciences, and the arts.
13. A format where people sent text messages to the newspaper to make comments, almost like today's social media platforms.
14. Equinor is required by law to send information about their operations to nearby inhabitants every five years but decided to send a new one ahead of time.

References

Arbo, Peter. 2010. "En Næring til begjær, en næring til besvær" [A desired industry, a challenging industry]. In *Oljevirksomhetens inntog i Nord* [The Petroleum industry's entry in the North], edited by Peter Arbo and Bjørn Hersoug, 15–44. Oslo: Gyldendal Akademisk.
Asplan Viak/Barlindhaug Consult. 2001. *Konsekvensutredning Snøhvit: Lokale samfunnsmessige konsekvenser i Hammerfest* [Impact assessment Snøhvit: Local societal impacts in Hammerfest]. Thematic report for Statoil.
Barry, Andrew. 2013. *Material Politics Disputes along the Pipeline*. Malden, MA: Wiley Blackwell.
Beck, Ulrich. 1992. *Risk Society: Towards a New Modernity*. London: Sage.
Callon, Michel. 1998. "Introduction: The Embeddedness of Economic Markets in Economics." *Sociological Review* 46(S1): 1–57.
Department of Finance. 2002. "Letter to Efta Surveillance Authority, Additional Information, 30.04.2002." Letter from the Department of Finance, Government of Norway.
Dolan, Catherine, and Dinah Rajak. 2011. "The Anthropology of Corporate Social Responsibilty." *Focaal: Journal of Global and Historical Anthropology* 60: 3–8.

Eikeland, Sveinung, Stig Halgeir Karlstad, Christen Ness, Trygve Nilsen, and Inge Berg Nilssen. 2009. *Dette Er Snøhvit: Sluttrapport Fra Følgeforsknigen 2002–2008* [This is Snøhvit: Final report from the accompanying research 2002–2008.] Report 2009:3. Alta: Norut.
Equinor. 2021. "Informasjon Til Allmennheten Om Risiko Og Beredskap: Hammerfest LNG" [Information to the public regarding risk and emergency preparedness: Hammerfest LNG]. Stavanger: Equinor ASA.
Finnmark Dagblad. 2008. "SMS Message. Unkown Sender." 27 August 2008.
Gullestad, Marianne. 1989. *Kultur og hverdagsliv: På sporet av det moderne Norge* [Culture and everyday life: On the trail of modern Norway]. Oslo: Universitetsforlaget.
Hammerfest kommune. 2001. *Snøhvitsamfunnet. Plan for Sosiale, Helse-/Trivselsmessige Og Kulturelle Forhold i Utbyggingsfasen 2002 – 2006.* [The Snøhvit Society. Plan for Social, Health-/Well-being and Cultural aspects of the Construction Phase 2002-2006]. Hammerfest: Hammerfest kommune.
Innst. S. no. 100 (2001–2002). 2002. "Innstilling fra Energi- og miljøkomiteen om utbygging, anlegg og drift av Snøhvit LNG" [Recommendations from the standing committee on energy and the environment regarding the construction and operation of Snøhvit LNG]. Oslo: The Standing Committee on Energy and Environment.
Johnsen, Alf Bjarne. 2020. "Regjeringen sier nei til å føre olje i land i Finnmark—Ap er rasende" [The government says no to bringing oil onshore in Finnmark—the Labor Party is furious]. *VG*, 7 October 2020.
KonKraft. 2016. "North and the Norwegian Continental Shelf—Introduction, Summary and Recommendations." Tromsø: Lundblad.
Kramvig, Britt. 2005. "Fleksible kategorier, fleksible liv" [Flexible categories, flexible lives]. *Norsk Antropologisk Tidsskrift*, no. 02–03: 97–108.
Lien, Marianne. 2001. "Likhet og verdighet, gavebytte og integrasjon i Båtsfjord" [Equality and dignity, gift exchange and integration in Båtsfjord]. In *Likhetens paradokser, antropologiske undersøkelser i det moderne Norge* [Equality's paradoxes, anthropological investigations in Modern Norway], edited by Marianne Lien, Hilde Vidén, and Halvard Vike, 86-108. Oslo: Universitetsforlaget.
Loe, Julia S. P., and Ilan Kelman. 2016. "Arctic Petroleum's Community Impacts: Local Perceptions from Hammerfest, Norway." *Energy Research & Social Science* 16 (June): 25–34. https://doi.org/10.1016/J.ERSS.2016.03.008.
Nilsen, Trond, and Stig Halgeir Karlstad. 2017. "*Når tillit brister*" [When trust is breached]. *Finnmark Dagblad*, 28 June 2017.
NTB. 2007. "Uttalelser om Snøhvit som terrormål skaper uro" [Statements concerning Snøhvit as a target for terrorism cause unrest]. *Sysla*, 28 September 2007.
———. 2020. "*Petroleumstilsynet: Melkøya-Brannen en av de mest alvorlige hendelsene i Norsk Petroleumshistorie*" [The petroleum safety authorities: The fire at Melkøya is among the most serious incidents in Norwegian petroleum history]. *Aftenposten*, 29 September 2020. https://www.aftenposten.no/okonomi/i/39jn9A/petroleumstilsynet-melkoeya-brannen-en-av-de-mest-alvorlige-hendelsene.
Olsen, Ingalill. 2018. 'Lei av å bli lurt – jeg konverterer'. In *Nordnorsk Debatt*, March 21.
Ottinger, Gwen. 2013. *Refining Expertise: How Responsible Engineers Subvert Environmental Justice Challenges*. New York: New York University Press.
Prop. 80 S (2017–2018). Utbygging og drift av Johan Castberg-feltet med status for olje- og gassvirksomheten. [Development and Operation of the Johan Castberg field with status for the oil and gas operations.] Green paper from the Ministry of Petroleum and Energy, Government of Norway.
PSA, Petroleum Safety Authorities. 2021. "Rapport etter gransking av brann i luftinntak til GTG4 på Hammerfest LNG, Melkøya" [Report following investigation into the fire in the air conditioning system to GTG4 at Hammerfest LNG, Melkøya]. https://www

.ptil.no/contentassets/3391c6686b2b4265abe8585294151335/2020_1862_rapport-equinor-hammerfest-lng-gransking.pdf.

Rajak, Dinah. 2011. *In Good Company: An Anatomy of Corporate Social Responsibility*. Stanford, CA: Stanford University Press.

Reginiussen, Arne. 2018. "*Færre søkere truer oljelinjer: –det er svært dramatisk*" [Fewer applicants threathens petroleum studies: –It is very dramatic.]. *Finnmark Dagblad*, 31 May 2018.

Rogers, Douglas. 2012. "The Materiality of the Corporation: Oil, Gas, and Corporate Social Technologies in the Remaking of a Russian Region." *American Ethnologist* 39(2): 284–96. https://doi.org/https://doi.org/10.1111/j.1548-1425.2012.01364.x.

Ryggvik, Helge, and Marie Smith-Solbakken. 1997. *Norsk Oljehistorie: Bind 3*. [Norwegian Petroleum History: Volume 3]. Oslo: Norsk Petroleumsforening.

Saue, Ole Alexander. 2020. "Hammerfest krever svar etter Equinor brann" [Hammerfest demand answers after Equinor Fire]. *Aftenposten*, 11 October 2020.

St.prp. no. 35 (2001–2002), 2022. "Utbygging, anlegg og drift av Snøhvit LNG" [Construction and operation of Snøhvit LNG]. Oslo: Department of Petroleum and Energy.

Statoil 2015. "Høringssvar fra statoil om eiendomsbeskatning av arbeidsmaskiner mv. i verk og bruk" [Statement for the public hearing on the motion to remove property tax on mills and factories]. https://www.regjeringen.no/contentassets/9298d2cf56064519a5 6a19690eb9e7d8/242_statoil.pdf?uid=Statoil.

Strathern, Marilyn. 1999. *Property, Substance and Effect : Anthropological Essays on Persons and Things*. London: Athlone.

Thesen, Gunnar, and Einar Leknes. 2010. "Nord-Norge i Norsk petroleumspolitikk—narrativer og politisk endring" [Northern Norway in Norwegian petroleum politics—narratives and political change]. In *Oljevirksomhetens inntog i Nord* [The Petroleum industry's entry in the North], edited by Peter Arbo and Bjørn Hersoug, 45-76. Oslo: Gyldendal Akademisk.

Tveiterås, Kathrine. 2010. "*Snøhvit—et megaprosjekt tar form*" [Snøhvit—a mega project takes shape]. In *Oljevirksomhetens inntog i Nord* [The Petroleum industry's entry in the North], edited by Peter Arbo and Bjørn Hersoug, 129-146. Oslo: Gyldendal Akademisk.

Vike, Halvard. 2018. "Politics and Bureaucracy in the Norwegian Welfare State: An Anthropological Approach." *Approaches to Social Inequality and Difference*. Cham: Springer International Publishing: Palgrave Macmillan.

Weszkalnys, Gisa. 2014. "Anticipating Oil: The Temporal Politics of a Disaster yet to Come." *Sociological Review* 62 (1_suppl): 211–35. https://doi.org/10.1111/1467-954X.12130.

— Chapter 10 —

STANDARDIZING RESPONSIBILITY THROUGH THE STAKEHOLDER FIGURE
Norwegian Hydropower in Turkey
Ståle Knudsen, Ingrid Birce Müftüoğlu, and Isabelle Hugøy

Oslo 1979: Facing strong opposition to the planned Alta power plant in northern Norway from the local Sami minority population as well as environmentalists nationwide, one of the Statkraft managers wrote in the agency's internal journal that he had "a strong belief in personal contact. We ought to pursue far more active information through for example schools, youth organizations, mass media, and other channels. ... It also seems evident that our organizational structure is not adequately prepared for the demands presented by our surroundings. If we are to succeed, we must find ways to cooperate with watercourse user groups to a larger extent than we have previously."[1]

Istanbul 2015: Statkraft was hiring a new Turkish CSR officer for their large construction site Çetin in southeast Turkey—a project that confronted a variety of challenges, including political conflict among impacted communities. In reviewing candidates, they were looking for someone familiar with international standards: "We already have a guy who can drink tea with the locals."

Why would even the most everyday interaction with local realities in rural Turkey in 2015 require knowing international standards, while management had not considered international standards when searching for new ways to do things in Norway back in 1979? In the short time span from the mid-1980s to around 2000, Statkraft went through momentous change, from being a Norwegian state agency to become a transnational corporation in pursuit of profit (see table

0.1 in the introduction to this volume). This change also implied a shift from rule-based governance to state "expectation" that corporate social responsibility (CSR) practice should be guided by international standards.

These two vignettes are suggestive of two major trends during the last couple of decades: corporatization and internationalization of economic activity, and the increasing degree to which the practice and language of CSR has become informed by and embedded in a multitude of international guidelines. These two trends are related: as governments lose control over capital, ameliorative soft governance is sought through international voluntary frameworks. How do these changes affect the way in which responsibility is handled by corporations? We pursue this question through a multisited study of Statkraft, a particularly "responsible" renewable energy corporation, owned by the Norwegian state. Being a fully state-owned company based in a Nordic corporate context raises the additional question of whether this makes a difference to the way in which the corporation relates to CSR standards and reporting. To what extent does the Nordic model inform Statkraft's practice of CSR in Turkey?

This study focuses on Statkraft's engagement in Turkey and the way in which they practice CSR. We have had longitudinal interaction from 2013 through 2018 (mainly but not limited to meetings) with staff at HQ in Oslo and local CSR staff in Turkey, as well as meetings with a range of persons who interact with Statkraft. Further, we have conducted ethnographic fieldwork in local communities in Turkey and surveyed corporate and government documents, relevant internet sites of the corporation, and international performance and reporting standards. Taking a multisited approach to the application of standards in Statkraft's work has enabled us to see beyond the tension between reality versus corporate presentation and to explore the multifaceted nature of CSR within and at the fringes of the corporation.

While CSR was once considered to be voluntary acts of "doing good," corporations now try to integrate social and environmental issues in risk management and decision-making systems, in performance standards, and in standardized reporting frameworks intended to ensure transparency and accountability (Shabana et al. 2017; Welker 2014). Critics—academics and activists—claim that, rather than securing transparency, the use of global standards, especially for reporting, tends to misrepresent or mask the way in which corporations perceive and act on local realities, to the extent that the standards organize, bureaucratize, and depoliticize the impact the corporation has on the world (see, e.g., Garsten and Jacobsson 2011). Taking the Global Reporting Initiative (GRI) as her prime example, Sally Merry concludes that "indicators produce readily understandable and convenient forms of knowledge about the world that shape the way policy makers and the general public understand the world … and new opportunities for governance through self-governance" (Merry 2011: 92–93).

This critical argument comes with several interrelated assumptions that may be problematic. First, it is largely based on a Foucault-inspired critique of neoliberal governance techniques (see the commentary in the introduction to this volume), which makes overly broad brush by incorporating into the narrative of a global neoliberalism ways of governance that have independent trajectories and are developed for aims other than "marketization of everything." It may also make overly strong claims about the effect of neoliberal governance, such as the inducement of "self-governance." Second, most of the literature on CSR, including studies of CSR as governance and in-depth ethnographic studies (e.g., Welker 2014; Rajak 2011) develop their arguments based on the assumption that corporations are privately owned shareholder firms. There is a certain Anglo-American bias to this literature that makes it hard to consider other possible "economic-institutional ensembles" (Foucault 2008: 167). For instance, Nordic state-owned corporations do not necessarily conform to the Anglo-American model. Third, the argument presupposes that we accept that corporations are unitary, that they consistently apply international standards throughout their organizations, and that standards actually work (for a critique, see Welker 2014). What does the use of performance standards and sustainability reporting really "do" for the corporations? It has been argued that an important character of standards is that they are "always already incomplete and inadequate" (Star and Lampland 2009: 14). Practitioners of CSR are often acutely aware of the tension between the complex reality they engage in and the standards that are assumed to guide their work and reporting. In keeping with this we will assume that the meaning, content, and character of CSR work is also contested and negotiated within the corporation.

Below we will first discuss how the Norwegian state manages its ownership of Statkraft, especially focusing on the evolving "expectations" for how the corporation should handle CSR. We show how Statkraft, at an overarching level, interprets these expectations in the context of increased international activity. Second, we outline Statkraft's use of the performance standards of the International Finance Corporation (IFC) and explain why the IFC-inspired focus on Project

Affected People (PAP) by many Statkraft staff is considered a better way to pursue "environmental and social management" than classical CSR. Third, we detail Statkraft's CSR work in Turkey through several case studies that show that the practice of CSR is flexible and pragmatic and often mixed with other agendas of the corporation. In doing so, we also show how Statkraft's CSR work feeds into reporting and public relations. Drawing on the case studies, we argue that the application of standards results in much less standardization than is often assumed, yet the elusive figure of the "stakeholder" plays an important role in holding together the heterogeneous field of CSR.

Statkraft: Internationalization and State Expectations to CSR

The corporatization of Statkraft was strongly interconnected with internationalization of the power sector. When the ministerial agency Norwegian Water Resources and Energy Directorate (NVE) split into several units in 1986, Statkraft became an independent economic entity. It was corporatized in 1992, becoming a state enterprise. This was motivated by a desire to make the entity a more effective, modern, and competent actor in the recently (1991) liberalized electricity market in Norway, but also by shifts in Norwegian and European power supply systems (Skjold 2009: 228). In 2004, driven by the desire to operate more easily internationally (Meld. St. 22 [2001–2]; Nilsen and Thue 2006: 371–73; Skjold 2015: 16), Statkraft became a limited liability, but unlisted, company. The state retains all shares, but the government has transferred judicial responsibility to the board and management of the corporation. The government appoints the chair of the board, which consists of nine members, three of whom represent employees (but not necessarily unions).

Statkraft's board had argued that "the state enterprise form is not known as a corporate form internationally" and that "the suggested reorganization allows Statkraft to present itself more clearly as a purely commercial actor in line with its most important competitors" (Prop. 53 [2003–4]: 26). Internationalization was the keyword in the new corporate strategy in 2006 (Nilsen and Thue 2006: 397). Building on a strong tradition in hydropower in Norway, Statkraft is now considered Europe's largest renewable energy corporation and has operations in Asia and South America as well.

The international expansion of Statkraft's operations, especially outside of Northern Europe, confronted the corporation with new challenges as regards responsible conduct and risk management, including violent local resistance (Skjold 2015: 212) or large-scale population resettlement (Laos). Its owner, the Norwegian state, provided only indirect guidance. Governments in Norway have been very concerned about the state managing its ownership "professionally." Therefore, the Ministry of Trade, Industry, and Fisheries, which "owns" the corporation, is expected to not interfere in daily operations but rather express its "expectations," which are to be interpreted and implemented by corporation management and reviewed by the board. The primary aim of the state's ownership of Statkraft, as expressed in a white paper on state ownership, is that "the company is to be run on a commercial basis and with the aim of delivering a competitive return" (Meld. St. 27 [2013–14]: 108).

However, governments have since 2006 also expected that corporations under state ownership should take a leading role in safeguarding CSR (Meld. St. 13 [2006–7]: 64), noting that if they do not, "the state's legitimacy could be weakened, for example as legislator and in matters concerning foreign policy" (Meld. St. 10 [2008–9]: 18). The 2013–14 white paper on state ownership is more specific in that it requires corporations in which the state has significant ownership and which have overseas operations to sign up to Global Compact, follow the OECD responsible business conduct recommendations for multinational corporations, take up ILO's core conventions in their business, and apply GRI reporting standards (Meld. St. 27 [2013–14]: 83). The government's specific expectations that Statkraft will conduct "responsible" business abroad is articulated in the public arena. A presentation by Monica Mæland (Conservative Party), minister of trade and industry at the Bergen Chamber of Commerce and Industry in 2013, included a slide that carried the title (in Norwegian) "Social Responsibility—a competitive advantage" and stated in bullet points: "Clear expectations that Norwegian business abroad takes responsibility"; "Increased awareness among Norwegian firms"; "Statkraft takes responsibility in Turkey." The text was accompanied by a photo from the signing of the energy agreement between Norwegian and Turkish ministers during the Norwegian state visit to Turkey in 2013, also showing the Turkish president and Norwegian king attending the ceremony.

Taking a Leading Role—With Multiple Models

The state's "expectations" about responsibility are communicated to Statkraft's board and management but are quite general, so they are open to a certain degree of interpretation and negotiation. In conjunction with the publication of the white paper on CSR (Meld. St. 10 [2008–9]), a Statkraft employee recalls discussions with fellow employees about how to present CSR to the corporation leadership and how to implement the white paper's requirement of taking "a leading role within the field." Similar concerns were expressed when we had our very first meeting with a senior CSR manager in Statkraft in 2013; he stressed that "since Statkraft is owned by the state, we are also partly Norway's ambassador. We are concerned about earning money in a decent way."

The explicit focus on CSR emerged in Statkraft around 2003 and then specifically within SN Power, which Statkraft established together with Norfund (Norway's Development Finance Institution) to invest in high-risk hydropower projects in developing countries (Skjold 2015: 203–4). It was, and is, a widespread idea that, while CSR was unnecessary in Norway since all relevant social and environmental matters were covered by law and regulations, operations abroad, especially beyond Europe, required more attention to issues such as local resistance, corruption, indigenous populations, and human rights. There was large overlap in personnel and operations between SN Power and Statkraft, and both recruited many non-Norwegians into the organization. Half of the approximately fifteen interlocutors we have had in Statkraft in Oslo were not Norwegian, and many of the Norwegians have gained extensive international experience.

Through international experience and staff, Statkraft came to engage various internationally circulating models of CSR. While CSR seems at first to have been the preferred label, corporate responsibility (CR) has since 2010 been used by management and in annual reports as a strategic term to broaden the corporation's work on responsibility, taking the attention away from the "social" of CSR to include environmental and economic responsibility toward owners (while the Norwegian term *samfunnsansvar*—societal responsibility—has been the overarching term all along).[2] All new Statkraft employees receive a week's training in Statkraft's "code of conduct" together with other core principles. Environmental and Social Management (ESM) has become an increasingly important corporate term; the internationally more widespread appellation Environmental and Social Governance (ESG) is also used. From 2004 to 2010, nonfinancial parts in annual reports were called "sustainability" reports, and the title CSR is still in use, both in documents and as vernacular.[3]

The several ways of talking about, implementing, and reporting so-called nonfinancial matters within Statkraft became apparent to us in pursuing a multisited fieldwork across different locations, documents, and websites. It is a complex picture, with standards and models coming from different places being used for different purposes. Those most frequently used in Turkey were the performance standards of the IFC and the reporting standards of the GRI—two of the most widely used standards in the private sector (Idowu et al. 2016; Shabana et al. 2017). In the following, we outline Statkraft's use of IFC performance standards (IFC-PS) and explain why this was preferred over classical CSR.

Doing CSR with IFC Performance Standards

When we first visited the project site in Turkey in 2013, the CSR coordinator in Turkey gave a presentation about their work, including the slide portrayed in figure 10.1. We came to learn that the language and approach presented in the slide was taken directly from the IFC-PS. IFC, one of five organizations within the World Bank Group, works to stimulate development in developing countries through credits, especially for private sector investments in large-scale infrastructure projects. Institutions receiving credit from the IFC are required to comply with IFC-PS and to report to and be audited by the IFC. "The Performance Standards ... are designed to help avoid, mitigate, and manage risks and impacts as a way of doing business in a sustainable way, including stakeholder engagement" (IFC 2012: i).

Statkraft's use of IFC-PS is voluntary. From at least 2009 the development of international projects in Statkraft's portfolio has been informed by IFC-PS and is included in the policy document *The Statkraft Way*.[4] Statkraft employs IFC-PS even though they are neither bound by loans to the IFC nor required to by their owner. This praxis seems related to the fact that hydropower, more so than extraction of hydrocarbons, has been made subject to international standards. Scandals and resistance related to construction of large dams resulted in the establishment of the World Commission on Dams in 1998 as well as the World Bank's establishment of standards for projects using IFC credit.

Statkraft's first activity beyond Europe had the character of development projects, especially its operations through SN Power with funding from Norfund. Statkraft's project in Nepal in the 1990s and SN Power projects in the 2000s (Skjold 2015: 212) received IFC funding, and they were thus obliged to follow IFC-PS and reporting guidelines. Although Statkraft no longer frames their projects abroad as also being development projects—considering them now

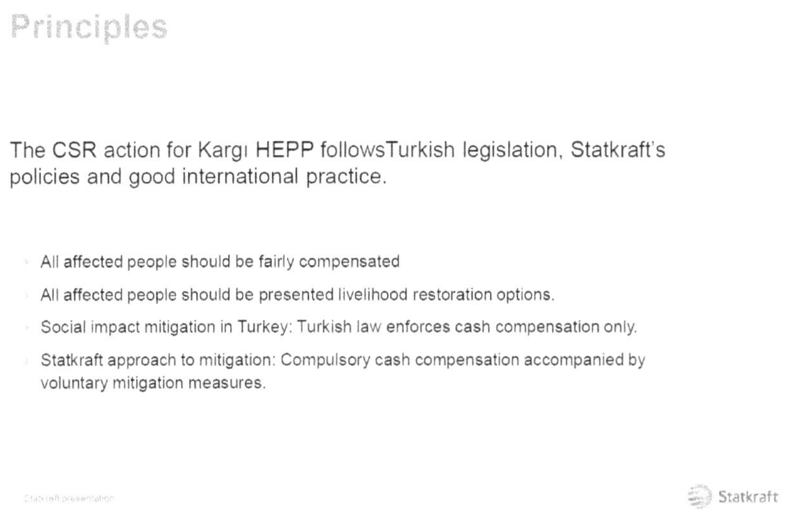

> **Principles**
>
> The CSR action for Kargı HEPP follows Turkish legislation, Statkraft's policies and good international practice.
>
> - All affected people should be fairly compensated
> - All affected people should be presented livelihood restoration options.
> - Social impact mitigation in Turkey: Turkish law enforces cash compensation only.
> - Statkraft approach to mitigation: Compulsory cash compensation accompanied by voluntary mitigation measures.
>
> Statkraft

Figure 10.1. Localizing IFC standards in Turkey. © Statkraft

to be business opportunities only—they continue to adhere to international IFC standards. The standards have been "lifted" from the development discourse into Norwegian state-speak about corporate responsibility. Government policy documents concerning CSR expect corporations to adhere to international standards. However, Statkraft considered UN Global Compact and OECD guidelines to be too vague to guide on-the-ground implementation of CSR and preferred to follow the international trend by adopting IFC-PS, the most widely recognized and used performance framework.[5] Statkraft management also considered that it was preferable to have consistent high-standards policies throughout the organization in place of following different local standards. Choosing to use IFC-PS, they replaced traditional CSR with a holistic and long-term perspective and plan for corporate responsibility while also branding Statkraft as being a serious and responsible player in the international energy landscape. Yet, it also meant something in practice: Through experience, Statkraft found IFC-PS to be a useful tool when they encountered new challenges, such as relating to indigenous populations in a project in Chile (Fribert 2018).

As a voluntary user, Statkraft is in a position to negotiate how to employ IFC-PS. Although not following full IFC protocol, Statkraft staff are trained in IFC-PS methodology and use its language for internal communication. This is, however, embedded within a broader policy for Environmental and Social Management (ESM) in Statkraft. Further, stakeholder management is seen to be of critical importance for ESM and, as will be discussed further below, has a wider framing than that provided by IFC-PS. Statkraft's experience with a large resettlement program in their Theun-Hinboun project in Laos, where "participatory planning" had helped secure "stakeholder acceptance" (Sparkes 2014: 65), has been formative in their approach to "stakeholder management."

The shift to IFC-PS in Statkraft was a conscious choice and reflects a position in Statkraft about what responsibility really implies. Most of the ESM people in Statkraft dislike the concept of CSR, which they describe as signifying "corporate excuse, twisted branding," and philanthropy verging on corruption. Although realizing that CSR can be a useful term to build reputation, they would typically assert that PR and the socioeconomic should ideally be "unmixed." "In the field CSR proves to be utterly useless," they contended. In place of CSR, they stressed the value of IFC-PS and its emphasis on project-affected people, mitigation, and livelihood restoration.

This is congruent with a broader shift in corporate circles (Edgecliffe-Johnson 2019) toward ESG and is mirrored by one of the leaders of the IFC, who in conversation with us stressed that the social and environmental policies of corporations should be "rights-based" and not manifest as charity (which he thought characterized CSR). This take on CSR stresses, rather, that it should be integrated in the way corporations do business; those working with ESM in Statkraft have argued internally for having CSR included in the risk-management process, motivated in part by a need to legitimize spending money on CSR. The following section explores what ensues when the IFC standards meet local realities in a concrete project.

"Statkraft Takes Responsibility in Turkey"

Statkraft bought a portfolio of three projects in Turkey in 2009, entering a power and electricity market that had been going through a radical liberalization and deregulation process since the early 2000s (see, e.g., Harris and Işlar 2014). In the face of Turkey's heavy dependence on imported oil and gas, a primary strategy of Erdoğan's governments has been to stimulate growth through the development of hydropower and other domestic energy resources. While the Turkish state remains the main driver for construction of hydropower, lack of domestic capital and competence has led to the invitation of foreign corporate investment in the energy sector. Statkraft is only one of many European corporations that started exploring this opportunity during the 2000s.

Statkraft's construction on the run-of-the-river medium-sized power plant Kargı (located between Ankara and the Black Sea coast) started in 2011, and the power plant was put into operation in May 2015. The smaller power plant Çakıt in Adana Province did not require construction work and began commercial operation in June 2010, while the construction of the third project in Çetin located in the southeastern part of the Anatolian region began in 2012 and was expected to be Statkraft's largest hydro asset outside of Norway. Statkraft reckoned that they had invested in a safe market within a growing economy and expected that they would expand further in Turkey.

Terror incidents, falling prices for electricity, the Syrian refugee crisis, and political uncertainty made Statkraft apply the brakes, and when the project in Çetin became imbricated in complex state-political-development processes and accumulated a composite of problems (technical, security, contractual, political), they halted construction and eventually sold the project in 2017 to a Turkish corporation, which has worked as Statkraft's contractor in their project in Albania. Although starting with ten to twenty employees, the local Statkraft staff working on CSR has, with the sell-off of Çetin and the shift to operation in Kargı, been reduced to only one person. We arrived when Statkraft was becoming uncertain about their strategy in Turkey, and, because we could not gain access to the field in Çetin, focused instead on Statkraft's Kargı project.

Overall, IFC-PS has been the main framework for Statkraft's CSR work in Turkey. At an overarching, national level, they have also supported World Wildlife Fund and Syrian refugees; at the local level they have organized training and public awareness concerning traffic and reservoir security and proved community support. The project in Çetin involved other initiatives as well. Adhering to the IFC requirement that "when host country regulations differ from" IFC-PS, "projects are expected to achieve whichever is more stringent" (IFC 2012),[6] Statkraft prepared social impact assessments (SIA) for their projects in Turkey (not required by Turkish regulation) (IFC 2015: 57). The Çetin SIA, prepared by international experts, was thoroughly informed by IFC-PS, elaborating, over a couple of pages, the details of stakeholder engagement and assessment using IFC-PS (Meadows and Helps 2010: 21–23). The emphasis on IFC-PS is also seen in documents prepared for the Kargı project. The "Environmental and Social Management Plan for Operation (2016–2020)" was "produced in line with *The Statkraft Way*" and the IFC-PS. Accordingly, the CSR work focuses, as we saw in figure 10.1, on project-affected people, impact mitigation, livelihood restoration, and compensation. Yet, the concept CSR is also used in the report, and the CSR-budget/reporting format includes several non-IFC topics, including "public relations." So, how is IFC-PS set to work in Kargı?

The main agricultural activity in the impacted districts Osmancık and Kargı is the cultivation of rice on irrigated banks along the river Kızılırmak. The Kargı hydropower project includes a relatively small reservoir in the district of Osmancık, from where a tunnel, shortcutting Kargı, transfers water from an outlet near the dam to a point farther downstream where the powerhouse is located. The areas inundated by the dam are not very extensive,[7] and had mostly been used for intensive high-value rice cultivation. Downstream, and mainly in the district of Kargı, the major impact is related to reduced flow.

During construction, the primary concern for Statkraft's CSR work was to compensate, according to Turkish law, for the loss of rice-farming land. However, compensation alone—based on state expropriation of land, a demanding and extensive process—was not sufficient to comply with the IFC-PS or *The Statkraft Way* guide for Environmental Management, which states: "Statkraft shall ensure that grievances from affected communities and external communications from other stakeholders are responded to and managed appropriately." Therefore, Statkraft established a grievance mechanism, operated out of a liaison office in Osmancık, whereby they assisted the farmers with the expropriation process. Statkraft also worked to help farmers find new sources of income through livelihood restoration projects. Farmers were provided equipment and training in horticulture, greenhouse farming, honey production, and other agricultural activities that require less water. After hydropower production started, the focus of CSR shifted to include the downstream issue, which was framed by a legal requirement to provide enough water for rice farmers.

When we met with Metin, one of Statkraft's CSR officers, in 2016, we were invited to join a meeting intended to stimulate livelihood restoration through beekeeping. Approximately twenty-five middle-aged and elderly farmers who had lost their rice farms to the dam attended. The beekeeping consultant engaged by Statkraft for the project talked about knowledge sharing and cooperation and explained that beekeeping "is quite difficult, but possible if you are willing to learn": "At first we will hold your hand, guide you through it; then we let go of your hand, help you when you need it; until, after a two-year period, our help is unnecessary." The farmers seemed to be interested and were keen to ask questions. The project was obviously considered promising, and Metin posted a "snapshot" (a photo with a short text posted on the internal web for those in Statkraft working in/with Turkey).

However, beekeeping was not a success. After only a year the project was discontinued. A few farmers continued the greenhouse project, but, otherwise, farmers, or PAPs according to IFC and Statkraft lingo, were not very keen on taking up the "livelihood restoration" opportunities presented to them by Statkraft. They preferred cash payments, which they could invest in property and/or their children's' education. Their attitude was related to the general economic and demographic structure: The agricultural sector in Turkey is increasingly marginalized, and the rural population is decreasing and aging. Most farmers in Osmancık and Kargı are over fifty years old, and, generally, their children have moved to larger cities in the west, particularly Istanbul. Although the beekeeping project was unsuccessful, Statkraft showed the ability to pragmatically extend CSR in various directions.

Pragmatic Extension of CSR

A Local Initiative: Recycling

When we returned to Osmancık in 2017 Metin was keener to talk about a new initiative than the failed beekeeping project. He wanted to show us the year's most successful environmental and social project: recycling projects at local schools. Statkraft had, on Metin's suggestion, initiated the projects in response to the problem with waste at the dam. In cooperation with local authorities, Statkraft trained two schools how to recycle. Pupils learned to gather plastic, paper, and metal and toss it all into a bin in the schoolyard. A recycling company gathered the waste once a week, sorted and weighed it, and reported back to Statkraft. For each ton collected, the school got a used Statkraft laptop computer.

Figure 10.2. "Good Neighbors." From article "Recycling Knowledge," p. 37 in Statkraft's magazine *People and Power*, issue 2, 2017. © Bahadir Sezegen

We went with Metin to the schools to deliver laptops. The primary school had managed to collect eight tons of waste, while the secondary school had collected two tons. Both schools wanted to continue the project after it was scheduled to be discontinued one month later, but Metin informed them that "there are unfortunately no more laptops to deliver." The principal argued that they did not care about the laptops only the project, because it had positive ripple effects in the local community, creating awareness about recycling and climate. After tea and small talk with the principal about the value of the recycling project for the children and the local community, Metin called the main office in Oslo, which confirmed that the schools could keep the bins. When we left the schools, Metin was happy: "This is a very successful project. The schools are taking responsibility—making the project their own."

The recycling project is more in line with the typical way for Turkish corporations to contribute to society. Some locals voiced opinions, such as: a "large foreign company like Statkraft" should invest more in "social projects" or "social funds" (newspaper article[8]); "I have not seen any social support from Statkraft" (conversation with local farmer). The concept "social support/projects/funds" here indicates a different approach to corporate responsibility than that practiced by Statkraft. Philanthropy remains the dominant form of CSR in Turkey, and "most family-owned conglomerates in Turkey have an associated foundation" (Ararat and Göcenoğlu 2005: 11) typically supporting "society," especially education, religion, and health. In Turkey, moral standards for the appropriate or expected behavior of business owners and leaders are strongly connected to ideals and practices of patron-client relations.[9]

A good example of how this Turkish framework for charitable giving informs the way in which large Turkish energy firms perform their responsibility to society can be found in the CSR prize of an annual Istanbul energy conference; in 2018 the prize was awarded to an energy utilities company that had successfully provided clothing and food for pupils at village schools and supported sports and Ramadan meals.[10] In the Turkish context, this is not usually "rights based" but considered a human duty, a moral obligation embedded in interpersonal relations. While Statkraft tries to embed ethics in systems and international standards, in Turkey, people tend to prefer to see ethics as embedded in persons and interpersonal relations. To the extent that "impact management" is considered anyone's responsibility, it would be in the government's implementation of state regulations. It is also notable that the Nordic model for a corporation's interaction with its environs is not activated. For instance, relating to or involving unions was totally outside of the scope of Statkraft's approach in Turkey.

In addition to the livelihood restoration projects, Statkraft also undertook what is regarded as classical CSR work, or locally as "social projects." Although the CSR personnel were ambivalent about it, they established community development funds (included in their CSR budget), which were used for a variety of purposes, such as funding for Ramadan meals. They realized that some such activity was needed to build and sustain good relations. Supporting schools—as Statkraft did in the recycling project—is also the kind of thing corporations are expected to do in Turkey. Unlike the livelihood projects, this initiative received a decent degree of local press coverage. Thus, the Turkish understanding of corporate responsibilities increasingly came to inform the CSR work of Statkraft. CSR became "localized" (Welker 2014) or "domesticated" (Knudsen 2015) as the recycling project emerged as a local success.

The cases discussed above relate primarily to the area directly impacted by the dam where it inundated rice fields near Osmancık. Another way in which Statkraft has pragmatically extended and adapted CSR work to fit new situations and agendas emerges as we turn attention to the downstream issue.

Rice Cultivation in Kargı

Early autumn is a busy period for rice cultivators in Kargı. Most open spaces are covered by rice spread out for drying. In 2016, we dropped in to visit our acquaintance İsmail at his camp and threshing ground. Learning that he was away on an errand, we were treated to a simple meal, including rice—from their own production—which they eat every day, year-round. İsmail's wife, an elderly woman, complained about her bad back and pain in her legs. Still, she was compelled to work; they needed money to marry their grandchild.

İsmail arrived on his motorbike. He was tired and morose. Long days and hard work for an old man. His fifty-year-old son was more talkative. The son operates the harvester they bought a few years back and is paid three *hak* ("rights," one *hak* equaling two six-kilogram bins of rice) for each acre (*dönüm*) that he harvests for others. Like many other families, their extended family works together to cultivate both their own fields as well as the sharecropped (*yarıcılık*) fields of more wealthy farmers. As is common in Kargı, their plots are small and widely dispersed, making the operation of the harvester cumbersome and costly. The rice cultivators desire a reorganization and consolidation (*toplulaştırma*) of their fields, but that is difficult to achieve without political will.

For many, rice cultivation has developed into a side income. Most rice cultivators are middle-aged or older. Young people are leaving Kargı, and the population of the small-town risks falling below five thousand, which is the threshold for being a municipality in Turkey. Although concerned about the dam constructed by Statkraft, rice cultivators find that they have enough water. Many farmers related that, when water stopped flowing a few years back, they called Statkraft, and the water flow resumed. They are more concerned about the costs of pumping water from the Kızılırmak up into the canals and their fields. There are also other costs involved: seeds, fertilizer and pesticides, guards, and more. Many complain that "the state does not support us any longer. We are not given a guaranteed price for the rice."

Interacting with a broad cross section of the society of Kargı, we tried to elicit the history and structure of the irrigation system in the district. Nobody seemed to really know. There are many institutions involved: General Directorate of State Hydraulic Works (DSI); the Kargı municipality; village heads; rice-farming cooperatives; the district office of the Ministry of Agriculture, Forestry, and

Livestock; the Agricultural Credit Cooperative; the Kargı Chamber of Agriculture, among others. Ownership of and responsibility for maintaining the irrigation structure is unclear. Does the DSI or the cooperatives own the channels? There is no overview of where water comes from and where it goes. There is no overall plan for irrigation and cultivation except for some limited measures administered by the state-organized District Rice Commission.

Surveying Irrigation, Enlisting Stakeholders

Statkraft is under contract with the DSI to release enough water for the seven hundred downstream farmers, mostly smallholders, to continue irrigation of their rice paddies during the May to October cultivation season. The contract stipulates the amount of water to be released as well as the periodicity. To help ensure that farmers receive enough water for irrigation, Statkraft organized and funded refurbishment of water-intake weirs. Beyond this, the CSR consultant's regular monitoring of water flow and agricultural activities convinced corporate leadership that it could be useful to make a detailed survey of the irrigation system and water use in Kargı. An international consultancy was contracted. The work basically involved walking up all channels, weirs, and the like and mapping them into a Google Earth template program to produce a detailed digital map of the irrigation system.

According to Statkraft personnel, "stakeholder mapping" was undertaken, and stakeholders were consulted in the process. The instrumental and managerial approach to "stakeholders" is demonstrated in this excerpt from an internal Statkraft presentation: "Engaging with stakeholders from the start (before operation) enables a proactive cultivation of relationships that can serve as 'capital' during challenging times." During our fieldwork in Kargı, it emerged that almost no one (except two leading local officers) knew about the irrigation survey, and even familiarity with Statkraft was limited. İsmail was relatively well-informed about Statkraft, but he and his fellow villagers knew nothing of the survey when we met him in late 2018, after the survey had been completed, which was striking given that he is a village head and village heads are identified by Statkraft as being among their primary stakeholders. A few meetings had been organized before the survey took place, but they did not focus on the survey. Only after a draft digital map had been produced did the CSR officer and an expert from the consultancy firm perform what they called "ground truthing," that is, checking their findings with local farmers, thus clearly serving Statkraft's rather than stakeholders' interests.

Statkraft's primary objective in doing the survey was, we were told, to "know the system better." The detailed knowledge gained about the irrigation system enabled them to start renegotiating the contract with the DSI with a view to becoming obliged to release less water during the irrigation season, in effect meaning that more water is retained for Statkraft to produce electricity and income. Although the project was not funded through the CSR budget but from "assets," it was managed by CSR personnel. It is a "win-win situation," a CSR officer told us. He thought it was natural that they, who were involved with stakeholders and community relations, handled this: "It is oftentimes the case that we have overlapping interests with other sections in the corporation." That Statkraft considers the survey of the irrigation system to be CSR activity demonstrates the flexible pragmatism of the corporation when it comes to implementing standards as well as the perceived importance of community and stakeholder relations for making things work locally (cf. Welker 2014).

Reporting CSR

Like performance, reporting CSR also involves a pragmatic approach. Although external reporting is not met with any significant sanctions, Statkraft is obliged to conform to the language of GRI for reporting purposes. Managed primarily by a small section at HQ, the GRI standards do not travel very far or deep into the Statkraft organization and are distinctly different from the IFC-PS language. Working for external reporting in Statkraft, therefore, involves considerable internal translation work to produce not only indicators but also stories in which "stakeholders" figure prominently.

Stories are, however, not only reputation-management material. They may also become important ingredients in Statkraft's reporting processes. Reporting in keeping with the law on accounting requires, according to the Office of the Auditor General of Norway, an annual report, a sustainability/CSR report, and quarterly results, but it can include information from the corporation's webpages (OAGN 2016-17: 151). According to personnel in the Statkraft CR division, stories in their magazines are considered to be "realistic" field reports and are used as the backdrop for annual reports and further CR strategy development.

The consideration of field reports as "realistic" depictions of CSR in practice makes internal reporting key to CSR officers. When Statkraft decided to keep only one of the two local CSR officers, they retained the one who was best at reporting. One of his superiors stressed that "quality in reporting is essential." Reporting, he maintained, is a skill that takes time to acquire, and Statkraft observes a strict reporting cycle. For instance, the plan for Environmental and Social Management in the Kargı project (2016–20) prescribed quarterly reporting on content and spending for a range of matters. Once a year the CSR officer is also asked to submit a standardized risk-assessment form. This reporting is not guided by GRI standards but works within an ESM framework.

Although internal reporting follows certain templates/formats, there is room for individual initiatives, such as the recycling project. As Metin left the meeting with the principal with whom he had discussed the future of the recycling project, he remarked, "I must report to Lysaker [Statkraft's HQ in Norway]." His next step was to gather photos and documents from the schools and prepare a presentation for the next CSR performance meeting in Lysaker. The recycling project, like the beekeeping project, was circulated internally as a "snapshot," but it was subsequently picked up for publication in the online *Statkraft Stories Collection* and the Statkraft magazine *People and Power*.[11]

The Kargı irrigation survey also traveled up through the organization to be included in Statkraft's Annual Report 2017, where a photo that had started out as an internal "snapshot" about ground truthing was displayed among "Highlights" with the caption: "Continuous dialogue with stakeholders was upheld, like in Turkey where downstream impacts were discussed with local farmers" (Statkraft 2017a: 3). The Kargı irrigation survey is presented as "a mitigation programme to improve irrigation systems downstream of the intake dam" (Statkraft 2017a: 30). The major motivation for the survey—the potential for making more profit—was underplayed, while the alignment with IFC-PS framework ("mitigation") and degree of interaction with stakeholders was exaggerated.

While "stories" travel up through the Statkraft organization and figure in external reporting, the formal framework for Statkraft's external reporting is GRI in accordance with the expectations of the Norwegian state (Meld. St. 27 [2013–14]: 83). GRI was established in 1997 as an independent international organization and has become the dominant framework for sustainability reporting. In order to simplify and ensure relevance of reporting, GRI established the "materiality" (i.e., essential) principle that implies that organizations are expected to address and report on matters that are central to its impact on society and environment. The latest version of GRI standards, G4, "guides companies in how to identify their major sustainability impacts, and then enter into a dialogue with key stakeholders—which they define themselves—to answer the question: 'What are the material aspects, and to whom?'" (GRI and Robecosam 2016: 8). Thus, it is left to each individual organization/company to design how it will organize stakeholder processes and identify material aspects. Process, not indicators, are imposed by GRI on Statkraft.

Statkraft started following the GRI recommendations several years before the state made it a requirement. In 2015, they undertook the materiality analysis, primarily by arranging workshops with key persons within Statkraft and with only limited input from stakeholders. Involved staff were asked by colleagues from the CR unit to "assess the materiality of all the corporate responsibility aspects … based on how important it is for Statkraft's ability to meet corporate strategies and goals and retain our 'license to operate.'" After categories and content were negotiated internally, the materiality assessment identified six aspects that were most "material," related to environmental issues, safety, human rights, and anticorruption.[12] The materiality analysis is meant to give structure to further CSR work: "Statkraft has developed ambitions and goals towards 2020 for the six material topics, and Statkraft's corporate responsibility report is structured according to the identified material topics" (Statkraft 2017b: 32).

Reporting to GRI does not really involve any content and review thereof by GRI—it essentially means submitting a GRI-structured report for publication on GRI's website. The 2017 CR report includes four pages that essentially list what has been reported by and to whom (e.g., the Statkraft board), organized by the categories and standards used by GRI.[13] The reporting recommendations by the state are not supported by any sanctions and leave Statkraft to decide how to involve stakeholders in materiality assessment and reporting. In their daily internal work, those responsible for reporting in Statkraft do not consult stakeholders directly but, rather, organize in-house studies of stakeholder perspectives and interact with Statkraft staff who can provide useful "stories" or other relevant information for their reports. They consider this robust enough since stakeholder engagement is integral to all phases of Statkraft's projects. Thus, Statkraft is very much at liberty to design the process and content of reports. Given the limited content and sanction relating to the use of the GRI standards, "stakeholder" perspective and "stakeholder" involvement stands out as a central legitimizing figure for Statkraft's approach to CSR.

Managing Stakeholders

What emerges from the discussion of the application of different standards above is the ubiquity of the figure of "stakeholder." It is one of the few concepts that has purchase across the different standards and models that Statkraft employs or relates to when enacting responsibility. However, that does not necessarily imply that its meaning is the same within different contexts. "Stakeholder" is a particularly open and negotiable concept with no clear denotational value—it is detached from larger structures of power, politics, and economy, which Giles Mohan and Kristian Stokke (2000) call "the dangers of localism." "The weakness of stakeholder theory lies in the underspecification of the organization/stakeholder relation in itself" (Friedman and Miles 2002: 15). It is precisely this underspecification that makes the frequent deployment of the term "stakeholder" across a variety of contexts and for different purposes possible and useful for Statkraft and gives a semblance of their CSR work being cohesive and unitary. But there is a huge difference between a property-less (e.g., not being entitled to membership in a cooperative) peasant in Kargı and the DSI ("our most important stakeholder"). Beyond this, the underspecification of the stakeholder concept also facilitates the enactment of multiple versions of the same stakeholder at different places in the corporation: the irrigation project stakeholders engaged by the CSR officer in Kargı are very different from the irrigation project stakeholders who figure into the 2017 annual report.

Although it is commonplace today to use the term "stakeholder" in a wide range of contexts, including environmental management and development projects, the concept had its roots in business and management science in the early 1980s (Jones and Wicks 1999; Grimble and Wellard 1997). But the management literature and its adoption by businesses has largely been insensitive to framing issues. Who defines the issue? What definition of stakeholder is to be employed? Which actors are affected by or have an interest in the topic? What is the "mandate" for stakeholder involvement? Every decision about who is entitled to be considered a stakeholder is, in the end, political. Company control of reporting processes means that the corporate perspective will dominate, and stakeholder dialogue can be transformed into the ultimate legitimating tool, since stakeholders carry legitimating authority in "participatory" processes (Cooke and Kothari 2001). Questioning the content of a report becomes more difficult if an organization can say that it has consulted stakeholders when preparing it.

The contrast between the minimal involvement of "stakeholders," lack of local consultation, and the profiling of—precisely—the "stakeholders" shows that, sometimes, the real concern about "stakeholders" is at the corporate level—in reports and reputational management. The local stakeholder is an important legitimizing figure in CR reporting and in corporate communication. The CSR consultants have an important position in this, doing in effect not only work directed at the community but also upward within the corporation.

While Statkraft's use of "stakeholder" may seem political, it does not have the "deep" effect "neoliberalism as governance" approaches sometimes assume. Few readers of Statkraft's CR report actually understand the indicators used, and hardly any of Statkraft's "stakeholders" realize that they are "stakeholders" and sometimes even "PAPs." They are not covertly guided toward self-governance (cf. Merry 2011) through internalizing Statkraft's use of standards and indicators. Statkraft does not organize the world of stakeholders through indicators—the indicators hardly organize things internal to Statkraft. That the indicators are produced is more important than what they reveal, since their existence is sufficient to fulfill reporting requirements. Therefore, the stories told in the report or in the Statkraft magazine are just as important as the indicators for conveying Statkraft's responsible approach.

Conclusion

CSR is many things in Statkraft. A multisited approach has enabled us to see that responsibility is engaged by different people with different agendas in a range of different places across the complex, geographically distributed corporation. CSR is transformed and transmuted and set to do different kinds of work. It is sometimes compartmentalized—in organizational structure, reports, and the like—sometimes merged or cross-fertilized with other activities. At other times CSR is seen as embedded within core activities (e.g., within risk management) or considered the responsibility of management and the board. There are several distinct, yet overlapping, communities of standardization practice (Star and Lampland 2009:

7) within Statkraft, and the transition from "doing" CSR (in line with IFC-PS) to "writing" CSR (according to GRI standards) is therefore blurry and involves translation work.

In Statkraft there are many different reasons for a move toward standardizing CSR work, but there are likewise many causes for the partial implementation of standards, be it flexible adaptation to local expectations (recycling), in-house pragmatic mixing of CSR and other agendas (such as in the irrigation project), or a consideration of what resources are "reasonable" to spend on aligning with international standards that are frequently upgraded. Heterogeneity of the CSR field is probably also reproduced by people wanting to hold on to their jobs and who are defending and expanding their turf. All the translation work going on within the corporation, between different standards and for reporting—much of it for internal purposes only— is very costly in terms of effort; not all find it meaningful. Reporting is demanding for Statkraft, not because it puts limitations on the way in which staff manage their projects but because of the translation work and internal mobilization necessary to produce stories, categories, and numbers that satisfy the externally defined standards and perceived needs for corporate communication.

CSR work is not as standardized as it may appear from the outside and as many analysts seem to assume (Merry 2011).[14] It is perhaps precisely the ability within Statkraft to keep CSR in "suspense"—or rather keep in suspense the ambivalences and dissonances concerning standardized CSR—that makes it useful and powerful. Standardization is thus partly a "make believe" standardization, and work related to CSR standards is characterized by flexible pragmatism. It is precisely because people in corporations are pragmatic and flexible that standards seem to be working, just as James Scott (1998) argued was the case for high modernist states' standardizing schemes, and Susan Star and Martha Lampland (2009: 4) have argued is generally the case in people's dealings with standards: "work must get done." Corporations may be less rigid than high-modernist state bureaucracies. Pragmatic flexibility is actually encouraged by persons in relevant senior or CSR positions in Statkraft who, taking a reflexive stance, do not find it problematic that there are many ways of doing and talking about CSR within the organization: "Those working in the field must themselves find the concepts that are most natural for them to apply"; "CSR will always be framed by local politics and culture"; "Our use of 'CSR' is pragmatic—we are looking to get things done." The pragmatic approach is even articulated in the CR report: "Statkraft has a decentralized approach to stakeholder management" (Statkraft 2017b: 9). That the border between CSR and other activities becomes blurred is even considered appropriate—that means that CSR has become integrated with other concerns and agendas in the corporation. Especially when it comes to reporting, it may be more important for the corporation to "be seen making the world legible" (i.e., transparent) rather than actually doing so.

Although Statkraft employees may stress that they act as "ambassadors" of Norway in their foreign operations, and the ministry stresses that it expects Statkraft to be responsible when operating in Turkey, there is not much trace of the Nordic model in the way in which Statkraft works in Turkey. The way they enact responsibility is informed by international standards, particularly those of the IFC and the GRI. Thus, the concept of "stakeholder," for example, has come into Statkraft's vocabulary through interaction with international standards and experience from managing international projects. Statkraft has never used the concept in its domestic activities. The "other" of Statkraft in a domestic context has not been standardized as "stakeholder." As a state agency in Norway, the work of Statkraft had been embedded in regular political and bureaucratic procedures and a complex sociopolitical landscape consisting of citizens and households, users, municipalities, other state agencies, unions, and various other organizations. There its activities were "already" political and not easily framed as Statkraft vs. stakeholders. But, operating away from home, Statkraft has needed both CSR and stakeholders—little of which has been explicitly informed by the Nordic model. However, the Norwegian state has not requested Statkraft to be "Nordic" when working abroad. They are tasked primarily with doing business. If one can argue that reference to universal norms for responsibility may be typical in the Nordic societal model, then one may perhaps also say that it is "Nordic" to expect corporations to be particularly responsible by requiring them to adhere to international standards and frameworks.

Acknowledgments

Research on which this chapter rests has been conducted within the frames of the project Energethics (2015–19), funded by a FRIPRO grant from the Research Council of Norway (grant no. 240617). We are grateful for the willingness of Statkraft representatives to interact with us and for giving us access to the project site. We also wish to thank the local population as well as officials in Kargı for their openness and willingness to teach us the sociomaterial dynamics of rice cultivation. Dinah Rajak and Simon Abram gave helpful comments to earlier drafts of this chapter. One of our main interlocutors at Statkraft read and commented on the final version of the text. This resulted in changes of some technical facts but did not alter any of the main findings or analysis. Some disagreement remains concerning interpretetions.

Ståle Knudsen is professor in the Department of Social Anthropology, University of Bergen, Norway. He was leader of the project Energethics (2015–19), from which this book emerges. Knudsen has, since the early 1990s, done ethnographic fieldwork in Turkey, focusing on topics such as fisheries, resource management, knowledge, technology, seafood and consumption, introduced species, environmental movements, and—more recently—energy and corporate social responsibility. A common thread running through all of his work is the vexing issue of identities. His publications include the monograph *Fisheries in Modernizing Turkey* (Berghahn, 2009).

Ingrid Birce Müftüoglu holds a PhD in ethnology and has done research within various fields, including the women's movement in Norway, nationalism in Turkey, and corporate social responsibility of Norwegian energy companies abroad. She is now working as a senior research and policy adviser.

Isabelle Hugøy was a research assistant for the Energethics project, and since 2020 she has been a doctoral fellow in the Department of Social Anthropology, University of Bergen, Norway. Her doctoral project deals with human-soil relations and explores how soil is actualized across different knowledge registers in the context of efforts to decarbonize agricultural sectors in Norway and Costa Rica.

Notes

An earlier version of this chapter was published as: Knudsen, Ståle, Ingrid B. Müftüoğlu, and Isabelle Hugøy. 2020. "Standardizing Responsibility through the Stakeholder Figure: Norwegian Hydropower in Turkey." In Theme Section, "Corporate Social Responsibility and the Paradoxes of State Capitalism," edited by Ståle Knudsen and Dinah Rajak. *Focaal: Journal of Global and Historical Anthropology* 88: 58–75.

1. Fossekallen 1979, no. 10: 5. http://publikasjoner.nve.no/fossekallen/1979/fossekallen1979_10.pdf.
2. https://www.statkraft.com/annualreport2014/Corporate_Responsibility/CR-in-Statkraft/, accessed 9 March 2019.

3. In this text we will for consistency continue to use CSR as an overarching analytical term, even when Statkraft employees would have preferred another term.
4. https://www.statkraft.com/globalassets/x-annual-report-2013/04-samfunnsansvar/02-styring-av-samfunnsansvar/01-the-statkraft-way/cr-hse-policy-for-report_tcm245-26148.pdf, accessed 22 January 2019.
5. https://www.statkraft.com/media/news/News-archive/2011/corporate-responsibility-and-new-projects/, accessed 19 January 2019.
6. https://www.ifc.org/wps/wcm/connect/115482804a0255db96fbffd1a5d13d27/PS_English_2012_Full-Document.pdf?MOD=AJPERES, accessed 25 February 2019.
7. According to Statkraft internal documents, loss of 4,271 decare of land, of which more than 3,000 decare are first-class agricultural land.
8. "Kargı HES'e Sosyal Proje Tepkisi," *Osmancık Haber*, 4 January 2013, retrieved 25 October 2013 from http://www.osmancikhaber.com.tr/haber-2082-Kargi-HESe-Sosyal-Proje-Tepkisi.html.
9. For an elaboration and discussion about CSR in Turkey, see Knudsen 2015.
10. http://beyazgazete.com/haber/2018/5/15/vedas-a-sosyal-sorumluluk-odulu-4487978.html, accessed 23 January 2018.
11. https://www.statkraft.com/globalassets/1-statkraft-public/media/pp_2_2017_engelsk.pdf.
12. https://www.statkraft.com/annualreport2015/Corporate_Responsibility/Managing-corporate-responsibility/Competence-and-training/, accessed 25 March 2019.
13. https://www.globalreporting.org/standards/.
14. See Welker 2014 and Sydow 2016 for more nuanced studies of CSR and standards.

References

Ararat, Melsa, and Ceyhun Göcenoğlu. 2005. "Drivers for Sustainable Corporate Responsibility, Case of Turkey." CSR WeltWeit.
Cooke, Bill, and Uma Kothari, eds. 2001. *Participation: The New Tyrant?* London: Zed Books.
Edgecliffe-Johnson, Andrew. 2019. "Beyond the Bottom Line." *Financial Times*, 4 January 2019.
Foucault, Michael. 2008. *The Birth of Biopolitics: Lectures at the Collège de France 1978–1979*. Translated by Graham Burchell. Basingstoke: Palgrave.
Fribert, Richard. 2018. "Differences Between and Differences Within—Community Engagement against a Background of Mistrust." MA thesis, Copenhagen Business School.
Friedman, Andrew, and Samantha Miles. 2002. "Developing Stakeholder Theory." *Journal of Management Studies* 39(1): 1–21. https://doi.org/10.1111/1467-6486.00280.
Garsten, Christina, and Kerstin Jacobsson. 2011. "Post-political Regulation: Soft Power and Post-political Visions in Global Governance." *Critical Sociology* 39(3): 421–37. https://doi.org/10.1177/0896920511413942.
GRI and Robecosam. 2016. *Defining What Matters: Do Companies and Investors Agree on What Is Material?* Retrieved 2 March 2019 from https://www.globalreporting.org/resourceli brary/GRI-DefiningMateriality2016.pdf
Grimble, Robin, and Kate Wellard. 1997. "Stakeholder Methodologies in Natural Resource Management: A Review of Principles, Contexts, Experiences and Opportunities." *Agricultural Systems* 55(2): 173–93. https://doi.org/10.1016/S0308-521X(97)00006-1.
Harris, Leila M., and Mine Işlar. 2014. "Neoliberalism, Nature, and Changing Modalities of Environmental Governance in Contemporary Turkey." In *Global Economic Crisis and the Politics of Diversity*, edited by Yıldız Atasoy, 52–78. London: Palgrave Macmillan.

Idowu, Samuel O., Ioana-Maria Dragu, Adriana Tiron-Tudor, and Teodora V. Farcas. 2016. "From CSR and Sustainability to Integrated Reporting." *International Journal of Entrepreneurship and Innovation.* DOI: 10.1504/IJSEI.2016.076687.
IFC. 2012. *Performance Standards on Environmental and Social Sustainability.* Washington, DC: World Bank Group.
———. 2015. *Hydroelectric Power: A Guide for Developers and Investors.* Stuttgart: Fichtner Management Consulting AG.
Jones, Thomas M., and Andrew C. Wicks. 1999. "Convergent Stakeholder Theory." *Academy of Management Review* 24(2): 206–21. https://doi.org/10.5465/amr.1999.1893929.
Knudsen, Ståle. 2015. "Corporate Social Responsibility in Local Context: International Capital, Charitable Giving and the Politics of Education in Turkey." *Southeast European and Black Sea Studies* 15(3): 369–90. https://doi.org/10.1080/14683857.2015.1091181.
Meadows, Kate, and John Helps. 2010. SIA Vol 3: *Social Assessment: Public Consultation and Disclosure; Plan for Feasibility Phase/EISA of Cetin Hydro Power Project.* The NRgroup Development Professionals.
Meld. St. 22. 2001–2. *Et mindre og bedre statlig eierskap* [A smaller and improved state ownership]. White paper from Ministry of Trade and Industry, Government of Norway.
Meld. St. 13. 2006–7. *An Active and Long-Term State Ownership.* White paper from Ministry of Trade and Industry, Government of Norway.
Meld. St. 10. 2008–9. *Corporate Social Responsibility in a Global Economy.* White paper from Ministry of Foreign Affairs, Government of Norway.
Meld. St. 27. 2013–14. *Diverse and Value-Creating Ownership.* White paper from Ministry of Trade, Industry and Fisheries, Government of Norway.
Merry, Sally E. 2011. "Measuring the World: Indicators Human Rights and Global Governance." *Current Anthropology* 52(3): S83–S95. https://doi.org/10.1086/657241.
Mohan, Giles, and Kristian Stokke. 2000. "Participatory Development and Empowerment: The Dangers of Localism." *Third World Quarterly* 21(2): 247–68. https://doi.org/10.1080/01436590050004346.
Nilsen, Yngve, and Lars Thue. 2006. *Statens kraft 1965–2006* [The state's power 1965–2006]. Oslo: Universitetsforlaget.
OAGN. 2016–17. *Riksrevisjonens kontroll med forvaltningen av statlige selskaper for 2015* [The auditor general's audit of management of state corporations 2015]. Oslo: Office of the Auditor General of Norway.
Prop. 53. 2003–4. *Statens eierskap i Statkraft SF* [State ownership in Statkraft SF]. Green paper from Ministry of Trade and Industry, Government of Norway.
Rajak, Dinah. 2011. *In Good Company: An Anatomy of Corporate Social Responsibility.* Stanford, CA: Stanford University Press.
Scott, James C. 1998. *Seeing Like a State: How Certain Schemes to Improve the Human Condition Have Failed.* New Haven, CT: Yale University Press.
Shabana, Kareem. M., Ann K. Buchholtz, and Archie. B. Caroll. 2017. "The Institutionalization of Corporate Social Responsibility Reporting." *Business and Society* (56) 8: 1107–35.
Skjold, Dag O. 2009. *Statkraft and the Role of the State in Norwegian Electrification.* Translated by Anna Paterson. Oslo: Universitetsforlaget.
——— 2015. *Beyond Borders: The Internationalization of Statkraft 1990–2015.* Oslo: Universitetsforlaget.
Sparkes, Stephen. 2014. "Sustainable Hydropower Development: Theun-Hinboun Expansion Project Case Study, Laos." *Water Resources and Global Development* 4: 54–66. https://doi.org/10.1016/j.wrr.2014.09.002.
Star, Susan L., and Martha Lampland. 2009. "Reckoning with Standards." In *Standards and Their Stories: How Quantifying, Classifying, and Formalizing Practices Shape Everyday Life,* edited by Martha Lampland and Susan L. Star, 3–24. New York: Cornell University Press.

Statkraft. 2017a. *Annual Report 2017*. Retrieved 26 January 2019 from http://www.nsd.uib.no/polsys/data/filer/aarsmeldinger/AE_2017_11203.pdf.
———. 2017b. *Corporate Responsibility Report 2017*. Retrieved 26 January 2019 from https://www.statkraft.com/globalassets/1-statkraft-public/1-about-statkraft/cr/statkraft-as-corporate-responsibility-report-2017.pdf.
Sydow, Johanna. 2016. "Global Concepts in Local Contexts: CSR as 'Anti-Politics Machines' in the Extractive Sector in Ghana and Peru." In *The Anthropology of Corporate Social Responsibility*, edited by Catherine Dolan and Dinah Rajak, 217–42. Oxford: Berghahn Books.
Welker, Marina. 2014. *Enacting the Corporation: An American Mining Firm in Post-authoritarian Indonesia*. Berkeley: University of California Press.

— Chapter 11 —

THE "NORDIC MODEL" IN THE MIDDLE EAST OIL FIELDS

How Shareholder Value Eclipses Corporate Responsibility

Synnøve Bendixsen

Norwegian energy companies are known to use the "Nordic model" as part of their self-representations, as a business strategy, and as a potential competitive resource in their operations and interactions outside the Nordic countries. Yet, while Corporate Social Responsibility (CSR) in a Norwegian context might be doing exceptionally well, this is not necessarily the case with Norwegian companies abroad. In this chapter, I will discuss DNO ASA (Det Norske Oljeselskap, the Norwegian Oil Company) to cast light on how a private, Norwegian oil company responds to and negotiates CSR expectations both from the Norwegian government and from the countries in which DNO is situated. DNO is an interesting case, because outside of Norway, it operates only in regions characterized by weak states and low levels of democracy as well as in countries that have issues in the functioning of governance and high levels of inequality among its citizens. Understanding the ways in which CSR practices by a private, Norwegian oil company are understood by various actors can shed light on the role of the state in how CSR is implemented, and whether the nature of CSR initiatives is shaped by the expectations of the corporations' "host" and "home" government.

Since the early 2010s, Nordic countries have been considered global leaders in CSR and sustainability (Strand, Freeman, and Hockerts 2015), placing high on rankings such as the sustainability-adjusted Global Competitiveness Index (GCI).[1] Accordingly, Nordic actors engage explicitly with CSR issues and build on long traditions of stakeholder engagement (Midttun 2005; Strand et al. 2015), and social actors' (such as corporations, trades unions, and social organizations) take on accountability to build an inclusive society (Maon, Swaen, and Lindgreen 2017). The Nordic corporate actors are thought to lead CSR engagement in Europe and are regarded as models and sources of inspiration for CSR development (Maon et al. 2017). The reason for this success might be related to the Norwegian, and Nordic, model based on stable economic management, a regulated labor market with strong labor unions, coordinated wage formation, and a redistributive, tax-financed welfare state (see the introduction to this volume). CSR may also be a way for the Norwegian state to try, with varying success, to export the Nordic model, as in the case of Equinor in Tanzania (see chapter 8).

The Norwegian state is a major owner of companies in Norway and expresses that it is concerned about the conduct of Norwegian companies abroad.[2] This chapter asks: How are CSR and the expectations of the Norwegian government concerning ethical practices pursued by Norwegian companies operating outside the Nordic countries? Does the Nordic societal model and it's reputation of conducting responsible business shape how Norwegian private companies operate outside the European context? While this chapter views CSR partly as a neoliberal governance technique that can be used by various actors and whose setup varies partly according to the character of the state(s) involved, it also focuses on how it is understood differently by different actors. At the focus of my analytical attention are the ways that people perceived, talked about, and understood the work of oil companies and CSR.

The chapter is based on fieldwork and interviews in the Kurdish region of Iraq in addition to online sources, reports, and media. I pursued two weeks of fieldwork in Erbil, Duhok, and Tawke in 2014 as part of the Energethics project. Contact was mainly established through a social network developed over years of working in the region as a university lecturer. While many people were nervous about the theme of oil companies, they also were eager to share their experiences with an outsider. I spoke to thirteen men living in the Tawke village, three people working for DNO ASA, two people working for a different oil company in the region, two journalists, three students, and the natural resources advisor to the government (Ministry of Natural Resources, Kurdistan Regional Government, KRG, Erbil). While some of the conversations were conducted with the help of research assistant Dunya Slahdin Mirdan, who also in some cases functioned as a translator, several were done in English.

Many Kurds are well acquainted with English, having worked for several years with international NGOs or having been to Europe as a migrant or as a student. In the village of Tawke, I used a male translator. Notably, my informants were almost all men, given that those in formal positions relevant to interview happened to be men; the field of oil industry in Kurdistan Iraq, as in several other countries, is dominated by males; and, in the village, my contact person was a male head of the village, who gathered the male inhabitants for a common discussion. Lengthier fieldwork would have facilitated more communication with the women living in that village and broadened my insights of the situation but would most likely not have altered the main findings and arguments of this chapter.[3] Further, I made several attempts, through emails and calls, to meet DNO officials, but no one was willing to talk with me. Additionally, DNO management in Oslo did not respond to formal emails from the Energethics project leader. The lack of response is unfortunate. It might suggest a different approach to communication with outsiders compared to Statkraft and Equinor, who were willing to talk to the researchers in this volume.

After briefly introducing CSR from an anthropological perspective, I discuss what kind of company DNO is. Subsequently, I will present two empirical cases, the first being DNO's establishment of the oil field in the Kurdistan Region of Iraq in which I discuss the discrepancy between the government and the local community's experience of the company's CSR operations. The second case, DNO in Yemen, examines a mediated labor union conflict that led to a court case. For this case, I draw upon online documents and news media. In the discussion and conclusion, I draw attention to how DNO focuses on shareholder values, disregarding all expectations of the Norwegian state as to how Norwegian companies should operate abroad. Both the Kurdistan Region of Iraq and Yemen cases are suggestive of the company's instrumental relation to CSR and ignorance of workers' rights.

A Short Outline of the Anthropology of CSR

Anthropological studies have emphasized that the meaning, substance, and character of CSR practices will vary in different places and among different actors (Maon et al. 2017; Campbell 2007; Garriga and Melé 2004), making ethnographic studies of the phenomena essential. Adoption, management, and orientation of CSR are pursued in different ways at different temporalities of the operation (see chapter 4) and by different sectors of corporations and industries as well as in different regional and national contexts. Gond, Kang, and Moon (2011) point to the chameleonlike character of CSR: companies can shape their CSR according to new ideas and to the sociopolitical and economic context of its application. Through encounters with diverse configurations of actors and institutions, CSR is transformed and reconstituted (Welker, Partridge, and Hardin 2011; Dolan and Rajak 2016) and is highly adaptable (Dolan and Rajak 2016). This metamorphic character of CSR has contributed to the view among researchers that CSR materializes into a "global assemblage" (Collier and Ong 2005), spreading and acquiring new meanings and modes of capitalism through its contact with and enactment of private and state corporations, multinational enterprises, nongovernmental organizations, development institutions, social enterprises, and consultancies (Thrift 2005; Collier and Ong 2005: 11).

Increasingly, research has examined how corporations pursue CSR and how CSR influences local communities (Rajak 2011; Rajak 2016; Welker 2014; see also the introduction to this volume). Empirical studies have shown the lack of intentionality and consistency in CSR practices and that CSRs are frequently operationalized in response to external pressures and thus transpire reactively (Welker 2014). In this chapter, research on the ways in which the state is challenged, bypassed, or strengthened through CSR is particularly relevant. Providing a historical contextualization of CSR, Djelic and Etchanchu (2017) recall a persistently blurry and shifting frontier between economy and polity and that firms have long played a political role. The political role and its nature, extent, and impact have altered over time and changed with shifting dominant ideologies. Djelic and Etchanchu (2017) suggest that Friedman's "null hypothesis"—that the corporate executive is only responsible to the shareholders (Friedman 1970)—as a distinct separation between business and state responsibilities does not describe a natural state of things but is instead a particular perspective with anchors in neoliberal ideology. Scholars have investigated the ways in which structures of political authority are shaped by modes of energy production (Mitchell 2013) and the way in which state ideas and practices are coproduced by state officials, transnational companies, and civil society (Schubert 2020). Resource-extractive enclaves can produce fragmented political and social orders where state power and corporate strategies become intertwined (Ferguson 2005; Watts 2004). Companies' CSR practices interweave corporate risk management and community engagement in ways that trigger indirect government when statehood is limited

(Hönke 2011). Thus, extractive industries become actors in governmentality through resource extraction. The conglomeration of state power and private capital produces particular configurations of control over territories and populations (Buu-Sao 2021). While CSR can be a technique for nation-states to indirectly govern their territories (Billo 2015), companies can also interject in such governmental "discharge" (Hönke 2011), seizing CSR principles and filling in for the state by conducting social functions. The multivalent character of CSR in some cases contributes to the functioning of companies as proxy states, providing jobs, social welfare, and infrastructure and managing environmental issues (Welker 2014) concurrently as companies are instrumentalizing corporate codes and global compacts (Dolan and Rajak 2016).

In these descriptions, the state is characterized as being both present and absent, giving the impression of being thinned or "hollowed out" (Bridge 2010; Ferguson 2006). Simultaneously, neoliberal processes of production and extraction are characterized by dispersion of "power away from geographically defined nation states" (Duffy 2006: 93). In some cases, extractive companies manage to sidestep the state by drawing on local enclaving (Ferguson 2005) or forming partnerships with nonstate actors (Gardner 2012); other researchers call attention to the ways in which companies mobilize new power arrangements by means of different forms of corporate and local infrastructure, through which companies represent themselves as a caring actor and blame the state for negative causes and effects (Appel 2012).

Recognizing that CSR is a particular form of business-society interaction with historical twists and turns opens new ways for ethnographically exploring and understanding CSR and its role in a global neoliberal market. As the introduction to this volume has well argued, researchers have not sufficiently recognized the various ways in which state actors and institutions relate and respond to CSR processes. While research has shown that some multinational corporations bypass governments and take over state institutions' roles through the ways they implement CSR, states can also try to increase their power through CSR. Just as with any tool, machine, or concept, if CSR is transferred to another setting, we as anthropologists need to study what it becomes and does at a specific location. CSR is not an "immutable mobile" (Latour 1987); it is not a thing that does not change when transported, nor is it a directly transferable mobile from one region to another. It becomes "localized" (Welker 2014) and "domesticated" (Knudsen 2015).

One could argue that the multifaceted and multisided character of CSR makes it hard to study. Who is to decide whether or not a company is performing CSR sufficiently in a region? What should the criteria be, and according to whom? While many actors outside of the site of production or operation have important roles in CSR policies, much of the initiation, implementation, and renegotiation of CSR is framed locally and thus must also be studied locally. This chapter provides one small but important contribution to the study of the role that CSR can be given by state actors, companies, and the local population, and how it is understood differently by the actors involved. The chapter also casts light on the various ways CSR is approached by nation-states of different characters. The states involved in the CSR process in this chapter include states that build their (various degrees of) sovereign legitimation from their population and the international community in very different ways: namely, a state in becoming (Kurdistan Iraq), a state in chaos or with minimum capacity (Yemen), and a state that fronts itself as moral and just (Norway).

The Company DNO: Attentive to Shareholders and Profit

The Norwegian oil and gas operator DNO ASA was established in 1971 and is Norway's oldest oil company. It is a small private corporation in the world of oil business and is largely dependent on financial capital in an international market. Its shares are distributed among several international owners, including the Government Pension Fund Norway (4 percent), with RAK petroleum as the largest owner (44 percent) and holding the greatest decision-making power. RAK petroleum is a public limited company established under the laws of England and Wales, listed on Oslo Børs in Norway, and registered in the Netherlands. The largest shareholder (36 percent) and CEO of RAK petroleum is the Iranian-born Bijan Mossavar-Rahmani (a US citizen who resides in the United States). In 2011, the company merged with DNO international, in which it already held a 30 percent stake, increasing its shares in the Norwegian company. Mossavar-Rahmani became executive chairman of the DNO board of directors. DNO ASA is Norwegian in the sense that is it listed on the Oslo stock exchange and headquartered in Oslo. Further, three out of five members of the board of directors and five out of eight members of the executive management are Norwegian citizens, all with higher education from Norway. In this capacity, DNO ASA is obliged to follow rules and regulations of the Norwegian state abroad because it is a company considered to be Norwegian and is expected, as other Norwegian companies, to follow international regulations.

DNO is known for pursuing a business strategy characterized by "who does not dare, does not win" and "Risk and Reward" (Bøe 2017: 121).[4] In the 1990s, the company focused on operations in the Middle East and Africa, with economic activities in Kurdistan North Iraq, Yemen, Oman, United Arabic Emirates, Tunisia, and Somaliland. Its business model is the diligent use of network strategies, cost-efficient collaboration, keeping costs down, and timing, including at what point to enter a potential oil field and operating quickly (Bøe 2017). As Mossavar-Rahmani stated to the media: "We are in the oil sector. You have to be a risk taker. You like risk, you have the ability to control it, you have a balance that allows you to survive and the rest are opportunities."[5] The cowboy approach of the company is suggested by the former administrative director, Helge Eide, who, reflecting back on DNO's early history, expressed: "It went pretty fast in the turns many times, and we did not have good enough contact with our networks at this time. We shot from the hip and missed" (Bøe 2017: 205).[6]

Online, DNO presents itself, under "Mission and Values," in the following way:

> Our mission is to deliver superior returns to our shareholders by finding and producing oil at low cost and at an acceptable level of risk. DNO's DNA is to be first, fair and firm. We are driven to stay ahead of our competition—and ahead of the opportunities. We treat stakeholders fairly by adhering to high standards of governance, business conduct, and corporate social responsibility. We meet our commitments efficiently and transparently and expect the same of our suppliers, contractors, partners, and host governments.[7]

Their self-representation appears in sharp contrast to that of Equinor, the largest operator in Norway, which Strønen (chapter 6) quotes as "doing business with a clean conscience" and a concern with having a social footprint. Equinor was partially privatized in 2001, and while it has international ownership, the largest shareholder is the Norwegian state, with 67 percent held by the Norwegian Ministry of Petroleum and Energy. Although Strønen argues well that what is meant by Equinor's clean conscience depends upon what the company considers as its responsibility; the Equinor corporation's *raison d'être* versus that of DNO's is strikingly different. In DNO's "Corporate Social Responsibility Highlights 2018," DNO's approach to CSR is represented in the following way:

Corporate social responsibility starts with identifying, understanding, and addressing the needs of all key stakeholders. Wherever we operate, we make a concerted effort to maintain mutually beneficial relationships with these stakeholders, achieved through open dialogue and efforts to balance their interests with our own as a public company with over 15,000 shareholders. In addition to balancing stakeholder interests, essential ingredients to DNO's success as a responsible and effective global player include our active engagement with local communities, the safety and security of our people and operations, a light environmental footprint, and zero tolerance for corruption.[8]

This online representation contrasts sharply with how DNO has been portrayed in the media and how local informants in the Kurdistan Region of Iraq talked about their experience with the company. Over the last two decades, DNO's operations have been under scrutiny by various actors, and their lack of openness concerning procedures and guidelines has been commented upon in the media and by the OECD National Contact Point for Responsible Business Conduct Norway. DNO has reached the public media both with titles related to charges on tax fraud ("Berge Gerdt Larsen [DNO Chairman of the Board] charged for fraud and tax evasion"[9]) and as the small oil company who is taking the lead in "The Race to Tap the Next Gusher" (*Time* May 2006).[10] DNO's operations in the Kurdish region of Iraq and in Yemen have been publicly critiqued and deemed controversial in different ways. To explore DNO's practice of CSR and how it responds to the Norwegian state's expectations of Norwegian companies, in the following I will discuss the cases in the Kurdish region of Iraq and in Yemen.

Case 1. The Kurdistan Region of Iraq: Expectations and Disappointments

Iraq holds the fourth largest proven oil reserves in the world, and in 2011, it was the ninth largest producer of oil globally. Much of that oil exists in the north, the Kurdish areas. After the fall of Saddam Hussein following the US-led invasion in 2003, the principle of federalism was included in the new Iraqi constitution in 2005. This legalized the Kurdistan Region of Iraq (KRI) as an autonomous federal region, which included a high degree of international sovereignty as well as its own parliament, armed forces, and government (O'Driscoll and Baser 2019). An oil and gas law was enacted by the KRG in 2007, based on Articles 111 and 112 in the Iraqi constitution (Hasan 2019). On this basis, the KRG signed more than sixty oil and gas contracts with international oil companies (IOCs). Consequently, a major dispute between the KRG and the federal government in Baghdad unfolded, as the KRG claimed a constitutional right to sign petroleum contracts and argued that the constitution decentralized the management of natural resources in Iraq (Natali 2012). Tension between the Kurdistan Region of Iraq and Baghdad concerning petroleum contracts in general continues and concerns the future of oil exploration and revenues; some of the large deposits of natural resources are in the disputed areas of northern Iraq.

The liberalization and opening of the petroleum fields as well as the constellation of production-sharing agreements brought new public and private partnerships to the Kurdish region (O'Driscoll and Baser 2019). Business deals with large oil companies began. This came with prosperity, bringing a level of political and economic stability that gave the impression of the KRI as "the other Iraq" (O'Driscoll and Baser 2019) or the "next Dubai." While the region has embarked on a long-term effort to build a democratic and well-functioning state structure, it is still characterized by corruption, high unemployment, distrust toward the government, kinship-defined power dynamics, and political turbulence. State investments in basic services have been fragmented and, in some places, scarce.

There are around six million inhabitants in the Kurdish region of Iraq who make up between 17 and 20 percent of the population of Iraq. After a short optimistic and peaceful period from around 2007 through 2010, the region again faced economic crisis, turmoil, and conflict as a consequence of strained relations with the Iraqi government in Baghdad and of the war against *Daish* (ISIS). Simultaneously, transnational cooperations have become important players in various sectors of the Kurdistan Region, including for infrastructure, construction work, and the oil industry. From being the source of war, violence, and suppression, oil is now transforming the semiautonomous state of the Kurdistan Region of Iraq into a global capitalist economy with neoliberal ways and means that have changed the patterns of production and consumption.[11] Its current economy is characterized by global connections, including investments by international oil and construction companies from China, Norway, South Korea, Turkey, and the United States, and the capital Erbil/Hewler is booming with construction work and migrant workers.

The Controversial Beginnings

As the first international oil company in the region, DNO signed what was to become a controversial production sharing contract (PSC) with the Kurdistan Regional Government in 2004. DNO's presence in Kurdistan was facilitated through networks and indirect contacts to the political leaders in the Kurdish region of Iraq, including the prime minister, Nechirvan Barzani. DNO country manager in Yemen Magne Normann contacted the Ministry of Foreign Affairs in Oslo before his visit to the Kurdish region of Iraq in 2004 to ask how the Norwegian government would respond to a possible oil engagement in Iraqi Kurdistan. Normann was warned unofficially that "to make a deal with the Kurds about oil in Kurdistan would be perceived as if a foreign oil company would make a deal with the [Norwegian] Sami about oil extraction in the Barents Sea" (Bøe 2017: 210).

For the KRG, cooperation with DNO was deemed important: the oil company entered a contract directly with the KRG rather than with the Iraqi authorities or "Baghdad," and this became part of the public discourse in statements from the Kurdish authorities in their struggle for greater autonomy and possible future independence. Iraqi authorities in Baghdad, on the other hand, sued DNO because it had negotiated with the KRG rather than with authorities in Baghdad. Thus, while national governments in some cases support nationally based corporations—both state and nonstate—as they seek to expand abroad (see the introduction to this volume), in this case DNO became part of politics by default: the Norwegian government stressed, if only unofficially, that any direct deals DNO made with the Kurds would be politically problematic, while for the Iraqi Kurdistan authorities (KRG), the company's direct contact was a welcomed political—as well as economic—support.

Today, DNO has three main explorations in the KRI (Tawke PSC, Duhok PSC, and Erbil PSC), with the Tawke area as a "world-class giant oil field" from which international export started in 2011. At the time of my interview with the natural resources government advisor (Ministry of Natural Resources, KRG, Erbil), the government was in the process of creating guidelines on CSR that the companies were to follow. That said, the local content included from the beginning an expectation that international oil companies should employ between 60 and 100 percent of their workforce locally. Yet, the government advisor argued that the nature of oil operations situated in remote areas made it difficult to fulfill this expectation: "It is local development in remote areas where people are conservative and poor—and so the government is not so strong in those regions. And they [locals] don't have so many skills. They are not sophisticated, and so it is difficult to implement it." He continued: "Qualified workers are not in that area. But the population see the oil companies in these areas, and they will have great expectations. They should not feel that they are ignored, they must be included." He argued that the KRG was developing a supporting infrastructure, although he did not provide any concrete examples: "The intention of the government is to draw up an instruction manual to follow up that role to local authorities in the area. To have good coordination with them. As a matter of courtesy, the companies must respect them [the locals]. This coordination is led by the major [in the area]. It needs to be localized."

The Kurdish region of Iraq has a so-called business-friendly climate that gives maximum rights to investors; there is, for example, no taxation system for international businesses. The natural resources government advisor told me during our interview that the KRG-implemented procedures, including complaints procedures, are followed by DNO. He suggested that "CSR from companies should not replace the government, but it should be a good gesture to the locality where you have invested."

In 2015, there was a financial crisis in the Kurdish region of Iraq, exacerbated by the influx of millions of refugees from Syria and budget cuts from Baghdad. Consequently, the government did not pressure the companies to pursue CSR activities. Further, KRG resolved part of their debt by selling KRG-owned shares to DNO, increasing DNO's share in the Tawke field from 55 to 75 percent.[12] Some years earlier, in 2008, a controversial sale of its shares led DNO to be investigated by Økokrim (the Norwegian National Authority for Investigation and Prosecution of Economic and Environmental Crime) for violating the obligations for ongoing disclosure.[13] Økokrim fined DNO NOK 20 million (approximately US$3.3 million) for market manipulation in connection with the sale of shares to the KRG.[14] DNO reached an out-of-court settlement. Bijan Mossavar-Rahmani said: "We agreed to pay a reduced fine, without admitting any liability, to bring an end to a protracted and costly distraction involving matters that predate the current executive management and board of directors of DNO International."[15]

The KRG natural resources government advisor told me that the Kurdish people demand so much from the government, expectations that the government cannot meet. The expectations from the KRG toward oil companies involve social investment projects: "The significant part of the project is to create coordination with the people." To do this, he told me, the production companies should conduct a demographic social study in the area and then draw up a plan for the social programs: "They have a plan that is renewable and can be redrafted based on the needs of the people. It's a localization policy:

that expats are to be replaced by local people." He explained that the community should be involved in the decisions of which projects to develop and the next steps. He expressed that the Kurdish population needs to distinguish between the oil companies and the government: if something goes wrong, "blame should be on the companies, not the government. The government must not be interrupted." As an advisor, he pays attention to that, and he is "very happy about what DNO is doing."

In contrast to the positive image of DNO provided by government representatives, journalists and scholars talked extensively about ongoing environmental issues—such as water shortage, air and water pollution, plastic waste, urbanization, geological imbalances, increasing numbers of cars, and destruction of agricultural areas—produced by oil companies in the Kurdistan Region of Iraq. What are the local population's expectations and experience of CSR conducted by DNO?

Local People's Experience of CSR: The Missing School

One day during my fieldwork in the Kurdish region of Iraq, I go to a village situated in Tawke to talk with the village inhabitants about their experience of the DNO oil drilling next door. The old road leading to the village is still a gravel road, but now village residents must also pass two roadblocks with security checks to enter and exit the village. The oil drilling is visible from the doorstep of the house of Ahmed, a man in his forties and father of three children.

The village men are gathered in Ahmed's living room; thirteen men are seated on the floor, leaning against the wall. The children are playing outside, and the women are not around except for Ahmed's wife, who serves us tea and water. After a short round of introductions and explanation of who I am and why I am there, Ahmed says, "We gave them our land, but they have not visited us even once." He is disappointed and frustrated. On the advice of the KRG and the village's muxtar (head of a village), he and his neighbors had leased land to DNO for an agreed amount of money. None of the measures promised had been met, they argue; the only thing they have gotten is a bad area for the children to grow up in. Living in a village situated some five hundred meters from Tawke—DNO's largest facility in Iraqi Kurdistan—the inhabitants no longer work in their fields, as these are occupied by pipes, other oil industry infrastructure, and grease. But they have no other work either. Ahmed, like his co-villagers, had believed they would receive better infrastructure for their remote

Figure 11.1. View from a village close to the Tawke field. © Synnøve Bendixsen

village and that the road from the village to the nearby town would be paved by the oil company, facilitating everyday life. They had also expected the company to build a school in the village. The villagers, I was told, had been informed that the men of the village would get jobs at the facility. But the only thing they had received, says Ahmed, was a new mosque.

The men in the village fear that the future will bring major health problems for all of them, in particular their children, because of living amid a whirlpool of gas, truck dust, and extraction dirt. They argue that a nearby village, where most inhabitants were Turkmen and thus Christians, had received a school built with money from DNO. They believe the differential treatment is due to the different ethnic and religious composition of the two villages. "All the villagers want today," Ahmed says, "is to move from the village, but they cannot afford it," continuing: "We feel like victims living in the heart of oil extraction without any of the benefits falling to us." The other men seated on the floor express feeling cheated by the government and believe the international oil companies are making a fortune on their land, while they are left without anything but a bleak future. The idea that they had been promised more than they had received was shared by everyone in the village. The men blamed the situation on the lack of control and follow-up on the part of the Kurdish authorities rather than on the oil company.

The village population's distrust toward international oil companies and the government as well as their pessimism about what the oil drilling had brought the region were replicated in various ways by other Kurds I spoke to, including journalists, students, and oil company workers. Many blamed the KRG for not being hard enough on the oil companies and letting them do as they wish: "The KRG doesn't push the companies, because they are new, and they don't want to push—they want companies to come to Kurdistan." A geologist in Duhok, whom I interviewed, told me:

> In 2003, when DNO started with oil here, they started very badly. They cut down many trees, with long-term impact. Protesters talked to the government, but the government just said: "It is also so in the US." "Yes, but there they have regulations—they follow the instruction there," the protesters had responded, but to no avail. The companies don't take care of the residential areas. ... And now people start to react. ... DNO gave $200 per family for hotel and transportation and for three days to evacuate the village. These people were evacuated for one to two days.

He believes that the muxtar (village head) took the compensation and did not give much of it to the villagers. Further, he adds, evacuation is not a matter of two to three days: "Oil wells are bad socially and for children. When you make a dam, for example, you must evacuate people for a long term, not short." Although the KRG tells the international oil companies to "please take care," the geologist believes that the KRG does not push the companies enough: "It is temporary solutions the whole time. The only permanent solution is about making oil fields." He talks about the environment, and how the last rain in the region included acid and oil: "The polluted rain is not from particular DNO activities or from one of the other companies—it is from all! The combination. Villages are very close to the oil activities, one kilometer." When we finish our talk, he adds that people are

> afraid to write about this in the newspaper. This is a matter of oil; it is a secret, so you will be under pressure. Security forces will tell you to be quiet. We only speak about this with a low voice. Sometimes there are demonstrations in certain areas. Then they give them money, and they will be quiet, they [the former protesters] then say: "It is not my problem, it is the problem of KRG." ... Because of high unemployment, a small amount of payment is enough to keep people quiet.

People in the villages and beyond expressed that they were overwhelmingly dissatisfied and disillusioned by the international oil companies and the government's policies on energy. One Kurdish journalist, who had investigated the CSR of companies in the Kurdish region of Iraq, commented on the CSR report of DNO: "A drop of water in the sea: they made a road which they needed for their own company and put that in the report! People are very religious, and so they made a small hall for religious meetings, for funerals, etc., and said that this is CSR!" He added: "The government has no clear plans for CSR. It is a matter of capacity building—they do not know how to raise this issue or work on it." His comment resonated with other informants in the region who believed that the KRG put blame on international companies for insufficient social responsivity without making sufficient efforts to ensure that their CSR expectations of these international companies were clearly stated and followed up. Many local informants also criticized the KRG for not engaging and interacting with the local communities affected by oil operations. They expressed dismay and distrust toward the KRG's management of international oil companies and had lost faith that the black gold would benefit their local communities in any way, for example by providing jobs.

Actors involved in CSR have different objectives and expectations. The government seeks CSR to create goodwill from its population and, ultimately, to facilitate continued expansion of oil operations. Governing in a fragile democracy, the KRG needs to make evident to its citizens that it is making demands on international companies with regard to CSR. Yet, its limited experience with international companies, malfunctioning government, and undeveloped legal regulations may be reasons for their failure to regulate and monitor the CSR practices of DNO ASA (and other multinational corporations).

Examining the CSR highlight reports available online, one finds the image of a company that is profit and shareholder-value oriented; the reports are directed toward the international financial market and show less commitment to CSR standards. Performing on-the-ground assemblages of CSR appeared important in the company's relation with the KRG. It seems as though the need to make things work locally involves transactions with local and national authorities, and that this is articulated as CSR. The company's approach to CSR looks to be more about continuing and expanding its business without interruptions from the government or population, expending as few resources as possible.

The locals' expectations of CSR included the implementation of projects in a way that will benefit the local community. The outcome of the CSR practices during my fieldwork was that representatives from the KRG claimed to be satisfied, though they were also concerned that any failure on the part of an oil company to meet CSR standards would boomerang on the government with increased distrust and dismay. We see in the village that, indeed, the government was held responsible for the disappointing CSR effects. It suggests that when CSR fails, the government risks being blamed.

The image left is that of an oil company preaching vague promises about CSR measures combined with a lack of control mechanisms from local, regional, and national authorities. This situation facilitates keeping costs for CSR down and limiting the time and effort expended on implementing CSR. For the oil company, talk of CSR is a way by which their presence in the region is legitimated. Yet, on the ground, the population expressed being exploited by the company, and the situation increased distrust toward the authorities. Poor management or potential mismanagement of CSR—here taking the form of a lack of concrete promises or creating a mismatch between expectations and implementation—can have serious ripple effects beyond the financial; there are negative effects on democracy building in weak states, such as the Kurdish region of Iraq.

I turn now briefly to the second case, from Yemen, to examine whether the low CSR input and lack of transparency in the Kurdish region of Iraq is an exception or part of more general trends and character in the operations of DNO.

Case 2. Yemen: Strike and Workers' Rights

Yemen is one of the poorest countries of the Arab world. Scholars have suggested that rather than calling Yemen a "failed state," actors in Yemen are using the production of chaos (Blumi 2011) to receive international funding (Dingli 2013). The strategy of simulating statehood, argues Dingli (2013), was one way in which the Yemeni regime ensured funding, facilitating the continuation of functioning power structures. The outbreak of civil war in 2014 exacerbated existing economic challenges, brought increased unemployment, and created a humanitarian crisis. At the same time, Yemen has large proven oil reserves, with the first commercial discovery in 1984. DNO had at one moment six oil fields in the country, yet their operations ended with criticism from labor unions and employees.

After a brief hesitation, DNO accepted an invitation from Dove Energy Ltd., a smaller English oil company, to collaborate on an oil project in Yemen in 1997 (Bøe 2017). Yemen was interesting because the price of licenses was cheaper than in other places and the costs of drilling wells less than offshore. Thus, the break-even price was lower than most other places. DNO budgeted the first operation to be $23 million, considered by other companies as unrealistically low. This, apparently, was to send a signal to those delivering tasks and activities that "nothing would be wasted": "Those who are not delivering will not be given a new chance" (Bøe 2017: 137). The time schedule was also made implausibly tight with the intention that work should be "quick and effective." To accomplish this, the company reduced the number of people engaged in the field to a minimum and made decisions hands-on, "with few negotiations, time-consuming evaluations and unproductive bureaucracy" (Bøe 2017: 138). Notably, the first Tasour field operation in Yemen was achieved with even lower costs than budgeted (at $13 million) and only two months delay. For some years, DNO's operation in Yemen was considered a success as explained by their "business model, the countercyclical network strategy, risk-reward philosophy, increased extraction and not least, timing" (Bøe 2017: 146).

Yet, in 2013 and 2014, workers went on strike because they were paid less compared to other companies. For example, an engineer was paid around NOK 5,000 (around $800 in 2014) per month by DNO, the lowest among all oil companies in Yemen.[16] DNO management responded with the written notification that they would fire all workers who went on strike. This violated the statutory right to strike in Yemen. Following the outbreak of war in the spring of 2015, DNO and several other international oil companies, such as Total and Dove, stopped all operations in Yemen. In June 2015, DNO notified the workers by SMS and email that they had been dismissed. This was in sharp contrast to the obligations DNO had accepted when initiating their operation: the law of Yemen states that if a company is granted a license to operate a field, the company must pay wages and honor social obligations to the workers so long as the company has a license. If the company wishes to terminate operations before the license period is over, the company must hand over the entire operation, including oil fields and workers, to the state.

Consequently, DNO faced a law court in Yemen, and in 2016 the company was ordered to pay their workers and to fulfill their obligations.[17] After losing their appeal, DNO was charged to forcibly recover the wages of the workers. Considering that DNO had in the meantime initiated new operations in Iran, the company's argument that their assets were too low to pay was not considered credible. The court seized DNO's properties, bank accounts, and cars in Yemen.[18] Nonetheless, according to the federal secretary of Industry Energy (the Norwegian trade union for those who work in the industry and energy sectors), the workers were not remunerated because at this point DNO did not own much in Yemen.

In an interview with Industry Energy, Ryadh Al-Gharady, the leader of the trade union for the workers in DNO Yemen, criticized DNO: "Our case is that DNO has treated us inhumanely and illegally. It is the only oil company in Yemen that has laid off workers and not paid wages. The families of the workers are suffering and lack money for food." He added: "We want to take the case not only on a national level but also internationally and hold DNO responsible for their actions."[19] Email campaigns and media coverage reporting bad treatment of workers in Yemen figured also in Norway. Industry Energy filed a complaint against DNO on behalf of the Yemeni trade union to the National Contact Point for Responsible Business Norway (NCP) whose primary task is to promote OECD guidelines for multinational companies and help resolve complaints that may arise in connection with an alleged failure of compliance with the guidelines.[20] The central point of the complaint was that DNO did not comply with OECD Guidelines: Chapter I, Section 2, "A company's first obligation is to comply with national laws," and Chapter V, Section 4a, "Comply with standards of employment and the employer-employee relationship which are no less favorable than those followed by similar employers in the host country."[21] DNO rejected participation in mediation and requested that most of the company's letters to the Contact Point be kept confidential, including in relation to complaints. In its final statement (22 March 2018), the NCP held that DNO did not comply with the OECD guidelines in parts of Chapter V.[22] Industry Energy also criticized the fact that DNO had opposed the employees' right to organize in trade unions and conduct collective bargaining in Yemen. The NCP did not find any grounds for DNO *not* to meet the expectations of the right of workers to join trade unions.[23] The NCP critique was extensive: "The National Contact Point recommends that DNO in future carry out risk-based due diligence assessments and show greater transparency in its guidelines and procedures for responsible business activities."[24] They also recommended that, in future, DNO "respect the National Contact Point Scheme's complaint mechanism, which is central to the OECD's guidelines, and co-operate with the National Contact

Point in good faith; map out what are comparable wage conditions in Yemen and apply these; follow up on its promise to enter into wage and post-payment agreements in keeping with Yemeni law."[25]

DNO responded initially that the complaint by the NCP was neither submitted by a party affected by the circumstances concerned by the complaint nor sufficiently founded or documented. They argued that the complaint was based on mere allegation.[26] In response to the final conclusions of the NCP, DNO argued that the Yemeni court decision had not been adjudicated correctly, arguing that toward the end of the process new judges had been appointed who had "questionable legal competence." DNO also expressed little confidence in the handling of the complaint by the NCP.[27]

The NCP does not have any sanctioning authority. Yet, the "unNorwegianness" of DNO's actions and lack of ethical approach overseas were highlighted, although not highly mediatized, in the media. The adviser to Industry Energy argued in the media that "we like to believe that Norwegian companies have ethical values that make them behave properly towards their employees. Here at home, they usually do. But not always abroad. The oil company DNO is one of the worst."[28] DNO was also depicted as particularly undesirable compared to other international oil companies in Yemen. As a consequence of the mismanagement of its workers in Yemen and the outcome of the court ruling, the Norwegian trade union, Industry Energy, warned shareholders and partners against DNO. So far, these warnings have had little, if any, effect on shareholder behavior, nor have they led to any real effects in the Norwegian government's approach toward DNO ASA, as will be discussed next.

Discussion: License to Operate and Its Depoliticizing Effect

How does DNO relate to the "expectations" set forth by Norwegian authorities? The Norwegian government highlights that companies are expected to develop their own CSR standards, establish mechanisms for whistleblowing, and show transparency in the economic, social, and environmental consequences of their operations. Stateand non-state-owned Norwegian companies are reminded that "Norwegian companies operating abroad are often equated with the Norwegian state, and their conduct is therefore also important for Norway's reputation."[29] The Norwegian minister for development aid (in 2018) has expressed great faith that Norwegian business and industry are the best in class in terms of social responsibility. The government also "considers it important that the trade union movement is involved in the company's work with social responsibility."[30] The Norwegian state does not require corporations abroad to follow a "Nordic model" but instead to follow universal standards, including applying the International Labor Organization's (ILO) core conventions to "establish notification routines for their activities abroad"[31] and pay attention to certain values (see the introduction to this volume). Companies that operate in countries that top the UN corruption index,[32] such as the countries in which DNO operates, are expected to take care to contribute to transparency concerning cash flows.

The two cases discussed here suggest that DNO initiates their operations and pursues their activities by accepting high risk and active use of social networks, personal contacts, and patronage in their region of operations. Disrespect of workers' rights is clear-cut in the Yemen case and conceivable in the Kurdistan Region case. CSR is not grounded in the operation of the company but, rather, pursued haphazardly to avoid the most stringent criticisms in the country of operation. While it becomes an informal requirement for license to operate (Nielsen 2013; see also chapter 7), it does not provide the company legitimacy to operate from the perspective of the local population due to its bad management or lack of implementation. Legitimacy is here understood as "a generalized perception or assumption that the actions of an entity are desirable, proper, or appropriate within some socially constructed system of norms, values, beliefs and definitions" (Suchman 1995, 574).

While the Norwegian authorities have expressed a particularly low threshold for corruption in companies both nationally and abroad, the court cases against DNO through the years suggest that this is of lesser concern to DNO. Additionally, the Sustainability Disclosure Database GRI reports that DNO has an "incomplete profile" and that "this organization has not yet disclosed their sustainability opportunities [and risks] on this profile."[33] DNO reports have frequently been criticized for incompleteness and lack of transparency. Its first country-by-country report is deficient according to the regulations on such reporting (Weum and Mohagen 2015).[34] Their land-for-land report for 2014, for example, lacks information, such as the status of internal interest costs, complete information on taxes paid in kind, the omission of tax information to the Kurdistan Region of Iraq, and the difference between income figures in the country-by-country report and the annual accounts, which should have been relatively easy to include (Weum and Mohagen 2015). DNO's corporate social responsibility highlight reports (2014, 2015, 2016, 2018) are characterized by being short, generic, and imprecise. While the court case in Yemen is closed (although the workers have yet to receive their salaries), there is an ongoing lawsuit by Iraqi lawyers against DNO in the labor court of Erbil. The lawsuit concerns the breaching of employment laws of the federal Republic of Iraq and the regional employment laws of the Kurdistan Region of Iraq.[35] It points to a lack of concern for labor rights and the lack of functioning mechanisms for whistleblowing as well as DNO's failure to follow Norwegian governmental expectations for the role of trade unions. DNO practices are important beyond the company's specific operations, considering that smaller companies on a world basis, such as DNO, might be seen as forerunners, laying the groundwork for larger companies that later buy the smaller companies' licenses when fields are up and running, expanded, and appear more stable.

Researchers have importantly alluded to the depoliticizing effects of CSR in other contexts, "that is, how it stops critique by bathing the corporation in a virtuous hue that masks the pathologies of capitalism" (Dolan and Rajak 2016, 21). In this case, there is another depoliticizing effect of CSR: namely, that national authorities in Iraqi Kurdistan and Yemen can blame the transnational corporations (TNCs) for a lack of real cooperation with the local population and for not paying heed to their own failure to standardize CSR through policies, laws, and regulations or to provide proper services themselves. One of the main consequences of the CSR practices of international oil production companies, such as DNO, and the KRG approach to international companies is the proliferation of distrust toward the local and national government by the population, detrimental to the ongoing formation of a well-functioning democracy.

Industry Energy reports that DNO has not complied with OECD guidelines for responsible business or with the UN's guiding principle for business and human rights (UNGP).[36] In his online blog, Leif Sande (former head of Industry Energy) states, "I would like to urge everyone who comes into contact with these bandits not to make any promises about licenses on Norwegian soil. This is a company that should have been kicked out—on their head and ass. After several court judgments, they continue to deny people the salary they owe them."[37] Yet, the Norwegian state has not blocked DNO from entering Norwegian waters: having not had a presence on Norwegian soil since 2007, DNO has recently been given licenses to operate in Norway and thus has been neither reprimanded nor penalized for their lack of following the Nordic model or more general CSR standards. The lack of adherence to expectations and a negative reputation apparently do not bear any consequences for their interests in the Norwegian waters.

Conclusion

The practices of social responsibility by DNO in the Kurdish region of Iraq and in Yemen reflect exceptionally bad divergences from the archetype known as the Nordic model. DNO's practices of CSR in the Kurdistan Region of Iraq and in Yemen are characterized by swift entrance to the market, limited CSR practices, and deep frustration among the local population. The locals' experience that DNO did not fulfil its CSR obligations in the Kurdish region of Iraq, a view that appeared to be shared by the broader population, was largely blamed neither on the corporation nor on the role of the Norwegian state but rather on the authorities in the Kurdish region of Iraq. CSR was thus not considered merely as the international corporation's responsibility, as in the case of Hydro in Brazil (see chapter 4).

While one might have expected that the lack of transparency, neglect of workers' rights, and limited CSR programs abroad could backfire as the company seeks to again become an actor in Norwegian waters, so far there have been no repercussions. Lack of compliance with the Norwegian government's expectations abroad has had little aftereffect in terms of access to licenses and thus economic consequences for misdeeds. So far, poor CSR has not limited this privately owned company's capacity to pursue business opportunities—even in Norway.

The acceptance, through the provision of licenses in Norway, by the Norwegian state of a company whose ethical practices and the reputation of its operations abroad are far from what is represented to be the Nordic model, signals a moral double standard by the Norwegian authorities. It might also suggest the limitations of the Norwegian state in promoting the Nordic model or their limited power of intervention when companies abroad are not following the Nordic model of corporate conduct. Yet, when the Norwegian state is less concerned with how Norwegian companies, although privately owned, operate abroad or whether the government's expectations beyond the international regulations are met, the Nordic model may turn out to be considered as only relevant when operating in the Nordic region and thus viewed more as an exception than a rule.

This is particularly the case if operation of the Nordic model is dependent upon a host state that is already familiar with the model—not only international CSR practices—and has state institutions with the means and power to ensure implementation. There may be little incentive for companies to follow CSR practices with a long-term perspective, but they may find it useful, rather, as a minimum practice for operations to facilitate and simplify the progress of an oil project in the short term. Lack of real (economic) consequences might contribute to erode the idea and ideal of a Nordic model in the longer run and dwindle its value as a resource.

Acknowledgments

Research for this chapter was supported by the project Energethics (2015–19), funded by a FRIPRO grant from the Research Council of Norway (grant no. 240617). The author also thanks Dunya Slahdin Mirdan and Mehmet Aktas for their important contribution during the fieldwork for this project.

Synnøve Bendixsen is professor in the Department of Social Anthropology, University of Bergen, Norway. She has a PhD from Humboldt University and Ecole des Hautes Etudes en Science Sociales (cotutelle) and has worked as senior lecturer at the University of Kurdistan—Hewler (2008–9). Bendixsen has conducted research on refugees and irregular migrants in Norway, Serbia, and Bosnia and Herzegovina; on young Muslims and religiosity in Germany; and on CSR in Kurdistan, Iraq. Her main research focus is on questions of marginalization processes, border constructions, urban life, and diversity. She is the coeditor for the Palgrave Macmillan series Approaches to Social Inequality and Difference.

Notes

1. The Nordic countries top the Transparency International Corruption Perceptions Index (with Denmark at a shared number 1, Finland and Sweden at number 2, and Norway at number 7 in 2020), suggesting low levels of perceived corruption across the Nordics. Midttun, Gautesen, and Gjølberg (2006) suggest that at the European level the Nordic corporations score best on CSR initiatives (see also Strand et al. 2015; Maon et al. 2017).
2. This is spelled out in their white paper on corporate social responsibility in a global economy: "The Government assumes that Norwegian business and industry will be

among the foremost in demonstrating social responsibility based on a good value base, awareness and reflection." Meld. St. no. 10 (2008–9) — retrieved 7 July 2021 from regjeringen.no.
3. My research intention was to return to the region in the following year; yet the *Daish* (ISIS) situation prohibited my return. Although I had not conducted fieldwork in this region in the past, I am familiar with the region as I worked as a university lecturer in Erbil for three semesters, 2008–9.
4. The book about DNO by Bøe (2017) was contracted by Berge Gerdt Larsen (DNO chairman of the board).
5. https://finansavisen.no/nyheter/energi/2015/05/forvalter-om-dno-loennen-spiller-ingen-rolle, [Manager about DNO: Salary does not matter], accessed 20 April 2021.
6. Author's translation from Norwegian: "Det gikk ganske fort i svingene mange ganger, og vi hadde ikke god nok kontakt med nettverkene våre i denne tiden. Vi skjøt fra hoften og bommet."
7. From DNO's online homepage: Mission and values | About DNO | DNO ASA, accessed 20 June 2021.
8. From DNO's online homepage Mission and values | About DNO | DNO ASA, accessed 2 May 2021.
9. In BT: Berge Gerdt Larsen tiltalt for bedrageri og skattesvik (bt.no) [Berge Gerdt Larsen charged with fraud and tax evasion], accessed 4 May 2021.
10. "The Race to Tap the Next Gusher," *Time*, 16 April 2006. From online: Kurdistan is rich in oil resources, Kurds are ready to deal (ekurd.net), accessed 20 June 2021.
11. There are more than 2,250 functioning foreign companies in the Iraqi Kurdistan region including Arabic companies (Ministries of Commerce and Industry, KRG). Oil companies include BP, CNPC, DNO, Lukoil, Eni, Occidental, Kogas, Shell, ExxonMobil, Petronas, Sonangol, and Total.
12. https://e24.no/olje-og-energi/i/jPynXn/dno-sjefen-kan-ha-skutt-gullfuglen-brikkene-falt-paa-plass [DNO boss may have shot the golden bird. Pieces fell into place], accessed 14 May 2021.
13. Økokrim etterforsker DNO-saken — Økokrim (okokrim.no) [Ecocrime investigates DNO case], accessed 14 May 2021.
14. Millionbøter til DNO for markedsmanipulasjon — Økokrim — Tips en venn (okokrim.no) [Million fines to DNO for market manipulation], accessed 12 May 2021.
15. DNO International Settles ØKOKRIM Claim | Announcements | Investors | DNO ASA, accessed 12 May 2021.
16. https://www.industrienergi.no/nyhet/dno-tvinges-a-betale-arbeiderne/ [DNO forced to pay the workers], accessed 15 June 2021.
17. Norwegian oil company DNO targeted by unions | IndustriALL (industriall-union.org), accessed 10 June 2021.
18. Arbeidere lider på grunn av oljeselskapet DNO — Industri Energi [Workers suffering because of the oilcompany DNO] (translated from Norwegian, accessed 2 February 2021), see also Dette selskapet må lempes på hode og ræva ut av norsk sokkel. (leifsande.no) [This company must be kicked in the head and ass off of the Norwegian shelf].
19. https://www.industrienergi.no/nyhet/dno-tvinges-a-betale-arbeiderne/ [DNO forced to pay the workers], accessed 15 June 2021.
20. The OECD guidelines are recommendations for responsible business and good practice for all types of companies in all sectors and builds on internationally recognized standards. The guidelines have recommendations for transparency, human rights, employment, and workers' rights, the environment, bribery and blackmail, consumer interests, science and technology, competition, and taxation. They contain voluntary, nonlegal recommendations, while there is a clear expectation from the authorities that companies comply with the Guidelines.

21. Industri Energi klager DNO inn for Norges OECD-kontaktpunkt—Industri Energi [Industry Energy complains DNO to Norway's OECD contact point], accessed 5 July 2021.
22. Slutterklæring-Industri-Energi-DNO-II-FINAL.pdf (regjeringen.no), accessed 6 July 2021.
23. Slutterklæring Industri Energi DNO ASA—Ansvarlig Næringsliv (responsiblebusiness.no), accessed 10 June 2021.
24. https://www.responsiblebusiness.no/nyheter/slutterklaering-industri-energi-dno-asa/?fbclid=IwAR3UvagvtVdXhxL8mX4xC9Ztkm0W3soAz8jo3PpsP9yuPzRRvdVO4AoPLvY [final declaration industry energy dno-asa], accessed 10 June 2021.
25. https://www.responsiblebusiness.no/nyheter/kontaktpunktets-slutterklaering-i-klagesak-industri-energi-dno-asa-ii/?fbclid=IwAR3ygNKtB8W_cLiAU61vGfCWitnSYKHSWJDyuScAAaclzHmDr2G26GSK-R4 [Contact point closing statement in complaint case, industry energy dno-asa], accessed 10 June 2021.
26. Specific-instance-DNO-Industri-Energi-English_090517_-1.pdf (regjeringen.no), accessed 7 July 2021.
27. Skarp kritikk mot oljeselskapet DNO (aftenbladet.no) [Sharp critique against the oil company DNO], accessed 7 July 2021.
28. Arbeidere lider på grunn av oljeselskapet DNO—Industri Energi [Workers suffers because of the oil company DNO], translated from Norwegian, accessed 2 February 2021.
29. Meld. St. no. 10 (2008–9)—regjeringen.no, accessed 7 July 2021.
30. Meld. St. no. 10 (2008–9)—regjeringen.no [Corporate social responsibility in a global economy—Report no. 10 (2008–9) to the Storting], accessed 7 July 2021.
31. Meld. St. no. 10 (2008–9)—regjeringen.no, [Corporate social responsibility in a global economy—Report no. 10 (2008–9) to the Storting], accessed 7 July 2021.
32. Global Corruption Barometer—2013—Transparency.org, accessed 8 July 2021.
33. See SDD—GRI Database (globalreporting.org), accessed 16 June 2021.
34. https://openaccess.nhh.no/nhh-xmlui/bitstream/handle/11250/2382953/masterthesis.pdf?sequence=1&isAllowed=y, accessed 17 June 2021.
35. https://telematique.co.uk/wp-content/uploads/2020/01/IraqLawyer_spokesperson_DNO_ASA_28-Nov-2019v2-2.pdf, accessed 16 June 2021.
36. https://www.industrienergi.no/2018/07/03/dno-asa-ein-omsynslause-profittjeger-eller-eit-ansvarlege-selskap/ [DNO ASA: a careless profit hunter or a responsible company], translated by the author from Norwegian, accessed 15 June 2021.
37. Dette selskapet må lempes på hode og ræva ut av norsk sokkel (leifsande.no) [This company must be kicked in the head and ass off of the Norwegian shelf], translated by the author from Norwegian, accessed 16 June 2021.

References

Appel, Hannah C. 2012. "Walls and White Elephants: Oil Extraction, Responsibility, and Infrastructural Violence in Equatorial Guinea." *Ethnography* 13(4): 439–65. doi:10.1177/1466138111435741.

Billo, Emily. 2015. "Sovereignty and Subterranean Resources: An Institutional Ethnography of Repsol's Corporate Social Responsibility Programs in Ecuador." *Geoforum* 59: 268–77.

Blumi, Isa. 2011. *Chaos in Yemen: Societal Collapse and the New Authoritarianism.* New York: Routledge.

Buu-Sao, Doris. 2021. "Extractive Governmentality at Work: Native Appropriations of Oil Labor in the Amazon." *International Political Sociology* 15(1): 63–82. https://doi.org/10.1093/ips/olaa019.

Bøe, Arnt Even. 2017. *DNO—Et norsk oljeeventyr. Elsket og fordømt* [DNO—A Norwegian oil adventure. Beloved and condemned]. Stavanger: Wigestrand Forlag, Larsen Oil & Gas AS.
Bridge, Gavin. 2010. "Geographies of Peak Oil: The Other Carbon Problem." *Geoforum*, 41(4): 523–30. https://doi.org/10.1016/j.geoforum.2010.06.002.
Campbell, John L. 2007. "Why Would Corporations Behave in Socially Responsible Ways? An Institutional Theory of Corporate Social Responsibility." *Academy of Management Review* 32(3): 946–67.
Collier, Stephen J., and Aihwa Ong. 2005. "Global Assemblages, Anthropological Problems." In *Global Assemblages: Technology, Politics, and Ethics as Anthropological Problems*, edited by Aihwa Ong and Stephen J. Collier, 3–21. Malden: Blackwell Publishing.
Dingli, Sophia. 2013. "Is the Failed State Thesis Analytically Useful? The Case of Yemen." *Politics* 33(2): 91–100. doi: 10.1111/j.1467-9256.2012.01453.x.
Djelic, Marie-Laure, and Helen Etchanchu. 2017. "Contextualizing Corporate Political Responsibilities: Neoliberal CSR in Historical Perspective." *Journal of Business Ethics* 131: 1–21.
Dolan, Catherine, and Dinah Rajak. 2016. "Introduction: Toward the Anthropology of Corporate Social Responsibility." In *The Anthropology of Corporate Social Responsibility*, edited by C. Dolan and D. Rajak, 1–28. New York: Berghahn Books.
Duffy, Rosaleen. 2006. "The Potential and Pitfalls of Global Environmental Governance: The Politics of Transfrontier Conservation Areas in Southern Africa." *Political Geography* 25(1): 89–112. https://doi.org/10.1016/j.polgeo.2005.08.001.
Ferguson, James. 2005. "Seeing like an Oil Company: Space, Security, and Global Capital in Neoliberal Africa." *American Anthropologist* 107(3): 377–82.
———. 2006. *Global Shadows: Africa in the Neoliberal World Order*. Durham, NC: Duke University Press.
Friedman, Milton. 1970. "The Social Responsibility of Business Is to Increase Its Profits. *New York Times Magazine*, 13 September.
Gardner, Katy. 2012. *Discordant Development: Global Capitalism and the Struggle for Connection in Bangladesh*. London: Pluto Press.
Garriga, Elisabet, and Domènec Melé. 2004. "Corporate Social Responsibility Theories: Mapping the Territory." *Journal of Business Ethics* 53(1/2): 51–71.
Gond, Jean-Pascal, Nahee Kang, and Jeremy Moon. 2011. "The Government of Self-Regulation: on the Comparative Dynamics of Corporate Social Responsibility." *Economy and Society* 40(4): 640–71.
Hasan, Qaraman Mohammed. 2019. "The Power of Constitution for Enacting Energy Law and Managing Natural Resources: The Case of the Kurdistan Regional Government's Oil Contracts, Energy Policy." *Energy Policy* 128: 744–51. https://doi.org/10.1016/j.enpol.2019.01.012.
Hönke, Jana. 2011. "New Political Topographies: Mining Companies and Indirect Discharge in Southern Katanga (DRC)." *Politique Africaine* 120(4): 105–27.
Knudsen, Ståle. 2015. "Corporate Social Responsibility in Local Context: International Capital, Charitable Giving and the Politics of Education in Turkey." *Southeast European and Black Sea Studies* 15(3): 369–90.
Latour, Bruno. 1987. *Science in Action: How to Follow Scientists and Engineers through Society*. Cambridge, MA: Harvard University Press.
Maon, François., Valérie Swaen, and Adam Lindgreen. 2017. "One Vision, Different Paths: An Investigation of Corporate Social Responsibility Initiatives in Europe." *Journal of Business Ethics* 143: 405–22. https://doi.org/10.1007/s10551-015-2810-2.
Meld. St. no. 10 (2008–9). "Næringslivets samfunnsansvar i en global økonomi" [Corporate social responsibility in a global economy], retrieved 7 July 2021 from regjeringen.no, https://www.regjeringen.no/no/dokumenter/stmeld-nr-10-2008-2009-/id542966/.

Midttun, Atle. 2005. "Realigning Business, Government and Civil Society: Emerging Embedded Relational Governance beyond the (Neo)Liberal and Welfare State Models; Corporate Governance." *International Journal of Business in Society* 5(3): 159–74.

Midttun, Atle, Kristian Gautesen, and Maria Gjølberg. 2006. "The Political Economy of CSR in Western Europe: Corporate Governance." *International Journal of Business in Society* 6(4): 369–85.

Mitchell, Timothy. 2013. *Carbon Democracy: Political Power in the Age of Oil*. London: Verso.

Natali, Dennis. 2012. "The Politics of Kurdish Crude." *Middle East Policy* 19: 110–18.

Nielsen, Anne Ellerup. 2013. "License to Operate." In *Encyclopedia of Corporate Social Responsibility*, edited by S.O. Idowu, N. Capaldi, L. Zu, and A.D. Gupta, 1585–1591. Berlin, Heidelberg: Springer.

O'Driscoll, Dylan, and Bahar Baser. 2019. "Independence Referendums and Nationalist Rhetoric: The Kurdistan Region of Iraq." *Third World Quarterly* 40(11): 2016–34.

Rajak, Dinah. 2011. *In Good Company: An Anatomy of Corporate Social Responsibility*. Stanford, CA: Stanford University Press.

———. 2016. "Theatres of Virtue: Collaboration Consensus and the Social Life of Corporate Social Responsibility." In *The Anthropology of Corporate Social Responsibility*, edited by C. Dolan and D. Rajak, 29–47. New York: Berghahn Books.

Schubert Jon 2020. "Wilful Entanglements: Extractive Industries and the Co-Production of Sovereignty in Mozambique." *Ethnography* 21(4): 537–58. doi:10.1177/1466138118802953.

Suchman, Mark C. 1995. "Managing Legitimacy: Strategic and Institutional Approaches." *Academy of Management Review* 20: 571–610.

Strand, Robert., Robert Edward Freeman, and Kai Hockerts. 2015. "Corporate Social Responsibility and Sustainability in Scandinavia: An Overview." *Journal of Business Ethics* 127: 1–15. https://doi.org/10.1007/s10551-014-2224-6.

Thrift, Nigel. 2005. *Knowing Capitalism*. London: Sage.

Watts, Michael. 2004. "Resource Curse? Governmentality, Oil and Power in the Niger Delta, Nigeria." *Geopolitics* 9(1): 50–80.

Welker, Marina 2014. *Enacting the Corporation: An American Mining Firm in Post-authoritarian Indonesia*. Berkley, CA: University of California Press.

Welker, Marina, Damani J. Partridge, and Rebecca Hardin. 2011. "Corporate Lives: New Perspectives on the Social Life of the Corporate Form." *Current Anthropology* 52(3): 3–16.

Weum, Inger Johanne, and Helene Mohagen. 2015. "Land-for-land rapportering i Norge: casestudier av land-for-land rapportene til Norsk Hydro, DNO og Statoil" [Country-by-country reporting in Norway: Case studies of country-by-country reporting by Norsk Hydro, DNO, and Statoil]. Master's thesis, NHH, Bergen. Available online: http://hdl.handle.net/11250/2382953.

Conclusion
Inactive State Ownership and the Nordic Model Recast as "Values"
Ståle Knudsen

In the introduction, we posed a number of questions about the relationship between the state, the Nordic model, and corporate responsibility. We asked whether state-owned or parastatal energy and extraction companies can pursue and implement corporate ethics by governance techniques that do not rely on and promote market rule, commodification, and privatization. We considered whether state entities take an active role in shaping the corporate social responsibility (CSR) of transnational corporations (TNCs), be it in their country of origin or operation. We questioned the extent to which the Nordic model actually travels with corporations when they operate abroad, even when the corporations are wholly or partly state owned. Underlying these concerns is the question whether CSR can be claimed "from below."

In addressing these questions, the authors have explored the relationship between transnational corporate capitalism, the Nordic model of welfare capitalism, and state ownership, between global diversification and notions about Norway as the "humanitarian superpower." The case studies do not provide any univocal answer, but two main tendencies can be teased out from the multifaceted stories told in this book. First, the Norwegian state is increasingly an inactive owner and otherwise refrains from sanctioning Norwegian corporations, which on the international scene—but also increasingly at home (see chapters 9 and 11)—are largely left to operate as any other TNCs. Second, in most contexts related to the international operation of TNCs based in Norway, the Nordic model is recast as a set of values, ignoring the history of contest through which it emerged and the institutional mechanism that came to characterize it. The main driver of these tendencies is the way the Norwegian economy has become increasingly integrated in the international economy in the neoliberal age.

The agenda of this book has not been to explore CSR in and of itself. Rather, the focus on CSR can be seen as a prism through which we can understand relations between states, capital, globalization, and corporate responsibility. In the introduction we argued for a more nuanced thinking about the dynamics between neoliberalism, governance techniques, and (traveling) models. The Norwegian case shows us the limits of conventional thinking about CSR as a neoliberal technology. What we are seeing here, we suggest, is not some ineluctable impulse of global capital driving Norwegian energy companies abroad according to a neo-Marxist rendering of the logic of transnational capital to escape the confines of the state and vanquish national regulation (e.g., Harvey 2005). Rather, internationalization of Norwegian corporations was a result of Norway's position/role in the global economy, which is characterized by surplus capital based on a prudently managed and technologically advanced natural-resource-based economy and an interest in maintaining an open economy. The state encouraged Norwegian state capital to internationalize through restructuring (read corporatize, privatize). This was matched with the state's own global ambitions as a humanitarian superpower, and the internationalization of capital at times mobilized a national identity as "Norwegian" as a key asset in achieving global expansion.

While internationalization—not a policy shift toward neoliberalism—was the main driver for Norwegian TNCs to seek opportunities abroad, once this process had got going, the way the corporations engaged with CSR was very much shaped by the international discourse about the CSR that they encountered. When we take a closer look, as Maraire and Hugøy do in chapter 2, at the development of the business concept of CSR in Norway, we see how it has evolved from a more locally embedded paradigm (and practice) informed by social values and expectations inherent in the Norwegian concept, *samfunnsansvar* (societal responsibility), to an agenda that has become increasingly aligned with international trends: with time evolving from "philanthropy" through "risk management" to "value creation."

It has been a political choice by Norwegian governments to let (partially) state-owned corporations play to the international tune.

Adapting to globalization, representatives of the Norwegian state have transferred power to corporate management and boards. In most cases, corporate boards are left to manage their organizations as any other TNC, pursing shareholder value and, in place of the Nordic model, latching on to international standards and frameworks for corporate responsibility, be it "sustainability," "environmental, social, and governance" (ESG), or "Sustainable Development Goals" (SDGs). Governments could have chosen to challenge the international framework and the international working of capital but have instead prioritized international business opportunities, partly to support the Norwegian state's international humanitarian ambitions. The reluctance of the Norwegian government to interfere in the operations and priorities of the corporations it (partially) owns is clearly demonstrated by the way state ownership enacted at arm's length gives Norsk Hydro license to operate as any other TNC in Brazil, focusing on shareholder value and mending problems by invoking the internationally acknowledged tool and language of CSR (chapter 4). It is also visible in the government's reluctance to interfere in Equinor's controversial tar sands and fracking operations in North America (Borchgrevink 2019: 415), and in the government's increasing unwillingness to use allocation of oil and gas licenses as a tool to constrain or punish unethical or problematic conduct of corporations (see chapters 9 and 11). Thus, the state's expectation that the state-owned corporations will be "ambassadors" for Norway abroad is only very vaguely expressed, and in practice the state has accepted that Norwegian state capitalism abroad largely plays to the tune of international capitalism, not to the Nordic model.

In the introduction, we suggested that the Nordic model could be considered one particular "economic-institutional ensemble" (Foucault 2008), characterized by institutional mechanisms such as the welfare state and the tripartite coordination between employers, unions, and the state. The case studies in this book give a mixed picture of the extent to which Norwegian TNCs have tried to transfer the model to its operations abroad. When the Nordic model, or elements of it, is made to travel by the corporations, the major aim has been to set up institutional frameworks that would facilitate long-term operational stability and success. In their factory in China, Norsk Hydro successfully mobilized management techniques informed by Norwegian models (chapter 5), yet only when there was a good business case for it. However, in neither this case nor in Equinor's promotion of a union in Tanzania (chapter 8) was the Nordic model part of the design or strategy from the outset. Rather, the corporations imported certain "Nordic elements," made the model travel, only when they confronted particular challenges. In short, the Nordic model was mobilized only when expedient.

What we have seen then is that piecemeal adoption of the Nordic model occurs, but the major trend runs the opposite way: Norwegian TNCs operate as "any other TNCs" on the global scene. This is clearly demonstrated in studies of Equinor's approach to the exploitation of tar sands in Alberta, Canada. In the extreme neoliberal political environment of pre-Trudeau Canada, corporations were given wide leverage for extractive operations, creating conditions under which corporations employed the tools of CSR, stakeholder management, and consultations away from and in place of the state. As governance was to a large extent delegated to industry, Wanvik (2016: 518) argues, Equinor became "an integral part of the new governance structure of Canada through their pragmatic quest for a social licence [sic] to operate." With an extremely low royalty rate, the government's "dependency on natural resource revenues lead [sic] directly to Northern Albertan's [sic] dependencies on CSR initiatives" (Gross 2019: 224). For instance, Equinor funded and operated in Conklin, Alberta, an E-learning center as well as a Local Opportunity Centre, providing, according to Equinor's 2012 sustainability report, "an innovative training and educational resource" used by more than twelve hundred individuals and contractors in 2012 (Gross 2019: 219). Thus, in the case of Alberta we see unfolding the kind of neoliberal CSR often described and criticized by anthropologists, the kind of CSR that bypasses the state and claims "a kind of collective moral guardianship over people" (Rajak 2011: 55). Equinor seemingly made no claim to its approach in Alberta being "Nordic."

Most of the studies in this collection show that, when Norwegian state capital is set to work abroad, there is not much "Nordic" left beyond the state's expectation that these corporations adhere to the highest international standards. There is scant evidence for CSR being used as a major channel or vehicle for the export of the Nordic model. What we do see, however, is the Nordic model recast as being first and foremost about values rather than institutional mechanisms. This matches well with current trends in corporate speak, which tend to accentuate "purpose" and "our values." We may, of course, question whether this emphasis on values casts a veil that disguises the actual institutional mechanisms at work.

Underlying much of Norway's international engagement is the assumption that "Norwegian values" should be the template for (or are consistent with the ideal form of) universal human rights. This is one version of the pervasive idea in Norway that "we do it better" (e.g., "our extraction of oil and gas is cleaner than others") (see Sæther 2017: 235, 319; Sætre 2009: 225). Thus, in the promotion of the Norwegian "way" internationally, the sociological understanding of the Nordic model—with tripartite negotiations, welfare state, and so forth—is glossed over, and the model is reborn as resting on certain values (trust, consensus, gender balance, and egalitarianism) that should ideally be universal. The ownership policy's support for global standards and reporting framework is consistent with this, as is the development policy.

The Norwegian state's approach to international relations has developed so "that the meaning of interest has broadened to include the concept of value and idealism" (Stokke 2012: 227). Norway has engaged in a specific kind of "value diplomacy" (Stokke 2012). It is the assumed Norwegian qua universal values that Norway seeks to export, not the Nordic tripartite organizational model. A cynical reading would be that Norwegian humanitarian diplomacy has not so much to do with the Nordic model but more with Norway's desired standing, impact, and reputation internationally.

Nordic energy and extraction companies sometimes deploy the "Nordic model" as a resource in their operations and interactions abroad. Such self-representations are mobilized as part of corporate narratives of sustainability and responsibility, which in themselves constitute key discursive assets in securing national contracts and social consent to land and resources overseas. But they are a double-edged sword, at the sharp end of which companies often find themselves when they are held to account for failing to meet the very standards they claim to export (chapter 4; for how this played out for Equinor in Brazil, see Borchgrevink 2019: 379–80).

While the effects of Norway's quest to be recognized as a "humanitarian superpower" are intangible, they do have some real and concrete implications for how Norwegian corporations proceed abroad. In 2005, the leading Norwegian daily reported that "the internationalization of the oil industry seems to determine where Norway has new embassies."[1] Business and aid/peace/foreign diplomacy are sometimes connected, but not everywhere: the connection is crucial for Equinor's involvement in Tanzania (chapters 7 and 8; Borchgrevink 2019: 381), while the Norwegian embassy in Ankara only learned through news media that Equinor had decided to invest in Turkey in 2016. Hydro's operations in Brazil were impacted in unforeseen ways by the Norwegian government's critique of Brazil's rainforest policies, as I detail in chapter 4.

The most significant coupling between the pursuit of humanitarian aims and Norwegian capital abroad has been the aid program, Oil for Development, administered by the Norwegian Directorate for Development Cooperation (Norad) and with an annual budget of approximately 20 million euros. Until it was recently discontinued, the program's ambition was to work for "poverty reduction through responsible management of petroleum resources" by supporting "capacity development through institutional collaboration."[2] While for decades Norwegian aid through Norad was not indexed to Norwegian business interests, this seemed to change around 2000. A study of the program argues that "it seems evident that several of the countries in Africa where Norwegian oil interests are present, primarily through [Equinor's] engagement, are also important aid recipient countries. Many countries have also experienced an increase in aid in periods when the Norwegian petroleum interests have appeared strong" (Tollaksen 2017).

The case studies in this book show that neither the Nordic model and the state's "expectations" toward Norwegian corporations nor the international institutional framework nor the way capital circulates globally explain the way the Norwegian corporations handle ethics abroad. There is considerable variation across the case studies: from Statkraft's work in Turkey (chapter 10), which is informed by international standards, to the Brazilian state dictating how Equinor should administer CSR (chapter 6). In Tanzania, Equinor, on the one hand, tenuously replicated the Nordic tripartite model when supporting the creation of a union branch (albeit without perhaps the most important actor, the state; see chapter 8); on the other hand, they somewhat awkwardly adapted to local expectations when designing its CSR program (chapter 7).

It goes without saying that bilateral relations cultivated and maintained by the Norwegian state with other states vary considerably, as the contributions in this book demonstrate. As Lange shows in chapter 8, the long history of donor-recipient relations between Norway and Tanzania is a key factor in the relationship between Equinor and the Tanzanian government as it plays out today. Juxtaposed with this, in Strønen's contribution (chapter 6), we find the same company pursuing divergent practices of CSR to very different effect in Brazil, where the legacies of neocolonial aid relations are absent. The variegated local unfolding of particular projects shows that even under neoliberal international capitalism local actors maintain significant agency in shaping and domesticating the way in which the corporations enact CSR.

Although state ownership and a Nordic background seem to give gentle nudges toward responsible business, these are no guarantees that corporations will act responsibly. So long as state capital is set to work in a corporate form and mandated to pursue profit, business logic will ultimately trump other concerns. This applies even to the fully state-owned corporation, Statkraft, which has been involved in various forms of tax planning. They avoided paying income tax on dividends to Albania by placing the mother company of their Albanian operations in the Netherlands (Hanssen and Haltbrekken 2014: 57).[3]

An exaggerated focus among corporations, governments, and scholars on CSR, sustainability, SDGs, and ESG can distract from more significant and fundamental ways that TNCs should be held responsible. Reporting, standards, telling stories, and so forth retain importance even as the business world and governance focus is shifting from CSR to new languages and mechanisms that—like CSR—come with nonbinding rules. Thus, a wider take on corporate responsibility should include how corporations are framed by and relate to rules, regulations, and taxation, which, ultimately, are the only mechanisms that can assure that TNCs act responsibly and provide benefits for society wherever they operate. Such regulations may be national, or preferably international. Successive Norwegian governments have striven to have the Nordic model "replicated" at a global level, but given the minimal influence that, for example, the UN Global Compact or OECD guiding principles for responsible business conduct really has on corporations (chapter 11; see also Welker 2009: 145; Welker 2014: 15; Orock 2013; Scholz and Vitols 2019: 239), this amounts to little relative to the power wielded by the TNCs. As seen in some case studies here (chapters 10 and 11), few current international frameworks are binding, and these largely have little effect. The ongoing process to create supranational regulations in the European Union is possibly one exception; another is the recent international agreement on a minimum 15 percent corporate tax, which is potentially more important than all CSR initiatives in total when it comes to TNCs' contribution to society.

As long as international regulations remain incapable of constraining TNCs, mechanisms to restrict the harmful effects of their activities remain equally hamstrung—limited to national laws and regulations, international nonbinding standards and conventions, and, not least, reputation—shame and blame—which very much depends upon public opinion and, ultimately, the news media. The Norwegian public's expectations may have a more significant impact on the behavior and actions of the Norwegian TNCs than the "expectations" expressed by the Norwegian state. One of the Turkish CSR managers of Statkraft told us that "if it emerged in Turkish newspapers that Statkraft does not treat local people decently, this can potentially explode in Norwegian newspapers, which may have adverse consequences for the corporation." Other case studies in this book (chapters 4, 6, 8) as well as investigative books by journalists (Sæther 2017; Borchgrevink 2019; Sætre 2009) report similar concerns. Nevertheless, it is challenging for journalists to report on Norwegian extractive and energy corporations abroad (Baumberger and Slaatta 2011), and the news media fail to report on important environmental consequences of Equinor's operations abroad (such as flaring in Nigeria) (Sæther 2017: 250).

Still, investigate journalists have published on various problematic aspects of the corporations covered in this book. In 2020, the major Norwegian business daily *Dagens Næringsliv* ran a long story about how Equinor, through bad management and flimsy handling of investments and assets, lost USD$20 billion in the United States before pulling out, raising concerns about whether the international adventure of Equinor actually is subsidized by operations back home (and then, in effect, by the Norwegian society).[4] A decade before this, another story about Equinor made the headlines in Norway. Angola was Equinor's economic success story abroad. But operating in a corrupt country also implied that the corporation paid signature bonuses (in total USD$0.4 billion) that were pocketed by the country's leaders, and USD$40 million in CSR support to an Angolan research center (Sætre 2009: 224–30; Borchgrevink 2019: 383–86).

As indicated in the introduction ("Corrupt Countries Line up for Statoil"), scandals exposed in the media can be an important driver for changes in state policies, and the management of corporate identity and reputation is a major concern for many corporations, especially the largest ones. That Norwegian businesspeople in the United Arab Emirates pay attention to the *VG* rule: namely, that what one does abroad must be able to withstand publicity in the Norwegian tabloid *VG* (Agnese Cimdina, personal communication); that Equinor is careful to respond "to the Norwegian society's demand for openness and information" (chapter 9) while also trying to mold the wider discourse about oil, gas, climate change, and the economy that informs the operational space of Equinor (see Sæther 2017) may testify a preoccupation with corporate reputation. At the end of the day, it is the Norwegian TNCs' reputation with those back home in Norway, rather than with "host" governments or communities in operation sites, that counts most. It is primarily in the eyes of the Norwegian public that the Norwegian societal model is considered relevant. But here also the Nordic model is increasingly equated with values (such as human rights) rather than institutional mechanisms.

In this book we have taken an ambivalent approach to CSR. Even as we researched in the field, the corporations themselves, the relevant entities of the Norwegian state, and the public debate moved away from the concept toward new languages and tools, especially "sustainability" and ESG. As I write this in June 2022, CSR is absent from the home pages of the corporations discussed in this book, while "sustainability" figures prominently (though not on DNO's home page). However, the aim of this book was never to contribute to narrow academic debates about CSR. Rather it was a prism through which to explore relations between states, capital, corporations, ethics, and the international economy. And therefore we focused as much on the Nordic model, with which CSR has only a tenuous relation. While the Nordic background is, on the one hand, considered by many in the corporations a mandate for being responsible when managing projects abroad, on the other hand, the "CSR" people with whom we interacted preferred to label their field "sustainability" (Equinor) or "environmental and social management" (Statkraft). CSR is not only a boundary object but also one of several flexibly overlapping concepts that all somehow speak to the same concern: corporate responsibilities. And, in this respect, I believe that our findings have generic relevance: whether they relate to CSR, ESG, or SDGs, corporations are primarily concerned about risk and reputation and are prepared and able to spend more resources than other actors to impact both reporting (and reporting regimes) and news media. While they promote transparency, they also subtly manage what is and what is not available in the public domain (Barry 2013; Appel 2019). This is especially the case for TNCs.

There is an important yet little recognized difference between "classical" CSR and the new concerns about sustainability. While the former was either a continuation of philanthropy with a new label or an approach directed primarily at the immediate impacts of corporations, such as affected communities and the surrounding environment, now, in the "climate conscious" age we have entered, corporations increasingly consider, and are expected to consider, global challenges. This concern about global sustainability makes it more demanding, but also easier for the corporations. Any corporation can document that they contribute to at least some of the SDGs, which makes it more difficult to specify relative to what a corporation should be held to account. When it was primarily about CSR, it was easier to define the constituency (although that could also be contested). For sustainability, there is less clarity.[5]

As with CSR, sustainability policies of corporations can be considered responses to critiques and demands from outside, but also to demands from concerned professionals within the corporations. We found many of our interlocutors in the corporations to be genuinely concerned about sustainability issues, and some people we have met make a real difference. One recent study found that energy elites in Norway "re-imagined energy futures and accordingly reoriented their careers" away from oil and gas (Rauter 2022: 1). Yet, "sustainability speak" seems to have become ubiquitous chatter in all kinds of businesses, and the incantation "sustainability is good for business" the new mantra. It is likely so widespread and so celebrated by professionals because it seemingly resolves the dilemma or tension between profit and ethics. You can earn (a lot of) money, and still feel good about it. The claim that "the businesses that are serious about sustainability do better (in the long run)" has advanced to become a taken-for-granted truth but also a rallying call, a statement, an encouragement. There are certainly clear affinities here with the "business case for CSR" (Welker 2014), but the statement "sustainability is good for business" makes an even bigger claim: it is in effect a defense of capitalism as a system. Thus, any anthropological take on this dynamic—Where does this idea come from? How does it operate? What effects does it have?—should be prepared to consider the larger "economic-institutional ensemble" in which it operates. One should also be reminded that it is important to analytically distinguish individual motivation and ethics of professionals in corporations from the real logics of corporate management, capital, and governance.

For anthropologists, it can be difficult to keep track of what is happening in and around the corporate world. On the other hand, we are good at being in the middle of things. But the kinds of projects we need for tracing the ways corporations handle sustainability, guided by the invocation "sustainability is good for business," are particularly demanding (see chapter 1), as they will usually involve multisited fieldwork, require the negotiation of access to risk-averse corporations, and demand considerable resources (for travels, attendance fees, etc.). Corporations have, to a large extent, the power to steer our research: We never received any reply from and were unable to interact with DNO management; Equinor were happy that we, after "gentle encouragement" from them, ended up with a case study in Brazil and not Venezuela; Statkraft closed their larger and more challenging project in Turkey to us on "safety grounds." This goes to show how little leverage researchers have relative to corporations and is a sharp reminder of where power rests. Even in the relatively egalitarian Norwegian context, where research is largely funded by the state and social distance between researchers and corporate professionals is short, research is demanding. We end this book with a note on the importance of available research funds "with no strings attached" and the critical assessment of the impact of externally imposed ethics rules (such as GDPR in Europe) on how we can go about studying corporations. With the resources corporations can muster, rigid ethics rules not well adapted to the practice of anthropology can easily become a tool for legitimizing further restrictions on how we can access and write about corporations.

Ståle Knudsen is professor in the Department of Social Anthropology, University of Bergen, Norway. He was leader of the project, Energethics (2015–19), from which this book emerges. Knudsen has, since the early 1990s, done ethnographic fieldwork in Turkey, and his publications include the monograph *Fisheries in Modernizing Turkey* (Berghahn, 2009).

Notes

1. "Vest-Afrika—Norsk oljekoloni: Oljeselskapene ønsker mer hjelp fra UD" [West Africa—Norwegian oil colony: Oil corporations requests more help from the Foreign Ministry], *Aftenposten*, 3 March 2005.
2. Retrieved 27 May 2022 from https://www.norad.no/en/front/thematic-areas/oil-for-development/oil-for-development-programme/'.
3. I have repeatedly asked our contacts in Statkraft whether their subsidiaries in Turkey pay tax to Turkish authorities, and how much. I have never received an answer.
4. "De hemmelige Equinor-rapportene" [The secret Equinor reports], *DN Magasinet*, 6 May 2020.
5. For ESG, though, the "constituency" is the corporation itself: ESG is about how environmental, social, and governance risks may affect the corporation itself. It is part of the business model.

References

Appel, Hannah. 2019. *The Licit Life of Capitalism: US Oil in the Equatorial Guinea*. Durham, NC: Duke University Press.
Barry, Andrew. 2013. *Material Politics: Disputes along the Pipeline*. Chichester: Wiley Blackwell.

Baumberger, Berit E., and Tore Slaatta. 2011. "Norsk Oljejournalistikk—Statoils Utenlandsvirksomhet som Transnasjonalt Nyhetsbeite" [Norwegian oil journalism—Statoil's foreign activities as transnational news field]. *Norsk Medietidsskrift* 18(1): 41–60.

Borchgrevink, Aage Storm. 2019. *Giganten: Fra Statoil til Equinor; Historien om selskapet som forandret Norge* [The Giant: The story about the company that transformed Norway]. Oslo: Kagge Forlag.

Foucault, Michael. 2008. *The Birth of Biopolitics: Lectures at the Collège de France 1978–1979.* Translated by Graham Burchell. Basingstoke: Palgrave.

Gross, Lena. 2019. "The Oil Sands Industry as Magnifier of Inequality: Tales of Land, Labour, Belonging, and Refusal in Northern Alberta, Canada." PhD dissertation, University of Oslo.

Hanssen, Thomas, and Tommy Haltbrekken. 2014. "Skatteplanlegging i Multinasjonale Selskap: En Analyse av Statkraft og Implikasjoner av den nye Norske Fradragsbegrensningsregelen" [Tax planning in multinational companies: An analysis of Statkraft and Implications of the new Norwegian tax deduction rule]. Master's thesis, NHH Norwegian School of Economics.

Harvey, David. 2005. *A Brief History of Neoliberalism.* Oxford: Oxford University Press.

Orock, Rogers Tabe Egbe. 2013. "Less-Told Stories about Corporate Globalization: Transnational Corporations and CSR as the Politics of (Ir)responsibility in Africa." *Dialectical Anthropology* 37: 27–50.

Rajak, Dinah. 2011. *In Good Company: An Anatomy of Corporate Social Responsibility.* Stanford, CA: Stanford University Press.

Rauter, Anna R. K. K. 2022. "Elite Energy Transitions: Leaders and Experts Promoting Renewable Energy Futures in Norway." *Energy Research and Social Science* 88.

Scholz, Robert, and Sigurt Vitols. 2019. "Board-Level Codetermination: A Driving Force for Corporate Social Responsibility in German Companies?" *European Journal of Industrial Relations* 25(3): 233–46.

Stokke, Kristian. 2012. "Peace-Building as Small State Foreign Policy: Norway's Peace Engagement in a Changing International Context." *International Studies* 49 (3&4): 207–31. https://doi.org/10.1177/0020881714532334

Sæther, Anne Karin. 2017. *De beste intensjoner: Oljelandet i klimakampen* [The best of intentions: The oil nation in the climate struggle]. Oslo: Cappelen Damm AS.

Sætre, Simen. 2009. *Petromania. En reise gjennom verdens rikeste oljeland for å finne ut hva pengene gjør med oss* [Petromania. A journey through the world's richest oil country to find what the money does to us]. Oslo: J. M. Stenersens Forlag.

Tollaksen, Tor Gunnar. 2017. "Olje for utvikling—hånd i hånd med norske oljeinteresser?" [Oil for development—hand in hand with Norwegian oil interests?]. MA thesis, University of Stavanger.

Wanvik, Tarje I. 2016. "Governance Transformed into Corporate Social Responsibility (CSR): New Governance Innovations in the Canadian Oil Sands." *Extractive Industries and Society* 3: 517–26.

Welker, Marina. 2009. "'Corporate Security Begins in the Community': Mining, the Corporate Responsibility Industry and Environmental Advocacy in Indonesia." *Cultural Anthropology* 21(1): 142–79.

———. 2014. *Enacting the Corporation: An American Mining Firm in Post-authoritarian Indonesia.* Berkeley: University of California Press.

INDEX

Albania, 277, 328
Alberta, 325
Ali, Sumaya Jirde, 82
Alta power plant, 268
aluminum, 5, 95–96, 115, 119, 124–25
Alunorte, 85, 115, 125–29
AMA PEA FOCO, 176, 179
  and CSR, 168–69
  and CSR, 180–84
  and Developing Countries, 168
  and Fishers, 171
  and marginalization, 178–80
  and oil and gas industry, 174
  and oil, 171
  and poverty, 179
  and Worker's Party (PPT), 173
Andersen, Dag Terje (Minister of Trade and Industry, Norway), 79
Angola, 202, 224, 226, 329
ANT (actor network theory), 139, 152–55
Arendals Fossekompani, 93–109, 111
audit, 4, 11, 21
authoritarian
  regime, 158
  state, 137
  ideology, 143

Barents Sea, 248
Barzani, Nechirvan, 304
bærekraft (sustainability) 83
Birkeland, Kristian, 95, 117
Bolsonaro, Jair, 170
boundary object, 4, 66–67, 71, 84, 330
Brandtzæg, Svein (Norsk Hydro CEO)

Brazil, 5, 18, 27–28, 52, 115–18, 121, 124–30, 145, 163–92, 196, 198–99, 208, 211, 225, 324, 326–27, 332
BP (British Petroleum), 24, 129
business case. *See also* CSR, Nordic model
  for gender equality, 194–95,
  for supporting unions, 221, 234–35
  for development, 197
business conventions, 43, 47–48

Çakıt hydroelectric power plant, 277
Campos basin, 163–5, 171–172
Campos dos Goytacazes, 163
Canada, 18, 325
capacity building, 29, 219, 228–34, 237, 309
Çetin power plant, 268, 277
Chama Cha Mapinduzi (CCM, Party of the Revolution, Tanzania), 227
charitable giving, 281
Chevron, 164
Chile, 275
China, 7, 11, 25, 203, 303
  audits, 11
  Norsk Hydro in China, 137–39, 141, 146–58, 162
  state capital, 23,
civil society organizations: 72, 168, 196, 211, 221, 229, 232, 235
collaboration, 67, 70, 72, 142, 146, 150, 152–56
collective bargaining, 232–35, 238, 312,
company boards, 5, 14, 96, 122, 127–28, 147, 156, 182–83, 200,

222, 227–29, 236, 239, 271–72, 286, 288, 300, 302, 304
compliance (with laws and regulations), 183–87, 199, 210, 312, 316
CONAMA, 169
Confederation of Norwegian Enterprise (Næringslivets Hovedorganisasjon, NHO), 74, 232
Conservative Party (Norway), 15, 69, 118, 128, 249
conventions (international-), 4, 21, 42, 200, 224, 272, 314, 328
corporate
　ethics, 4, 6, 42, 322
　democracy, (*bedriftsdemokrati*), 123, 222
　governance, 75, 77, 79, 82, 87n5, 87n10, 120, 122, 140
　responsibility, 2–4, 17, 67, 75, 79, 120, 273, 275, 281, 286, 322–24, 328
　scandals, 18–19, 75, 85, 115, 125–28, 274, 329
　time, 49, 59
corporations
　as moral guardians, 1, 6, 325
　as proxy states, 299
corporatization, 15–16, 24, 118, 269, 271
　struggle over, 139–42
corruption, 19, 21, 52, 126–27, 129, 168, 177, 185, 226, 276, 286, 305, 314, 317n1, 330
Covid-19, 70, 73, 245, 261
　crisis package, 258
CSR, 142–147, 153, 158, 253–55. *See also* corporate ethics, corporate responsibility, *samfunnsansvar*
　adoption by Norsk Hydro, 120–22, 144–46
　business case for, 1, 3, 20–21, 182, 331
　"explicit," 94, 109–10, 144–45, 158
　history and theory of, 3–5, 6, 12, 27, 42, 56, 60n3, 63–66, 93–94, 101, 104–5, 107, 109–10, 140–41, 145, 165–70, 176, 185, 194–95, 197–99, 210, 222–23, 255, 269–70, 281, 295–99, 323
　"implicit," 94, 138–139, 144, 158, 170, 185
　multivalent character of, 299
　and neoliberalization/as neoliberal governance technique, 3–4, 42, 140, 299, 323, 325
　Norwegian state's approach to, 19–21, 74–77, 79–85, 141, 269, 272–73, 276,
cultural encounters, 137–139, 153, 157

Daish (ISIS), 303
democracy, 6, 69, 123, 142–44, 147–150, 156–57, 222, 224, 232, 310
democratic, 137, 138, 142, 144, 147, 150, 155
developing countries, 168, 236, 273–74
development aid, 22, 24–25, 122, 200, 228–29, 238, 326–27
　importance of, 55, 58, 63–65, 73–77, 79–85, 196, 203, 250, 252, 274–76, 278, 284–87, 312–313
DNO (Det norske oljeselskap), 5, 29, 295–21, 331
dugnad (voluntary work), 67, 70–71
Duhok, 296, 304, 308

"economic-institutional ensembles," 9, 20, 270. *See also* Foucault
egalitarianism, 14, 67, 70–72, 92–93, 130, 255, 326
embeddedness of capital, 98–101, 117, 122–24, 147, 257, 263
entrepreneurship, 205–6
environmental NGOs, 53, 54, 251
environmental, social, and governance (ESG), 4, 6, 66, 110, 324, 328, 330, 332n5
Equinor Book, 202–203
environmental impact assessments (EIA), 169, 202, 213n2
environmental and social management (ESM), 271, 273, 276, 278, 285, 330

Erbil, 296, 303–4, 315
ethnographic extended case, 137
EU taxonomy for sustainable activities, 66
European Union (EU), 236, 328
European Works Council (EWC), 236,
"extreme northern periphery," 244
Exxon, 199
Eyde, Sam, 95–96, 111n5, 112n8, 117

fertilizer production, 119
Filho, Sarney (Brazilian minister), 128–29
Finnmark (county), 244, 248–50, 256–57, 262–63
fishermen's colonies, 178
fishers, 171–72
Fjær, Unni, 246
foreign direct investment (FDI), 23, 76–77
Freire, Paulo, 174
follow-on research, 251
Foucault, Michael, 8–10, 270, 324

gender, 69, 163, 179, 193–218, 221, 224
gift economy, 255, 281
Gjølberg, Maria, 63–64, 75, 165–66
Global Compact, 21, 42, 81, 197, 222, 272, 275, 328
Global Competitiveness Index, 295
global framework agreement, 224, 232, 236
Global Reporting Initiative (GRI), 21, 29, 42, 81–82, 169, 200, 270, 272, 274, 284–87, 289–90, 314
Global Work Council, 221, 236
Goliat field, 264n3
Government Pension Fund Global ("Oil Fund"), 5, 23–24, 31n6, 51, 300
Greenpeace, 53
Grønhaug, Reidar, 110

Hammerfest municipality, 251
Harvey, David, 8–9
Helgesen, Vidar, 128
Heroes of Tomorrow, 193, 205–6, 208, 264n2, 265n12

Herøya, 144, 148–152, 156–157
high-fidelity models, 148, 155
Hilson, Gavin, 168
Holte, Johan B., 124, 144, 147
human rights, 25, 145, 203, 224, 273, 286, 325, 330
humanitarian superpower (Norway as), 2, 19, 22–25, 79, 158, 322–24, 326–27
hybrid, 138–139, 142, 150, 152–153, 157
Hydro. See Norsk Hydro
hydro(electric) power, 5, 16, 22, 24, 49, 92, 94–95, 97, 103, 112n8, 268–94
Hydro model, 138, 158

IBAMA (Brazilian Institute of Environment and Renewable Natural Resources), 128, 164, 173, 174–76, 185, 187, 188n2, 198
"income-political settlements" (inntektspolitiske oppgjør), 14, 230, 237
India, 19, 122, 144
Industrial Democracy Law of 1973 (Norway), 142, 232
Industrial Democracy Program of 1962 (Norway), 123, 143–44
IndustriAll, 226
Industri Energi, 220, 222, 224, 226, 230–31, 233, 236, 238, 312
infrastructure, 244–45, 248, 254, 257, 259, 263
international companies. See transnational corporations
International Finance Corporation (IFC), 22, 270, 274–79, 284–85, 289–90
ILO (International Labor Organization 236–37
  core convention, 21, 200, 224, 272, 314
Isaksen, Torbjørn Røe (minister of trade and industry, Norway), 127–28
Istanbul, 268

Jacobsen, Alf E. (major of Hammerfest), 247

Jagland, Thorbjørn (prime minister, Norway), 24
Johan Castberg (oil field), 256

Kargı, 277–79, 282–83, 285, 287
Kızılırmak (river), 278, 282
KOMPAKT, 19
Kurdistan Region of Iraq, 297, 301–10
Kurdistan Regional Government (KRG), 296, 302–4, 306, 308–10, 315

labor, 25, 99, 101, 103, 105–6, 108–9, 123, 143, 178, 220, 222, 226, 311
  movements, 14, 107, 219
  regulations, 166, 225, 311,
  rights, 42, 101, 103, 179, 223–24, 227, 312–315,
  strikes, 25, 236, 311,
Labor Party (Norway), 15, 24, 11n4, 118, 224, 256
labor unions, 7, 13–14, 17, 20, 25, 68, 70, 117, 121, 123, 142, 147, 152, 156, 160n10, 219–39, 265n8, 281, 296, 312, 315. *See also* collective bargaining, Industry Energi, IndustyAll, National Union of Mine and Energy Workers (NUMET), Trade Union Congress of Tanzania (TUCTA)
  representative at corporate level, 152, 223, 227, 271
Lama, Dalai, 25
Laos, 272, 276
legitimacy to operate, 314
Leira, Torkjell, 126, 128
license to operate, 172, 183, 193–99, 202–5, 209, 286, 311, 313–16, 324
Listhaug, Sylvi (minister of petroleum and energy, 257
LO (Landsorganisasjonen i Norge, Norwegian confederation of trade unions), 14, 69–70, 82, 121, 147, 222, 236, 265n8
local content, 22, 29, 45, 201–2, 209, 256, 263, 265n11, 304
London, 48

low-fidelity models, 148, 155
LNG (liquefied natural gas), 195, 212, 221, 226, 244–51, 256, 259–60, 262
Lula (Luiz Inácio Lula da Silva), 173
Lund, Helge (Equinor CEO), 54

Management (business)
  American, 140, 143, 149
  and Nordic model, 137, 142–43, 150–58
  by objectives (*målstyring*), 15, 139–40
managerialism, 7, 11
material expectations, 250
materiality assessment, 286. *See also* standards, GRI
Matten, Dirk, 170, 185
Mazzucato, Mariana 7
Mæland, Monica (minister of trade and industry), 21, 273
Mendes, Chico, 173
Menstad battle, 117
Merry, Sally, 270
Millennium development goals (MDGs), 197
mining, 201, 207, 227
Ministry of Foreign Affairs (Norway), 19, 80, 304
Ministry of Trade and Industry (Norway), 18, 81, 272
Moon, Christopher J., 170, 185
Mossavar-Rahmani. Bijan, 5, 300–1, 305
Multinational corporations/companies (MNCs), 21, 44, 193–95, 198, 210, 219, 222–23, 232, 236, 272, 298–99, 309, 312. *See also* transnational corporations
multisited ethnography, 29, 40–41, 43–45, 57–58, 137, 221, 269, 273, 288, 331

Nader, Laura, 43
narrative, 122, 127, 252–53, 260. *See also* stakeholder-in corporate stories
National Contact Point for Responsible Business (OECD), 302, 312

National Natural Gas Policy Tanzania, 201–3
national oil companies (NOCs), 16, 43, 195, 199, 219, 223
National Union of Mine and Energy Workers (NUMET), 228–38
neoliberalism, 4, 11, 15–16, 147, 299, 303, 323, 325, 327
  and CSR, 1, 3, 4, 44, 64, 93, 140, 185, 325
  and the state, 3–6, 298
  theories of, 7–12, 270
neoliberal governance (techniques), 1, 3, 6, 8–12, 44, 270, 288, 296, 323
Nepal, 274
news media, 29–30, 64, 69–70, 73–74, 78, 207, 260, 298, 306, 326, 328–30
Nobel Price, 24–25
Nonnini, Donald, 11
Norad (the Norwegian Directorate for Development Cooperation), 236, 327
Nordic model, 2, 9, 12–14, 17, 116, 123, 129–31, 186, 219–20, 281, 290, 296, 316–17, 322, 324–28. *See also* Norwegian model
  business case for, 324
  and CSR, 20, 141, 153–54, 158, 296
  export of, 137–139, 147, 156, 158, 325 (*see also* Norwegian model)
  history of, 13–14, 25–26
  in India, 19, 122, 144
  traveling, 26, 322
  tripartite collaboration, 70, 142, 144, 219 (*see also* "income-political settlements")
  values, 92, 124, 126, 130, 138–39, 144–47, 151, 155–58, 323, 326, 330
  welfare model, 75, 144, 152
  of work and organization, 137–39, 141–44, 147–49
Nordkapp municipality, 256–57, 263
Norfund (Norway's Development Finance Institution), 273–74
Norsk Hydro, ix, 5, 16, 19, 23–24, 68, 85, 93, 95, 115–31, 137–39, 141–50, 152–59, 186, 324

Normann, Magne, 304
Norwegian confederation of trade unions. *See* LO
Norwegian model, 14, 21, 121, 124, 126, 130, 137–39, 142–44, 147, 150–52, 155–58, 219–25, 227, 230–32, 235–38
Norwegian Parliament. *See* Stortinget
Norwegian Water Resources and Energy Directorate (NVE), 271
Norwegian Work Environment Act, 115
"null hypothesis," 298
Næss, Marianne Sivertsen (major of Hammerfest), 261

OECD guidelines for responsible business conduct, 21, 42, 72, 77, 87n5, 200, 272, 275, 312, 315, 318n20, 328. *See also* national contact point
Oil and gas (sector), 5, 16–17, 21–22, 24–25, 43, 115, 118, 127, 163–64, 169–171, 173, 179, 185, 188n2, 189n7, 199, 206, 210–11, 223, 236, 238, 256–58, 260, 265n8, 256n11, 276, 297, 300–13, 318n10, 324, 326–27, 331
Oil for development, 327
"Oil Fund." *See* Government Pension Fund Global
Olsen, Ingalill, 256
one-dimensional man, 142
Ordoliberals, 9–10. *See also* Foucault
Økokrim (the Norwegian National Authority for Investigation and Prosecution of Economic and Environmental Crime), 305
organization
  hybrid, 142, 156–57
  management, 137
  model, 139, 143, 148, 151–52
  work, 137
Oslo (as headquarters of corporations), 47, 119, 148, 181, 222, 236, 268–69, 273, 280, 297, 300

Oslo stock exchange, 17, 125, 300
Osmancık, 278–81
ownership reports (*eierberetning*), 18, 75, 79, 83
PCAP (Compensation Plan for Fishery Activities), 172, 176
PEA FOCO, 163, 175–83, 186
PEA projects (Environmental Education Projects), 172, 176
Peregrino field, 163, 164, 172
Petrobras, 164, 169, 171, 174
Petroleum Act Tanzania, 201, 203, 211
Petrorio, 164
philanthropy, 4, 63, 65–66, 81, 101, 165, 169, 183, 187, 189n11, 204, 276, 281, 323, 330
Plan for Development and Operation (of petroleum fields), 248
popular education, 174
port, 172
privatization, 6, 15–16, 42, 73, 118, 120, 224, 322
"project affected people" (PAP), 271, 279, 288
proper dynamics, 9, 102–6, 109–11
public relations (PR), 56, 183, 271, 276, 278

Quisling, Vidkun, 117

REDD+, 25, 128
regulations, 4, 14, 20, 28–29, 75, 93, 102, 139–40, 166–68, 175, 186, 193, 195–96, 201–3, 210, 219, 225, 273, 277, 281, 301, 308, 310, 314–16, 328
reporting (CSR/sustainability-), 4, 10, 21, 58, 74, 83, 145, 169, 194, 198, 201, 210, 212, 213n3, 269–71, 274, 278, 284–90, 314–15, 326, 328, 330. *See also* Global Reporting Initiative
rice cultivation, 278, 281–84
Rio Declaration on Environment and Development, 173
ripple effects, 252

risk
    assessment/management, 4, 44, 49, 54, 66, 145, 199, 209–10, 236, 269, 272, 276, 288, 298, 323, 330
    perception of, 193, 196, 203
Rjukan, 101, 115, 121–22, 145
Russia, 20

samfunnsansvar (societal responsibility), 21, 26, 63–87, 115, 127, 253–55, 257, 263–63, 274, 323
    and cultural resonance, 27, 63, 65, 71–74, 80, 84
Sámi, 268
Sande, Leif, 315
Sandvik, Andreas, 261
Scotland, 54,
SDGs. *See* sustainable development goals
Sen, Amartya, 25
shareholder, 22, 66, 77, 300
    state as, 18, 24, 138, 195, 199, 263
    value, 29, 65, 118, 122–23, 126, 130–31, 140–42, 147, 186, 297, 309, 324
Shell, 164, 185, 189n9, 213n2, 224, 318n11
Simonsen, Marie, 79
SN Power, 273–74
Snøhvit LNG (liquefied natural gas) project, 244–46, 248–53, 257–60, 264n5
social fields (theory of), 9, 102–4, 107
social footprint, 183
social license to operate. *See* license to operate
social responsibility, 67, 80–81, 137, 139–41, 144–48, 153–55, 157–58
social welfare, 65, 152, 299
SSU (safety and sustainability), 164, 180–83
stakeholder
    in corporate stories, 284–86, 288
    engagement/involvement, 44, 274, 277, 283, 286–87, 296
    figure of, 167, 271, 288, 290

management, 276, 286, 289, 302, 325
mapping, 283
researcher as, 50
perspective (as opposed to shareholder perspective), 66, 141
theory, 287–88
standards (CSR performance-), 2, 12, 19, 21–22, 42, 48, 76, 79, 84, 268–71, 274–78, 281, 284–90, 309–10, 313–14, 324, 326–28. *See also* Global Reporting Initiative
state capitalism 17–19, 324
state corporations, 110
   state ownership of 5, 17–19, 23, 116, 119–20, 128–30, 138, 147, 210, 324, 328
   state expectations towards corporations, 19–20, 73, 210, 272, 314
Statoil (Equinor) Book, 202
Stoltenberg, Jens (prime minister, Norway), 24
Stortinget (the Norwegian Parliament), 18, 25, 127–28, 244, 250, 258, 263
structural adjustment, 205
sustainable development goals (SDGs), 83–84, 169, 194, 197, 200, 212, 324, 328, 330
"sustainable value creation," 65, 84
Sætre, Eldar (Equinor CEO), 54

Tawke, 296, 304, 306–8
Tanzania, 51–52, 121, 193–243, 326–27
tax, 24, 314, 328, 332n3
   property tax, 246–47, 251, 255–56, 263
   fraud, 302, 328
Telenor, 19, 23
Temer, Michel (Brazilian president), 128
The Statkraft Way, 275, 278
Thorsrud, Einar, 142
TNCs. *See* transnational corporations
trade unions. *See* Labor unions

Trade Union Congress of Tanzania (TUCTA), 227
TRANS FOR MAR, 164, 177, 178
translation (between cultures, models), 84, 137, 139, 149, 152–53, 155–57, 181, 285, 289
transformation, 137, 138, 152–53, 157
transnational cooperations (TNCs), 1–2, 4–6, 12, 22–23, 42, 130, 137, 149, 153, 298, 315, 322–25, 328–30. *See also* Multinational corporations/companies (MNCs)
transparency, 183, 269, 312–16, 317n1, 330
Transparency International Norway, 126
traveling, 137–39, 147
traveling model, 148, 154–55
tripartite collaboration/cooperation, 14, 17, 68, 70, 72, 103, 118, 123, 130, 142, 144, 219, 232, 237, 324, 326–27. *See also* Nordic model, Norwegian model
Turkey, 47, 49, 129, 268–90, 326, 332, 332n3

UN Global Compact. *See* Global Compact
UN Guiding Principles on Business and Human Rights, 202
UN Sustainable Development Goals. *See* sustainable development goals (SDGs)
Unions. *See* Labor unions
United Arab Emirates, 329
United States (of America), 11, 52, 148
   and concept of CSR, 3, 65–66, 68, 166
   operations of Norwegian corporations in, 18, 52, 181, 226, 329

Varieties of Capitalism, 7

Wallenberg family, 96, 117

welfare state, 1, 14, 17, 27, 101, 130, 219, 222, 296, 324, 326. *See also* Nordic model
   culture, 98, 102, 107
   democracy, 123, 157, 158
   environment, 157
   groups, 143, 156
   humanization, 142, 144
   life, 46, 49, 51, 78, 99, 102, 139, 142–43, 282
   meaningful, 156
   organization, 156
   perception of, 177
   power at, 48
   relations, 142
   voluntary (*dugnad*), 67
white paper on CSR, 19, 21, 79–81, 273, 318n2
white paper on ownership (*eierskapsmelding*), 18, 73–75, 81, 83–84, 128, 272
Worker's Party Brazil (PPT), 173
World Bank, 22, 194, 198, 274. *See also* International Finance Corporation
World Commission on Dams, 275
World Wildlife Fund (WWF), 57, 277

Xi'an, 139, 147, 149–154, 156–158
Xiaobo, Liu, 25

Yara, 23, 19
Yemen, 29, 311–16

Politics, resources, combinations

MANAGING AND LEAD EDITOR:
Luisa Steur, *University of Amsterdam*

EDITOR-AT-LARGE:
Don Kalb, *University of Bergen*

berghahnjournals.com/focaal

Volume 2023, 3 issues p.a.

www.ingramcontent.com/pod-product-compliance
Lightning Source LLC
Chambersburg PA
CBHW051525020426
42333CB00016B/1781